BUDAPEST and NEW YORK

BUDAPEST
and NEW YORK

Studies in Metropolitan Transformation:
1870–1930

Edited by

THOMAS BENDER and CARL E. SCHORSKE

Russell Sage Foundation / New York

The Russell Sage Foundation

The Russell Sage Foundation, one of the oldest of America's general purpose foundations, was established in 1907 by Mrs. Margaret Olivia Sage for "the improvement of social and living conditions in the United States." The Foundation seeks to fulfill this mandate by fostering the development and dissemination of knowledge about the country's political, social, and economic problems. While the Foundation endeavors to assure the accuracy and objectivity of each book it publishes, the conclusions and interpretations in Russell Sage Foundation publications are those of the authors and not of the Foundation, its Trustees, or its staff. Publication by Russell Sage, therefore, does not imply Foundation endorsement.

Library of Congress Cataloging-in-Publication Data

Budapest and New York :   studies in metropolitan transformation, 1870–1930 / edited by Thomas Bender and Carl E. Schorske.
  p. cm.
  "The conference that produced this volume was held in Budapest in 1988"— Acknowledgments.
  Includes bibliographical references (p.) and index.
  ISBN 0-87154-113-0
  1. Budapest (Hungary) civilization.   2. New York (N.Y.)—Civilization.   3. Budapest (Hungary)—Popular culture—Congresses.   4. New York (N.Y.)—Popular culture—Congresses.   I. Bender, Thomas.   II. Schorske, Carl E.   III. Russell Sage Foundation.
  DB988.B8   1994   93-13533
  306'.09439'12—dc20   CIP

The paper used in this publication meets the minimum requirements of American National Standard for Information Sciences—Permanence of Paper for Printed Library Materials, ANSI Z39.48-1984.

Text design by JOHN JOHNSTON

RUSSELL SAGE FOUNDATION
112 East 64th Street, New York, New York 10021

10 9 8 7 6 5 4 3 2 1

To the Memory of

HERBERT G. GUTMAN AND GYÖRGY RÁNKI

Two extraordinary scholars and citizens,
collaborators in the initiation of this project,
who did not live to see the fruits of their dreams
of free international movement of scholars and scholarship

Contents

Part V

THE HIGH ARTS: METROPOLITAN AUTONOMY AND MODERNISM

$\mathcal{W}$ HEN Budapest celebrated the millennium of the Hungarian monarchy in 1896, New York's most famous newspaper reporter, Richard Harding Davis, was there, in part because he had been in Europe to cover the coronation of Czar Nicholas II. He was unprepared for what he saw in Budapest. The energy and modernity of the city, as well as the drama of the celebration, deserved to be known beyond Hungary's borders. He explained to his New York readers that Budapest was nearer to New York than they supposed. While he found it "interesting" that civic leaders "delighting in electric tramways" dressed themselves "in the chain armor of their ancestors" for their millennial festival, that did not cause him to exaggerate the differences between New York and Budapest. Indeed, only a few years later, in 1909, New Yorkers themselves dressed in period costume to celebrate the tricentennial of Henry Hudson's discovery of the river named for him and the centennial of Robert Fulton's successful steam navigation of that river.

Davis informed his readers that Hungarians were considered to be the Americans of Europe and that Budapest was the old world's "Yankee City." The celebration was held in Pest, the newest part of the city. Built in the nineteenth century and across the river from the ancient city of Buda, Pest was, according to Davis, "the most modern city in Europe; more modern than Paris, better paved and better lighted; with better facilities for rapid transit than New York; and with Houses of Parliament as massive and impressive as those on the banks of the Thames, and not unlike them in appearance." *

Davis was writing against the common view that assumed the distance between Budapest and New York to be very wide, virtually unbridgeable. We too are writing against a sense of the nearly absolute otherness of the two cities shared by Hungarians and Americans, historians and urbanists included. Of course, Americans and Europeans have always emphasized the distinctiveness of the New World and, by implication, New World cities. In our own century, the Hungarian

---

* Richard Harding Davis, *A Year from a Reporter's Note-book* (New York, 1898), 71–74.

experience with fascism and communism has further encouraged this subjective sense of absolute difference. Such an inherited structure of perception makes it difficult to recognize the substantial objective ground for comparison.

With the hopeful prospect of a single world of scholarship at the close of this century, it becomes both possible and necessary to rethink this categorical isolation. The point is not to deny the real and substantial differences between Hungary and the United States, Budapest and New York, but rather to bring the history and historiography of these two nations and cities into a single scholarly conversation. Only by opening academic discourse in this way will the possibilities of a fruitful comparison become available to the Hungarian and American historical imaginations.

The comparisons between the two cities are drawn in a general Introduction and, more explicitly, in the introductions to each of the five parts. The several studies that make up the bulk of the volume, however, are coordinated rather than comparative. Hungarian historians present studies of Budapest while American historians offer comparable accounts of New York. Although these essays are not formally comparative, the writers on each city consulted with their counterparts in establishing the terms of discourse and the boundaries of their topics.

Consistent with its origins as a project in international scholarly exchange, the book illuminates the differences in historiographical traditions and practices that derive from two different intellectual cultures that have had little previous contact. The reader should keep alert to these differences in the substantive work that follows. In an Afterword, the emergent historiographical differences are probed for their wider significance.

*T*HIS book reports the fruits of an unusual effort in international scholarly collaboration among historians. A common historiographical conversation embracing Hungary and the United States, Budapest and New York, it grew out of a wider concern: the need to counter the disruption of the cosmopolitan Republic of Letters imposed on scholars through the political isolation and intellectual distortions occasioned in both East and West by the Cold War. By bringing Budapest and New York into a comparative frame we have, at least for a moment, exemplified our task and, we hope, made a contribution to the reinternationalization of the community of humanities and social science scholarship.

The origins of this project date from 1979, with the launching of a series of scholarly exchanges and conferences devoted to broadening mutual professional understanding and overcoming the intellectual liabilities of a divided world of scholarship. We wish to thank those who nourished and sustained it as well as the Hungarian and American historians who participated in it.

Let us now be specific about our debts. The framework for the exchange was established by the American Council of Learned Societies and the International Research and Exchange Board, then a part of the ACLS but now independent, and the Hungarian Academy of Sciences. For over a decade these sponsoring organizations have been generous with the necessary funds and hospitality that facilitated participation of Hungarian and American historians in a series of conferences on various themes, ranging from "Ethnicity, Social Class, and Cultural Change in Hungary and America" (1982) to "Intellectuals and the Left" (1985). The conference that produced this volume was held in Budapest in 1988. It was the most ambitious yet. From the outset it aimed to go beyond the normal conference conventions of individual papers to the production of a systematic topical exploration of a common object, the modern metropolis, in order to cystallize a common historiographical discourse focused on the modern city.

This volume provides only a sampling of the rich feast of contributions to that conference, and we wish to emphasize that the editors and authors of this volume have absorbed and profited from papers not published here. By way of acknowledging the role of the participants not included, we have listed the titles of their work in an appendix. Among them, particular thanks go to John Kasson and Alan Trachtenberg, who played a crucial part in shaping the intellectual exchange.

As we planned the conference and volume, innumerable scholars responded with great generosity to a wide range of questions, and we appreciate their help, even if we cannot name them here. Gloria Deak clarified and polished the translations of those chapters written in Hungarian and translated into English. Alice Fahs undertook to make the format and scholarly apparatus of the papers uniform. Maps to orient the reader to the two cities were drawn by Kimberly Santini. The Getty Center for the Study of the History of Art and the Humanities provided support in the final stages of putting together the book, particularly in regard to the maps and illustrations. An editorial committee formed from among the conference participants contributed graciously of their time and advice as we converted the conference results into the constituents of a book. On the American side we thank Neil Harris and Roy Rosenzweig, and on the Hungarian side Péter Hanák, Zsuzsa Nagy, Gábor Gyáni, and Miklós Lackó. Attila Pók of the Hungarian Academy of Science's Institute of History has a gift for scholarly organization that proved indispensable. Vivien Abbott, the director of IREX's Eastern European Programs, was an enthusiastic and ever-helpful supporter of this project from beginning to end. Finally, we wish to thank Lisa Nachtigall and the publications staff of the Russell Sage Foundation for their critical and ever-generous contribution to the making of the book.

Budapest and New York Compared

THOMAS BENDER and CARL E. SCHORSKE

*I*N 1870 NEW YORK AND BUDAPEST were peripheral cities, one on the western perimeter of the European core, the other on the eastern. Yet both harbored metropolitan ambitions. Their civic leaders were eager to have them join the select company of Western European metropolises (London and Paris in New York's case, Vienna and Paris in Budapest's). Political events in the United States and Hungary, moreover, propelled—and facilitated—this civic aspiration. The consolidation of a more clearly defined, empowered, and aggressively modernizing national state effectively enhanced the authority, ambition, and political significance of the two cities. The creation of the Austro-Hungarian Dual Monarchy in 1867, after a generation of contention, conferred substantial autonomy on Hungary and removed important obstacles to Hungarian national development. In the United States, the Civil War, which ended in 1865 with a victory by the urbanizing and industrializing North, had much the same significance. The rapid growth of banking and finance (and its concentration in these two cities) followed hard upon these political events, making Budapest and New York the administrative centers for national economic modernization.

The metropolitan expansion and ambition of the two cities came to be symbolized by the construction of two bridges across the Danube and the East rivers, vastly expanding the aspiring metropolises beyond their historic centers. The Iron Bridge in Budapest (completed in 1849) and the Brooklyn Bridge (begun in 1867 and completed in 1883) each preceded and forecast the eventual political consolidation of the greater cities. Buda, Óbuda, and Pest were united in 1872; Manhattan and the Bronx were unified in 1876, with Brooklyn, Queens, and Staten Island added in 1898 to form Greater New York. The bridges

1

Figure I.1 New York, *View of New York from Brooklyn*, 1906. Museum of the City of New York, Gift of Mrs. A. C. Johnson.

were both the work of non-natives: Adam Clark from Scotland designed the Chain Bridge; German immigrant John Roebling and his son Washington designed and built the Brooklyn Bridge. Celebrated for their technological innovation, both bridges came to signify the modernizing enthusiasm of their respective cities. Later, the subway would symbolize urban modernity to New Yorkers, but that took place in 1904, eight years after Budapest had opened Europe's first electric subway line. In Budapest, both of these modern symbols, the bridge and the subway, were in fact mediators, standing for the unification of the traditional aristocratic elite identified with Buda and the emerging bourgeois elites identified with Pest. In New York, bourgeois values were shared at both ends of the bridge and at all subway stations.

These two peripheral cities outpaced the growth of all their European and American counterparts. Budapest, growing twice as fast as Vienna and three times as fast as Paris and London, dramatically changed its position in the European urban hierarchy in the fifty years following the establishment of the Dual Monarchy. Europe's seventeenth largest city in 1869, Budapest had risen to its seventh in 1910.

Figure I.2 Budapest, *Pest from Buda.* Parliament to left, Chain Bridge center, factory stacks in background, 1900. György Klösz, *Budapest Anno* (Budapest: Corvina, 1979).

This extraordinary rate of growth prompted a German geographer writing in the 1920s to remark that Budapest was unique in Europe, exhibiting an "American pattern" of growth.

New York and Budapest grew by absorbing inmigrants and immigrants. Budapest's inmigrants and many of New York's immigrants were drawn from the same regions of Central and Eastern Europe. But the consequences for urban demography were quite different. While this immigration increased the diversity of the population of New York (adding to its mid-century core of Dutch, British, German, and Irish), Budapest became more Magyar because of the ethnic origins of the immigrants and because of the powerful commitment of both authorities and immigrants to Magyarization. In 1880, 18 percent of Budapest's population spoke only Magyar; in 1910, one generation later, 47 percent of the population spoke only Magyar, with nearly all of the remaining Budapesters speaking Magyar as a second language.

Budapest grew so rapidly that by 1930 one in eight Hungarians lived in the capital. Part of the explanation for this remarkable figure is Hungary's substantial loss of territory and population in the settlement of World War I, but it remains a striking figure, even with this qualification. In the United States no more than one in twenty Americans lived in New York.

Hungary was ascendant in a rural nation; there were few secondary urban centers and those lagged far behind Budapest. New York, by contrast, capped the urban hierarchy in a nation that had developed a richly differentiated system of cities, with many large ones continually challenging New York's leadership. Because New York, unlike Budapest, was not the national capital and because the American state was less centralized, the relationship of city to nation was less direct in the United States than in Hungary. Perhaps this gave New York more space to define its own metropolitan identity.

The metropolitan dominance achieved by New York and Budapest by the 1890s depended upon their near-monopolies of the import and export trade (initially agricultural) of their respective nations. They consolidated this trade and its related financial activities because of their exceptional access to water transport in their regions; but after the political consolidations of the 1860s, both cities became the hubs of national railroad systems. This dominance in trade provided the foundation for the development of their large and sophisticated banking and financial sectors. Both cities were national leaders in industry, and the industrial organization that prevailed (especially in New York but in Budapest as well) emphasized many small units of production rather than the huge factories characteristic of Manchester, Pittsburgh, and Chicago. Both cities manufactured goods for export, but the development of their manufacturing sectors was heavily dependent upon their large local consumer markets. The vast populations of New York and Budapest supplied both labor and a market for industrial production. This role of the local market was reflected in their leadership in food processing, clothing, and other consumer items, although Budapest, unlike New York, was a leader in heavy industry, including locomotive building. The growing industrial bases of Budapest and New York were crucial to their social development; they enabled them to absorb a continual flow of inmigrants and immigrants. The national cultural leadership of the two cities was evident in their dominance in entertainment, printing, and publishing.

4

These similarities in the ambitions and the paths by which Budapest and New York became modern metropolises provide a foundation for our comparative inquiries. But the cumulative findings reported in the following chapters stress that these similar metropolitan economic and demographic transformations produced quite different results in those areas of politics and culture that are the focus of our inquiry. Although these differences vary in particulars, the main axis of difference is defined by the distinct historical relations between metropolitanism and nationalism. This unexpected finding sustains our notion that city-making and state-making are intertwined processes, deeply affecting each other. Because New York was less constrained by the nation than was Budapest, it was able to develop fully into a modern metropolis, becoming a symbol and standard for metropolitan modernity in the twentieth century. Indeed, New York even extended its values into general characteristics associated with American nationality during the interwar years.

Budapest, by contrast, although developed with nation-building intent, found itself continually struggling against nationalist imperatives that denied the "Hungarianness" of the city—even though Budapest was demographically more "Hungarian" than New York was "American." By the 1930s, New York had won national tolerance, even acceptance, of its modern, liberal, and cosmopolitan culture and politics, while Budapest had not. Conservative nationalism snuffed out metropolitan values of modernism, liberalism, and cosmopolitanism in Hungary. After Hungary's defeat in World War I; two failed revolutions, one liberal, the other Communist, in 1918–1919; and the conservative reaction which by the 1930s blended into Fascism; the carriers of Budapest's metropolitan culture, especially those of Jewish descent, emigrated in significant numbers, stocking the scholarly, artistic, and entrepreneurial communities of London, Paris, Los Angeles, and New York. New York, it is true, sent a generation of writers and artists to Paris in the 1910s and 1920s, but by the 1930s they had returned. The American culture that had seemed too provincial and inhospitable in 1910 had become more congenial, partly because New York was the acknowledged capital of the century's modernity.

New York, so different from Budapest in the 1930s, seems to share certain vulnerabilities with Budapest in the past two decades. It is pertinent to note this because one must take care that comparative history not dissolve into mere ideological justification of one city, nation, or people against another. Comparative history, like other histories, addresses contingent outcomes. In the 1930s it seemed that New York had overcome American unease about the city and its people. The city rose to a commanding position in the world economy after World War II, maintaining a liberal commitment to social welfare policies in a way that Budapest did not.

But more recently, particularly during the 1970s and 1980s, national politics in the United States turned conservative, parochial, and anti-urban. The city's symbiotic relation with the nation and national government was weakened, and for many, including some New Yorkers, the city came to represent not modernity to be emulated but past errors to be avoided. Moreover, New York, like Budapest, became increasingly vulnerable to the globalization of the international economy, a transformation brought about partly through the agency of Wall Street. Ironically, the financial sector's success threatens New York's larger economy and social welfare.

It is, of course, premature to predict the demise of New York, especially in view of the results of the 1992 national elections in the United States. Yet one cannot escape the thought that as the twentieth century closes, New York and Budapest, as was the case at the end of the nineteenth century when Richard Harding Davis visited Budapest, are more similar than one might have guessed. But this time they share international and national vulnerability rather than modernizing energy.

These reflections may well be based upon much too pessimistic readings of both Hungarian and American political and economic developments. Yet a larger point holds even if the present signs of distress are only temporary: it is that the seemingly universal process of metropolitan development is historically specific and contingent, and thus a proper object for comparative study.

The more one inquires into the particularities of our two cities in the era of metropolitan transformation, the more one finds fruitful axes of comparison that bring out differences in the development and urban pattern of the two cities. These specific comparisons illuminate a variety of general issues associated with the study of modern urbanism: the relationships between politics, ethnicity, and class, as well as between ethnicity and culture; the spatial organization of urban social life; the culture of politics and the politics of culture; metropolitanism and cosmopolitanism in their relationship to nationalism; and the connections among modernization, modernism, and traditional culture. These are themes by which we track the meaning of metropolitan development in Budapest and New York.

Budapest and New York in Their National Contexts

A comparison of New York and Budapest becomes, in part, a comparison of the United States and Hungary. New York was the metropolis of a nation distinguished by a relatively weak central government (by European standards), yet one in the process after 1870 of becoming a world power—and ultimately internationalizing itself. By contrast, Budapest was the capital of a Hungary working to build a modern national state within a larger imperial framework. For these reasons, and because Budapest was a national capital and New York was not, the Hungarian state was more central to the structure of Budapest society and to the forms of metropolitan life. The national government, predictably, was more directly involved in urban affairs yet. national problems, especially national politics, seem to have overshadowed municipal or civic ones in the life of the city. Some of the implications of this pattern appear in the newspapers of the two cities. The Hungarian press emphasized national as opposed to urban affairs. There was more national political coverage in Budapest journalism than in New York, where, as Neil Harris's chapter shows, "softer" urban lifestyle and cultural reporting were more prominent, feeding a strong consciousness of local identity.

New York had universal male suffrage throughout the period and universal suffrage after 1920, while Budapest had a very limited suffrage. Even though residence and citizenship requirements in New York (a city of immigrants) kept many disenfranchised, there was a fundamental difference between the political culture of the two cities based upon the residents' differential access to suffrage. With a strong government and a restricted electorate, the major political objective for the mass of the citizenry in Budapest was the securing of broader access to formal political power. The integrative role of political institutions was correspondingly different from that in New York. The limited suffrage in Budapest promoted a working-class solidarity on political issues. In New York more particularistic outlooks prevailed in urban politics. With a large electorate to be mobilized and organized, New York had highly developed though almost unmanageably diverse local political institutions, often organized by a political machine, which performed the civic task of social and political integration, forming political identities that emphasized neighborhood and ethnic concerns over those of class.

The New York elite was bourgeois in its values and aspirations, strongly influenced by a Protestant tradition of service. In the eighteenth century New York City had been dominated by landed families or families with important rural bases, but these were largely eclipsed after 1850 by business and intellectual (protoprofessional) leaders. In Budapest, by contrast, gentry authority and values survived longer, with modern bourgeois social groups playing a lesser role, especially at the beginning of the period under study here.

Private power and elite patronage made a larger impact in New York than in Budapest. There were fewer and less influential organizations of Budapest businessmen, and compared to their New York counterparts, the range of their public activity was narrower. New York was distinctive among the world metropolises in giving control and responsibility for "higher culture" to private, not-for-profit organizations—from the Metropolitan Opera to the Metropolitan Museum of Art to Columbia and New York Universities. With "official" culture somewhat weak and diversified, there was more room for entrepreneurial ventures into the cultural realm in New York. Commercial culture, as a result, was more highly developed.

In both cities Germans as well as Jews who had been assimilated to German culture played important roles. But the circumstances and identity of these groups were complicated and distinctly different. In Budapest there were German-speaking Jews in the middle of the nineteenth century who, by the second half of the century, had become Magyarized, becoming the very model of linguistic assimilation. The German Jews of New York (defined by religion and national origin rather than by language) were, after 1890, rapidly outnumbered by East European Jews, who were Yiddish-speaking, generally poorer, and less assimilated. In New York this flow of immigrants was substantial but it was only a portion of a larger immigration of pan-European dimensions.

Ethnic identity was defined differently in the two nations, a difference manifested in their census categories. Hungarian authorities kept count of religious and linguistic groups; Americans paid little attention to language and were prevented by the First Amendment of the Constitution from inquiring into the religious identification of immigrants or citizens. Americans were interested in national origins and were tolerant enough to enable the development of hyphenated Americans. Such identities survived more publicly in New York than in Budapest. The Americanization process was less transformative in New York than was the Magyarization process in Budapest. While the native elite in New York City shared power with new groups, out of necessity as much as by choice, they did not really seek to incorporate ethnic minorities fully into "their" culture. Only in comparative perspective does one recognize how limited the Americanization campaigns in the city and the city's schools, especially, were. In Hungary, however, the Magyar elite proposed to make everyone a Hungarian, with a linguistic standard accorded such primacy as to preclude a double identity. Americans asked not for linguistic uniformity but for common allegiance to the principles of the Constitution, something that allowed for the double identity represented by the hyphenated American and the American who maintained his or her native tongue. There were no hyphenated Hungarians in Budapest. One was an Hungarian or one was not, and the measure was linguistic.

The differential impact of World War I on the two cities produced and revealed some of the most striking differences between them. New York consolidated itself as the metropolis of a much enhanced international power, and the city's intellectuals and business leaders became major voices of American internationalism. Budapest, in contrast, shared the traumatic fate of a defeated nation drastically reduced in population, size, and international significance. If the effect of World War I's outcome was unambiguously positive for New York, Budapest lost and gained. While its hinterland was greatly reduced by the Trianon Treaty, the city's relative significance in a small, newly independent nation was proportionately enhanced. Before 1918, 5 percent of the national population resided in Budapest; after the Treaty, 12 percent. One-fifth of all industrial enterprises and 80 percent of all larger shops and department stores were in Budapest. Yet the metropolitan values that had been developing in Budapest were strongly challenged by resurgent national and traditional values that were identified with rural Hungary.

The Hungarian circumstance was not without irony. Precisely because Budapest was a metropolis, populist critics of the city's metropolitan values had to move there (often from Debrecen, the "capital" of the Great Hungarian Plain) in order to mount their attack upon the metropolis.

The period of 1919–1921, the era of revolution and counterrevolution, was marked by especially intensive expression of antimetropolitanism in Hungarian political culture—when the "western" values of the capital were blamed for the Communist Revolution and for the disastrous terms of the Trianon Treaty that redivided the Danubian Basin. At the very moment when the New York intellectuals were articulating a theory of American national culture rooted in the cosmopolitanism of New York, Admiral Miklós Horthy, representing Hungarian reaction and provincialism, entered Budapest, calling it a "sinful city." He promised that the new regime he headed would give it "well deserved" punishment for its errors, which had led to crisis and revolution.

Hungarian intellectuals assumed the burden (or had it imposed upon them by circumstances) of justifying the values of Budapest in a national—or nationalistic—context. Metropolitan values, they felt compelled to argue, were compatible with vernacular Hungarian culture. New York, too, was perceived by many in the United States as a city of sin, radicalism, and foreigners; but New York intellectuals felt free to embrace the city's provocative distinctiveness. They gloried in New York's difference from heartland America. Against what they considered American provincialism, they argued that the cosmopolitanism and modernity that characterized the culture and politics of the metropolis ought to become the basis for a transformed American culture. Neither the party of parochialism nor that of cosmopolitanism wholly succeeded in the United States. But by the late 1930s it was clear that New York's cosmopolitanism had found a national constituency in the United States, while Budapest's cosmopolitanism, identified as it was with urbanism, liberalism, and Jewishness, was being crushed in Hungary.

It is not that New York liberalism and cosmopolitanism were not challenged by provincial values. Always somewhat suspect beyond the Hudson River, New York's values were subject to sustained attack in the decade following World War I. The period began with a "Red Scare" against alien ideas and groups. It was a time of resurgent Protestantism, heavily fundamentalist; a time of renewed Ku Klux Klan activity against blacks, Jews, and Catholics; a time of nativism, when the United States changed its immigration laws, closing the doors especially to immigrants from Eastern and Southern Europe, most of whom were Jews or Catholics. In the 1928 presidential election New York City's Al Smith, who symbolized in his own person the immigrant in politics, was defeated in part because a provincial America rejected the non-Protestant, urban, cosmopolitan, and "liberal" values he represented. Yet, by the 1930s the political and cultural values of New York had turned back this provincial attack, spearheading the New Deal liberalism of the era.

New York was a metropolis in a nation with a highly developed national urban system (probably unmatched in the world) with twelve cities exceeding one-half-million population in 1920. Hungary had only two cities outside of Budapest in excess of 100,000 people. New York thus found itself with more urban competitors, but it also had important urban alliances that bolstered the national influence of metropolitan political and cultural values. In New York, journalism (newspapers and magazines, especially the *New Yorker*) and advertising were able to establish a "brassy style" and modern attitudes that set the terms nationally for urban sophistication and for metropolitan lifestyles.

The trajectory of New York's growth had been steadily upward well before the period of 1870–1930. Since the American Revolution New York had experienced more or less uninterrupted development, and World War I represented a moment of consolidation of the city's political and economic power and of its cultural autonomy and identity. The war was a benchmark, not a dividing line. For Budapest, 1919 was a dividing line, one of many historical disjunctures. If New York's long pattern of growth nourished a sense of civic self-confidence, Budapest's sense of repeated crises and disruptions produced a sort of civic neurosis. Although Budapest was able to reorient its economy and to prosper in its new relationship to the Danube Basin after 1919, its intellectual and cultural leaders were demoralized by the war, many becoming exiles.

Power and Governance

How does political identity relate to political structures and urban processes? More particularly, what is the relative significance of class and ethnicity in shaping political culture in Budapest and New York? From the American perspective, the limited salience of ethnicity in Budapest as a source or determinative element of political identity is striking. The organization of American political culture attenuated class and heightened ethnic consciousness, and immigration, which kept making the city more heterogeneous, furthered this tendency. The opposite was the case in Budapest, where immigration reenforced conservative, nationalist political identifications.

Since American urban politics is territorially based (voters are registered by residence, and representatives live in the areas from which they are elected), the class and ethnic patterns of residence encouraged and sustained an ethnic and localistic pattern of politics organized by local political leaders. The very large, diverse, and constantly changing New York electorate was managed with great difficulty by coalition-building political parties, and, as David Hammack points out in Chapter 2, ethnicity rather than class or ideology increasingly shaped the political identity of voting groups within the coalitions. It was to these identifications that politicians appealed. In Budapest, by contrast, the powerful national pressure for Magyarization dissolved ethnicity as a viable political category. In Chapter 1, Zsuzsa Nagy reports that while there was an identifiable Jewish voting pattern, before World War I it was not understood by voters or by the politicians courting them to be a specifically Jewish political identification. Nor did German voters vote as an ethnic political group.

In New York ethnic political identity and ethnic competition were common, and they were understood to be positive measures of dem-

11

ocratic politics. By 1930 the practice of ethnic politics was given important symbolization in the ethnically "mixed ticket." A similar politics did not emerge in Budapest. In fact, ethnic identification became increasingly dangerous, at least for Jews, well before the late 1930s. After 1918, Nagy indicates, no Jew could hold high municipal office in Budapest, even though many controlled considerable wealth, played major roles in the economy, and were therefore entitled to the vote by the franchise system of *virilism*, which based suffrage on tax-paying status. More important, a series of legislative acts in the 1930s made the ethnic/religious identification of Jews a matter of state, not self, definition. In America ethnic identification was increasingly, if still ambiguously, voluntary, except for blacks (who are more appropriately compared in their exclusion with Hungary's Gypsies than with Jews).

The progressive political ideology of New York was less isolated from that of other parts of the United States than was Budapest's. In both countries the relationship of the politics of the metropolis to the larger nation was complex and changing, but New York's liberalism found support in other regions. The emergence of progressivism in the United States drew upon New York's earlier experience with social and political problems, but it was a national movement in 1900, with midwestern and western urban and agrarian components, as well as an eastern, or New York, thrust. In time, especially after World War I, urban liberalism came to be more specifically associated with New York, but it still had a broad national urban constituency.

In Hungary the movement for municipal progress was identified with Budapest, particularly with the mayoral administration of István Bárczy (1906–1918). His policies were similar to those of American municipal progressivism, and probably both Americans and Hungarians were heavily influenced by German municipal developments— housing, municipal ownership of public utilities, improved education, libraries. City leaders assumed responsibility for enabling inhabitants of the city, in the words of Zsuzsa Nagy, to "enjoy the benefits of technical civilization regardless of their social status." Bárczy's supporters included lower-middle-class and middle-class voters, including a large Jewish constituency, and the intellectuals involved with the political sociologist Oscar Jászi and his reformist Association of Social Sciences. Much of this sounds familiar to American students of urban progressivism, except that this pattern was replicated in many American cities—in Chicago, Cleveland, San Francisco, Minneapolis, Philadelphia, Atlanta, St. Louis, Madison, Milwaukee, and others, as well as in New York. In Hungary such urban liberalism was more or less confined to the one metropolis.

12

The agendas of Hungarian and American liberalism in the prewar years were strikingly similar, but their genealogies were different. These historical differences contributed to their postwar divergence. In the United States liberalism was associated with the internal development of large industrial cities. Liberalism was equally central to political life in Budapest and Hungary before the war, but it had a different trajectory. Hungarian liberalism, initially supported by the nobility, was less clearly identified with the metropolis.

Since the turn of the century, liberalism in New York addressed the social problems of the city. It promoted an increase in the role of government in economic and social life and a cosmopolitan acceptance of ethnic minorities and their cultural practices. Hungarian liberals confronted these issues, but much of the appeal of liberalism in Hungary derived from another source. While American liberalism was grounded in democracy, the Hungarian variant was impelled by the experience of a strong, even oppressive, central government. Liberalism held out the possibility of carving out space for personal, intellectual, and entrepreneurial freedoms as well as providing the basis for a modern national culture. For a decade following the creation of the Dual Monarchy in 1867, national liberalism flourished with gentry support. Nationalism and liberalism seemed more comfortable with each other than they would later be. The traditional elite envisioned a transformation of the gentry into entrepreneurs. This liberal movement for modernization in fact weakened the gentry, as "foreigners"—assimilated Jews and Germans—established themselves in dominant positions in the Hungarian economy. With this development, the brief marriage of liberalism and nationalism within the gentry dissolved, and the latter turned away from classical liberalism, branding it foreign, non-Magyar, and metropolitan. This wounded liberalism became identified with Budapest and urban culture, leaving it more vulnerable to resurgent traditional nationalism after the First World War. New York's liberalism was founded on a stronger democratic base, which gave it a different character and made it less vulnerable.

In New York and Budapest the whole array of social issues associated with capitalist urbanization and industrialization were first and most intensely confronted in the United States and Hungary. Out of that confrontation an interventionist liberalism (as opposed to laissez faire liberalism) emerged in the 1880s. This new liberalism had many confluent sources, some shared by both cities: academic, including the important influence of the German historical economists; social activists, including charity workers and religious groups; and working-class or trade unionist activism. The great metropolitan achievement of New York, supported by other large and some smaller cities, was to transform this new liberal ideology into a national ideology, something confirmed by the political success of the New Deal in the 1930s. Budapest did not duplicate this achievement.

If anything, the experience of World War I in the United States furthered the development of the ideas that would be realized in the 1930s as New Deal liberalism. The war pointed the way toward greater governmental intervention, and after the war there was an increase in governmental urban activity. During the 1920s in both Budapest and New York there was tension between the municipal government and the national regime. But in New York, with the elections of Roosevelt as president (1932) and Fiorello LaGuardia (who had been employed as a clerk in the American consultate in Budapest in 1901–1903) as mayor in 1933, tension gave way to an extraordinarily successful collaboration between city and nation. New York intellectuals, social workers, politicians, and labor leaders played a large role in the presidency of New York's Franklin D. Roosevelt, whose New Deal defined and institutionalized modern American liberalism.

The war and the failed revolution of 1919 discredited both Budapest's liberalism and its municipal progressivism as ideologies. After World War I many of the urban development policies of the Bárczy mayoralty were continued, but without liberal ideological explanation or justification. The context had so changed that the development of municipal services was occasionally supported as a strategy of discrimination against Jewish and other liberal businessmen who had provided various social services (transportation, for example) on a private basis. Municipalization was a means of using the power of government to punish targeted groups. Usually, though, postwar policy aimed to enhance the "splendor" of Budapest as the capital of the Danube Basin. The issue here is not the modernizing policies themselves, but rather the dissolution of a liberal ideology as the basis for infrastructure development and other urban improvements.

In New York liberalism fared better, surviving even the Red Scare of 1919; and it played a strong role in municipal and national affairs in the interwar years. New York's liberalism, articulated weekly by the *New Republic* after 1914, set the terms of national liberal political debate between the wars. The metropolitan point of view was not without challenge. Indeed, the 1920s were, as we have already noted, a time of provincial reaction against New York. Yet the cosmopolitan and liberal values identified with New York survived to define the 1930s. While New York emerged as the center of liberalism, cosmopolitanism, and modernism after the war, Budapest failed to legitimate these metropolitan values. New York found its political culture incorporated into national political practice, but Budapest found itself suffering from external intrusions—first from Hungarian authoritarian nationalism, later from European fascism. The two cities that developed along a common political trajectory before World War I took different paths thereafter, even while continuing to pursue common programs of infrastructural development and technical services.

Cultural Politics
and the Social Construction of Space

Within the two cities there were distinctive ways in which politics and culture defined themselves in relation to each other. Not only was there a difference in the character of the political systems (most importantly the limited suffrage in Budapest), but there was a contest over culture in New York that our studies do not detect in Budapest. For the American city Roy Rosenzweig and Betsy Blackmar in Chapter 4 explore the importance of a cultural politics in public spaces, even a politics *of* public spaces. The working classes resisted some of the cultural assumptions and initiatives of the dominant classes in New York. Or put differently, New York's lower classes tended to politicize cultural issues that ranged from school curricula to the regulation of social drinking and the use of public space. In doing so, as David Scobey suggested in a paper presented at the conference, they were responding to an elite cultural politics. The Protestant elite, distrustful of an electoral politics much influenced by immigrants and "bosses," used voluntary and philanthropic means to reform the culture and the environment with the goal of "improving" the masses. The clearest example is provided by Frederick Law Olmsted, the co-designer of Central Park in 1858 and a leading social thinker in his day.

There seems to have been no Hungarian Olmsted—or, perhaps, Hungarian historiographical tradition has made it difficult to discover him. American historians have seen Olmsted as representing a Protestant and bourgeois ideal of uplift, working through the cultural realm. His efforts seem to exemplify an effort to establish bourgeois cultural hegemony, and this cultural side of urban progressivism is treated, therefore, with suspicion by American historians. What might be seen as civic improvement is suspected of being an expression of class politics.

Hungarian historians appraise Budapest's urban and park planners—and reformers generally—from a less suspicious perspective. They suggest that one reason the style of politics associated with Olmsted in New York is not evident in Budapest may relate to the differing

15

role of the elites in the two cities. The traditional elite in Budapest was more effectively and comfortably incorporated into the political structure, which had, after all, far fewer actors because of the limited electorate. Conversely, American workers who were incorporated into the political system by virtue of wide suffrage may have been able to advance their own agenda: they could define and defend their own ethnic cultural values against elite challenge.

The lower classes in Budapest had, understandably, a narrower political goal—to achieve suffrage and formal power in the political system. In 1912, only 10 percent of the adult population could vote; in the interwar years under the conservative Horthy regime, somewhat surprisingly, the figure rose to 30 percent, still well below the New York level. Those elected to municipal offices became more representative of the population at large with the expansion of the Budapest electorate, and cultural issues became more prominent on political agendas. For example, one of the actions of the brief revolutionary government in Budapest in 1919 was to abolish the admission charge to Margaret Island, one of the city's most beautiful parks. After the revolution the fee was restored, but access remained a political issue in the interwar years. This suggests that the more open the political process the greater the likelihood, assuming considerable cultural diversity, that cultural politics will find expression inside and outside of the formal political structures.

Historians of New York argue that social conflict was expressed not only regarding public places but also over spatial issues, over competing visions of how space should be developed in the city. In Budapest, according to Gábor Gyáni in Chapter 3, one finds only conflict *in* public spaces, not a politics *of* the development of public space. Some areas of Budapest, he explains, were appropriated by one class, which was acknowledged and accepted without promoting conflict. Where a given space was used by a mixture of classes, Gyáni points out that conflict was again avoided or diffused by dividing space internally—different areas of a park, for instance, for different uses and classes.

Public spaces in New York were more mixed in their clientele and more the object of contention. The work of John Kasson and Kathy Peiss that was presented to the conference demonstrated that the new semipublic spaces associated with commercial leisure—Coney Island's amusement complexes, dance halls, nightclubs, and the like—multiplied this process of mixing. While urban space became more sharply differentiated, certain categories of space—commercial entertainment zones, particularly those in central places (Times Square) or defined as resorts (Coney Island)—experienced more intermixing of peoples. Such places, Kathy Peiss explained, "brought together people of different classes, sexes, and ethnicity from different parts of the city." We do not have comparable research on Budapest, but it seems likely that New York's pattern was not fully matched by that of Budapest. At the same time, one should not overemphasize the difference. There was a "choreography" of the use of public space in New York that was structured by class, gender, and ethnicity.

The spatial elaboration of social life in the two cities differed in important respects, particularly before 1910. In part, the differences were the product of the cities' different physical scales and demographic composition. New York had much more territory for the development of ethnic enclaves, as well as larger numbers and varieties of immigrants. In Budapest, only Jews were able to develop a substantial complement of cultural institutions, but in New York a half dozen or more ethnic groups had sufficient numbers and resources to sustain such distinctly ethnic cultural ensembles. Besides the factor of scale, the insistent assimilative politics of the political elite in Budapest doubtless contributed to this difference. Protected by a smaller electorate which meant a relatively secure electoral position, the political elite of Budapest were not compelled to develop ethnic appeals as were their New York counterparts, who had to compete for popular votes to sustain their political power.

New York was marked by distinct patterns of geographical segregation by class and ethnicity. Such patterns were less evident in Budapest before the war. There was some class segregation by district or *arrondissement*. But ethnicity was a factor only in tandem with class. The distribution of Jews in Budapest, for example, can be identified with districts, but class defined these districts of Jewish concentration as much as ethnicity. Poorer Jews lived in the Teresváros (Theresia district), the middle class in Lipótváros (Leopold district), and the elite on Andrássy utca near the City Park. Gyula Zeke, in a study of the residential patterns of the city presented at the conference, argued that where Jews lived was a function of their class affiliation and only secondarily of their ethnicity. There were no multiclass ethnic settlements such as the Lower East Side of New York surrounding East Broadway, where a Jewish elite lived a fairly comfortable middle-class life in a sea of impoverished immigrant Jews living in tenements. By the 1920s, however, the residential patterns of Jews in both cities showed signs of convergence. The Teresváros was like Williamsburg in Brooklyn or the Lower East Side; Lipótváros may have found its analogue in the Grand Concourse in the Bronx; West End Avenue and other parts of the Upper West Side and Ocean Parkway in Brooklyn may have roughly corresponded to the Andrássy utca district of Budapest.

The most significant difference in residential patterns in the two cities is the absence of the ethnic neighborhood in Budapest. Small, place-oriented group identity seems to have been alien to the Budapest experience, with identity focused more narrowly on the apartment building and more broadly on the district.

After 1910 there is evidence of a sharper segregation in Budapest. Distinct residential districts for the elite and working classes emerged. The timing suggests that industrialization rather than urbanization was the variable. New York industrialized earlier; perhaps that is why the segregated pattern emerged there earlier. The pattern of residence one finds in Budapest in 1880 more closely approximates New York of a half-century earlier, before industrialization had had much impact on the spatial distribution of work and residence. What we usually recognize as a metropolitan phenomenon may in fact be specific to the industrial metropolis.

In the physical expansion of New York, the neighborhoods of the city explicitly defined their ethnic composition. In her chapter, Deborah Dash Moore observes that "New Yorkers reckoned their ethnicity as part of the common coin of urban discourse and as a feature of the urban landscape." Such was not generally the case in Budapest. The St. Imre colony, studied here by István Teplán in Chapter 6, is an especially revealing case of the relation of nationalism to metropolitan identities. Built for Magyar émigrés from the territories lost after World War I, St. Imre embodied an ideology associating nationalism with traditional family values as the basis for what Teplán calls a "partially accepted" bourgeois pattern of life.

The residential mobility of New Yorkers (apparently higher than that of the inhabitants of Budapest) had consequences for ethnicity and place. Such mobility "constantly reshuffled the ethnic composition of the city's neighborhoods," encouraging, in Moore's words, "the reinvention of ethnic identity." When ethnic groups moved to new, upwardly mobile neighborhoods (such as Jews to Manhattan's Upper West Side), they appropriated it, giving it an ethnic identity, even if they did not constitute a clear majority of the population in the area. Ethnic bonds did not have this degree of authority in Budapest.

Cultural Unity and Cultural Differentiation

The incorporation of new migrants to the city, the assimilation of ethnic groups, emerges from our study as a historically situated and differential process, not a universal one. Our study reveals a much greater persistence of public ethnic identity in New York than in Budapest. Part of the reason is the institution of the ethnic neighborhood, with its connection to the ethnic-oriented political machine in New York. Yet such an explanation may be insufficient to account for the much stronger and successful process of Magyarization in Budapest. The Hungarians turned more firmly to state power to enforce Magyarization than did the Americans, and they had a more limited criterion of assimilation—the adoption of the Magyar language.

Hungarian nationality demanded the Magyar standard, both at the level of culture and as a state policy. Here again, a factor external to the metropolitan process itself may be relevant. In the Danubian Basin, filled as it was with nationalistic rivalries and preoccupied with the "minority question," it may well be that an intense nationalism, which implied a strong insistence on assimilation, was a necessary defense against both domination and fragmentation—or, later, reaction to dismemberment. By contrast, the United State's nineteenth century tradition of free security, a gift of two oceans, may have made it easier for New Yorkers to declare themselves permanently multiethnic and cosmopolitan, making room for the hyphenate in America.

At any event, metropolitan cultural pluralism was sharply limited by national identity in Hungary. Magyar remained the standard, whether because urbanites were so willing to assimilate or because they saw no alternative to assimilation. By contrast, in New York Americanization failed to fully assimilate immigrants. A compromise position, probably deriving from the relative weakness of traditional culture, seems to have emerged in New York. Instead of the Americanization of particular ethnic groups, ethnicity itself was Americanized. The general identity of "ethnic" (with no clear or specific ethnic heritage, only ethnicity itself) emerged in the 1920s as an inclusive metropolitan type, and this was apparent in emerging forms of mass culture, as Robert Snyder shows in Chapter 7.

Responding to the opportunity or imperative of an ethnically diverse mass audience, vaudeville, movies, and newspapers emphasized the commonalities even while playing on stereotypes of difference. Portrayals of ethnicity, as Snyder observes, were "multisided and could mean different things to different members of the vaudeville audience." The popular entertainer Sophie Tucker exemplified the American approach when she used Yiddish words (hence signaling difference) to evoke mass audience response to the universal of motherhood in her famous song, "My Yiddisha Mama." This use of ethnicity had the effect of depoliticizing it in mass culture. As Snyder argues, the mass culture forms that emerged in early twentieth century New York "could speak *to* many different New Yorkers, but only rarely could they speak *for* them." What Snyder shows in the case of vaudeville is true of the movies as well.

These different patterns of assimilation in Budapest and New York had large cultural, even political, consequences. Cosmopolitanism was never fully legitimated by metropolitan life in Hungary, as it was in the United States, where this definition of ethnicity was associated especially with New York City. In representations of America emanating from New York, nothing was more American than being ethnic. Ethnicity thus generally defused conflict, while the sharpness of definitions in Budapest deepened conflict, both in popular culture forms, as Géza Buzinkay suggests in Chapter 9, and in politics—ultimately with tragic consequences.

The process of ethnic interaction in New York proposed a novel model of ethnic relations. By 1930 no dominant group could represent the culture into which minorities or newcomers were to be assimilated. There was a double process of creolization at work. The dominant culture itself was plastic and pluralistic, and a certain degree of ethnic particularism was legitimized in politics and culture. While Jews, who constituted in excess of 20 percent of the population of Budapest, never made the particular interests of the Jewish "community" a political issue, pressing ethnic interests in a context of ethnic rivalry was the stuff of New York City politics. Circumstances in Budapest discouraged such particularism among the Jews. For them the advancement of general rights of toleration would be at once a general and a particularistic interest of greater importance than the issues of ethnic advantage so important in New York City politics.

In 1880 there had been a dominant Protestant ethos in New York, which was lost by 1930. Demographic patterns by then supported a more complex model of group relations. By 1930 there was no dominant culture group by numbers; Protestants (including blacks), Jews, and Catholics were represented in roughly equal numbers in New York. While Budapest represented an *incorporation* model of assimilation, New York offered a new kind of pluralism. Beginning with Randolph Bourne's famous essay on "Trans-National America," published in 1916, intellectuals in New York began to project onto America a cosmopolitan American culture, unified but an ongoing product of multicultural interaction. American culture in this view was not something to be discovered in the past, but rather to be made in the future with the collaboration of immigrants. Behavior, of course, did not fully correspond to this prescription, even if it was well grounded in experience. But the point is not behavior; rather it is a conception pro-

Figure I.3 Budapest, *Kálvin Tér (Square) and Museum of Fine Arts*, 1900. György Klösz, *Budapest Anno . . .* (Budapest: Corvina, 1979).

posed and widely embraced by New York intellectuals that was inconceivable in Budapest.

The development of commercial forms of culture in New York seemed to further undermine Americans' sense of their historical culture, and it provided a meeting place for native and immigrant populations, especially among the young. Many of the new forms of cultural expression that in New York became the foundation of popular, commercialized culture were in Budapest much more closely associated with traditional or elite culture. Early Hungarian films, for example, were made in close association with major Hungarian writers and actors; 90 percent of early Hungarian motion pictures were based on literary works. Though a popular medium in Budapest as well as in New York, cinema had a greater impact upon "high" culture in Budapest than in New York or, perhaps, anywhere else in the world. In New York, by contrast, movies were made by new people, marginal to established elite culture, often in fact from immigrant backgrounds.

The audience partly and significantly shaped American commercial culture, often using it for larger social and cultural as well as personal purposes. Behavior that was encouraged or at least permitted in the marketplace of commercial culture facilitated major changes in the culture, particularly the development of heterosocial entertainment and public display of sexuality in entertainment and leisure activities. Moreover, films from the era portraying the two cities suggest that the public spaces of New York were, in comparison with Budapest, significantly charged with erotic expectancy. In her paper presented to the conference Kathy Peiss explained the manner and degree to which New York's commercial entertainment zones brought about and legitimated new relationships of the sexes in public.

American commercialized culture broke boundaries in a way that unified much of the population as "modern" consumers, but it also sharpened other boundaries, particularly between itself and an increasingly self-conscious, self-contained, and sacralized "high" culture. Commercial culture came to be associated with the metropolis, representing excitement and cultural promiscuity. Through the commercial organization of national culture, headquartered in New York and covered by the media (including advertising) in New York, the city profoundly influenced the national culture, nourishing modern values.

In both cities the process of the sacralization of culture occurred in tandem with an opposite effect—the popularization of culture. While the former process contributed to the segregation of metropolitan society, the latter, mostly performing arts, movies, musical theaters, sports, and newspapers, nourished a broad metropolitan identity. This identity, often associated with nationalist as well as with metropolitan themes, encouraged a collective sense of national culture. Because of the linguistic diversity in East Central Europe, music proved the most effective artistic medium in the creation of a cosmopolitan cultural language transcending class and national differences, not only in the city but throughout the Habsburg Empire. In Paris and London, cities at the center of relatively homogeneous national cultures, operetta provided "social and political satire." But in Budapest, a heterogeneous city in a multinational empire, operetta offered integration as well. Péter Hanák in Chapter 8 reflects that "with the 'Merry Widow' and some other works Lehár performed a real feat. . . . He managed

Figure I.4 New York, *Herald Square*, 1909. Broadway looking north from 34th Street. Museum of the City of New York. The Byron Collection.

to reintegrate a very differentiated city culture in the rejuvenated operetta," appealing to all classes.

Modernism, the Metropolis, and Nationality

Because the history of modernism in the arts is so much associated with the urbanism of Haussmann's and Baudelaire's Paris, one's first impulse is to assume such a connection for all great cities. In New York the city's modernist aesthetic in art, photography, and literature was very much associated with a sense of the unprecedented newness of the city, drawing upon specific images to project this vision. The artistic expression of modernity in New York drew upon the technological and architectural transformation of the city, particularly the development of the skyscraper. Skyscraper and skyline became both favored subjects of art and provocations to formalist experimentation.

Budapest had no skyscrapers. Its artists, though they generated modernist works, did not develop a self-consciously urbanist modernism. In architecture, for example, there was a great receptivity to European modernism in Budapest. Modernist architecture in the city was powerfully original, yet it produced no symbols for the representation of the city itself that corresponded to the skyscraper in New York. Nor did the painters of Budapest create images of the city comparable to those with which New York painters defined for Americans the modernity of New York.

Since Hungarians, as Éva Forgács points out in Chapter 12, were ambivalent about modernization and modernism, their representations of modernity were often cloaked in ornamentation that suggested a pseudocontinuity with the past, pseudo because it claimed popular folk roots but denied much of Hungary's premodern past. The architectural avant-garde, Ödön Lechner, for example, reached back to folk motifs as decorative elements for modern buildings, while in music modernist Béla Bartók went even further in developing modern structures out of national folk elements. These were not nostalgic gestures; they were modernist in intent, seeking to define a new Hungarian culture. But the weight of history and, especially, the struggle for defining a new national consciousness compelled modernists to find the roots of a new Hungary in the past. Yet much of the past had to be denied: that past which was identified with the traditional nobility of Central Europe. In order to challenge the past of this immediately premodern history and culture, Hungarian modernists went back behind it to previous and presumably more pure popular cultures. This "archaization" created a popular idea of the nation that was an alternative to the traditional ideas of the ruling nobility.

24

While there were efforts in the 1910s, 1920s, and 1930s in New York to recover a "usable past" to be enlisted in the task of creating a new American culture, one is struck by the confidence with which New York intellectuals let a historical definition of American culture recede in favor of a conception of an American culture yet to be made out of the diverse materials, social and aesthetic, made available by metropolitan life.

New York intellectuals did not seek to establish historical roots for the cosmopolitan and modern culture they proposed. Nor did they seek to redefine traditional American culture. Rather, they embraced New York's cosmopolitan and modern culture as a standard, as an example for Americans who would seek to revitalize the nation's culture. Hungarian artists and intellectuals had a much more complex task: they felt compelled to balance tradition (or history) and modernity, Hungarian nationalism and European cosmopolitanism. How to be modern but still rooted in the Hungarian past? How to be European but still national?

American modernists were anxious to escape from the suffocating world of small-town America, and their revolt against the national mythology of small-town life is a major theme of much of the literature of the period. In contrast, Hungarian writers often brought traditional values to bear against the mechanical and alienated life of the metropolis. Few Hungarian writers saw the new values of the metropolis as the basis of a transformed national culture, something New York intellectuals, such as those associated with the magazine *Seven Arts,* indeed envisioned.

The hold of the past in New York was weak, and it offered no resistance to the quest for modernity. New York's artists, Wanda Corn explains in Chapter 11, stressed, in the pictorial language they developed, those New York qualities that were different from European capitals as well as from the rest of the United States. They were buoyed by the comments of European critics and artists who associated New York with, in the phrase of Francis Picabia, "extreme modernity." For New York artists as well as for European visitors, there seemed to be a link forged between "modernity, New York, and Americanness." Hungarians were not inclined to associate modernity with Budapest, nor Hungarian nationality with modernity or the city. Neither modern nor traditional artists made Budapest an important source of imagery or form. Indeed, as Éva Forgács points out, the special character and social problematic of Budapest's modernity did not find an appropriate language of local, urban visual expression.

The Hungarian avant-garde learned from Paris but not from its urbanism. They adapted French formal developments to the painting of

Hungarian landscapes and figure painting. The weight of traditional culture was simply much stronger in Budapest than in New York—a place where its weakness may have been frightening to some. Budapest was a historical city; New York was a modern city, hectically so.

Between the famous Armory Show of 1913 and the founding of the Museum of Modern Art in 1929, modern art found a secure home in New York. Such was not the case in Budapest. There was no continuity or organic development of Hungarian art, with the events of 1918–1919 marking an especially important break. Advanced or avant-garde Hungarian artistic development, Éva Forgács argues, was "severely broken and discontinuous," and this, she further observes, symbolizes the "lack of consensus" that marked Hungarian history in this era.

Writers in Budapest were less engaged with urban themes than were their New York counterparts. Few made the description and evocation of the city's life and form a focus of their writing. Their urban concerns were phrased in terms of a tension between novel urban values and those of a familiar rural past. The subject of most Hungarian writing, Miklós Lackó argues in Chapter 14, was the resolution of the play of tradition versus liberalism. Metropolitanism was rarely celebrated for itself. Nationalism and national political and cultural traditions were more powerful than metropolitanism in Budapest. New Yorkers, less certain about what tradition or even nationality were, were quicker to embrace modern (and cosmopolitan) definitions of American culture.

In Hungary, because of its "late and limited modernization," provincial and nationalist associations persisted longer and more strongly than in America. It was more difficult, therefore, to establish alternative metropolitan versions of national identity. Metropolitan writers, whether Magyar, German, or Jewish, unlike, for example, the Jews and gentiles associated with *Seven Arts* in New York, hesitated to assume a role as formulators of a cosmopolitan national culture.

New York writers, like the early twentieth century New York painters, were fascinated by the newness of the metropolitan life being developed in the city. Hungarian writers did not find a similar appeal in Budapest's metropolitan innovations. More often they evoked the old city of their youth, emphasizing the "homelike appeal of the streets." It is precisely this older, family-oriented culture, the culture of the small town, that New York City writers resisted, rejecting, in the phrasing of Philip Fisher in Chapter 13, the "small town norm of family life."

The greater number of both New York and Budapest writers were from provincial towns, not the metropolis, but the American writers turned against the small town in a way the Hungarian writers did not. In the work of Endré Ady, Hungary's finest writer, there is an impulse, in the words of Miklós Lackó, to "bridge the conflict between urban and provincial literature." One finds no analogue among major New York writers, though many "local color" writers, some of whom made New York a base after achieving success, played this theme, as did the writers of the Southern "agrarian" movement in the 1920s and 1930s.

Ady, Lechner, and Bartók modulated modernist and traditional elements in literature, architecture, and music, while the American writers considered by Philip Fisher sought to remake their lives out of the metropolitan experience, with its offer of Bohemian freedom. In Fisher's account of Theodore Dreiser we follow the writer's shift from a realistic novel of urban social concern (*Sister Carrie*, a novel of provincial migration to the city) to the pleasure and freedom of modernism in *A Gallery of Women*. Hungarian writers, by contrast, were little inclined to turn away from public life and move into this realm of subjectivity and individualism. There were some expressions of an individualistic modernism between 1925 and 1933 in the work of Gyula Krúdy, for example, but the movement was less intense than in Western Europe or even in New York. Hence the experience of literary culture in Budapest in the 1920s was radically different from the increasingly aesthetic, subjective modernism of Paris and New York that the New York critic Edmund Wilson criticized in *Axel's Castle*.

In both cities cultural innovation and elite culture owed much to the participation of Jews. The cosmopolitan and modern ideal of American culture was the product of a Jewish/WASP collaboration. It is important, however, to keep in mind the sequence and character of Jewish participation in early twentieth century New York culture. Before World War I, culminating perhaps with the establishment of the 291 Gallery by Alfred Stieglitz and the *Seven Arts* magazine by James Oppenheim, Waldo Frank, and the gentile Van Wyck Brooks, the key Jewish presence was from an earlier German-Jewish migration, now comfortably upper middle class, cultivated, and assimilated. Later, the Eastern European Jewish community populating the dense precinct of the Lower East Side would make its mainstream cultural impact, with the founding and phenomenal success of the *Partisan Review* in the late 1930s and the development of Abstract Expressionist painting in the 1940s. Although it is clear that assimilated Jews collaborated with secularized gentiles of similar persuasion in the development of Budapest's cultural and political modernism, the gentry nonetheless tended to identify cosmopolitanism and cultural modernism in Hungary with Jewishness and often with transnational ideologies like liberalism and socialism as well. This pattern of associations made metropolitan culture more vulnerable during the nationalistic and anti-Semitic postwar years. The metropolitan and self-consciously modern culture of New York found native WASP spokesmen (Edmund Wilson, Randolph Bourne, and John Dewey, for example) as often as Jewish spokesmen, and this may have made it less vulnerable.

Our studies suggest that the two cities underwent similar processes of metropolitan transformations. But the results were profoundly and revealingly different. With regard to infrastructure development and urban services, one finds a reasonable degree of parallelism in the two cities, but in respect to politics and culture there is a striking divergence. In New York the political and cultural dimensions of metropolitan development proceeded in an autochthonous fashion, little deflected (perhaps even sustained) by external influences, whether from European or American sources. Budapest represents a different pattern, far more subject to the impact of extraurban constraints and pressures that often undermined the apparent logic of metropolitan development. Especially after World War I, the significance of circumstances outside of or more extensive than the metropolitan process itself—the war and the terms of the peace, nationalism, and the weight of historical culture—are visibly determinative. Our focus on the city, then, leads us back, as perhaps it should, to broader questions inherent in the consideration of the relation of a metropolis to its nation, and a nation's relation to its metropolis.

Part I

POLITICS: PARTICIPATION AND POLICY

*T*HE DRAMATIC expansion of the population and territory of Budapest and New York and the restructuring of their economies put enormous pressure on traditional social and political institutions. The two cities were mercantile/administrative centers in 1870, but by 1900 they had become industrial centers and national financial and business administration hubs. The resulting enlargement of social life—both in scale and in degree of differentiation—occurred at all levels.

This growth complicated inherited categories of political identity. Would existing political institutions accommodate the newcomers and these structural changes in society? What political means were available to traditional elites and to the new middle and working classes? Did all of these changes alter the meaning and role of politics in the context of the metropolis? What was the capacity of politics to integrate and unify the growing population of the two cities? Or, to invert the historical question, is there evidence that political practice not only represented the underlying social divisions of the modern metropolis but even constituted these divisions?

The dimensions of economic and population change can be quickly sketched for both cities. Between 1870 and 1910, Budapest grew from about 300,000 to just under 1.1 million residents, while New York, larger to begin with, grew from 942,000 to 4.7 million. The absolute numbers are of significantly different orders but the ratios of the new to the old populations of the two cities are comparable in magnitude. The number of new arrivals in Budapest amounted to almost three times the 1870 population of the city; New York absorbed a new population nearly four times as numerous as its 1870 population. These migrant populations, equal to a new city of more than three-quarters of a million people in the case of Budapest and almost four million in New York's, had to be housed and integrated into urban social institutions. It was an unprecedented political and technical task shared by all late nineteenth century metropolises.

Most of the inmigrants found the means of making their livelihoods in the expanding industrial sector. But not all were relegated to industrial labor. The expanding middle classes absorbed many of these immigrants and inmigrants. Most of those who moved into the middle stratum were in the lower rungs of that stratum, mostly in petit bourgeois occupations, but growing numbers found employment in the growing bureaucracy (particularly in Budapest). Others joined the managerial ranks of larger incorporated economic enterprises increasingly concentrated in Budapest and, especially, in New York, where the growth of business administration was represented by the emergence of Lower Manhattan's famous skyline of tall buildings. The United States census of 1910 indicated that 37 percent of all employed males in New York City followed professional, managerial, clerical, or entrepreneurial pursuits. All ethnic groups shared in this trend, albeit in varying degrees and at different levels. The new middle class of Budapest expanded too, but the specifically industrial workers in the city expanded more rapidly, constituting nearly 60 percent of the city's gainfully employed in 1910. These workers in Budapest represented 28 percent of all Hungarian industrial workers in 1910. By contrast, only about 37 percent of the gainfully employed of New York in 1910 were industrial workers, and the proportion of the American industrial labor force employed in New York dropped from 16 percent in 1890 to 14 percent in 1900, where it remained into the 1930s.

When considering the political implications of these large numbers of industrial workers, it is important to note that in both cities the majority labored in enterprises with fewer than fifty employees. But there were more large factories (1,000 or more employees) in Budapest than in New York. Both cities were centers for the financing and management of large national industrial enterprises, but more of the Hungarian factories were actually located in Budapest itself (50 percent of all large Hungarian factories). New York's financial and managerial elite directed a geographically dispersed national network of factories. By far the greater number of large factories were located in other parts of the nation, even if the corporate headquarters were in New York. For example, U.S. Steel, the first billion-dollar corporation, was created in New York in 1901 by J. P. Morgan and his partners, but the plants were in Pittsburgh, Pennsylvania; Gary, Indiana; and other locations.

The demographic impact of growth was different in Budapest and New York. The influx of migrants to the city of Budapest, especially after World War I, were heavily ethnic Hungarians from various parts of the Austro-Hungarian Empire or its successor states, and they tended to increase the ethnic homogeneity of the city. In New York, the influx, especially after 1880, brought new groups without significant previous representation, and they changed the ethnic map of the city in fundamental ways. The German, Irish, and native-born New Yorkers of 1870 were reduced to minority status with the arrival of large numbers of Russian (Jewish), Austro-Hungarian, and Italian immigrants. These new groups increased the heterogeneity of New York, making integration of the population more difficult. Yet—and this is surely counterintuitive—this fragmentation may have facilitated political stability. The relative homogeneity in Budapest may, again counterintuitively, have clarified and sharpened the basis for group conflict in that city.

Social life in New York was divided at all levels. Spatial segregation by ethnicity, class, and race produced a complex mosaic that was further divided by the number and variety of workplaces. This pattern of fragmentation was as evident at the top of the social structure as at the lower strata. New York had no unified elite; rather, it had several elites associated with various functional sectors (or interests) in the economy—trade, finance, manufacturing, landowning, corporate management, railroads and communications, lawyers, and so on. Budapest's elite, by contrast, was divided into only two classes whose members operated across the functional sectors: the traditional landed aristocracy, whose urban base was old Buda; and the rising, heavily German and Jewish, entrepreneurial elite of Pest. Bipolarity in Budapest, reenforced by ethnoreligious differences, may have given focus to conflict, particularly when the landed aristocracy and gentry became disenchanted with the non-Magyar (Jewish) modernizers.

Fragmentation in New York seems to have diffused both power and conflict. Members of New York's various elites had significant power, but no one group could achieve control. Nor did they share enough interests and social circles to form a unified front that would enable them to govern. This fragmented pattern of elite politics, evident in New York even in the eighteenth century, opened the way for other groups to claim important, if always partial, access to political power.

In Budapest the narrowness of the suffrage encouraged a working-class and lower-middle-class politics focused on the vote, and this unified a large portion of the city's population, making them susceptible to ideological mobilization. But in New York the combination of wide suffrage (universal after 1920) and fragmentation seems to have encouraged the proliferation of localistic and ethnic political identities. It is often remarked that American politics emphasizes ethnicity over class and is less ideological than European politics. That view finds support in these studies. There is, however, another way to phrase the difference between the political cultures of New York and Budapest. If the political culture of New York was *structured* by the diffusion of political power from the center to a myriad of smaller and particularistic nodes of power, the *work* of politics in its metropolitan context was to harmonize differences in the interest of holding together diverse political coalitions. Far from encouraging harmonizing negotiations, politics in Budapest worked to give expression to social cleavages that sharpened with time and increasingly divided the metropolis against itself.

So far in this introduction the meaning of participation has been emphasized, but in their chapters, Zsuzsa Nagy and David Hammack invite us to ponder the relationship of participation to policy result. To what extent did democratic participation shape urban policy in either city? Two very different urban political cultures, with different relations to the nation-state, seem to have sustained rather similar technical and "progressive" municipal initiatives. What ought we make of this puzzle? Or is it a puzzle? Can one say that among the professional fields engaged with urban issues a translocal municipal expertise circulating in the international systems of cities shaped actual municipal policy at least as much as democratic politics?

One is tempted to ask to what extent formal political practices deserve credit or blame for metropolitan stability or conflict. Do other social and cultural phenomena explain or at least contribute to these outcomes? Did urban sociospatial patterns and cultural expression work in tandem with politics or did they counter the work of politics? Did these other metropolitan phenomena further the diffusion of power and nourish harmony in New York while sharpening the focus of conflict in Budapest? These broader issues link the chapters in this section with those in the following sections.

Zsuzsa Nagy and David Hammack collaborated very closely, and have organized their chapters descriptively, treating topics in Budapest and New York in parallel fashion. The two chapters lay out the political and economic context for the whole book. They also raise, indirectly, some fairly broad questions about the changing nature of politics and political power, and their relationship to other dimensions of metropolitan life and culture.

Chapter 1

Transformations in the City Politics of Budapest: 1873–1941

ZSUZSA L. NAGY

ETWEEN 1873, when Budapest officially became the capital of Hungary, and 1941, when the country entered World War II, Hungary witnessed fundamental changes which deeply influenced the city's politics. The national political system changed dramatically three times in that period. The liberal dualistic system was followed by a bourgeois democratic revolution and a soviet-type dictatorship. Then came the conservative nationalistic regime headed by Regent Miklós Horthy. Two themes in the city's history remained unchanged, however: (1) the ambition to develop Budapest as much as possible; and (2) the fight for universal suffrage, since urban workers and even members of the lower middle class lacked the right to vote. The life of the city became politicized: ideological concepts shaped civic perceptions. After the turn of the century, when ethnic diversity and identification of the population lessened, class and group interests and rivalries took political forms.

The capital became not only the center of state administration but that of the economic and cultural life of the nation as well. It had no rival among the towns of the country, and the consequences of the peace treaty of Trianon even strengthened this special role.

A Half-Century of Growth and Transformation

The desire to create a unified capital by combining Pest, Buda, and Óbuda was first launched by the revolutionary government of 1848.

At least three events prepared the realization of this: the opening of the first permanent bridge, the Chain Bridge, connecting the two banks of the Danube in 1849; the 1867 Compromise between Austria and Hungary, which created the Dual Monarchy; and the setting up of the Capital Public Works Commission for financing and managing city development in 1870. Of these events, the 1867 Compromise was the most important; and on November 17, 1873, the newly named city of Budapest officially became the capital of Hungary. By the turn of the century Budapest had become a metropolis, and in it were concentrated all the changes and results brought about by the capitalist and bourgeois developments of the country.[1]

Apart from their geographical situation, Pest and Buda differed significantly. Four-fifths of the population lived on the Pest side, and the majority of industrial and commercial enterprises and banks were located there as well. According to contemporary description, "Pest was in possession of the masses and the tools that defined the spiritual and moral outlook of the city." On the other hand, "Most of Buda represented the conservative traditions that were still attached to the past and existed far from the noise of Pest."[2] Each district had its own special character. The real heart of the capital, the financial and commercial center, could be found in District V. District IV represented metropolitan fashion and style with elegant shops, hotels, and promenade on the riverbank. The Royal Palace and the ministries, the governmental buildings and elegant palaces ruled District I in Buda. The former Óbuda became District III, dotted with factories; its inhabitants comprised workers, shopkeepers, and craftsmen.

The dynamic economic development and the building boom of the late nineteenth century drew migrants to the city. Between 1870 and 1910 the capital's population grew by more than 600,000 people. Later on, this growth slowed down—but it never stopped. By 1910, 5 percent of the country's population lived there. From the very beginning, people arriving from the rural countryside were the largest migrant group. In 1880, 47 percent of Budapesters were born in Hungary. By 1930, this ratio had risen to nearly 60 percent.[3]

That Budapest was the center of the country's whole life can be demonstrated by a few examples. The railroad and the highroad system built up by the turn of the century were centered radially on Budapest, while the capital became the greatest Hungarian port on the Danube, a position maintained up to the end of World War II.[4] Five great Budapest banks controlled nearly 60 percent of the country's banking capital. In 1910 almost 36 percent of the large factories, those with more than one thousand workers each, could be found in Budapest. At that time more industrial workers lived in Budapest than

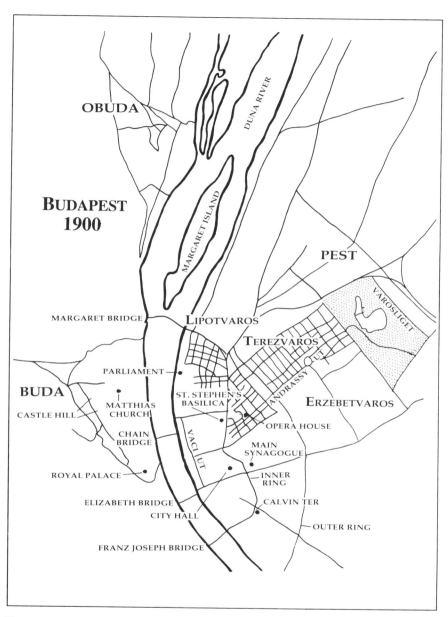

Figure 1.1 Map of Budapest, 1900. Drawn by Kimberly Santini.

Figure 1.2 Budapest, Pest from Buda, Parliament to left, St. Stephens to right, factory stacks in background, 1900. György Klösz, *Budapest Anno* (Budapest: Corvina, 1979).

the total population of Kolozsvár (Cluj), the capital of Transylvania. Twelve percent of the shopkeepers and 19 percent of the craftsmen of the country worked in the capital.[5]

Budapest's long history is rich in dramatic changes and catastrophes, a pattern that continues in the present century. World War I and its consequences represented a drastic turning point. As part of the Austro-Hungarian Monarchy, and as a member of the defeated Central Powers, Hungary suffered in the peace treaty, losing 70 percent of its territory and 60 percent of its population. What is more, the Romanian Army occupied the capital for a short time in 1919, a humiliation for a city that had not been under foreign rule since the Turks in the sixteenth and eighteenth centuries.

The Peace Treaty of Trianon changed not only the country's position in the Danubian Basin but that of Budapest within Hungary. A city that had been envisioned for a great country became the capital of a small one. The sphere of influence of Budapest was consequently sharply curtailed, but its importance and role in the country's life became even more dominant than it had been.

Its population passed the one million mark, while only two other cities in the nation had as many as 100,000 inhabitants: Debrecen and Szeged. The historical dominance of Hungary's capital city was increased after 1918, and in the postwar era 12 percent of the country's population was concentrated there.[6] Now, almost a fifth of all industrial enterprises, more than half the great factories, a quarter of the trading companies, and 80 percent of the department stores and large shops were located in Budapest. And the economic life of the country came under the control of only four or five metropolitan banks.[7]

The capital functioned like a melting pot and, in a few decades, had created a practically homogenized Hungarian society out of an ethnically diverse population. In 1873 the German-speaking people constituted the most numerous national minority, but by the beginning of the twentieth century they were only a small community. The Slovaks, the second largest minority, less numerous than the Germans and with weaker bourgeois and intellectual strata, were nearly completely absorbed by the Hungarian society of the capital. At the time of unification, Budapest was "much more Hungarian" than the country, and this characteristic feature became more visible later on.[8] By the beginning of the twentieth century the ethnic diversity of the capital had practically disappeared, and ethnicity lost its significant role in city life and city politics.

The occupational structure of Budapest society differed considerably from that of the country as a whole. Between 1873 and 1941 two groupings absorbed Budapesters: the urban workers and the lower-middle-class strata. Nowhere in Hungary was the concentration or proportion of urban workers, shopkeepers, craftsmen, clerks, and civil servants as high as in the capital.[9] This social division—more than ethnic difference—gave shape to the city's politics. Every political party declared itself to be the real representative of the interests of the city and its population. Their social bases were very similar. What really differentiated them was political argumentation and ideology.

The process of assimilation went on spontaneously, inspired by capitalist development and the new metropolitan conditions of life. For all the newcomers of Budapest, the Hungarians and the historical Hungarian social strata, mainly the gentry, offered the model of assimilation. Assimilation embodied primarily an identification with Hungarian national language, values, and aims. The question of giving up ethnic culture and traditions was not considered significant.

Here we should note the case of Budapest's Jews, who were a religious group, not a national minority, as in Poland. Jews were a substantial population, but they never considered themselves a national minority group nor did the rest of the society so consider them. One of the most prominent representatives of the new Jewish bourgeoisie, Vilmos Vázsonyi, declared many times that the Jews were first of all Hungarian and only after that Jews, with the same confessional distinction accorded to Roman Catholics or Protestants.[10] Jews were concentrated in Budapest. They made up only 5 percent of the country's population, but in Budapest they constituted 20 percent of the population.[11] Since the Jews of Budapest declared themselves to be Hungarians, their presence raised the proportion of Hungarians among the capital's inhabitants.

Yet, the "Jewish question" did not disappear from political life. Anti-Semitism developed mainly after 1919, in Trianon Hungary. Jews were seen as competitors of the Christian middle class, and they were resented because they were more fully urbanized and had more important positions in professions engaged in directing Hungary's capitalist development. At the same time, the Jews were attacked because they played a large role in the working-class movement, including the Communist Party, and in the radical bourgeois democratic organizations, principally in the intellectual group led by Oscar Jászi. All kinds of social tensions were channeled against the Jews, mainly after 1919 and especially in the thirties. Conservative and right-wing-oriented elements attacked Jews both as capitalists alien to the traditional Hungarian society and as revolutionaries (Social Democrats and Communists).

Budapest had a twofold and contradictory place in public opinion. The capital, with its rapid development, urban achievements, and modern appearance, was considered to be representative of the nation's talent and productivity. This strengthened the pride and self-esteem of the nation. At the same time, strong hostility toward the city emerged, some reflecting real problems, some rooted in the traditional and conservative mentality. Nobody could deny that Budapest was oversized, especially in Trianon Hungary. There was such a large gap between the urbanization and modernization of the capital and the rest of the country that Budapest almost did not fit into the general conditions of Hungary. Though the city hall government suffered under the omnipotence of the state, Budapest appeared to the rest of the country to be part of or representative of the central state power. Budapest, with its modern social structure and new metropolitan values, seemed to be alien from the point of view of national society and a traditional mentality. Moreover, Budapest was the center of the two revolutions. Therefore, not only was a bourgeois democratic revolution attached to the city but also the existence of a Soviet-type dictatorship headed by Béla Kun.[12] In November 1919 when Admiral Horthy, later the Regent of Hungary, marched with his army into Budapest, he declared the capital a culpable city which deserved punishment and purging.[13]

Anti-Budapest feeling could not be maintained in the long run. Before 1918, Budapest had assumed a competitive role with Vienna in the Austro-Hungarian Monarchy. After 1918, Budapest acquired the function of representing the regime's aspiration to regain authority in the Danubian Basin. That ambition maintained Budapest's centrality in Hungary. Nothing can better demonstrate the place of Budapest in the country than the dilemma of the so-called Populist movement, which had its origins in the countryside. Although it was the sharpest critic of the capital's dominant role and modern values, it was forced to act mainly in the maligned city if it wanted to influence public opinion. What did not happen in Budapest did not, in effect, happen at all.

The Social Basis of Politics

When Budapest became the capital, the structure of the municipal leadership, particularly access of the inhabitants to city politics, reflected previous social-political conditions. As the capital changed, the tensions between the old structure and the new demands became even sharper and deeper.

The key question was the franchise system, including the system for electing aldermen. Between 1873 and 1920, municipal suffrage was limited by conditions of age, level of education, and financial position. The requirement of several years of city residence prevented a great number of the inhabitants from voting because they were newcomers. During this period, only about 5 percent of the population had the right to vote.[14] The other weak point of the franchise system was *virilism/virilismus*.[15] Virilism was well known in Central Europe and not a special Hungarian phenomenon. In this system the payers of the highest taxes had privileges that other groups of inhabitants, including great parts of the lower middle class and urban workers, did not have. These groups were closed out from the franchise system and consequently from influencing city politics. According to the franchise system, half of the aldermen had to be elected from among the greatest taxpayers, the virilists, though their number (1,200) represented only 0.4 percent of the capital's population. Such was the context for the demand of the bourgeois strata and the industrial workers for general suffrage and the secret ballot. Under the mayorship of the well-known liberal politician István Bárczy,[16] the City Hall supported this demand by official proposals addressed to the government. Bárczy also joined the different demonstrations organized by the Liberals, Democrats and Social Democrats.[17]

Who were the virilist aldermen? Between 1873 and 1914, their largest and gradually growing section was composed of homeowners who owned apartment houses and whose income derived from the apartments that they rented. In 1914 nearly half of the aldermen (48.5 percent) came from this group, reflecting the building boom of the city.[18] The second major group was made up of merchants who invested their profits in industry and partly in real estate. As time went on, the ratio of general managers and directors of companies and stock corporations as well as lawyers grew simultaneously. This expressed the growing importance of the professionals and the vocational intelligentsia. Law was a path of social mobility, a path followed by many Jews.

The virilist system has been attacked and declared conservative and antidemocratic by contemporaries and in current Hungarian historiography. But perhaps nothing can better demonstrate the contradictory political and social situation than the composition of the virilists themselves, of whom the greater part came from the new bourgeoisie. They were representatives of economic modernization and held modern liberal ideas. Most of them were Jews. This antiquated system, in fact, opened up the road to city politics for a new and modern social stratum. While the pauperized former gentry maintained power in the countryside, this system in the capital made such a pattern impossible. The great taxpayers of the city lived overwhelmingly in Pest, the bourgeois, modernizing part of Budapest. (There were eight times as many greatest taxpayers in Pest as in Buda, and those actually paying the highest taxes lived only in Pest.)

Among the freely elected aldermen, the professionals and intellectuals of the middle class dominated; this condition permitted Vilmos Vázsonyi, organizer of the urban-middle- and lower-middle-class strata, to be elected member of the Municipal Assembly in 1901. Craftsmen, shopkeepers, junior clerks, or industrial workers could not get into the Municipal Assembly before 1920.

There was another important characteristic feature—before 1920, women could neither vote nor serve. In the interwar period there were a few women in the Municipal Assembly with different party memberships, but the dominant pattern hardly changed.

Before World War I, the inhabitants and voters of Budapest were not organized in independent municipal political parties. Those who were granted suffrage gathered in municipal districts headed by "chiefs" and followed the lines of the national parties based on constitutional and not social interests. By the end of the nineteenth century, such politics did not serve the perceived needs of the city, and political parties emerged, which began to represent class interests.

Part of the industrial and urban workers were organized into the Social Democratic Party (SDP).[19] The middle-class and lower-middle-class bourgeoisie concentrated mainly in the Democratic Party (DC) headed by Vilmos Vázsonyi, though some of this stratum were in the Free Bourgeois Party led by the Roman Catholic former civil servant Péter Kasics.[20] The high bourgeoisie, which was part of the ruling elite in coalition with the great landowners and aristocracy, did not take part in this political movement.

The DC was the first bourgeois political party based on social or class interests. It sought to represent the interests of the lower and middle strata of the urban bourgeoisie. It was this party that formed the political base for the modernizing and liberal administrations of István Bárczy between 1906 and 1918.

The DC was organized on the Pest side, and four Pest districts defined its social background (Districts V, VI, VII, and VIII). In these districts, the greater part of the inhabitants were shopkeepers, craftsmen, clerks, and some workers. These districts were also the place of residence for 68 percent of the Jewish population of Budapest.[21] Though the leaders and the members of this party were mainly Jews, the party did not represent special Jewish interests. On the contrary, it defined itself as the voice of the lower middle class and the urban population in general.

Liberal and modern ideas influenced the policy of the City Hall in the first two decades of the century due to the activities of Mayor Bárczy and that of the DC. The conservative and Catholic Free Bourgeois Party commanded little influence in city politics before 1918, largely because the franchise system did not reflect the social transformations that had occurred in Budapest since 1873. Yet, in the first two decades of the century, liberal and modern ideas influenced the policy of the City Hall due to the activities of Mayor Bárczy and of the DC.

The task of organizing the inhabitants into municipal political parties and of changing the franchise system fell to the Horthy regime. This process was not without contradictions. One of them was that a conservative and antiliberal regime democratized the franchise system and abolished virilism. The other, equally important, was that the SDP, the political representative of the working class, got into the Municipal Assembly in 1925.

By Act 9:1920 the number of voters in Budapest rose sharply, partly because women were given the franchise and became members of the Municipal Assembly. The parliament sanctioned this act as a necessary step on the road to the regime's consolidation after the two revolutions. Subsequent legislation concerning Budapest narrowed the circle of voters.

The abolition of the virilist system radically reduced the proportion of Jews among the aldermen. From that time onward Jews could get into the Municipal Assembly only on the list of the liberal-democratic bourgeois parties and that of the SDP. The Christian national parties, which became the dominant power at City Hall, never had a Jewish candidate.

In the interwar period there were many municipal political parties in Budapest, but only three major political trends stand out. First, a definite conservative and Christian national trend was manifested by the Christian Municipal Party. Its conservatism produced an oppositional position against the governments when they seemed to be either too liberal in the twenties or too right-wing during the thirties. Second, up to 1939 there was a more moderate direction than that of the Christian Municipal Party with some liberal remnants. The United Municipal Party, the local branch of the government's party, had some liberal elements during the twenties. The third trend opposed the other two. The liberal-democratic bourgeois parties and the SDP were its representatives, and both endorsed the ideology of the Western-type bourgeois democracies.[22]

Made up of smaller Catholic groups, including the former Free Bourgeois Party, the Christian Municipal Party played a decisive role in city politics from 1920 until 1939. The government party could organize its local branch only in 1925, and its seats in the Municipal Assembly fell far short of those of the Christian Municipal Party.[23] There was a certain competition between these two parties, and the majority of the aldermen and the leading officeholders belonged to them.

The left-wing opposition, composed of the liberal-democratic bourgeois parties and the SDP, had strong representation in the Municipal Assembly and obtained a majority at the municipal elections in 1925.[24] Yet the left-wing opposition could not take over the city leadership. According to Act 6:1924 there was to be a large body of assigned members in addition to elected members. The proportion of assigned members of the Municipal Assembly was close to 20 percent, and they supported the Christian and government parties.[25] This explains why the left-wing parties could not elect István Bárczy mayor in 1926.

The distribution of mandates according to the place they were received reflects the social basis and character of the parties. Available sources make it possible to examine this distribution in 1930.[26]

Out of the elected aldermen, only 14 percent had seats in the Municipal Assembly before 1918. Their majority belonged to the Democratic Party. Almost 78 percent of the aldermen were elected from the Pest side. As in the pre-1918 period, this side of the city offered the social basis to the liberal democrats and the SDP. Pest provided 82 percent of their mandates while the Christian and government parties received only 70 percent. Four of the Pest districts (V, VI, VII, and VIII) had great importance for the left-wing parties. While the Christian and government parties got 47 percent of their mandates in these districts, the left-wing opposition won 65 percent. The particular features of these districts had not changed since the beginning of the century. If the left-wing parties had strength in Budapest, that was due to the lower-middle-class strata and the workers and last, but not least, to the Jews. While the Christian Municipal Party got half of the mandates of the 1st district in Buda, it won only a quarter of them in the District VII in Pest.[27]

The transformation of the aldermen's professional and social composition started before 1918, but the real turn came after that time. The highest taxpayers practically disappeared from the Municipal Assembly, their places taken by professionals who were independent or employed (lawyers, physicians, journalists, etc.). Representatives of other occupations appeared who were completely missing from the Municipal Assembly before 1918, including Roman Catholic ecclesiastic leaders and priests on the list of the Christian Municipal Party; party functionaries of the SDP; and industrial foremen and skilled workers. Leading government or public officials, as well as all people who were attached to the government by their jobs and incomes, belonged to the Christian and government parties. At the same time, private capitalists and freelance intellectuals had a distinguished place among the liberal-democratic aldermen.[28]

Between 1873 and 1941, there was no quota or stipulation of any kind that regulated the nationality and denominational division of the aldermen, and no official statistics were kept regarding nationality or religion. However, the first generation of the city's leaders and aldermen, including the lord mayors and the mayors, were largely of German origin. But this had no political significance, even at the end of the nineteenth century. There were quite a number of Jews among the elected aldermen before and after 1918. Before 1918, they came in mostly as virilists and on the list of the DC. After 1918, Jewish aldermen could be found among the social democrats as well as among the liberals. Before 1918 it was still possible for a Jew to be among the leading functionaries of the capital, like Ferenc Heltai, who was lord mayor in 1912; this was not true after 1918.

Beside the political parties, there were social organizations that influenced the political relations of City Hall. The majority of the liberal party members belonged to Freemason lodges despite the fact that their activity was banned by the Horthy regime. Freemasonry in Hungary was entwined with the democratic bourgeois movement from the turn of the century. The liberal-democratic aldermen could be found in the English-patterned Cobden Society as in the Fabian Society, and among the functionaries of the neologist Jewish community.[29] The leading members of the Christian Municipal Party and of the United Municipal Party played a primary role in the Roman Catholic social organization.[30]

City and State

The relationship between city and state was never harmonious during the period under discussion: conflicts emerged in political and economic fields. The municipality wanted to enlarge its autonomous rights, and the state wanted to maintain its paternalist and controlling role. In the long run, only the state could be successful.

Before 1918, the state had been the initiator of capitalist transformation and modernization; the first beneficiary of this activity was the capital. After 1918, under the conditions created by the Peace Treaty of Trianon and during the Great Depression, the capital needed the state's help even more. The City Hall accepted state intervention that would help develop the city and improve the conditions of metropolitan life. But it rebelled against intervention, which touched the political sphere and the city's autonomy.

The government, as an important contributor to the building up of Budapest, wanted to keep the City Hall under its control, particularly because the political character of the city leadership and the Municipal Assembly differed from that of the government. In the first decades of the twentieth century, in the era of Mayor Bárczy, the municipality moved in a very determined liberal-democratic direction, while the national government took a conservative turn under the leadership of Prime Minister Count István Tisza. At that time the fronts were clear: the City Hall stood on one side and the state government on the other.

After World War I, the situation changed and became more complicated. At that time the Christian Municipal Party took over the city leadership, representing a more conservative political trend than the government of Count István Bethlen. The policy of curtailing of autonomous rights was directed partly against the leading position of the Christian Municipal Party. The left wing opposition judged these conflicts to be a battle between two groups in power. The left, therefore, kept up a two-sided fight against both of them, although it was somewhat sympathetic toward Bethlen.

During the first half of the thirties, Prime Minister Gömbös tried to reorganize the country's entire political life following the Italian Fascist model. This unsuccessful attempt threatened the existence of the Christian Municipal Party and also the left wing opposition. For this reason the conservative municipal parties joined the left wing parties against the government under the slogan of defending constitutional order and rights. Finally, because the Christian Municipal Party could not defend its independence, the right wing government party of Prime Minister Béla Imrédy incorporated it in 1939. This was the end of a long and important era of the capital's political life.[31]

When the government brought the municipality more and more under its control, it employed only constitutional means. There was no need for drastic dictatorial measures because the Parliament, dominated by the government party, sanctioned every act concerning Budapest.[32]

Between 1873 and 1918, the lord mayor could be elected only from among the king's candidates and, later on, those of the regent. From 1934 on, the lord mayor was appointed by the regent. In 1934 only the joint efforts of the municipal parties could maintain the right of electing the mayor because Prime Minister Gömbös wanted to take it away from the Municipal Assembly. After 1918, the acts relating to Budapest gradually reduced the number of the elected aldermen, while the number of the assigned members remained the same. The institution of the assigned members itself strengthened the conservative trends and the influence of the central state power in the City Hall. The Municipal Assembly was called together less and less often and, from the mid-thirties on it was not allowed to deal with general or national political issues, only with special local problems.

All acts regarding the capital authorized the ministry of interior to suspend autonomy and to have a government commissioner appointed the head of Budapest. This happened once before 1918 (in 1906) and twice after 1918 (in 1920 and 1924).

After 1938 the state intervened harshly into city life by enacting anti-Jewish laws which touched the whole country. Jewish employees had to be dismissed from municipal firms and schools according to Act 4: 1939. On the basis of Act 19: 1941, 24 of the 108 elected aldermen were deprived of their mandates since they qualified as Jews by this act. This action profoundly changed the composition of left-wing aldermen.[33]

The economic conflicts between the municipality and the state were less spectacular but not less important. The City Hall's economy, taxation, its degree and use were regulated by acts passed by the Parliament. The taxation system was always harmful to city administration because Budapest and all the other towns had to pay an excessively higher proportion of the direct taxes than the rest of the country. To change the system was one of the aims of the Congress of Towns convened by Mayor Bárczy.[34]

In the twenties, when the Bethlen government executed the reorganization of the national economy, laws were laid down prescribing a reform of the capital's administration and the reduction of its staff members and their wages. The right to control municipal companies was given to the minister of the interior. The state was authorized to put a so-called reorganizing lord mayor in power at any time. Although the capital had the highest tax rates in the whole country, it could dispose of only part of the revenue. The leading parties of the city considered these restrictions unconstitutional and protested against their application to Budapest.[35] By doing so, the City Hall did not take into consideration that these were exceptional times. Only unified principles, which did not permit an exception in the favor of the capital, could set the country on solid economic grounds. First thought to be temporary, the state intervention became permanent because of the Depression and then the war. The municipal parties feared that state intervention on the economic field would spread to political intervention. And their fears were well based since that was what occurred.

Politics and Physical Development

The conditions of city development differed very much before and after 1918. The earlier period was long and prosperous, and the capital could be judged a metropolis by any European standard. That was the time when the main streets, thoroughfares, squares, parks, and official buildings were constructed, and when the basis of the urban infrastructure was laid down. Quantity and expansion characterized this era.

After World War I, Budapest experienced a fundamental halt in its expansion, as did the whole country. The interwar period did not have lasting prosperous phases. The economic stabilization of the country and the city were realized only around 1925, and then the Depression stopped a boom that had hardly started. During the first half of the thirties, lack of capital and high unemployment shadowed the activities of the municipality. Yet the building and modernization of the metropolitan infrastructure continued. Quality and technical modernization, rather than massive expansion, were the characteristic features, and many more inhabitants became beneficiaries of technical improvements than had been the case earlier.

The growth of the population was not followed by an increase of the city's territory. The size of the latter changed only slightly in the thirties. The city had been divided into ten districts from 1873 on. When Act 18: 1930 ordered the creation of four more districts, it was carried out by reorganizing the former territory, and only a few additional hectares were added to the capital. However, this reform accelerated the building activity in District XIV of Pest and Districts XI and XII of Buda.

Since the nineteenth century a suburban area of twenty-two locales around Budapest developed more rapidly than did the capital. These areas were attached to the city in the conduct of everyday life but had independent municipalities. The City Hall would have liked to create a "larger Budapest" by incorporating them into the capital, but this happened only after World War II.

The city, accompanied by the state in almost every field (i.e., housing, schooling, mass transportation), tried to meet the needs of the inhabitants for modernization. The efforts were not without some success. Budapest's late start in development actually had certain advantages, allowing the use of new technical means and the adoption of modern, liberal-spirited ideas of city politics. Mayor Bárczy and his followers believed that the city leaders were responsible for ensuring that all inhabitants of Budapest enjoyed the advantages of new technology regardless of their social status. Therefore, they thought it important to municipalize ownership of the most important public service companies.[36]

Budapest had a well-built mass transportation system. Though the first electric metro on the continent opened in 1896 in the Hungarian capital, transportation was based mainly upon streetcar lines. But with accelerated motorization, the bus lines increased in the interwar period. After long preparations, the City Hall took over the management of the different companies and created the unified metropolitan transport firm. Before World War I, four Danube bridges connected the two parts of the city. After the war, only one was opened and the construction of another one started.[37]

Due to the investments of private capital, banks, insurance companies, the City Hall, and the state, the increase in the number of apartments kept up with or even exceeded the growth of the population during the whole period discussed. However, the building activity had a certain periodicity. Between 1869 and 1900 the number of buildings rose by 74 percent. (In 1869 there were 9,351 buildings.) At the turn of the century, this process slowed down and prosperity returned only in the second half of the twenties. Up to 1941, 13,821 new buildings were constructed. Yet, because of the high prices of apartments, they were inaccessible to certain groups of the lower middle classes and the industrial workers.[38]

The appearance of the city was determined by the fact that 56 percent of the buildings were single stories, even in 1935. Houses with three or more stories could be found mainly in the inner districts.

The City Hall's program for the construction of small apartments, started by Mayor Bárczy, continued and was joined by large companies who built residential colonies for their workers. In the interwar period, the state's share in apartment buildings increased considerably. By the end of that period, 6–7 percent of all apartments were in the management of the city.

The development of new technologies accelerated in Hungary in the interwar years. By 1930 there was electric lighting and water in about 85 percent of the houses; gas in more than half of them. Before World War II, 60 percent of the country's telephone sets were in Budapest, as well as almost half of the country's automobiles.[39]

Education was considered important by the city leaders as a means of modernization and of Magyarization as well.[40] Before 1918 the City Hall spent a higher proportion of the municipal budget on the Budapest schools than the government spent of the state's budget on the whole country's schools. In this period the emphasis was on the elementary schools where education was free. The high schools' importance increased, and the social composition of their students changed. The lower high schools (die Bürgerschule), dedicated to the children of the bourgeoisie in the late nineteenth century, became more and more the typical school of the lower middle class and urban workers in the interwar period. At the same time, only a few new schools opened, and these were primarily high schools and technical schools. As part of the modernization process, physical training was introduced as a new subject and gymnasia were added to the school buildings.

The enlarged educational system and the easier access to it for the lower social strata helped to eliminate illiteracy in Budapest, but only partly lessened the social differences reflected in the students' social composition in the different types of schools.[41]

The basic institutions of the public health system were built up before 1918, but the interwar period brought significant improvements. Some special new hospitals opened, such as the first hospital to be dedicated exclusively to children as well as an emergency hospital, and new buildings were being added to the already existing hospitals. The City Hall built up the network of school physicians in the elementary schools and enlarged the mother and child welfare systems. By reforming the insurance system, the health care conditions of the lower classes and strata improved significantly.[42] Yet social differences did not disappear even from this field. The middle classes, for example, had their own hospital and insurance companies.

Within the framework of technical modernization, the country's only radio company started transmitting its program in Budapest.

Broadcasting and films played a great role in standardizing the cultural level of the society.

In the interwar period, comfortable conditions of life depended not so much on one's social place or financial resources but on whether one lived in a town or a village. And Budapest dwellers enjoyed the most privileged position. To be a metropolitan inhabitant meant that one enjoyed all the achievements of technical development and urban facilities at a level superior to that of the rest of the country. A contemporary observer noted: "Maybe he is only a simple worker . . . yet he gets plenty of public services, good paved roads, lighting, transportation, etc. . . . he can live and experience the dynamism of the highest standards of life to be found in Hungary."[43]

The collapse of the Austro-Hungarian Monarchy and the dismemberment of the old Hungarian kingdom brought drastic changes into the whole Danube Basin. Among the newly established independent states there were only two capital cities who lost their former hinterlands—Vienna and Budapest. The other old/new capitals (Prague, Bucharest, Belgrade) became growing and flourishing centers of countries with greatly enlarged territories and populations.

In Budapest city building was interrupted. After 1918 the state as well as the City Hall became impoverished, and the Great Crisis caused serious difficulties. Yet the conditions of city life improved due to the persistent efforts of the city leadership and the national government.

With the appearance of the municipal parties after 1918, the capital's inhabitants became more organized. The reform of the franchise system introduced by the new political regime enlarged the circles of voters: the lower middle class and industrial workers could now elect their aldermen.

Before 1918 liberal politicians and ideas dominated the City Hall. After 1918 conservative and Christian parties took over the leadership, but the liberal-democratic bourgeois parties and the SDP maintained a strong position in the Municipal Assembly.

The City Hall of the interwar period inherited a capital on the European level built up before 1918. It has to be judged a great achievement that the city leaders could preserve this European level while the demands of the period became sterner and harsher in every aspect of life in Budapest.

Notes

1. I. Illyefalvy Lajos, *Budapest 1873–tól Napjainkig* (Budapest since 1873 to our present days) (Budapest, 1945); Károly Vörös, ed., *Budapest Története a Marciusi Forradalomtól az Őszirózsás Forradalomig* (The history of Budapest from the March Revolution to the Asters Revolution), Vol. IV (Budapest, 1978); Miklós Horváth, ed., *Budapest Története a Forradalmak Korától a Felszabadulásig* (The history of Budapest from the epoch of the revolutions to the liberation), Vol. V (Budapest, 1980); Mária H. Kohut, ed., *Források Budapest Múltjából, Források Budapest Történetéhez 1873–1919* (Sources from the past of Budapest, sources to the history of Budapest, 1873–1919), Vol. II (Budapest, 1971); József Szekeres, ed., *Források Budapest Múltjából, Források Budapest Történetéhez 1919–1945* (Sources from the past of Budapest, sources to the history of Budapest, 1919–1945), Vol. III (Budapest, 1972); Antal Balla, *Budapest Szerepe Magyarország Történetében* (The role of Budapest in Hungary's history) (Budapest, 1937).
2. Endre Szigethy, ed., *Wolff Károly Élete, Politikája, Alkotásai* (The life and politics and works of Karoly Wolff) (Budapest, 1943), 24.
3. Illyefalvy, *Budapest,* 44–45.
4. The corn production of the country was brought to Budapest on the Danube. The capital was the center of the milling industry.
5. *Magyar Statisztikai Közlemények* (Hungarian statistical publications). New series. 52: 1022, 1042; 42: 12–13.
6. The size of the country without Croatia in 1910 was 282,870 km^2; in 1920, 92,963 km^2. The population in 1910 was 18,264,533; in 1920, 7,615,117. See *Magyar Statisztikai Közlemények* 83: 12–13.
7. *Magyar Statisztikai Közlemények* 72: 272–274; 94: 210, 212. On the industrial development and the role of Budapest, see Iván T. Berend and György Ránki, "A Budapest Környéki Ipari Övezet Kialakulásának és Fejlődésének Kérdéséhez" ("To the question of emerging and development of the industrial zone around Budapest") in *Tanulmányok Budapest Múltjából* (Studies from the past of Budapest), Vol. XIV (Budapest, 1961).
8. *Magyar Statisztikai Közlemények* 42: 563–564; 69: 216–217; 83: 186–187. The ratio of Hungarian in the country was 46.6 percent in 1880 and 92.1 percent in 1930.
9. *Források Budapest Múltjából,* 2: 170–171; 3: 590. In the country the occupational structure was dominated by agriculture. Before 1920 more than half (later on, less than half) of the population lived on agriculture.
10. Vázsonyi was the son of a Jewish school teacher in the countryside. He became a popular and well-to-do lawyer in the capital, an alderman and MP by the turn of the century, and Minister of King Károly IV in 1917 and 1918. See Vázsonyi's biography in Hugo Csergő and József Balassa, eds., *Vázsonyi Vilmos Beszédei és Irásai* (Speeches and articles of Vilmos Vázsonyi), Vol. 1 (Budapest, 1927).
11. *Magyar Statisztikai Közlemények* 42: 563–564; 83: 186–187.
12. These ideas were represented by Gyula Szekfú, the most influential and conservative historian of the interwar period, as well as by the populist writers of the thirties.

13. *Források Budapest Múltjából* 3: 21.
14. *Források Budapest Múltjából* 2: 307–310.
15. See Act 36:1872. On the virilists, see Károly Vörös, "Budapest Legnagyobb Adófizetői 1873–ban" (The greatest tax-payers of Budapest in 1873), in *Tanulmányok Budapest Múltjából* (Studies from the past of Budapest), Vol. XVIII (Budapest, 1971); and Károly Vörös, "Budapest Legnagyobb Adófizetői 1903–1917" (The greatest tax-payers of Budapest, 1903–1917), in *Tanulmányok Budapest Múltjából* (Studies from the past of Budapest), Vol. XVII (Budapest, 1966).
16. Bárczy's father was Polish (Smolensky) and his mother was Hungarian. Having been a teacher in Vienna, the father changed his name to Sacher. After the family moved to Budapest and the son started to serve the capital, he took his mother's family name, Bárczy, which was a name of Hungarian gentry. About his activity see *Források Budapest Múltjából,* Vol II.
17. *Források Budapest Múltjából* 2: 81–85, 296–304, 307–313.
18. There was also another practical reason for this phenomenon: i.e., it was easier to determine the house tax than the sales tax, at least at that time. Therefore the house tax was fixed higher than the sales tax.
19. The SDP was established in Budapest in 1890.
20. Zsuzsa L. Nagy, "Politikai Erők, Politikai Harcok Budapesten a Századfordulótól a Második Világháború Végéig" (Political powers and political fights in Budapest from the turn of the century up to the end of World War II), in *Studies,* Vol. XX, 67–78; Ferenc Harrer, *Egy Magyar Polgár Élete* (The life of a Hungarian citizen) (Budapest, 1968), 70.
21. Based on the 1910 census. At that time the proportion of Jews to inhabitants was 28.9 percent in District V; 32.5 percent in District VI; and 38.5 percent in District VII.
22. Zsuzsa L. Nagy, *The Liberal Opposition in Hungary, 1919–1945* (Budapest, 1983), Part I. A more detailed account can be found in Zsuzsa L. Nagy, *Bethlen Liberális Ellenzéke* (Bethlen's liberal opposition), 1919–1931 (Budapest, 1980), Chap. IV.
23. The last municipal election before World War II was held in 1935. At that time the Arrowcross Party had no strong influence. This situation changed by the 1939 national election when many Budapesters voted for the Arrowcross Party. See György Ránki, "Az 1939–es Budapesti Választások" (The elections in Budapest in 1939), *Történelmi Szemle* (Historical review) 4 (1976).
24. *Források Budapest Múltjából* 3: 149.
25. The assigned members were among others: lord mayor, mayor, deputy mayor, leaders of departments, chief commissioner of police, chief medical officer, the delegates of the Hungarian Academy of Sciences, chambers of physicians and engineers and lawyers, the universities, and other institutions.
26. The analysis of the mandates and the professions of the aldermen is based on the data of *Amíg Városatya Lettem* (As I became an alderman), Endre György, ed. (Budapest, 1930).
27. Based on data from György and the 1930 census.
28. See *As I became an alderman.*

29. Zsuzsa L. Nagy, *Szabadkőművesség a XX. Században* (Freemasonry in the 20th century) (Budapest, 1977); Ludwik Hass, "The Socio-Professional Composition of Hungarian Freemasonry 1868–1920," *Acta Poloniae Historica* 30 (Warsaw, 1974).
30. *Források Budapest Múltjából*, Vol. III, 112; Ferenc Harrer, *The life of a Hungarian citizen*, 453–454.
31. Zsuzsa L. Nagy, *A Budapesti Liberális Ellenzéke, 1919–1944* (The Budapest liberal opposition, 1919–1944) (Budapest, 1972), 144.
32. Mainly two acts had a great role in transforming the activity and structure of the city leadership: 18: 1930 and 12: 1934.
33. Zsuzsa L. Nagy, *The Budapest liberal opposition*, 152–160.
34. *Források Budapest Múltjából*, Vol. II, 78–80; Ferenc Harrer, *The life of a Hungarian citizen*, 177–180.
35. Zsuzsa L. Nagy, *The Budapest liberal opposition*, 75–78.
36. Bárczy's policy speech on June 19, 1906. From *Források Budapest Múltjából*, Vol. II, 66–67.
37. See Note 1 and *Források Budapest Múltjából*, Vol. II, 94–98, 170–173; Vol. III, 587–600.
38. The housing problem is described in Péter Győri, "Social Welfare and Housing Policy in Budapest from the Unification of the Town until the 1930s." Paper presented at the 3rd meeting of American and Hungarian Historians, Budapest, August 1988.
39. István Weiss, *A Mai Magyar Társadalom* (The present Hungarian society) (Budapest, 1930), pp. 51–53; Elemér Radisics, *A Dunatáj. Történelmi, Gazdasági és Földrajzi Adatok a Dunatáj Államainak Életéről* (The Danube region. Historical, economic and geographical data on the lives of the states of the Danube region) (Budapest, 1946). Volume I gives detailed data on Budapest and the largest non-Hungarian towns of the region on every field.
40. About the schooling system see Lajos Timar, "School System and Social Mobility in Budapest, 1873–1941." Paper presented at the 3rd meeting of American and Hungarian Historians, Budapest, August 1988.
41. *Magyar Statisztikai Évkönyv* (1929), 200: Ibid. (1938), 270, 272. The universities nearly completely and the high schools to a great extent remained the schools of the middle class and high middle class.
42. See Note 1 and Csaba Ory, "Poor-Relief or Social Policy, Budapest 1873–1936." Paper presented at the 3rd meeting of American and Hungarian Historians, Budapest, August 1988.
43. Cited by István Nemeskürty in *A Képpé Változott idő* (Time transformed into picture) (Budapest, 1983), 418.

Chapter 2

Political Participation and Municipal Policy: New York City: 1870–1940

DAVID C. HAMMACK

ETWEEN 1870 and 1900, New York City changed with bewildering speed. Its area was increased by 713 percent, its population ballooned, and its people became more diverse. It created new industries in the manufacture of women's ready-to-wear clothing and in commercial entertainment. Its great merchants ceased to dominate the nation's economy, yet the new national manufacturing corporations located their headquarters in the city. Once controlled only by the state of New York, it became more and more subject to the influence of federal resources and federal policy.

But the more New York changed, the more it remained fundamentally the same. Its people have always been more diverse than those of any other American city. Through all the changes that have occurred in the American economy, New York has remained the central commercial, information, and financial market. Despite significant political changes (including the extension of the franchise to all white men in the 1830s, to black men after the Civil War, and to women in 1920), it has remained an integral part of a nation that has avoided invasion and retained its basic form of government.

New York City's government was remarkable in many ways, but the city was not a major center of government. In contrast to most of the great cities of Europe, it was neither a national nor a provincial capital. Its leaders, whatever their own preferences, have always had to take into account the nation's larger political culture, with its resistance to taxes and opposition to vigorous government. But in the fifty years between the collapse of Reconstruction and the Great Depression, governments at all levels in the United States were weak; and this weakness of government allowed New York, the national marketplace, to wield great influence over the rest of the country.

In this general pattern of continuity and change, 1870, 1898, and 1933 mark three great divides in the political history of New York City. 1870 was the year of the "Tweed Charter" for the city, a charter that returned many municipal powers, including control of its police, fire, public health, and public works development projects, from the state of New York to the municipality: it was also a year of renewed political activity by a mercantile elite that had a clear vision for New York's development. 1898 was the year Manhattan pursued a great civic and mercantile vision by consolidating with Brooklyn, Queens, and Staten Island to form Greater New York: it was also very close to the time when the mercantile elite began to pass from the New York scene. The Depression year of 1933 saw Fiorello LaGuardia put an end to the long-standing electoral coalition created by Tammany Hall's greatest leader, Charles F. Murphy, and win election as mayor. These dates serve admirably to frame an inquiry into the history of political participation and municipal policy in New York.

Sixty Years of Economic Growth and Transformation: New York: 1870–1930

New York City reigned supreme over the business affairs of the United States in the years between 1870 and 1930 through a continuous process of change and expansion. Until the turn of the century, New York's harbor provided the symbolic image of the metropolis; after about 1910, the Wall Street skyline formed its most familiar representation. Both of these images captured New York's dominant role in American business. The shift from harbor to skyscraper also caught the extraordinary transformation that was taking place in the way American business was organized, and in the nature of the New York economy. In 1870 New York was above all a mercantile city, the entrepôt for America's vast and rapidly growing trade with the Atlantic world, the locus of America's great international bankers and merchants. By 1900 New York was more deeply involved in the management of American industry than in the Atlantic trade. It housed many of the great corporate headquarters; it provided the great markets for industrial and railroad bonds and stocks; and it handled much of the advertising and marketing of industrial products to the United States as well as to Europe. New York was also a very considerable manufacturing center, but its manufacturing was subordinate to its port.

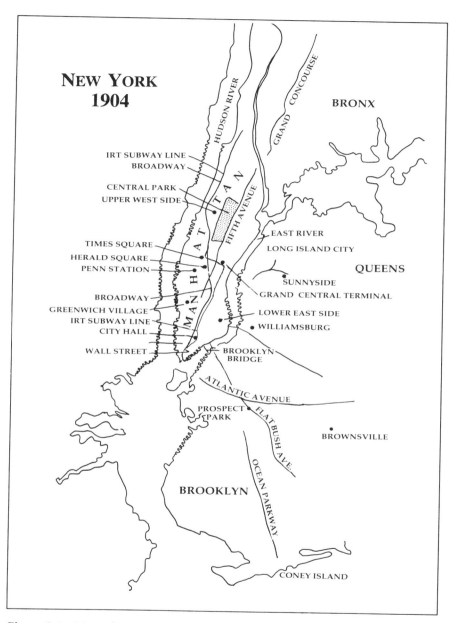

Figure 2.1 Map of New York, 1904. Drawn by Kimberly Santini.

Figure 2.2 New York, Manhattan from Brooklyn, 1909. I. N. Phelps Stokes, *The Iconography of Manhattan Island, 1498–1909* (New York: Robert H. Dodd, 1918), Volume 3, Plate 28A.

Economically, New York was transformed between 1870 and 1930 from a great port to the center of America's new manufacturing corporations.[1]

New York's economic dominance was the result of its long-established advantages as the center of communication, trade, and finance within the United States and between the United States and its great trading partners in Europe. Before 1800, nature and the economic demography of colonial America had supplied these advantages: New York lay on America's best Atlantic coast harbor, midway between the intensively developed New England and Chesapeake regions. Human innovations reinforcing New York's position through the nineteenth century included a regularly scheduled shipping service to Europe after 1807; the Erie Canal linking New York via the Hudson

Table 2.1 Population of New York City: 1880–1940

Year	Population	Growth (percent)
1880	1,843,785	
1890	2,507,414	+36%
1900	3,437,202	+37%
1910	4,766,883	+28%
1920	5,620,048	+18%
1930	6,930,446	+23%
1940	7,454,995	+8%

SOURCE: Data for the territory that became the five boroughs of Greater New York in 1898, calculated from information in Ira Rosenwaike, *Population History of New York City* (Syracuse, N.Y., 1972).

58

River to the Great Lakes after 1825; and a significant railroad network by the late 1840s. From the 1780s on, New York was the nation's central collecting and distributing point for information of all
kinds.[2] As a result, it attracted North America's largest aggregation
of merchants, publishers, investors, and speculators—and, to serve
them, the largest and most sophisticated groups of bankers, lawyers,
insurance brokers, engineers, writers, and artists as well.[3]

By 1870, railroad leaders had joined the great merchants and international bankers at the top of New York's economic pyramid: Cor-
nelius Vanderbilt and Chauncey Depew of the New York Central and
Jay Gould and Russell Sage of the Erie had joined bankers like J. P.
Morgan and merchants like Morris K. Jesup in the Chamber of Commerce of the State of New York. In 1870 New York reached its statistical peak as America's leading port, handling 57.6 percent of the nation's entire import and export trade. Ten years later there were 56
wholesale, import-export, and shipping firms capitalized at more than
$1 million in New York, 27 private bankers and brokers with assets
at that level, 8 railroads, and over 100 banks with comparable assets:
but only 11 national and perhaps 32 New York manufacturers oper-
ating with capital assets of $1 million.[4]

Merchants led the city. To celebrate their status and house one of
their key markets, they built, in 1884, the great Produce Exchange
Building, a vast iron-framed, red brick-and-terracotta pile whose cam-
panile was, for a time, the only structure except the Trinity Church
steeple to tower over Manhattan's four- and five-story warehouses,
counting houses, brownstones, and tenements.[5] But like many other
elites at other times and in other places, New York's merchants were
in a relative decline even before they built their great monument. By
1895 there were already more million-dollar manufacturing firms (102)
than shippers and wholesalers (77) in New York, and by 1910 there
were well over 500 manufacturing firms of that size, compared to
only 135 merchant companies. A great majority of the manufacturers
carried on a national business, using New York as a financial and
marketing base.[6]

New York City and its region was a great center for manufacturing
as well as for management. According to the best estimates, in the
1880s it housed 16 percent of all production workers in the United
States, and it continued to house 14 percent for many years after 1900,
even as industrial production boomed in the Midwest and in parts of
the South and the Pacific Coast. Some of New York's manufacturing
was strongly tied to its port, especially the processing of bulky, imported raw materials, such as molasses, copper ore, hides, and hoofs.
Some, including the production of printing presses, elevators, pumps,

pianos, and gas fixtures, depended on the great metropolitan market itself.[7]

Increasingly, New York's manufacturing was linked to the city's central place in the American communications system. As a leading manufacturer explained to a Columbia University investigator early in the century, "Those industries which produce products of a standard pattern can locate anywhere . . . but industries whose products differ with each particular order must be located in or very near their market, in order to be under the constant supervision of their customers."[8] As the total number of industrial workers in the New York region grew from 425,000 in 1880 to 630,000 in 1910, they concentrated increasingly in three industries for which New York provided the information and facilities of a central market for the nation: clothing, printing and publishing, and specialty and luxury trades, including all forms of commercial entertainment.[9]

This emphasis persisted even as the number of manufacturing jobs in the New York region rose to nearly 1,000,000 by 1920. In each of its major manufacturing industries, success required current information about fashions, and New York provided both the largest local market and the best access in the nation to information about fashions both in the U.S. and in Europe. With a few exceptions (Steinway pianos, Otis elevators, the Havemeyer family's American Sugar Refining Company, Peter Cooper's glue factory), New York's industries were organized not into large, heavily capitalized plants but into very large numbers of small, fragile, competitive firms, capable of responding quickly to new consumer demands.[10] Thus, New York City was a major manufacturing center in which few manufacturers had large numbers of employees or commanded large resources.

The Social Basis of Politics

In sum, New York's economy created and attracted a changing variety of economic elites whose members possessed the means needed to influence local affairs. From the 1870s into the 1890s merchants, brokers, international bankers, and railroad leaders constituted the most prominent of New York's economic elites; they were very active in its politics as well. A turning point occurred at about 1898, as the managers of national manufacturing corporations replaced merchants and brokers as the city's largest group of economic leaders. But many of these managers, like the very considerable number of investors who were attracted to New York as the center of American economic life, had little interest in New York itself apart from its facilities for carrying on their business. Nor did the city's own burgeoning manufac-

60

turing industry create many notable new fortunes: most of its firms remained very small. After 1898, a large, diverse, fragmented, varied, and often preoccupied set of wealthy men could be found to join the contest for power in New York. They were not united by a common mercantile, industrial, or civic vision, and, to an even greater extent than had been the case before 1898, they pursued diverse and individual strategies in their quests for advancement.

Anyone who sought political leadership in New York—before or after the turn of the century—had to face a bewildering and rapidly changing population which not only enjoyed but made enthusiastic use of universal male suffrage. Elections played a truly important role in New York City politics between 1880 and 1940. Elected officials played significant roles in decision-making, and elections were generally open and honest. The electorate was limited to male citizens over the age of 21, thus excluding women, the young, and recent immigrants. Those who did belong to the electorate participated actively: 90 percent or more of the eligible voters turned out in general elections in the 1890s. Election officials were sometimes accused of fraud, but serious charges of fraud were quickly and vigorously prosecuted, in part because local and state offices, including law-enforcement offices, often shifted from the Republican Party to the Democratic Party.[11] The parties existed to nominate and seek majorities for candidates; to obtain those majorities they had to appeal to real voters.

New York's rapidly changing economic activity created a growing and diverse electorate. The city grew so rapidly that it was little wonder that it could hardly keep up with itself. Despite a heroic surge of construction, streets, trams, houses, schools, and public facilities of all kinds were crowded to an appalling degree. In Budapest and several other European cities there were periods of rapid population growth: New York grew more continuously, uninterrupted by great political or military upheavals. Spared the direct impact of war and revolution, New York kept on growing throughout the entire period between 1870 and 1940, though at a somewhat slower rate after 1920 (see Table 2.1).

New York's continuous growth was fed by sources of ever-increasing diversity. In the seventeenth century the city was already famous for its ethnic and religious diversity. "Our chiefest unhappyness here is too great a mixture of Nations, & English the least part," Governor Dongan's oft-quoted remark of the 1680s states. He added that the city contained not only Dutch Calvinists, Anglicans, French Calvinists, and Dutch Lutherans, but also "Singing Quakers, Ranting Quakers; Sabbatarians; Antisabbatarians; Some Anabaptists some Independants; some Jews; in short all sorts of opinions."[12] The mix became ever more diverse (and less Protestant) throughout the nineteenth century and into the twentieth as well. And the dramatic changes in the composition of Greater New York's population were the result of new waves of immigration rather than of selective outmigration or differential birthrates: the city's population was growing (from 1.8 million in 1880 to 7.5 million in 1940) as rapidly as it was becoming more diverse (see Table 2.2).

Overall, Greater New York changed from a "native-stock" (largely British and Dutch), Irish, and German city of 1.8 million in 1880 to an Irish, German, Eastern European, and Central European city of 3.4 million in 1900, to an Eastern European, Italian, Central European, Irish, and German city of 6.9 million in 1930. New York City's population has continued to change, so it is important to keep in mind that African Americans constituted only 3 percent in 1920, and that African Americans, Hispanics, and Asians together made up only 7 percent as late as 1940. African Americans did vote, but before the mid-1930s their numbers were so small that they could be only a minor factor in elections.

New York's increasing ethnic diversity encompassed increasing religious diversity as well. Perhaps 40 percent of the German immigrants, 5 percent or 10 percent of those from Austria-Hungary, and nearly all of the Scandinavians (who comprised 1 percent of Greater New York's population in 1890 and 2 percent from 1900 through 1940) and African Americans were Protestants, as were a large majority of the "Native Whites of native parentage" who were present in 1880. Nearly all of those from Russia and Poland were Jews, as were perhaps half of those from Austria-Hungary and 10 percent of the Germans. Some of those reported in the U.S. census as Irish were in fact Protestants from Ulster, but most were Catholic, as were nearly all of the Italians, French (1 percent from 1890 through 1940), and Puerto Ricans, half of the Germans, and perhaps 40 percent of those from Austria-Hungary and adjacent regions. A few of the Russians and others from Eastern Europe belonged to Orthodox churches. By 1920 many of the "Native Whites of Native Parentage" were the grandchildren of immigrants, and increasing proportions of them were Catholics or Jews. According to one very careful estimate, New York City's population was half Protestant, one-third Catholic, and one-sixth Jewish in 1900, but 37 percent Protestant, 34 percent Catholic, nearly 2 percent Orthodox, and 27 percent Jewish in 1930.

These ethnic and religious identities had a profound influence on

Table 2.2 New York City Population, by Major "Nationality Groups": 1880–1940

	Native Born/ Native Parents	German	Irish	Russian/ Polish	Austro/ Hungarian	Italian	Other European	African Americans	Puerto Rican	Asian
1880	NA	23%	27%	0%	0%	0%	6%	2%	0%	0%
1890	20%	26	25	3	1	3	6	1	0	0
1900	21	23	21	9	6	6	5	2	0	0
1910	19	15	14	15	10	11	4	2	0	0
1920	21	10	11	18	11	14	5	3	0	0
1930	22	9	9	21	8	15	6	5	1	0
1940	29	7	7	18	8	15	7	6	1	0

SOURCE: Calculated from data in Ira Rosenwaike, *Population History of New York City* (Syracuse, N.Y.: Syracuse University Press, 1972).
NOTES: "Nationality Groups" derived by Rosenwaike from U.S. Census data based on self-reported birthplaces of individuals and their mothers. For this table, Russia, Poland, and Lithuania are grouped under "Russian/Polish"; and Austria, Hungary, Romania, Czechoslovakia, and Yugoslavia are grouped under "Austro/Hungarian." The "Other European" category consists primarily of immigrants from Great Britain, Scandinavia and France. "New York City" is defined as the Greater New York of five boroughs established in 1898; data for 1880 and 1890 include New York City, Kings County (Brooklyn and adjacent towns), Queens County, and Richmond (Staten Island), and the numbers presented for those years are somewhat incomplete.

NA = Not available.

politics in Greater New York. But the American social environment was in many ways voluntaristic: it was an environment in which people were to a large extent free, unless they were black or Asian, to define their own identities and organizational affiliations. This environment created a complex set of limits and opportunities for each individual. Robert F. Wagner, one of the most influential members of the United States Senate between the world wars, was born of Lutheran parents in Germany in 1887, moved with his family to New York City in 1886, became a Methodist in his twenties, married an American-born woman of Irish Catholic origin in a Catholic ceremony, and converted to Catholicism in 1946. His son, Robert F. Wagner, Jr., served as mayor of New York from 1955 to 1965.[13]

Fiorello LaGuardia, mayor of New York from 1934 to 1945, was born in New York City to immigrants; his father was born a Catholic in Italy, and both of his mother's parents were Jews from the region near Trieste that was under Hungarian control when they lived there before World War I. Fiorello and his siblings were raised as Episcopalians.[14] Such stories are an essential part of New York's ethnic and religious history. In the fragmented and rapidly changing political arena of New York City, ethnic, religious, and class identifications were symbolic resources that successful political leaders used as—and when—they could.

Paying scant attention to these inconveniently complicated facts about the rapidly changing social basis of politics in New York City, and relying too heavily on the rhetoric of literate and often anti-democratic partisans, historians of New York and other American cities have long based their studies on four assumptions:

> That wealthy, well-educated people, the "best men," withdrew from politics and public affairs sometime in the nineteenth century.

> That unitary political machines, tightly controlled by powerful "bosses" of immigrant, often Irish, background, replaced them.

> That ordinary working people had little direct influence on public affairs.

> That small bands of "reformers" provided the only real opposition to the "bosses."[15]

We now know that none of these assumptions is true for New York. In fact, wealthy people were continuously, prominently, and very influentially involved in New York City's politics throughout the nineteenth century and into the twentieth. Historians have been unable to find any period between 1870 and 1940 in which Tammany Hall or any other political machine was effectively dominated by a single leader or a coherent group of leaders, and was capable of controlling nominations to the most important citywide offices and to the city and state legislatures. The people who made up New York City's electorate were never passive, ignorant, or easily manipulated: rather, they were deeply engaged in debates over the merits and uses of various forms of "artisan republicanism," "workerism," socialism, Catholicism, the single tax, and other ideological commitments. From the 1840s onward, the debate within working-class communities was at least as intense as any debate between workers and capitalists; even in Henry George's extraordinary 1886 campaign for mayor, no single political view shaped the political thinking of a majority of the city's working people. Finally, although many politicians did seek to draw the mantle of "reform" over their shoulders, these politicians did not form anything like a coherent group; indeed, they sometimes differed more widely from one another than they differed from their "machine" opponents.

Daniel Greenleaf Thompson, a successful lawyer and literary figure in late nineteenth century New York City, provided the most accurate account of the efforts of New York's political leaders to deal with its maddening diversity and ceaseless change. Tammany Hall, Manhattan's Democratic Party organization, was simply a "syndicate," a "business combination for business ends," Thompson wrote in a remarkable book published in 1893. As a syndicate, Tammany Hall, like New York's other leading political organizations, responded both to voters who sought respect and representation and to businessmen who sought opportunities to make money through contracts for public works as well as through commercial and manufacturing activities in the city of New York.[16]

The divided, contentious, changing character of New York's politics persisted through the changes that distinguished one period from the next. Brief accounts of key events in the 1870–1898 period, the last years of merchant ascendancy, and in the subsequent period dominated by increased ethnic and religious diversity and by something of a response to the needs of ordinary workers, illustrate the point.

In the twenty years or so before 1870, wealthy New Yorkers, alarmed by what they saw as mounting class conflict and social disorder in the city and by the political events of the Civil War, continued to run for local office but hedged their bets by working effectively, at the same time, to shift powers away from municipal government. They successfully argued for the reassignment of several municipal respon-

sibilities to state commissions after 1857, and they obtained expanded public support for several key private, nonprofit organizations,
including the Metropolitan Museum of Art and the American Museum of Natural History.[17]

The so-called Tweed Charter, passed in response to the efforts of
Tammany Hall leader William Marcy Tweed by the state government
in 1870, abolished the state commissions and restored their powers
to the municipality. With more now at stake in municipal elections,
wealthy men—especially the great merchants who sought to use municipal government to build port facilities in New York and to press
the federal government for low tariffs and commercial services abroad—
redoubled their interest in municipal elections, without, however, re-
ducing their participation in business and professional firms and associations, or in nonprofit organizations.[18]

In many ways the mayoral election of 1886 and the subsequent
two-year administration of Abram S. Hewitt was the high point of
mercantile influence in New York City politics. The 1886 election
campaign is one of the most famous in New York's history because
it pitted three extraordinary candidates against one another. Theodore
Roosevelt, who later served two terms as president of the United States,
was the Republican candidate. Henry George, the advocate of what
he called the "single tax" on land, led one of the largest coalitions of
labor organizations, socialists, and social reformers ever assembled in
the United States—a coalition that even included a significant group
of Democratic district leaders. The highlight of George's campaign
was a torchlight parade of delegations from at least fifty unions of
skilled and semiskilled workers. Carrying slogans, banners, American
flags, union regalia, and more than one red flag, the marchers passed
by George's reviewing stand for more than two hours. Flanking the
candidate on the stand were Patrick Ford, editor of the *Irish World
and American Industrial Liberator*; German-American leader Theodore von Bremsen; and several Democratic district leaders. Despite a
last-minute denunciation by the Catholic Church as a man whose
ideas "would prove the ruin of the working men he professes to be-
friend," George received over 68,000 votes.[19] But he did not win.

The winner, Abram S. Hewitt, is much less well remembered. But
he was a remarkable man who was widely known and respected in
his own time; during his service in the U.S. House of Representatives
in the 1870s and 1880s, no less an observer than Henry Adams called
him "the most useful public man in Washington."[20] Hewitt won the
1886 mayoral election with over 90,000 votes because he represented
an even broader coalition than the one that supported George. Three

important groups of Democrats joined in his nomination: wealthy merchants known as Swallowtails after their commitment to formal dress; a citywide network of Democratic district leaders, the County Democracy, which had often worked with the Swallowtails; and Tammany Hall, New York's oldest and most Irish citywide Democratic organization.[21]

Henry George ran especially well among second-generation Irish, Germans, and Jews, particularly those who lived in the relatively prosperous districts of artisans, bookkeepers, and shopowners.[22]

Hewitt won the election by attracting a more diverse coalition, a coalition that included both middle- and upper-class voters who opposed tariffs and other high taxes and Catholics who opposed government actions that interfered with their religion and culture. Both of these groups favored government action to develop New York's harbor and transportation facilities, financed by bonds to be paid for with real estate or users' taxes. Hewitt's campaign statements praised Tammany Hall for its work on behalf of "the rights of Ireland," celebrated the American system of "free government," and insisted that "all over the world men are looking to this land as the great example of what may be done for the elevation of the masses" through the provision of economic opportunity. As a member of Congress, he reminded voters, he had effectively opposed tariffs and other taxes on consumer goods, and had supported harbor development and other measures to promote commerce. Hewitt's Catholic constituents understood that the limited government he favored would leave their church alone.

Hewitt's positions won the enthusiastic support of Tammany Hall, the County Democracy, and other political and civic organizations, each of which was particularly effective with specific groups of voters. Tammany Hall and the County Democracy brought him pluralities among the poor, recent immigrants from Ireland and Germany in the districts along New York's long waterfront. Tammany helped him win majorities or pluralities among the prosperous second- and third-generation Irish, Germans, Jews, and native-stock middle class on the Upper West Side and in newly built Harlem; the other Democratic organizations helped him in Upper Manhattan and the South Bronx. And Swallowtail support enabled him to secure pluralities among the wealthy native-stock, British, German, and German-Jewish residents of mid-Manhattan's "silk-stocking" district.[23]

Hewitt articulated a durable vision of New York's future, setting the agenda for public improvements in the city over the next twenty years. Following discussions of the city's transportation, commercial, financial, and social problems and opportunities with his colleagues in the Chamber of Commerce of the State of New York, he offered the following peroration in his annual message of January, 1888:

> With its noble harbor protected from injury, and the channels of its approach straightened and deepened; with its wharves and docks made adequate for the easy transfer of the vast commerce of the country; with its streets properly paved and cleaned, and protected from destructive upheavals; with cheap and rapid transit throughout its length and breadth; with salubrious and attractive parks in the centers of dense population; with a system of taxation so modified that the capital of the world may be as free to come and go as the air of heaven; the imagination can place no bounds to the future growth of this city in business, wealth, and the blessings of civilization. Its imperial destiny as the greatest city in the world is assured by natural causes, which cannot be thwarted except by the folly and neglect of its inhabitants.[24]

Hewitt uttered these words not long after the opening of the Brooklyn Bridge, built by a state commission of which he had been a member. In the next ten years the metropolis would consolidate with Brooklyn, Queens, and Staten Island largely to "protect its harbor from injury" and speed the improvement of streets and public facilities in outlying areas. It would plan and finance an extensive electric rapid transit system. It would open new parks in crowded tenement-house districts and move toward tighter regulation of tenement buildings, expand its water supply and sewers, and adopt a rigorous system of street cleaning and public health inspections. And—again with Hewitt's support—it would centralize the administration of its public education system, expanding the number of schools and, after 1900, adding secondary schools to the primaries that had so long constituted nearly all of the city's free public school offerings.

Despite his influential vision, Hewitt was unable to sustain his personal prominence in New York. Nor was the coalition he managed to assemble in 1886 to last. Hewitt's own ethnic group, that of native-stock Protestants, was rapidly dwindling as a percentage of New York's population. But even as it dwindled, many of its members adopted new, restrictive moral and political positions and sought to impose these positions on the city. In part, this was a response to the arrival of so many newcomers. Before the end of his term, Hewitt himself was denouncing the Irish who had elected him; in the next few years he often endorsed efforts to impose Protestant cultural practices on Catholic immigrants. Such actions quickly forced him out of elective politics in New York City. Other Protestant merchants—dry goods purveyor William L. Strong and Seth Low of a great Brooklyn shipping family—did, however, win almost every other election between 1888 and 1902.

The greatest political syndicator—to apply Daniel Greenleaf Thompson's term—in New York's history was Charles F. Murphy, who led Tammany Hall from shortly after the consolidation of Greater New York in 1898 until his death in 1924. Murphy succeeded Richard Croker, under whom Tammany Hall enjoyed only intermittent success between 1888 and 1900. Croker put together an Irish-German, unskilled/skilled white collar coalition that was unable to win majorities for his mayoral candidates in 1894, 1897, and 1901, and managed only a 44 percent plurality in 1897.[25] Murphy's candidates won mayoral elections in 1903, 1905, 1909, 1917, 1921, and, even after his death, in 1925 and 1929; and they won because Murphy put together a broader coalition of voters and paid closer attention to the demands of New York's economic leaders. To create this coalition, Murphy built on Croker's initiative. He consolidated and retained Tammany's hold on the first- and second-generation Irish, strengthened its appeal to German Catholics, and sought a way to attract much larger numbers of Jews and people from the many provinces of Austria-Hungary. The effort to appeal to the non-Irish groups was critical: whereas the first- and second-generation Irish had amounted to 27 percent of Greater New York in 1880, they were only 14 percent in 1910, and Germans had fallen from 23 percent to 15 percent. Meanwhile, the largely Jewish Russian and Polish population had increased from under 0.5 percent to 15 percent, people from territories under Austria and Hungary had increased from under 0.5 percent to 11 percent, and the Italian population had increased from negligible to 11 percent. Murphy and his contemporaries had to appeal to a much more diverse electorate than the one that had faced Hewitt and Croker.

Historians J. Joseph Huthmacher and Nancy J. Weiss have shown that Murphy was increasingly willing to support departures (first broached in the 1897 mayoral campaign) from Tammany's traditional laissez faire approach to government. As Weiss put it, by 1911 Murphy had come to favor positive government action to provide "social welfare and economic reforms for the masses." His shift was without doubt due, as Huthmacher and Weiss argue, to his simple recognition of the fact that housing, working conditions, and wages were appallingly bad for very large numbers of workers. Great events like the fire that killed 146 women at work in the Triangle Shirtwaist Company's factory in 1911 certainly influenced Murphy and his most famous protégés, Alfred E. Smith and Robert F. Wagner. These Tammany leaders also responded to the barrage of publicity and argument put forward by labor and social welfare leaders in the years after the turn of the century.[26]

But Murphy and his associates were also well aware of the need to seek the votes of more recent immigrants from Central and Southern Europe. Unlike the Irish, many of these immigrants held anticlerical views or were Jewish: they did not share the Irish concern that strong government might harm the Catholic Church. And whereas many Irish voters identified a strong government with hostile, Protestant Britain, many immigrants from Central and Eastern Europe identified strong governments with the traditions that a good Czar protected minorities and the poor, or that the Austro-Hungarian empire protected its minority groups and provided them with educational opportunities. As a Swallowtail Democrat who supported Low observed in 1901, many of New York's new immigrants came "from European cities that are as progressive as we are backward" in providing municipal services. And a considerable portion of the immigrants from Central and Eastern Europe subscribed to one or another socialist tradition.[27]

Murphy and his associates learned that these voters would respond to candidates who promised to expand the powers of government—to tighten the regulation of housing and public health and working conditions, to build public parks, to expand the public schools, to build rapid transit lines. The successful anti-Tammany "fusion" campaigns of William L. Strong in 1894 and Seth Low in 1901 had made such promises. (Between 1890 and 1940, fusion campaigns brought together Republicans, dissident Democrats, certain labor organizations, advocates of social and religious change, and often the leaders of organized charity including key women leaders.)

William Randolph Hearst's frequent and colorfully disruptive forays into New York City's politics also forced Murphy to move Tammany toward support of a more active municipal government. An extraordinary Californian who inherited British ancestry, a mining fortune, and a taste for politics from his father, a United States senator, Hearst had by 1900 put together a string of major newspapers from San Francisco and Seattle to New York and Boston and had conceived an overwhelming desire to become president of the United States. He confounded his contemporaries in New York: and because his ideas were neither Republican, Democratic, Socialist, nor very consistent, he has confounded many historians as well.

Hearst won election to the U.S. Congress in 1902 and 1904 (on the Tammany ticket), and ran for mayor of New York City (against Tammany and other candidates) in 1905 and in 1909. In his mayoral campaigns Hearst stressed such issues as the right of workingmen to organize unions, the need for government to regulate the great new corporations, and the desirability of municipal ownership or close control of such utilities as rapid transit and gas in the interest of low charges to the poor. In 1905 these positions brought Hearst the active support of many labor union and social welfare leaders, and he came within 4,000 votes of victory. 1905 was the one year in which fraud (Tammany destruction of ballots for Hearst) may well have changed the outcome of a major election in New York.

Hearst promoted the same ideas in 1905, in his less successful campaign of 1909, and in his support of John Purroy Mitchel's victorious fusion campaign of 1913. In each of these three elections his notions attracted significant numbers of German, Central European, and Jewish voters, particularly those whose skilled or white collar occupations gave them a middling sort of prosperity, as political scientist Kenneth Finegold argues.[28] In occupation, income, and literacy, Hearst's voters resembled those who had favored Henry George in 1886. But Hearst's voters were very different in ethnic background: Hearst and his followers found it almost impossible to attract the Irish to their continental coalition in 1905, 1909, and 1913.

Murphy responded by advancing non-Irish candidates who were often quite independent of Tammany Hall, and by supporting legislation that strengthened the powers of government. His first two successful mayoral candidates had gained prominence outside Tammany Hall, and they retained considerable independence in office, even to the extent of publicly denouncing Murphy and refusing to appoint his nominees. George B. McClellan, Jr., who won in 1903 and 1905, was a Princeton graduate whose father had been a famous Civil War general and the Democratic presidential candidate in 1864. William J. Gaynor, the independent Democrat from Brooklyn who won the mayoralty in 1909, had represented business interests, gained fame as an advocate for consumers, and been elected to the state's second highest court. His support for municipal ownership of rapid transit facilities had, in earlier years, attracted favorable comment from Hearst and his newspapers, and helped him defeat Hearst quite soundly in 1909. Gaynor's father had been born a Catholic in Dublin, and Gaynor attracted many Irish voters even though he himself had renounced the Catholic faith and, like McClellan, attended the Protestant Episcopal church.[29]

Murphy's candidate lost to Mitchel's fusion campaign in 1913. But Murphy was consolidating his position by sponsoring the rise of German-born (and Columbia University-educated) Robert F. Wagner and Irish-American Alfred E. Smith, who emerged as remarkable political leaders and social welfare advocates in the New York State legislature during the years before World War I. Murphy may well have intended to nominate Wagner for mayor of New York City in 1917, a move that would have appealed both to Germans and German-speakers and to Eastern European Jews who appreciated the efforts of Wagner and Smith to improve their working and housing conditions. Once again, however, unanticipated events threw rational political plans off course. As the United States entered World War I on the side of the Allies in the spring of 1917, Mayor Mitchel asserted that certain of Wagner's legislative actions were "in the service of the German government."[30]

Denied the candidacy of German-American Wagner in 1917, Murphy's Tammany nominated John F. Hylan, an obscure judge whose vehement advocacy of municipal ownership of subway lines had attracted Hearst's notice. With 47 percent of the vote to Mitchel's 23 percent, Hylan won a resounding victory. Mitchel had alienated far too many voters with his miserly administration, disregard of Irish and German self-esteem, personal affiliation with Protestant friends from Columbia University and the Rockefeller-supported, efficiency-minded Bureau of Municipal Research, and noisy advocacy of the British cause in World War I. Hylan enjoyed the noisy support of Hearst's newspapers as well as Murphy's Tammany Hall, and did very well among both the Irish and the Germans, among skilled workers and shopkeepers and the semiskilled and unskilled, and among both Jewish and Italian voters. (Many of Hearst's German, Jewish, and Italian voters did, however, shift to the Socialist, Morris Hilquit, who received nearly 22 percent of the vote.) Hylan was reelected in 1921.[31]

Meanwhile, Wagner was elected to the New York State Supreme Court in 1918 and to the U.S. Senate in 1926. Al Smith consciously or unconsciously helped enlarge the Democratic coalition by cultivating close ties with such Jewish advisors as Prussian-born Belle Moskowitz and American-born, Yale- and Oxford-educated Robert Moses, as well as with Protestant social worker Frances Perkins, who would go on to be, as Franklin D. Roosevelt's Secretary of Labor, the first woman to serve in the Cabinet of the United States. In 1918 Smith obtained a nomination sought by Hearst and was elected governor of New York; he served in that post again from 1921 to 1928. In 1928, Smith became the Democratic nominee for president of the United States, and Jewish Democrat Herbert H. Lehman was elected lieutenant governor of the state of New York.[32] In 1925 Smith finally ended Hearst's influence over New York City politics when he persuaded Tammany to replace Hylan with Jimmy Walker, who won in that year and again in 1929.

With Walker, Wagner, Smith, and Lehman as its top vote-getters, Murphy's Tammany held its Irish/German/ Jewish, lower-middle-class/

lower-class coalition firm through the 1920s. But the city's ethnic composition continued to change. By the mid-1930s people of Irish and German descent together constituted only about 20 percent of New York's population, whereas perhaps 30 percent were Jews from Eastern Europe and nearly 20 percent were Italian. The city's electorate changed even more with the introduction of woman suffrage by constitutional amendment in 1920. Although Murphy, Smith, and Wagner had worked closely with such women as Belle Moskowitz and Frances Perkins, even under their leadership Tammany retained a distinctly masculine style.

Thus, an opportunity awaited Fiorello LaGuardia when financial scandals and the Great Depression threw Tammany into disarray in 1933. Discouraged by Irish control of the city's Democratic Party, LaGuardia had affiliated with the Republicans; and the support of Republican leaders in 1933 helped him win a large share of the votes of the relatively prosperous Protestants of British and German stock who usually supported that party. He also received the votes of a majority of the wealthiest and a large fraction of the middle-class Jewish voters. And he won nearly 90 percent of the Italian vote.[33] We do not know whether women voted disproportionately for LaGuardia, but his wife was a celebrated member of his political group and the press made much of the fight-scene crudeness of Tammany Hall. With this coalition—one that would have been inconceivable as recently as 1910—LaGuardia defeated the divided Democrats and established a new political regime that remained in office until 1945.

The political impact of Greater New York's increasing ethnic diversity is evident in these arduous efforts to form political coalitions capable of electing mayors and other citywide officials. The city's ethnic and social composition changed with bewildering speed, and no coalition provided a stable source of electoral success. Just as one political leader seemed to find the skills and tactics needed to win local elections, a new situation demanded new skills, new tactics, new combinations of voters, and new policies.

City and State

The political forces of New York City expressed themselves through governmental structures that significantly limited the city's autonomy: that is probably why municipal politics turned so frequently on questions of cultural identity rather than economic or development policy. Politics in New York City was not only highly contentious, competitive, contingent, fluid, and unstable—it was a game that took place in several distinct arenas. The American Constitution created a set of institutional arrangements that were very different from those on the continent of Europe, and certainly different from conditions in Hungary. The doctrines of separation of powers, federalism, and the separation of church and state, as well as nonconstitutional factors, such as the rise of the political parties and a persistent hostility to government action and taxation, imposed strict limits on New York's freedom of action.

As a "minor civil subdivision" of the state of New York, New York City enjoyed precious little autonomy. The state legislature, rather than the city council, passed most important legislation, including the laws that controlled the city's taxing and borrowing; and the city had significantly fewer legislative seats than its population might have justified under a strict one man–one vote apportionment. Within the state legislature, New York City economic and political elites did have a certain leverage through their roles in financing and getting out New York City's vote for presidential and gubernatorial election campaigns. Apart from other factors, the patronage provided by the U.S. Customs House rivaled that of City Hall. Other units of government, notably state-controlled regional commissions and neighboring municipalities and counties, also provided important public arenas for decision-making.

Also important were state-chartered and often city-supported non-profit religious, cultural, and welfare organizations. Devoted to service and cultural functions more usually provided by the established church and the ambitious state on the continent, many nonprofits served in effect as privately managed government agencies. Private business and law firms, business and professional associations, and labor and trade organizations also provided important political arenas in New York. The phrase of political scientist Norton Long applies to the multiple arenas of New York politics in the second half of the nineteenth century: it was a complex "ecology of games."[34]

Like other American cities, New York used its powers in the last three decades of the nineteenth century to build great physical improvements: bridges, docks, streets, public buildings, and water and sewer lines. The policy of local responsibility for the construction of public works was so widely adopted in the era of laissez faire that local debt greatly exceeded federal and state debt combined in 1902.[35]

Municipal governments had used these vast sums to build the facilities needed for commercial growth. This fact explains why Abram S. Hewitt and other Swallowtail merchants involved themselves so actively in municipal politics.

Greater New York alone accounted for between one-fifth and one-

Table 2.3   Total Government Debt Outstanding at End of Fiscal Year 1902

Local Government	1,877,000,000	57%
State Government	230,000,000	7%
Federal Government	1,178,000,000	36%
All U.S. Governments	3,280,000,000	100%

quarter of all municipal borrowing in the early years of the twentieth century. So it is no surprise to find that the federal government also involved itself in the city's affairs during years of financial crisis. State governments had set debt limits for cities throughout the nineteenth century, and the courts had often limited the purposes for which municipalities could spend money. The federal government assisted many municipalities with major projects to improve navigation in rivers and harbors, but it played no other important role in municipal affairs before 1900. The expansion of federal power over the cities is one of the great stories of American urban history.

Federal power over New York's affairs became apparent during the fiscal crisis that accompanied the outbreak of World War I in 1914. New York's chief financial officer, businessman and fusionist William A. Prendergast, inadvertently laid the groundwork in 1912 and 1913 when he rejected the terms offered by New York investment bankers J. P. Morgan & Co. and Kuhn, Loeb & Co., and used the city's own facilities to place $80 million in notes in London and Paris. Investors in those cities were willing to accept interest rates lower than the rates demanded in New York, provided the notes contained a clause obliging New York to redeem them in gold if requested. Prendergast agreed to this clause. Early in 1914 he could claim to have saved the city a good deal of money through astute "business-like" management.

But Prendergast had not anticipated the guns of August. At the beginning of World War I, the United States was caught in an international exchange crisis. And New York was at the center of America's international trade. By the middle of August it was clear that the British and French holders of New York City notes would not renew them but would demand payment in gold. As Morgan partner Thomas W. Lamont put it, "the good name of the City of New York was involved in meeting those obligations promptly. She did not have the gold to ship . . . and she could not have got the exchange."[36]

At this point the federal government stepped in to insist that the city of New York take immediate action. The Federal Reserve Board had just been created in the summer of 1914. At the end of August the Board, alarmed about the international financial crisis and eager to establish its own authority, called for a conference on foreign exchange problems and for a full accounting of American debts abroad. New York City alone accounted for about half of all the U.S. debt due to be paid in the autumn of 1914. Under pressure from the Federal Reserve, J. P. Morgan & Co. and Kuhn, Loeb & Co. announced a few days later that New York City officials had agreed to special arrangements. The bankers would organize a syndicate to buy $100 million in New York City notes, using the proceeds to pay the city's gold obligations. Because this action covered half of the nation's European debt it satisfied Federal Reserve officials. In return for the bank's help with its financial problem, New York City officials agreed to a "pay-as-you-go" policy that prevented borrowing for public works projects that did not yield income. New York City officials also agreed to tax and expenditure policies designed to guarantee prompt payment of its debt.[37]

The 1914 fiscal crisis had two long-term consequences. It reinforced fusion mayor John Purroy Mitchel's tendency to emphasize economy and efficiency, rather than public service, in government.[38] This tendency not only contributed to his defeat in 1917 but to the discrediting of all other fusion candidates until Fiorello LaGuardia's campaign in 1933, in the midst of a second fiscal crisis (one that was also largely brought about by federal policy). More significantly, the fiscal crisis of 1914 defined the limits of policy in New York City for many years, for anti-fusion as well as for fusion candidates. If the city could not borrow for public works projects that would not yield sufficient income to repay the borrowing, it could not build and operate its own subway system, as William Randolph Hearst and Mayor John Hylan wished.

Nor could the municipal government move very rapidly to develop other municipal facilities. Under constant pressure from ordinary voters, real estate developers, and the managers of municipal services, city officials used their limited resources for the construction of streets and water and sewer lines in newly developed areas, and for fire and police stations, schools, and an excellent public health service. They left many medical services to private nonprofit agencies, like the Murray and Leonie Guggenheim Dental Clinic for school children, and nearly all cultural activities to nonprofits like the New York Public Library, the Metropolitan Museum of Art, the Brooklyn Museum, the Brooklyn and the New York Botanical Gardens—or to entrepreneurial groups in the performing arts like the Metropolitan Opera and the many theaters of Times Square. And they left tunnels across the

Hudson to special bistate commissions, and failed to develop large-scale transportation systems for the other parts of Greater New York.[39]

The result was a great backlog in the building of the sort of municipal public works projects championed by Abram S. Hewitt—highways, bridges, parks, high schools, and colleges. All this, as well as the need for low-cost housing, came quickly to the attention of Fiorello LaGuardia and his great public works manager Robert Moses. Journalist Robert Caro has described how Moses used state authority, bonds backed by the promise of tolls and fees, and federal funds provided by Franklin D. Roosevelt's New Deal to build many of these projects in the years after LaGuardia's election in 1933. The limited-expenditure policy of the teens and twenties was largely responsible for creating such a great opportunity for Moses—but to pursue the story of participation and policy in New York City's government into the LaGuardia-Moses era would take us far beyond the limits of this chapter.[40]

Notes

1. For histories of New York City's economy, see David C. Hammack, *Power and Society: Greater New York at the Turn of the Century* (New York, 1982; 1987), Chap. 2; and Eric E. Lampard, "The New York Metropolis in Transformation: History and Prospect. A Study in Historical Particularity," in H. J. Ewers, ed., *The Future of the Metropolis* (Berlin & New York, 1986), 40–90. In effect this chapter is part of the effort to create "a truly systematic urban history," a history that identifies "the relationships among local economies, social structures, spatial arrangements, and political cultures," as Kathleen Conzen has described it; Kathleen Neils Conzen, "Quantification and the New Urban History," *Journal of Interdisciplinary History* 13 (1983): 653–677.
2. Allan R. Pred, *Urban Growth and the Circulation of Information: The United States System of Cities, 1790–1840* (Cambridge, Mass, 1973), 28–42.
3. Hammack, *Power and Society*, 45.
4. Hammack, *Power and Society*, 47.
5. Hammack, *Power and Society*, 31; John A. Kouwenhoven, *The Columbia Historical Portrait of New York: An Essay in Graphic History* (New York, 1972), 358.
6. Hammack, *Power and Society*, 44–51.
7. Hammack, *Power and Society*, 39–41.
8. Edward Ewing Pratt, *Industrial Causes of Congestion of Population in New York City* (New York, 1911), 94.
9. Hammack, *Power and Society*, 40.
10. Hammack, *Power and Society*, 40–41.
11. Hammack, *Power and Society*, 122–129. For an account of the way that partisan rivalries helped police election fraud in New York, see David

C. Hammack, "Edward M. Shepard and the Gravesend Affair," *Columbia Library Columns* XXIII, 3 (May 1974): 3–10.

12. Quoted in Patricia U. Bonomi, *A Factious People: Politics and Society in Colonial New York* (New York, 1971), 25.

13. J. Joseph Huthmacher, *Senator Robert F. Wagner and the Rise of Urban Liberalism* (New York, 1971), 14–15, 22.

14. Charles Garrett, *The LaGuardia Years: Machine & Reform Politics in New York City* (New Brunswick, N.J., 1961), 117.

15. Hammack, *Power and Society*, Chap. 1.

16. Daniel Greenleaf Thompson, *Politics in a Democracy* (New York, 1894).

17. See Amy Bridges, *A City in the Republic: Antebellum New York and the Origins of Machine Politics* (Cambridge, Mass., 1984); James C. Mohr, *The Radical Republicans and Reform in New York During Reconstruction* (Ithaca, N.Y., 1973), 38, 274–275, and *passim;* and for brief accounts of the Metropolitan Museum of Art and the American Museum of Natural History, *The Columbia Encyclopedia* (New York, 1950). For a discussion of the role of the Charity Organization Society, another private, nonprofit organization, in mayoral politics during the 1890s, see Hammack, *Power and Society*, 178.

18. Bridges, *A City in the Republic;* Hammack, *Power and Society.*

19. Hammack, *Power and Society*, 112–113, 173–176.

20. Quoted in Hammack, *Power and Society*, 137.

21. Hammack, *Power and Society*, 113–115, 135. On the platform at Tammany Hall when Hewitt was nominated were some of New York's most successful German, Jewish, and Irish businessmen, including Joseph Pulitzer, publisher of the *New York World*, Oswald Ottendorfer, publisher of the *New York Staats-Zeitung*, banker August Belmont, brewer Jacob Ruppert, tea importer Joseph J. O'Donahue. The list of notables was read by Tammany's secretary, Thomas F. Gilroy, whose mother had brought him (along with his numerous brothers and sisters) from Ireland when he was five years old.

22. Martin Shefter, "The Electoral Foundations of the Political Machine: New York City, 1884–1897," in Joel Silbey et al., eds., *American Electoral History: Quantitative Studies in Popular Voting Behavior* (Princeton, N.J., 1978).

23. For a detailed discussion of the social and economic character of voting districts and of their political organizations, see Hammack, *Power and Society*, 135–137, 346, and the sources cited there, especially Daniel Greenleaf Thompson, *Politics in a Democracy*, Chap. 10.

24. Quoted in Hammack, *Power and Society*, 192–193.

25. For accounts of Croker's career and the mayoral elections in which he figured, see Hammack, *Power and Society*, 163–169; Shefter, "The Electoral Foundations of the Political Machine"; William L. Riordan, *Plunkitt of Tammany Hall* (New York, 1963, first published 1905). Also useful are Richard Skolnik, "Civic Group Progressivism in New York City," *New York History* 51 (1970): 411–439; and Augustus Cerillo, Jr., "The Reform of Municipal Government in New York City, from Seth Low to John Purroy Mitchell," *New-York Historical Society Quarterly* 57 (1973): 51–71.

26. Hammack, *Power and Society*, 115–117, 151–154, 166–170, 273 (the

Tammany view on school centralization); Martin Shefter, "The Emergence of the Political Machine: An Alternative View," in Willis D. Hawley et al., eds., *Theoretical Perspectives on Urban Politics* (Englewood Cliffs, N.J., 1976), 35–50, and Shefter, "Electoral Foundations," 273, 280; Nancy Joan Weiss, *Charles Francis Murphy, 1858–1924: Respectability and Responsibility in Tammany Politics* (Northampton, Mass., 1968), 90; J. Joseph Huthmacher, *Senator Robert F. Wagner and the Rise of Urban Liberalism* (New York, 1968).

27. On Irish political traditions, see Oscar Handlin, *Boston's Immigrants: A Study in Acculturation* (Cambridge, Mass., 1941); on European traditions of positive government see John DeWitt Warner, "Municipal Betterment in the New York City Elections," *Municipal Affairs* 5 (1901): 625–627; on the political traditions of Jewish immigrants from Eastern and Central Europe, see Moses Rischin, *The Promised City: New York's Jews, 1870–1914* (Cambridge, Mass., 1962). Huthmacher notes that during the First World War opponents of social welfare legislation denounced it as "Germanic," and that after the Bolshevik revolution they added that it was "Communistic" (*Senator Robert F. Wagner*, 39–412). American historians who favor such legislation may have refrained from emphasizing the continental origins of many social welfare ideas out of a desire to protect social welfare ideas from criticism on such grounds. Also relevant on this point is Thomas M. Henderson, *Tammany Hall and the New Immigrants: The Progressive Years* (New York, 1976), 108–112.

28. Hammack, *Power and Society*, 142–145, 155–156; W. A. Swanberg, *Citizen Hearst* (New York, 1961), 231–236; Kenneth Finegold provides the most recent and statistically most ambitious study of voting patterns in New York City in this period in his recent Harvard University Ph.D. dissertation, a portion of which he describes in "Progressivism, Electoral Change, and Public Policy in New York City, 1900–1917." Paper presented to the annual meeting of the Social Science History Association, Washington, D.C., October 1983.

29. The best work on McClellan is *The Gentleman and the Tiger: The Autobiography of George B. McClellan, Jr.* Harold C. Syrett, ed. (Philadelphia, Pa., 1956). On Gaynor, see Lately Thomas, *The Mayor Who Mastered New York: The Life and Opinions of William J. Gaynor* (New York, 1969).

30. Huthmacher, *Senator Robert F. Wagner*, 41.

31. For a brief account of Hylan's campaigns, see Melvin G. Holli and Peter d'A. Jones, *Biographical Dictionary of American Mayors, 1820–1980* (Westport, Conn. and London, 1981).

32. Huthmacher, *Senator Robert F. Wagner*; Oscar Handlin, *Al Smith and His America* (Boston, 1958); Robert A. Caro, *The Power Broker: Robert Moses and the Fall of New York* (New York, 1974); Elisabeth Israels Perry, *Belle Moskowitz: Feminine Politics and the Exercise of Power in the Age of Alfred E. Smith* (New York, 1987).

33. Arthur Mann, *LaGuardia Comes to Power, 1933* (Chicago, IL.: University of Chicago Press, 1965), Chap. 5.

34. Norton E. Long, "The Local Community as an Ecology of Games," *Amer. J. Soc.* 64 (1958): 251–252.

35. U.S. Department of Commerce, Bureau of the Census, *Historical Statistics of the United States, Colonial Times to 1970, Bicentennial Edition, 1975* (Washington, D.C., 1975), 1123, 1130, 1132.

36. *Proceedings of the Academy of Political Science in the City of New York* 5 (1915): 638–642.

37. *New York Times*, August and September 1914; letter from J. P. Morgan & Co. and Kuhn, Loeb & Co. to William A. Prendergast, September 4, 1914, and related press release from Prendergast, September 5, 1914, in the George McAneny Papers, Princeton University Library.

38. Edwin R. Lewison, *John Purroy Mitchel: The Boy Mayor of New York* (New York, 1965), provides the best account of Mitchel's career; it touches briefly on the 1914 fiscal crisis, pp. 125–129.

39. On New York City's transportation system, see Jameson W. Doig, *Metropolitan Politics and the New York Region* (New York, 1966); on the consequences of limited investment in facilities for higher education, see Selma C. Berrol, *Getting Down to Business: Baruch College in the City of New York, 1847–1987* (New York, 1989), Chap. 1.

40. On Moses, see Robert Caro, *The Power Broker*. On the federal impact on cities during and after the Great Depression, see Mark L. Gelfand, *A Nation of Cities: The Federal Government and Urban America 1933–1965* (New York, 1975).

Part II

SPACE: SOCIETY AND BEHAVIOR

THE NINETEENTH CENTURY emergence of the modern, large city in Europe and America sharpened the distinction between private and public life. The forms and extent of public life multiplied in the new metropolises. Scale, mobility, the market, and much else contributed to the development of a new world of strangers who shared the spaces of streets, parks, cafés, train stations, hotels, department stores, amusement parks, and the like. This novel social experience, organized neither by family ties and values nor by the hierarchy of the workplace, posed difficult questions about the maintenance of order. The elaboration of unprecedented social forms contributed to the invention of a new academic discipline, sociology, to find new modes of understanding, organizing, and controlling city people in public. Regulating the new public of large cities also became a focus of public policy.

The examinations of public spaces in New York and Budapest use the great urban parks in the two cities to examine how "the public" came to be defined in the everyday life of the metropolis. Both Gábor Gyáni, on Budapest, and Elizabeth Blackmar and Roy Rosenzweig, on New York, raise the question of definition at the outset and then show how actual social practice came to fill out and expand the notion of the public. In both cities the bounds of the public and the elements that constituted it became more comprehensive over time, finding space for more diverse values and behavior.

The expansion of the public did not, however, follow the same course in the two cities. A more promiscuous pattern of social interaction prevailed in New York. In Budapest, different classes of people were accommodated by separating them. Fairly rigid spatial boundaries reenforced the social differences the visitors brought with them to the park. Conflict was managed in the forms of accommodation characteristic of each city, but there were very different implications for metropolitan political culture. The experiential yield for users in New York may have been some enhancement of intergroup understanding, perhaps even a blurring of difference. But spatial politics in Budapest, like formal politics, may well have reenforced class difference.

The bourgeoisie, who largely shaped the development of the physical cities in their private and public capacities, envisioned an infinite expansion of their own values and way of life. That was the public for them: their own culture writ large. The lower classes had no such universalizing aspiration, but they insisted upon their right to carve out and appropriate a terrain where they might express themselves in public—culturally and politically.

The two essays address the problem of defining the park as a public space differently. Gyáni, like most historians of parks, evokes the meaning or core definition of Városliget Park in Budapest by probing the intentions of its designer, Christian Nebbien. Historians of New York's Central Park have customarily proceeded in the same fashion, explicating the writings of Frederick Law Olmsted. Blackmar and Rosenzweig, however, emphasize instead the user point of view. Method in this case may shape interpretation in an important way. A user perspective is more likely to pick up evidence of a politics of public space, something Gyáni professes not to find in Budapest. He stresses instead the importance of significant public spaces as the site of public discussion of—even conflict over—more general political issues. Yet, in both cities there is a trend over time for the cultures of the parks themselves to become politicized, suggesting that there is a politics of public space in both cities, even if it is less fully developed in Budapest.

The different conceptions of the designers' plans for the parks reveal important differences between the two cities. The original intent for Central Park precluded monuments, exhibitions, and other organized activities. Conforming to the romanticism to which the New York elite subscribed, the park was to provide an escape from the conditions of modern city life. It was to be the opposite of everything suggesting materialism and power. In time, of course, many of the proscribed activities were admitted to the park, but each one constituted a contestation of the park's original conception. Városliget, by contrast, was intended to be a site for national monuments, exhibitions, and celebrations.

This pattern of difference can be pressed farther. Central Park was developed, at least in part, as an alternative to emerging forms of commercial culture and entertainment. Middle-class New Yorkers, worried about the fate of culture in the intensely commercial society they had created, wanted to distinguish culture (which, for them, was a repository of moral value) from commerce. The very bourgeois who earned a living from the commercialization of so much of American life worried that an all-pervasive commerce would undermine all value. Some absolute values must be secure in a market society. For Victorian Americans the family served that end. So did nature and high culture, representing, as it did, absolute beauty and religious value. Because Hungarian society was less extensively commercialized and high culture more secure, there was less of a quest for purity in the park.

Both parks represent the bourgeois democratization of an aristocratic tradition of pleasure grounds. But Central Park was more fully or exclusively embedded in a municipal context. The making of Városliget was an act of national affirmation; it was, in Gyáni's phrase, a "national monument to the country." The creation of New York's Central Park was a civic, not a national, act. If it represented American democracy, it was a distinctly urban version of it. It addressed specific urban problems—social fragmentation and division, the pace and tension of urban life, and the challenge of a commercialized culture.

Chapter 3

Uses and Misuses of Public Space in Budapest: 1873–1914

GÁBOR GYÁNI

*T*HROUGHOUT EUROPE in the nineteenth century, and in Hungary during the late nineteenth century, the norms of conduct in public life came to be sharply separated from conduct in the private domain. The bifurcation meant that the kind of sociability found in family domestic circles was less and less tolerated on the public scene. The underlying difference in modes of private and public life, as Richard Sennett has argued, was that:

> In "public" one observed, one expressed, in terms of what one wanted to buy, to think, to approve of, not as a result of continuous interaction, but after a period of passive, silent, focused attention. By contrast, "private" meant a world where one could express oneself directly as one was touched by another person; private meant a world where interaction reigned, but it must be secret.[1]

With the limitation of sociability in public spaces, a completely new code of social behavior emerged, one that defined precisely the way that individuals should appear in public. The new rules were based on the imperatives of self-restraint and passivity. The transformation of rowdy theatrical audiences to passive, silent, and disciplined spectators denied them the possibility of making personal contact with the actors on the stage, anticipating a process soon to dominate everyday life. That transformation of audience behavior to a level of conduct where clapping is the single manifestation of inner feelings, occurred around the mid-nineteenth century. During the subsequent decades, "the rules for passive emotion which people used in theatre," Sennett remarks, "they also used out of it."[2]

This new code of public behavior was closely allied to class and gender identities. In terms of the English middle class of the early nineteenth century, Leonore Davidoff and Catherine Hall demonstrated that the notion of public "coincided with the world of productive work, of politics and men; the private with the world of home, of women, children and servants. Men had access to both spheres and moved constantly between them. Women, on the other hand, were supposed to occupy only the private sphere." True, it was an ideal rather than ubiquitous practice. Nevertheless, as Davidoff and Hall stressed, "the idea of public and private, with its close relation to gender difference, was extremely influential in the creation of a specifically middle-class way of life and self-identity in this period."[3]

Even within the scope of the private domain, there was a clear distinction between the space maintained for intimacy and the space used for communal ends. Thus, the privacy afforded the family from the outside world and from other members of the household was provided by the bedroom(s) and the living room; while the reception room(s) or the parlor were devoted to receiving visitors.[4]

The extreme and unambiguous distinctions between private and public, even within the confines of the home, remained a more or less Anglo-American peculiarity; much less emphasis was laid upon that sort of spatial differentiation in continental urban centers.[5] Although there were some variations in the rigidity assigned to the use of social space, self-discipline and self-control in shaping social interaction seemed to be universal characteristics in bourgeois culture.[6] They were meant to display and support the bourgeois sense of superiority and distinctiveness. The life of the working class, as it was reflected in the minds of members of the middle classes, was full of vivid, corrupting habits, exuberant sociability, noise, alcoholism, unregulated sexuality, which rendered them deviants, or even barbaric— a "dangerous class" to be feared.[7]

The middle-class fears of the fragility of their own respective social ideals and the protection from contamination with the vulgarity of the lower classes led to the determination of a constant vigilance over bourgeois morality on the one hand, and a patronizing attitude toward the lower classes on the other.[8] These notions directed the middle and upper middle classes to the belief that they alone were entitled to policing the common people and that it was their mission to impose new standards on the urban masses so as to create order in a chaotic urban setting.

The separation of public and private spheres brought fundamental changes in both the ecological structure and the visual layout of modern cities. The spatial segregation of various social classes and the striking architectural otherness of public buildings in comparison with residential buildings were clear manifestations of the divergence of public and private arenas. For that reason, the meaning and scope of the street as a public space was also narrowed with the passing of time. In short, the streets of the metropolis, especially the boulevards and the avenues, were to exclude not just private actions but even unregulated sociability. As the streets came to be used more and more by vehicular traffic alone, public life was multiplied and became spatially fragmented. Functionally separated public and semipublic scenes began to substitute for the single public domain: parks, places of excursion; cafés, clubs, societies, casinos used by a definite group of customers; museums, galleries, libraries available to the public, and circuses, movies, sport stadiums and the more traditional theaters housing spectacles; restaurants, saloons, pubs, music halls, and department stores; big railroad stations, bus terminals, and finally airports.[9]

In all these newly established public spaces the rigid rules of public behavior tended to decline, albeit they could not invalidate the dominant notion of propriety. The main concern of this present study is to demonstrate how some of the urban public spaces were controlled by the authorities and how they were used by the city's residents. A further concern is whether the conflicting uses of public spaces resulted in the concomitant tensions between diverse social groups or between certain social groups and the authorities. Friction was most likely to occur quite frequently at those urban junctions to which diverse social classes had equal access. Accordingly, this study focuses on the street and public parks instead of semipublic spaces like cafés or clubs.

Notions of Public Space

Municipal authorities' notions on public space can be gleaned through a series of negative definitions. The prohibitions included in single urban bylaws and regulations are the major sources leading to these definitions. Among the most relevant are the Public Sanitary Rules (issued in 1879, renewed in the 1890s), which prohibited littering, urinating, killing and feeding animals, or drying clothes in public places. These rules did not permit the engagement of the sidewalk for private ends. Exceptions to the latter were separately regulated.[10] One 1883 bylaw ordered silence everywhere in public, particularly at night, and held out the prospect of a fine to any who would dare to break the regulation. A statute promulgated in 1891 defined the limits of vehicular traffic by prohibiting cycling on sidewalks.[11]

Guides and manuals of manners are also instructive in grasping the dominant notions of what constituted public space. One of the most popular of these guides, first published in the mid-nineteenth century and reprinted many times since, focuses on the rules that should be followed in theaters or concert halls while barely dealing with requirements of street behavior. It stresses the necessity of self-restraint, sobriety, and above all, silence.[12] The same standards were generally applied to the public sphere from the late nineteenth century onward. The continuation of this pattern is clearly reflected in guides issued in the early twentieth century where we come upon characteristic passages such as the following: "A cultured man is distinguished from an uncultured person in the street, streetcar, bus, pastry shop, restaurant, and theatre or concert hall mainly by his formal conduct."[13] In the street "we are expected to keep silent . . . (there) one doesn't eat (but) smoking is permitted; (this is true) for women, too, should they happen to stroll in a city or neighborhood; where it doesn't attract much attention."[14]

Notions of the public realm held by the authorities were, in fact, ambiguous. When applied to single cases in everyday life, widely variant interpretations could be expected, something evident in the spirited debates over use of the sidewalks for private ends. A municipal statute passed in 1882, obviously inspired by the police authorities, forbade the cafés and the restaurants (saloons) to enclose an area of the sidewalk with fences or flowers. Before the suspension of these licenses, there had been forty-three cafés and twenty-four saloons that sprawled out onto the streets. Of them, not more than fourteen cafés (located mainly at the city center) and five saloons tended to enclose the maximum of two-thirds of the sidewalk territory in front of them.[15]

Police held the view that such enclosures might make it impossible to control street life, resulting in the dominance of immorality and indecency in public spaces. Order in the streets was seriously threatened, the police suggested, by night vagabonds and other suspicious figures who were supposed to lurk in these enclosures in front of the cafés or restaurants. The restrictive statute, the police commissioner added, honored women passersby who had been regularly harassed by male café customers from within the enclosed spaces. Others asserted, however, that the enclosures were necessary for establishing the semipublic nature of the cafés. They created a transitional space. While they were visible to others in the café, sidewalk patrons could be isolated within the enclosures from the masses of strangers on the streets. As one of the leaders of the Trade Chamber of the Cafés once remarked:

. . . the fence enclosed the place to be maintained for the customers, defending them against the gaze of the gaping pedestrians . . .
and shielding them against the thieves recently more numerous in
the capital . . . ; it made it convenient to sit in the street which
was avoided by many who did not wish to be publicly seen.[16]

The municipal council did not fully accept the views held by the police commissioner, and some years later reestablished the right of the
coffeehouses to the enclosures.

Apart from the sidewalk debates, it might safely be argued that a
real consensus existed about the meaning of public space and how to
use it. But it is interesting to explore which of the methods and techniques available to the authorities were used most regularly in the
enforcement of this consensus. Before doing so, however, it is necessary to provide a sketchy overview of the park and promenade system
of Budapest in the late nineteenth and early twentieth centuries.

Parks and Promenades in Budapest

According to reports dating from 1900, there were twenty-eight so-
called public spaces around the turn of the century.[17] The official statistics, however, list forty-eight parks and promenades.[18] Here we are
mostly concerned with those public places that have been well documented in various sources.[19]

Creation of the Városliget (City Grove) goes back to the close of
the eighteenth century and the beginning of the nineteenth. The area
at this time was covered by forest and was transformed after 1816
into a garden modeled on the English style. Throughout the nineteenth century and even up to the present day, the Városliget was and
has been the only urban public park of the city that can be compared
to well-known urban gardens elsewhere, like Hyde Park and Regent's
Park in London, the Tiergarten in Berlin, or Central Park in New York
City. The key factor leading to its early and constant prominence over
any other public park of Budapest lay in its highly favorable location
and its extensive size (600,000 square meters). In the course of re-
building and extending the built-up areas of the city after 1870, what
was once an outside, suburban "resort" was suddenly completely en-
gulfed by the city. Városliget became the terminal point of a fashionable thoroughfare, the Andrássy Avenue. In addition, quite a few luxury cottage houses were erected around the park during the 1870s and
1880s for middle- and upper-class families. The park gained its final
inner spatial structure during the 1880s by the establishment of the

famous Stefánia Promenade, by converting some neighboring areas into a garden, and by erection of most of its permanent structures (exhibition halls) and monuments.

The distinctive feature of the Városliget was that it was planned from the outset for the entire town's population. Most of its European counterparts had formerly been owned by aristocrats who used them as hunting grounds. The Városliget was the result of a project carried out by the Embellishment Commission, which announced a competition for a public park in 1813. This was probably the first competition in the history of landscape architecture ever held. Christian Heinrich Nebbien, a park planner of German origin who submitted a plan in 1816, won the competition. Nebbien's project embodied a conscious attempt to establish a public garden on behalf of the town's inhabitants with their active participation. Nebbien himself was fully aware of his pioneer role in park planning, as evidenced by a text he wrote at the time. In this manuscript, first published by Dorothea Nehring in 1981, Nebbien expressed his intention to dissociate himself from the dominant park notion of the eighteenth century, which had emphasized the "contemplative and edifying recreation of the individual."[20] For Nebbien, as Nehring pointed out, "the aim of his planning was to make Városliget a public park which was not, as was customary in the eighteenth century, created out of magnanimity toward the public by those in power, but which was 'to be the immediate possession and creation of the people' " as a place providing "common recreation in the fresh air" for all classes of urbanites. Considering park-going as a form of physical training became a widespread idea after the mid-nineteenth century, but when Nebbien proposed it for Budapest in the 1810s, it was still a novel notion.[21]

The Városliget was also unique in that it was devised not just as a framework for single monuments that would be erected there, but was to form, in and of itself, a national monument. Nebbien laid great emphasis on the idea that the Városliget should be "the purest expression of the great virtues of a people and the product of the spirit, the taste, the patriotism and the culture of a noble nation." To achieve his ends, he planned a large number of monuments to be dedicated to major historical personalities of Hungary. The urban public park, as an embodiment of patriotism in the form of a national pantheon, was also a new idea during the early nineteenth century and anticipated the projected "national gardens" of the 1850s.[22]

The development of the park was slowed by the insufficiency of the funds available from the city; it was not completed during the 1820s, and between the 1820s and the 1870s little work was done to finish the half-completed park. The work, with minor deviations from

Nebbien's plan, was resumed in the 1870s. And the planner's spatial and social visions for the park were retained in the work of completing it in the late nineteenth century. We will show how the availability of the park to all kinds of visitors became a reality at the turn of the century.

Nebbien's concept of a park dedicated to the national idea was also realized in the 1890s. The park gained importance in the life of the city and nation by serving as a staging ground for nationwide exhibitions, such as those held in 1885 and the Millennial Exhibition held in 1896. Városliget could meet every need of the various segments of society, since it could offer extensive cultural, amusement, and ceremonial facilities.

In sharp contrast to Városliget, both the Városmajor (City Manor) on the Buda side or the Népliget (People's Grove) on the Pest side, had much more limited appeal and were used by the lower classes alone. The Városmajor (98,000 square meters) also dated from the eighteenth century (1787), but its transformation into a public park that drew visitors mostly from the lower classes occurred only after 1825. At that time, licenses were given to sideshows, and Városmajor gradually became a Wurstl (amusement park). Much later, in 1867, a decision was made to establish the Népliget, an extensive (743,000 square meters) public park. It was intended chiefly to serve residents of the two neighboring working-class districts, Ferencváros and Kőbánya. The transformation of the area into a park modeled on an English-style garden took place following 1893 when Ilsemann Keresztély's plan was approved by the city council. Its development was, however, very slow, as reflected in a statement of the council in 1907.

> In the Népliget the population turnover is so modest and the conditions so primitive that circus and other sideshows do not survive. It is no wonder that a great part of the visitors who sought amusement in shows frequented the Népliget in small numbers only both in the past and current years; presumably out of habit they preferred, even from this part of the city, the Városliget.[23]

There were two additional parks, although they have been partially or entirely removed from the public park system. The Orczy-kert (Orczy Garden) was founded in 1790, but owing to the creation of the Ludovica Akadémia (Military Academy) of that area in the 1830s, and as a result of the gradual development of the Népliget in its vicinity, the Orczy-kert eventually lost its public status and was closed to the public by 1891.

Nebbien was the planner, too, of the Margitsziget (Margaret Island)

91

in the 1820s. This privately owned park was taken over by the state in 1909; from that time on it was opened to the public, although its use was tied to an entrance fee in subsequent decades.

The parks were rarely used by city dwellers during the week and had a greater following on Sundays only. As a circus owner commented in 1910: "The turnover in the Népliget is exclusively on Sundays."[24] The statement can also be applied to the other parks. Of great importance were the promenades or walks—tiny gardens that were hedged in the dense street system of Budapest. Frigyes Podmaniczky, vice president of the FKT (Board of Capital Public Works) after 1873, had earlier conceived of an idea to establish such public spaces everywhere possible. "Where space exists in our capital which may deploy, it ought to be transformed into a promenade, thus following the English example."[25] And he proposed to convert every sort of square or market, even ones in front of churches, to this end.[26]

Fortunately (or perhaps unfortunately) his suggestions were not completely carried out, but there were thirty-three such public spaces by the turn of the century. Of these, we can single out those that have been the more intensely used by city dwellers and for which relevant historical data is available.

On István Széchenyi's initiative, a promenade was established in the mid-1840s with a territory of 18,500 square meters. Located outside the historical city center but near to it, in Lipótváros, the promenade was named for Széchenyi. Initially privately owned, it passed into the hands of the town of Pest in 1870.

Erzsébet sétány (Elizabeth Promenade), on the fringe of the old city center of Pest, might be considered the most extensive (23,000 square meters) of its category. The area had previously been used as a marketplace, and its conversion into a promenade lasted until 1873. Adjoining it was József tér (Joseph Square), a tiny park that was labeled "the most preferred playground for children" around the turn of the century.

On both banks of the Danube several walks were created during the last decades of the century. The Dunakorzó (Danube Walk) on the Pest side was opened in 1873.[27] On the opposite side, in Buda, numerous smaller and less fashionable walks were usually frequented by neighborhood residents. Among these were the walk around the Margit Bridge abutment; the walks in front of the two baths (Lukács and Császár); and those on the hills (Várhegy-Castle Hill and Gellérthegy-Gellért Hill). Due to the expansion of vehicular traffic, many of them have since disappeared.

The Question of Surveillance

The burden of the surveillance of these parks and promenades was shared by civilian and police authorities. Following tradition, the municipal council assigned park duty partially to inmates of asylums and partially to its own employees. In turn, the fines levied against those who were guilty of inappropriate use of the parks were all transferred to the asylums. According to data from 1905, there were forty-six civilian guards and day laborers employed by the council, twelve from each category employed either in Városliget or in Népliget.[28] With few exceptions, however, they all were involved in gardening and not in the guarding.

What about police control? During the 1880s, eight guards held permanent posts in Városliget, but during the period of the national exhibition (1885) this figure jumped to sixteen.[29] By the next decade the police staff had increased to eighteen; four in the daytime and two constables at night. The other guards were involved in the patrols that controlled the whole area: one during the day and two at night.[30] In the Népliget, in the 1880s, where the turnover lagged significantly behind that of the Városliget, not more than one civilian guard and one policeman were employed day and night, to supervise the order of the park.[31] This number seldom increased except in 1894 for a period of six weeks. The aim then was to eliminate unauthorized itinerant traders.[32]

As for promenades, they seem not to have come under a strict control; an 1895 report of the police on the Erzsébet promenade indicates this:

> The police guard who holds a post at the corner of Fürdő Street and the Erzsébet Promenade passes around the area every hour by day, and every half an hour in the evening and at night; beyond that, the patrol monitors the promenade twice before midnight and twice after that.[33]

The same holds true of the Széchenyi Promenade and the others.[34] How strict was this police supervision? Reading the ever-repeated complaints of the city council concerning the police, surveillance seems to have been quite lax. In response to the complaints, the police superintendent usually referred to the heavy shortage of police and refused to increase the number of guards in either the parks or the promenades. Yet the number of guards more than doubled during the period 1881–1895, the initial number of 620 jumping to 1,463.[35]

Policemen, in addition, were often reproached for their indifference and indulgent attitude. The guards, as someone remarked, "calmly watch, and do not intervene even when some people damage trees" and other park property.[36] According to the president of the Committee of Városliget, not just patrols but constant guards were required to be on hand everywhere in Városliget.[37] On another occasion, municipal authorities called upon the police superintendent "to command those guards assigned to duty in Városliget . . . to watch every person very closely all day, especially between 8 and 10 o'clock in the morning when unreliable, work-shy tramps lie about on the lawn thus heavily threatening decency, public morals and the public order."[38]

Elsewhere, too, policemen allegedly showed similar indifference to turbulence caused by the parks' population. "The police guards in Népliget," reads a council memorandum of 1897, "are unable to maintain order . . . and are indulgent towards those doing mischief; they do not intervene, not even when they are called upon."[39]

Since the beginning of the twentieth century was an era of political liberalism, especially in the capital, this undoubtedly contributed to the less rigid surveillance of public behavior. True, that situation substantially changed with the coming of World War I, its aftermath, the revolutions of 1918 and 1919, and with their suppression. During the short period of the "White Terror" in 1919–1920, even the city council, a highly liberal-minded body heretofore, tended to follow a much more severe policing of the public. In 1920, for example, the council made an attempt to have local military forces assigned to controlling public spaces. Its request was denied.[40]

The more severe attitude of the authorities toward public behavior in the beginning of the 1920s was a result of bitter experience during the time of the revolutions. Constant street riots and frequent mass meetings in 1918–1919 were responsible for this severity. Of much greater importance, however, was the fact that both the scope and the meaning of public space came to be altered as a result. Making the Margitsziget available without any entrance fee, especially to the children of the proletarians, was one reflection of this change in attitude. The complete transformation of the Millennium Monument at the entrance point of the Városliget was another. These symbolic acts were designed for the purpose of carrying out a total reinterpretation of the public realm. When the Habsburgs' statues were removed from the kings' gallery of the Millennium Monument to be replaced by monuments portraying common people who participated in the May Day ceremonies held in the square; or when the statues of Árpád, the conquering leader of the Hungarians in the ninth century, and those of his suite were concealed by drapery, the Communist regime wished to demonstrate and symbolically express a negative attitude toward the nation's history and a firm commitment to the emancipation of the proletariat.[41]

A rigid policing of public space that prevailed in England at that time was not practiced in Budapest prior to 1920.[42] Not even indications of the moralistic attitude of the upper classes and the authorities toward the appearance of the lower-class masses in public can be discerned in Hungary in connection with public space. The commitment to the notion of stewardship advanced by Frederick Law Olmsted and his political supporters in New York City was almost totally absent in Budapest, or perhaps it emerged much later and in other versions. The effort to uplift manual laborers in Budapest focused less on making them behave correctly than on teaching them to think more rationally. This was the impulse behind the foundation of the Free School of Social Sciences, established in Budapest in 1906. This school, operated by a group of radical and socialist intellectuals, offered lectures and seminars to the public.[43]

Appropriation and Division

Conflict concerning the use of public space can be classed according to three categories: vehicular use of the space, use of the space by military officers, and the character of the population using the parks and promenades.

Conflicts emerged if particular public spaces were shared by diverse vehicles, some of which were eventually prohibited. During the 1890s, police authorities repeatedly excluded carts, freight traffic, and hearses from the Stefánia Drive.[44] At the same time, municipal authorities worried about vehicular traffic in Városliget and pondered over its ban. They argued that:

> recently cyclists are not satisfied with exercising their sport in Stefánia and the other drives, but run up the walkways and even the roads of the Körönd; and with this they seriously threaten the physical well being of the pedestrians.[45]

The special place of the Városliget among the public parks of Budapest is shown by parallel situations. A request of the residents of Városmajor in 1897 to prohibit cycling on the walkways of that park was denied by the municipal authorities. Yet horseback-riding on the walkways was tolerated by the city council, despite the protests of the district council.[46]

During the 1880s and 1890s, complaints were often lodged regarding the Népliget that army officers (those serving either in the common K.U.K. army or in the Hungarian Honvéd army, as well as students of the military academy) deliberately rode into the park on horseback, trampling down plants and parading through the walkways, sometimes insulting the civil guards who attempted to warn them off.[47] These offenses usually occurred in parks used chiefly by the lower classes, reflecting sharp divisions between civilians and the army officer corps, which formed a castelike social group with an aristocratic self-consciousness. This attitude was encouraged even in the less prestigious Honvéd army where:

> volunteer and officer couldn't be in contact with the rank and file outside the barracks; the officer couldn't visit the same cafés or restaurants and what is more, it was derogatory to his position to take the same horse tramway and streetcar, or to travel via the same class that was prescribed in the ranks.[48]

An officer's attitude was extended to the public parks whose order, he reasoned, did not concern him.[49]

Tensions also arose from an unrestricted mingling of the parks' visitors, especially on the promenades. Problems arose when the most diverse social strata began to visit a public space that had previously been frequented only by the middle or upper classes.

Which of the social groups were considered to be the most vexing park patrons? A police report, dated from 1886, answers the question. The promenade around the Margit Bridge abutment, it declared:

> is used every hour of the day by residents of Buda, especially by the more educated segments of society. But the public, who seeks recreation here is quite bothered by domestic servants, children and ragamuffin laborers who occupy the benches and break the silence with their cries.[50]

Therefore, the police asked the city council to exclude domestic servants and the children from this area, just as they had been from the Danube Walk in Pest. The city council complied only partially, reluctantly excluding cycling children and drunkards. The argument of the city council in supporting its decision was as follows:

> We do not endorse the idea of excluding honest laborers, because nowadays they are just as much taxpaying citizens as everybody else and the proposition advanced by police is contrary to recent humanistic principles.[51]

The "honest laborers" in the quotation referred to every sort of working person, not only the "ragamuffin laborers" but the female domestics, too. True, notions of the promenade without children and servants had some popularity beyond the police.[52] Their exclusion, however, was not achieved with any completeness. But what was to be done if their presence was barely or not at all tolerated by the upper-class park users? One possible solution was to appropriate or reclaim a space for elite groups. Such a strategy can be discerned in respect to the Széchenyi Promenade.

At the close of the 1850s, when the Széchenyi Promenade was still a privately owned public space, an ambitious effort was made to sustain its exclusivity, as recorded in an 1858 issue of *Budapest Daily:*

> The plan is to bring together here the more educated classes of Pest and to this end . . . twice a week, on Wednesday and Saturday at 6 o'clock in the afternoon, exclusive promenade parties will be held. For a month, everybody may subscribe to eight parties . . . all who are going to attend any party may rest assured that the temper and composition of the assembly won't be disturbed by anybody whose presence is undesirable.[53]

When the plan was put into practice, around 800 persons, representing the "most prestigious society," participated in the parties. As a consequence, "the common audience: servants and the lower class, all who had been in the habit of visiting the square, now took a seat outside the fence."[54]

The promenade parties, however, were of short duration, and after some months the place was again dominated by the lower classes. According to police remarks in the 1890s, "domestic servants and soldiers gather in great number here and . . . therefore the upper-class audience avoids its use."[55]

In summary, it can be said that the public spaces studied here rarely served as suitable channels for uniting diverse social groups. The efforts of the upper classes to separate themselves from the lower classes, even in recreational public spaces, precluded any democratic mingling. To enforce separation, the strategy of appropriation was applied. Other techniques were also employed, especially where exclusive availability could not be established. In such cases, particularly where the Városliget was concerned, a strategy of division or distribution prevailed. Briefly, this entailed a rigid social topography within the confines of the park. A "recreational segregation" effectively channeled the movements of the park's population. A contemporary vividly describes the scene for us:

At the entrance where a fountain squirts its jets in an arched form, the masses divide: the gentlefolk tend towards the Stefánia Drive, the middle classes move towards tiny islands of the lake, and the common people in their best clothes, eager to amuse themselves, push on to the pleasures of Eldorado: the fireworks square. But, the surroundings of the fountain also have their own public . . . an army of children dressed in their best with Swiss governesses on the benches. . . . Tens of thousands of people (dressed up clerks and apprentices among them in the boats) are milling down along the banks of the lake. . . . Hundreds of marriageable girls from Teréz-város are sitting on the island around white tables with their mothers. . . . Gentlemen, merchants by trade dressed in white vests, dance close to the big statue of our great Széchenyi. . . . Beyond that, masses dominated by soldiers throng in the line of the trees leading to the Wurtlprater (amusement center).

The fireworks square is marked by "sideshows, a circus, a photographer, a shooting-gallery, the big-lady and a self-acting theatre all of which operate peacefully side by side." Large families enjoy the shade lying on the grass beyond the railway substructure. They are "dwellers of narrow streets in the outskirts who have their open-air picnic here." In sharp contrast to them:

a different kind of life is to be found . . . where the very fashionable Stefánia Drive looms white. Stefánia is a preferred place for walking beginning with the more genteel folk and high society. [They come] not during holidays in sunny summer time, but on beautiful spring afternoons and evenings. It is fashionable to drive, ride and walk here or to watch and judge those who do so.[56]

Appropriation and internal division of public places by various social groups were the usual methods by which society coped with the recreational problem. Since opposing classes tended to separate from each other even in parks and promenades, the conspicuous tolerance of the authorities in approaching the conflicting uses of public spaces is not surprising. The actual lack, or rather rare occurrences, of confluence of the classes made it unnecessary to impose a more severe control. And even though one or another of the authorities tended to urge much closer surveillance, such insistence was insufficient to require a change of official policy. Intervention by the police authorities was limited. They were "forced to apply proper standards everywhere in public which serves as a gathering and amusement site for lower classes . . . and could intervene only if indictable behavior took place."[57]

98

Conflicts concerning the recreational use of public space were, therefore, largely contained. The picture is less bright when we turn to public space as a political arena, and when we consider the violence of collective uprisings that occurred in Budapest between the 1860s and 1914. Briefly, the main social basis of these uprisings initially concerned the working class (1869–1871); subsequently, the provocation came from university students; and from the mid-1890s on through World War I, it was at the instigation of the industrial laborers again. Issues ranged from purely economic grievances to anti-Semitic demonstrations (around 1882), from nationalistic sentiments to the persistent demand for universal and secret suffrage.

The Political Use of Public Space by the Working Class

Community networks within the working class were so deeply imbedded in the world of the saloons and restaurants that initially every political and trade union activity was concentrated there. Consider the turbulent year of 1898, when increasing repression against the socialist movement and the movement's reactions to it contributed to the general restlessness. In that year, the Hungarian half of the Monarchy commemorated the fiftieth anniversary of the revolution of 1848; that year also represented the fiftieth anniversary of Francis Joseph's accession to the throne. Celebration of the two diametrically opposing anniversaries kept tempers astir.[58] Concerning the anniversary of the revolution, the socialists, in tactical unity with the independent political parliamentary forces, stressed the demand for universal and secret suffrage.

The socialist mass meetings that eventually led to a frontal clash with the government were still held primarily in restaurants and cafés; sometimes they were staged in theaters, but more often they took place in the urban public parks. On February 13, as a response to anti-socialist government measures, the socialists held a mass meeting in Café Mautner.[59] On March 17, the socialists disturbed some of the performances in theaters where patriotic plays were being staged.[60] Finally, the Social Democratic Party (SDP) applied to the city council for the approval of meetings to be held twice in the Városliget and twice in the Városmajor.[61] Their requests, however, were denied just as were those of laborers in Buda who attempted to hold a mass meeting in the Városmajor some months later. The laborers were told that: "The capital is not willing to yield leisure spaces to mass meetings, because they are used by visitors to such a degree that the permission would prevent them from enjoying the place."[62] On another occasion, in 1902, butcher shop assistants wished to set up the headquarters of a planned strike in the Népliget: their application was also denied.[63] Restaurants and parks alike were often used as headquarters of strike committees. In the great streetcar strike of 1906, headquarters were set up in a restaurant called the Zöld Vadász (Green Hunter).[64]

Following the turn of the century, a new location for meetings appeared on the scene—workingmen's clubs or casinos. They were founded either by single employers, societies, or the trade unions and the Social Democratic Party.[65] The clubs were gradual replacements for public spaces like the restaurants, saloons, or cafés. However, they were not suited for big mass meetings, where tens of thousands of people were present. These events continued to be held in public parks and, from the 1910s on, they moved to the roofed hall called *Tatter-saal*. This was an establishment that alternatively served as an arena for horse exhibitions, horse fairs, and much later, as a racecourse.[66]

The struggle for domination of the street as public space culminated in collective actions motivated politically. Use of the street for political ends is best revealed through the paradigm of the barricade and the demonstration. The barricade, a specifically nineteenth century phenomenon, which was closely tied to Paris, frequently divided the city into two distinct parts; it separated the outskirts from the city center, with the former defended by restless lower-class residents against the professional army attacking them. The line of barricades sharply and visibly distinguished the territories that belonged to the working classes and those attached to the bourgeoisie and the state power; the latter two represented the world of order. By cutting the cities in half, the barricades created totally new spatial relations. As Vidler suggested: "Within the space closed off by the barricades, the street took on the air of communal property, an open-air room adopted by the community as its own."[67]

Street demonstrations that were frequently accompanied by wide-scale strike movements, however, did not totally appropriate any public space, although they transformed the neutralized, depersonalized public domain by temporarily repudiating the dominance of a bourgeois code of public behavior. The imposition of official order could be most effective when the demonstrations happened in the heart of the city, occupying urban areas where the residences of the upper classes were usually located side by side with the buildings of the state and municipal authorities. Here, combined wealth and power held sway over the spatial domain. Such areas, usually characterized by wide and long thoroughfares or forumlike squares, housed a majority of the political public events. By a temporary suspension of traffic, they regularly served as a staging ground for all public ceremonies, mass marches, military parades, community rituals, and every kind of celebration that was approved of and initiated by the authorities. When the same place was used "unofficially" for similar ends, the demonstrators were, in fact, seizing control of the space "as a medium for contesting power."[68] For this reason, organizers of the workers' May Day parades chose a marching route to the city center. At the outset of the twentieth century, the most customary route of the May Day celebration in Budapest was via the principal boulevards:

> In the early afternoon, the laborers regularly rally on the Kálmán Tisza square with flags and banners grouped by industrial trades. From here they start the long march that passes through the Rákóczi Avenue, the Great Boulevard and the Andrássy Avenue, finally arriving in Városliget. There, behind the park in a spacious restaurant, they completely engage the gardens. Festive speeches are delivered here; the red feast is then concluded by music, singing, dancing and parlour games.[69]

May Day, says Eric Hobsbawm, is a "regular public self-representation of a class," an assertion of power, indeed in its invasion of the establishment's social space, a symbolic conquest.[70] The self-representation of laborers through the class organizations of their own parties or trade unions on May Day, can be seen as a demonstration of self-control, a control that can facilitate its gradual legalization.[71]

The Hungarian capital, however, abounded in riots that were not so peaceful as a May Day ceremony. The events of May 23–24, 1912, for example, lead us to spatial implications of another kind.

Spatial Choreography of "Blood-Red Thursday"

The most vehement of the riots that occurred in the period of the Dual Monarchy (1867–1918) was provoked by events inside the Hungarian Parliament a day before the riot. István Tisza, a talented, conservative-liberal politician of the time (leader of the governing party and ex-prime minister) was elected president of the Parliament. His election meant an open challenge to the opposition both in and out of Parliament. Since the new president immediately adopted measures against any obstructive tactics, the opposition applied a parliamentary technique to delay the discussion of the so-called Armed Forces Bill, which it also used in the ongoing struggle for the passage of a universal and secret ballot. The Social Democrats (a party not represented in the Parliament), soon responded to Tisza's election by calling for a general strike and a "demonstration walk" to be held on May 23, 1912.

The decision to stage a strike and a demonstration was made during meetings of delegates who represented both the party and the trade unions, and the decision involved the use of public space. The preliminary meetings were held in various restaurants and saloons. On May 23, people rallied not in the customary points (Garay and Kálmán Tisza squares or Városliget), but started out from their residences, so a crowd gathered on the thoroughfares (Váci and Soroksári roads) that led to the city center. Elsewhere the masses marched on the side streets (on Wesselényi Street and toward the Margit Bridge in Buda) by which they could also get to the center.[72] Their common destination was the forumlike square in front of the Parliament. The police also concentrated their main forces there.

> Two hundred foot and forty mounted policemen under the immediate personal command of the police superintendent were ordered (to Parliament Square); they were even supported by two squadrons of hussars. Beyond that, one infantry battalion was kept in reserve in the neighboring barracks, in the Nádor one with a command to go there if necessary.[73]

The united forces of the police and the military endeavored to occupy all strategic points along the Great Boulevard so that not many succeeded in getting to the vicinity of the Parliament. Those who did came to a sudden halt and soon clashed with the police and the soldiers. Indeed, bloody clashes also occurred around the Nyugati railway terminal and in Szabadság Square, where rioters prevented the streetcars from going through and, by piling up wagons, park benches, and other objects, put up barricades.[74]

By afternoon the center of events shifted as the SDP called a mass meeting on Petőfi Square, in the heart of the historic city center. The police and the military forces were also sent to this area to occupy the strategic points along the line of the Inner Boulevard, which surrounds the historic city center.[75] The defensive cordon around the city core, where the thrust of events subsequently shifted, proved to be even more effective than the one around the Parliament set up in the morning. Accordingly, the mass meeting planned here had to be finally cancelled.[76]

Because of the cancellation and subsequent withdrawal, the sites of the riots (mobilizing some 100,000 rioters) moved back to the outskirts and the working-class suburbs. Here the rioters entrenched themselves, and by evening had completely appropriated the area. How was it accomplished? In the so-called "Chicago" section, "in that part of Erzsébetváros (Elizabeth district) . . . in half an hour the entire district was darkened, because the gas lamps were all knocked down." By piling up the booths of the market in Garay Square, people put up road blocks

> thus barricading the roads; in addition somebody obtained cables with which they closed down almost every street in Chicago. . . . The most threatening trap in a dark street is an invisible wire entanglement.[77]

Factory owners, meanwhile, came to a common decision to lock out all of striking employees for two weeks. This led to additional riots the next day, which were confined, however, to the working-class districts. The restless workers then began to dominate entire streets within the borders of their residential areas; and they did not restrain their tempers.

> They have smashed in the factory gates with the lamp-posts pulled down and are intent on breaking, crushing and destroying. Around forty streetcars are turned over when the masses manage to possess a loaded carriage with oil drums, and burning begins. . . . The masses erect barricades as high as three floors; by piling up streetcars and loaded carriages they try to impede the fire-brigade from fulfilling their duty.[78]

The center of the riots then moved to Angyalföld, one of the most characteristic working-class districts of Budapest. But the other outer districts, like Kőbánya or the suburbs of Újpest and Budafok, were also involved to some extent in the events. The barricades that were constructed in Angyalföld were rudimentary; they did not form an uninterrupted line of defense. Yet, although they could not provide a permanent shelter against the military troops, they were able to slow down their intrusion.[79]

Overheated tempers began to cool down when the SDP called upon the rioters to appear at a mass meeting to be held in the afternoon on May 24. The general upheaval then came to an abrupt end in the same place where it had started a day earlier: in a restaurant. Obeying the SDP, around 4,000 workers assembled in and around the restaurant *Zöld Vadász*, located in the Városliget. During and after the meeting, some smaller clashes with the police were registered, but these were the final chords of the notorious "Blood-Red Thursday."[80]

In all of the riots, three or four people were killed, about 180 were wounded. Women were not involved in large numbers in the events; and only nine women were wounded.

The topography of the events of "Blood-Red Thursday" closely resembles that of the Commune of 1871 in Paris or of the configurations of some of the notable riots in various North Italian cities, like the I Fatti di Maggio in Milan in the 1890s or the Fatti di Torino of 1917.[81] A common factor in these events was that the rioting working-class masses first attempted to conquer the city center and, failing that, returned to their residential areas to prepare for their defense. The populace of these districts encircled by the barricades was, thus, united in a common cause. Use of the social space within the barricades even further stressed the differences between the two halves of the city—the area dominated by the bourgeoisie and the state authorities, and the area ruled by the working class, whose behavior behind the borders of the barricades caused them to be perceived as a "dangerous class."

We cannot conclude that the bourgeois city center and the working-class outskirts of Budapest represented a total polarity of the social space within its metropolitan setting. As Danile Jalla correctly demonstrates in the case of Torino, "The notion of a simple correspondence between geographical location and type of community, working class barrier and bourgeois center, is very misleading."[82] There are many strong functional links between the city center and each of the outer districts (sometimes divided into more homogeneous, smaller units), though these links might appear temporarily eroded when violent collective action dominates the scene. Such erosion, however, took place infrequently in Budapest during the years of the Dual Monarchy.

Notes

1. Richard Sennett, *The Fall of Public Man* (New York, 1977), 148.
2. Sennett, *The Fall of Public Man*, 212.
3. Leonore Davidoff and Catherine Hall, "The Architecture of Public and Private Life: English Middle-Class Society in a Provincial Town, 1780 to 1850," in D. Fraser and A. Sutcliffe, eds., *The Pursuit of Urban History* (London, 1983), 327. More elaborately, *idem, Family Fortunes, Men and Women of the English Middle-Class, 1780–1850* (London, 1987).
4. Martin J. Daunton, *House and Home in the Victorian City: Working-Class Housing 1850–1915* (London, 1983), Chaps. 2 and 11; Clifford E. Clark, Jr., "Domestic Architecture and the Cult of Domesticity in America, 1840–1870," *Journal of Interdisciplinary History* 7, 1 (1976): 33–56.
5. Donald J. Olsen, *The City as a Work of Art: London, Paris, Vienna* (New Haven, 1986), 101–132.
6. Scandinavian evidences are shown in Jonas Frykman and Orvar Löfgren,

Culture Builders, A Historical Anthropology of Middle-Class Life (New Brunswick, 1987), 106–118.

7. Sennett, *The Fall of the Public Man*, 214.
8. F. M. L. Thompson, *The Rise of Respectable Society, A Social History of Victorian Britain, 1830–1900* (London, 1988), 89.
9. See Paul M. Hohenberg and Lynn H. Lees, *The Making of Urban Europe, 1000–1950* (Cambridge, Mass., 1985), 300.
10. *Budapest Főváros Törvényhatóságának Szabályrendeletei, I. Rész* (Statutes of Budapest capital city), Part I. (Budapest, 1881), 167 ff.; *Fővárosi Közlöny* (Capital gazette) (January 13, 1899), 4–20.
11. *Budapest Főváros Törvényhatóságának Szabályrendeletei, II. Rész* (Budapest, 1888), 147 ff.; *Budapest Főváros Törvényhatósága Által az 1888–1891.Ik Években Alkotott Szabályrendeletek, Szabályzatok és Utasítások, V. Rész* (Statutes decrees and regulations of Budapest capital city in the years 1888–1891), Part V. (Budapest, 1892), 51 ff.
12. *A Pesti Művelt Társalgo* (The cultured manual of Pest) (Budapest, 1986), 62–64, 65–67.
13. *Az Új Idők Illemkódexe* (Rules of conduct of new times) (Budapest, 1930), 199.
14. *Művelt és Udvarias Ember a XX. Században* (The cultured and polite man in the 20th century) (Budapest, n.d.), 169 ff.
15. *Budapest Főváros Levéltára* (Budapest capital archives), IV, 1407, b. 465/1874–VII.
16. *Budapest Főváros Levéltára*, IV, 1407, b. 465/1874–VII.
17. J., "Budapest Nyilvános Parkjai" (Public parks in Budapest), *Kertészeti Lapok* (1900), 92.
18. Gusztav Thirring, ed., *Budapest Székesfőváros Statisztikai Évkönyve*, III: 1897–1898 (Budapest, 1901), 22.
19. Here I consulted the following printed sources: Anna Zádor, "Az Angolkert Magyarországon" (The English garden in Hungary), *Építés-Építészettudomány* 5 (1973), 32, 49; Aladár Edvi Illés, ed., *Budapest Műszaki Útmutatója* (Technical Guide Budapest) (Budapest, 1896), 257 ff. and 261 ff; *Budapest Lexikon* (Budapest, 1973) *passim;* Gusztav Thirring, *Statistical Yearbook of Budapest Capital*, III: 1897–1898.
20. Christian Heinrich Nebbien, *Ungarn Folks-Garten der Koeniglichen Freystadt Pesth* (1816), Dorothee Nehring, ed. in the series *Veröffentlichungen des Finnish-Ugrischen Seminars an der Universität München*, Reihe C, Bd. 11, (Munich, 1981).
21. Dorothy Nehring, "The Landscape Architect, Christian Heinrich Nebbien, and his Design for the Municipal Park in Budapest," *Journal of Garden History* 5, 3 (1985): 269–270.
22. Dorothy Nehring, "The Landscape Architect, Christian Heinrich Nebbien, and his Design for the Municipal Park in Budapest," 271–272.
23. *Budapest Főváros Levéltára*, IV, 1407, b. 3105/1901-VI.
24. *Budapest Főváros Levéltára*, IV, 1407, b. 3105/1901-VI.
25. Frigyes Podmaniczky, *Egy Régi Gavallér Emlékei. Válogatás a Naplótöredékekből 1824–1887* (Reminiscences of an old gentleman. Selection from diary fragments 1824–1887) (Budapest, 1984), 414.
26. Frigyes Podmaniczky, *Egy Régi Gavallér Emlékei*, 415.
27. Károly Vörös, "A Dunakorzó Regénye" (Novel of the Danube walk), *História* 1, 1 (1979): 21–24.

28. *Budapest Főváros Levéltára* IV: 1407, b. 114/1880-II.
29. *Budapest Főváros Levéltára* IV, 1407, b. 3087/1885-I.
30. *Budapest Főváros Levéltára* IV, 1407, b. 1241/1889-VI.
31. *Budapest Főváros Levéltára* IV, 1407, b. 1241/1892-II.
32. *Budapest Főváros Levéltára* IV, 1407, b. 6972/1874-VII.
33. *Budapest Főváros Levéltára* IV, 1407, b. 1143/1895-I.
34. *Budapest Főváros Levéltára* IV, 1407, b. 1071/1890-I.
35. "Az Ötven Éves Budapesti m. Kir. Állami Rendőrség Története 1873–1923" (History of the fifty-year-old Hungarian royal state police of Budapest 1873–1923), in János Baksa, ed., *Rendőrségi Almanach* (Police almanac) (Budapest, 1923), 31, 54.
36. *Budapest Főváros Levéltára* IV, 1407, b. 1241/1892-II.
37. *Budapest Főváros Levéltára* IV, 1407, b. 3087/1885-I.
38. *Budapest Főváros Levéltára* IV, 1407, b. 3087/1885-I.
39. *Budapest Főváros Levéltára* IV, 1407, b. 1730/1897-II.
40. *Budapest Főváros Levéltára* IV, 1428, gy. II 250/1920.
41. András Gerő, "Az ezredévi emlékmű" (The Millennium Monument), *Medvetanc* (1987): 33–34.
42. See Robert D. Storch, "The Policeman as Domestic Missionary: Urban Discipline and Popular Culture in Northern England, 1850–1880," *Journal of Social History* 9, 4 (1976): 481–510; Martin J. Daunton, *House and Home in the Victorian City*, 266 ff.
43. Judit Szapor, "Egy Szabad Egyetemért. A Társadalomtudományok Szabad Iskolája" (For a free university. The Free School of Social Sciences), *Medvetánc* (1985/4–1986): 1.
44. *Budapest Főváros Levéltára* IV, 1407, b. 1588/1897-I.
45. *Budapest Főváros Levéltára* IV, 1407, b. 899/1897-VI.
46. *Budapest Főváros Levéltára* IV, 1407, b. 1131/1897-VI, 877/1888-II.
47. *Budapest Főváros Levéltára* IV, 1407, b. 148/1889-II; 154/1897-II.
48. Tibor Hajdu, "Avtisztikar Társadalmi Helyzetének Változásai, 1848–1914" (Changes of social position of the officers' corps, 1848–1914), *Valósag* 4 (1984): 77.
49. We found only one case when the officer was, in fact, fined for such an offense. See *Budapest Főváros Levéltára* IV, 1407, b. 154/1897-II.
50. *Budapest Főváros Levéltára* IV, 1407, b. 219/1886-II.
51. *Budapest Főváros Levéltára* IV, 1407, b. 219/1886-II.
52. Concerning the Erzsébet promenade, see *Budapest Főváros Levéltára*, IV, 484/1885-II.
53. *Budapesti Hírlap* (Budapest Daily), April 24, 1858.
54. *Budapesti Hírlap*, May 7, 1858.
55. *Budapest Főváros Levéltára* IV, 1407, b. 1071/1890-I.
56. Zs. Sz., "A Városliget. Verőfényes Ünnepnapon" (The Városliget. On a sunny holiday), *Fővárosi Lapok*, June 15, 1888.
57. *Budapest Főváros Levéltára* IV, 1407, b. 1071/1890-I.
58. Péter Hanák, "1898. A Nemzeti És Az Állampatrióta Értékrend Frontális Ütközése a Monarchiában" (1898: Frontal clash between the national and the state-patriotic value order in the monarchy), in *idem*, *A Kert és a Műhely* (Garden and the workshop) (Budapest, 1988), 112–130.
59. *Rendőrségi almanach* (Police Almanac), 80.
60. *Rendőrségi almanach* (Police Almanac), 71.
61. *Budapest Főváros Levéltára* IV, 1407, b. 133/1898-VI; 316/1898-VI.

62. *Budapest Főváros Levéltára* IV, 1407, b. 316/1898-VI.
63. *Budapest Főváros Levéltára* IV, 1428, gy. VI, 894/1902.
64. Béla Gadanecz, "Adalékok a Budapesti Villamosvasutasok 1906. Évi Sztrájkjának Történetéhez" (Data to the history of streetcar strike in Budapest in 1906), *Tanulmányok Budapest Múltjából* XV (1963): 529. The saloon owners who were reluctant to yield their businesses to socialist meetings were regularly boycotted around 1900. *Rendőrségi Almanach* (Police Almanac), 80.
65. József Kovalcsik, *A kultúra Csarnokai* (Halls of culture) (Budapest, 1987), Vol. II, 86, 235ff; *Budapest Főváros Levéltára* IV, 1409, b. 4076/1905.
66. *Budapest Főváros Levéltára* IV, 1428, gy. VIII, 3/1910.
67. Anthony Vidler, "The Scenes of the Street: Transformations in Ideal and Reality, 1750–1871," in S. Anderson, ed., *On Streets* (Cambridge, Mass., 1978), 82.
68. David Scobey, "Boycotting the Politics Factory: Labor Radicalism and the New York City Mayoral Election of 1886," *Radical History Review* 28–30 (1984): 310.
69. Rezső Vigand, *Budapest Útmutatója* (Guide to Budapest) (Budapest, 1909), 317.
70. Eric Hobsbawm, "The Transformation of Labour Rituals," in *Workers: Worlds of Labor* (New York, 1984), 76; on French cities, see Michelle Perrot, "The First of May 1890 in France: the Birth of a Working-Class Ritual," in P. Thane et al., eds., *The Power of the Past: Essays for Eric Hobsbawm* (Cambridge, 1984), 157.
71. Eric Hobsbawm, "The Transformation of Labour Rituals," 76.
72. László Remete, *Barikádok Budapest Utcáin 1912* (Barricades in the streets of Budapest 1912) (Budapest, 1972), 111, 118, 120ff.
73. *Budapest Főváros Levéltára* IV, 1428, gy. 4421/1912-XI.
74. *Budapest Főváros Levéltára* IV, 1428, gy. 4421/1912-XI; László Remete, *Barricades in the Streets of Budapest 1912.* 136ff.
75. László Remete, *Barricades in the Streets of Budapest,* 167ff; *Budapest Főváros Levéltára,* IV, 1428, gy. 4421/1912-XI.
76. László Remete, *Barricades in the Streets of Budapest 1912,* 174.
77. *Rendőrségi almanach* (Police Almanac), 124.
78. This day, on the whole, approximately 10,000 police and especially military forces were deployed in the streets of Budapest. *Budapest Főváros Levéltára,* IV, 1428, gy, 4421/1912-XI.
79. László Remete, *Barricades in the Streets of Budapest 1912,* 245ff.
80. *Budapest Főváros Levéltára* IV, 1428, gy, 4421/1912-XI.
81. See Anthony Vidler, "The Scenes of the Street: Transformations in Ideal and Reality," 100, 105; Louise A. Tilly, "I Fatti di Maggio: The Working Class of Milan and the Rebellion of 1898," in R. J. Bezucha, ed., *Modern European Social History* (Lexington, Ky., 1972), 124 ff; Danile Jalla, "Belonging Somewhere in the City—Social Space and its Perception: The Barriere of Turin in the Early 20th Century," *Oral History* 13, 2 (1985).
82. Danile Jalla, "Belonging Somewhere in the City—Social Space and its Perception: The Barrière of Turin in the Early 20th Century," 20.

Chapter 4

The Park and the People: Central Park and its Publics: 1850–1910

ELIZABETH BLACKMAR and ROY ROSENZWEIG

*I*N JULY 1901 New Yorkers rioted. Through the nineteenth century New Yorkers had rioted over the price of bread, the abolition of slavery, and the draft. This time, the issue seemed trivial: a new park policy licensed a private entrepreneur to charge five cents to rent chairs in the city's parks. The practice, common in European (including Budapest's) parks, had been imported to the United States in June and met immediate howls of protest. In the city's most famous public space, the 843-acre Central Park, the chair rental agents faced jeers and verbal abuse. "Some park patrons," one newspaper reported, "were so enraged that they used knives . . . to deface and break the chairs." In Madison Square Park, tensions ran particularly high, as dozens of people refused to pay the rental fees and thousands joined in smashing the chairs as well as taunting the rental agents and chasing them from the park.[1]

Park Commissioner George C. Clausen, who had initiated the chair scheme, soon backed down. He noted that he had received "hundreds of letters from ladies and gentlemen commending" the new policy. But "the great public of New York . . . seems to condemn the innovation." As a "public servant," Clausen was now bowing to "the public will" in order to maintain "the public peace" and "public property . . . for the use and enjoyment for all the people."[2]

Clausen's repeated use of the word "public" was hardly coincidental. The ambiguous meaning and ideological use of the term "public" was central to the park chair controversy as it was to numerous debates involving New York's public parks—particularly Central Park.

This chapter traces the development and transformation of New York's best known "public park" and the shifting meaning of that seemingly simple phrase.

Like many others before and since, Park Commissioner Clausen used the word "public" in more than one sense. In his description of himself as a "public servant" responsible for maintaining "public property," "public" referred to municipal ownership and control of property. Such usage contrasted public (state-owned) property to both privately owned property and to "common property"—land or resources from which no member of the community could be excluded. State ownership delegated exclusive authority over the management and use of public spaces—in this case parks— to government officials (like Clausen) who claimed to represent the interest of all citizens. Control of parks (and similar public spaces like streets and wharves) was thus negotiated through the political system. In this sense, the people on whose behalf this property was administered constituted the sovereign or political public.[3]

Yet Clausen also invoked a more inclusive "great" public, when he spoke of preserving the public property for "the use and enjoyment of all the people." In this sense, "public" referred to the organization of parks as relatively nonexclusive territories, which assumed their character not through political powers of ownership or administration but rather through patterns of social use. The people who claimed access to this public space thus constituted the "user" or cultural public. Such a meaning of public space overlapped with its property-based definition in sometimes confusing ways. Although nonexclusive spaces could be privately owned (as in the case of a theater or saloon), the notion of public space as open to all members of the community had its ideal type in the village commons.

Property-based definitions of "public" and "private" tend to be absolute and are rooted in matters of ownership and control. But the idea of public space as nonexclusive territory is a more relative concept. Few, if any spaces, can be said to be entirely open or entirely restricted in access. Degrees of exclusivity and access are shaped by economics, politics, and culture. First, access is determined by a variety of structural constraints; that is, by whether people possess the resources to make use of public space. Ostensibly, a park may be open to the entire community, but some people may lack the time or money (for example, the price of transportation) to enjoy it, or at least to enjoy it equally with others. Second, formal prescriptive rules can regulate access to public spaces. For instance, in some Southern cities before the mid-1960s, segregation laws prevented black Americans from making use of public accommodations, including parks. Third, informal rules or codes of social conduct structure the willingness of particular groups to make use of different public spaces. In mid-nine-teenth century New York City, a poorly dressed Irish laborer might avoid Washington Square Park, located in the midst of one of the city's wealthiest residential districts, just as an elegantly attired law-yer might feel unwelcome in Tompkins Square Park, situated in the city's working-class German ward.

Concepts both of public space (as state-owned and nonexclusive territories) and of the public (as political and cultural bodies) affected the resolution of the chair riot controversy. Large numbers of New Yorkers, Jewish and Italian immigrants prominent among them, re-fused to pay for the rental of chairs themselves and, in some cases, obstructed the rental of chairs to others. In this admittedly minor protest, park users insisted on their common right to sit in shaded seats despite a government policy that licensed a private entrepreneur to collect rent on those chairs. "I will not pay five cents for what I have always had free. . . . This is a public park," declared Abraham Cohen when he was arrested for refusing to pay.[4]

Yet the public was not an undifferentiated mass. Indeed, some New Yorkers defended the rental chair scheme precisely because it allowed for distinctions within the public, because it offered, as one letter writer to the *Times* put it, an alternative to "the ordeal of sitting next to unclean, often drunken, and generally foul-mouthed loafers."

Nevertheless, protesters who insisted on their right to free seats created political pressure that led Commissioner Clausen—the ser-vant of the state and the political public—to modify his original pol-icy and revoke the chair franchise. Appointed by the Tammany (Dem-ocratic) organization's mayor, Clausen (who had mayoral aspirations himself) could ill afford to offend the voters who had put his backers in office.[5]

The outcome of the chair riot rested, therefore, on both political and cultural definitions of the public. Those definitions, however, were subject not only to contest but also to change over time. Between 1850 and 1910, New Yorkers continually negotiated Central Park's political management as public property and its cultural value and use as a public space. The interplay of these two dimensions of the public shaped the park's creation, design, use, and subsequent modi-fication. Conflicts over the meaning of "the public" were thus part and parcel of struggles over Central Park in its first sixty years of existence.

The movement to create a large public park had emerged in the early 1850s when New York City's economy was booming. In explaining why the city needed a park, a coalition of newspaper editors, politicians, leading merchants, landowners, and philanthropic "gentlemen" had stressed the symbolic value of a grand landscaped park in enhancing the city's image as a world-class metropolis. Comparing New York to European capitals—which themselves were undertaking extensive public works programs in the mid-nineteenth century—editors claimed that such an amenity would attract visitors, customers, and wealthy residents to the city and simultaneously stimulate its economy and elevate local tastes and manners. Arguments on behalf of the park also revealed class cultural divisions. Wealthy New Yorkers insisted that the city needed a park because they needed a safe and scenic place to drive their carriages, while middle-class reformers contended that a park would improve public health and morals by providing laboring families with fresh air, exercise, and an alternative to the saloon. Workers in the Industrial Congress, housing reformers, and the German press were less enthusiastic about the proposal to establish a large public park. The *Staats-Zeitung*, for example, urged "many smaller parks in different parts of the city," which would be "equally useful and accessible to all citizens," instead of a "mammoth park" that would only be used by "the heirs of the upper Tendom."[6]

Although debates about whether New York should build a large scenic park revolved around competing conceptions of the "public" good, it was private real estate interests that secured passage of the actual park legislation. East Side and West Side landowners battled each other (as well as downtown taxpayers) over the park's cost and site. Central Park, located between Fifth and Eighth avenues from 59th to 106th streets, won out over an already-landscaped, private estate on the Upper East Side called Jones Wood due to the former's natural and social features. This rocky and swampy "waste" land three miles from the center of settlement would be expensive to grade for streets or construction.[7] Furthermore, the current occupants of the land—poor black, Irish, and German families—were perceived as "public nuisances," whose shanties, piggeries, and subsistence gardens interfered with the surrounding neighborhood's development as an elite residential enclave. Rejected as the site of a public park, the private Jones Wood estate acquired new life as popular commercial pleasure ground.

Once land for Central Park was taken through the state power of eminent domain in 1856, the political question shifted to who should administer it. For decades, the New York State legislature had routinely authorized municipal appropriations of money to manage public works, which the local party in power often used for patronage.

But in the mid-1850s, antislavery sentiment and nativism recast party alignments in New York. Republicans, drawing heavily on a rural constituency, organized an antislavery party. Within the city, Republicans also opposed themselves to Irish and German immigrant voters, who had made New York City a Democratic Party stronghold. When Republicans gained control of the state legislature in 1857, they immediately wrested control of Central Park from the Democratic mayor in order to establish their own channel of party patronage in the city. Thus, in the name of "reform," the legislature removed the park from city politics by replacing the Democratic mayor's park commission with one appointed by state lawmakers.

Republican merchants, bankers, and lawyers dominated the new eleven-man Board of Commissioners of the Central Park. In addition to their personal wealth, the commissioners' Protestant and predominantly rural roots reinforced their credentials as gentlemen of taste and refinement under whose stewardship the park might fulfill its "destiny" as the ornament of a great metropolis. Stewardship, of course, was a classical Republican concept: those who obtained wealth could return it to the community through public service. Yet the move of state politicians to appoint ostensibly bipartisan administrative commissions to oversee city affairs also coincided with a shift in the social composition of New York City's elected political leaders. In the 1840s and 1850s, wealthy men retreated from local elective office and campaign frays, but in the 1860s they regained control of critical city institutions (including the police, fire, and public health departments) through state administrative bodies insulated from Democratic control.[8] Because the Democratic Party's command of city government depended on the immigrant working-class vote, the struggle for party power intersected with issues of class power.

After nearly a decade of political debate over the value of creating a public park and how it should be administered, the new commissioners' first exercise of power came from their authority to determine what after all a park was—what it should contain, what it should look like, and how it should be arranged for public use. In 1857, there were no obvious answers to these questions.

As they lobbied for a new park, most newspapers invoked European models. Like Hyde Park in London or the Bois de Boulogne in Paris, the *Herald* insisted, the Central Park should offer a grand concourse for a "varied, animated and attractive promenade . . . crowded with the beauty and fashion of our city." To the *Tribune*, the republican application of European models would instruct and rationally amuse citizens, for instead of resorting to saloons, "the workingman and his working wife and working children" would find relief and be "softened by the beauty of the scene; civilized by the good manner which would spontaneously be the rule, and be enforced when wanting." Other advocates imagined a park to be the public equivalent to private Hudson Valley estates with artistically landscaped grounds and picturesque rural scenery. The *Irish News*, looking to a model yet closer to home, suggested that there should be two parts to a public park: a landscaped "pleasance" with drives and walks, and a "commons" or "public diversion ground"—open terrain (like that of nearby Elysian Fields pleasure ground in Hoboken, New Jersey) that could flexibly accommodate picnics, sports, games, ice-skating, and militia drills. "New York wants a place to play leap-frog in," the *News* urged, "not a mere ornamented place to pass through."[9]

The process of selecting a plan for the park's design, however, focused attention on the question of what the park would look like as much as how it would be used. Choosing a plan from thirty-two widely varying conceptions submitted in a design competition, the commissioners defined Central Park as a beautiful "rural" landscape set apart from the city. They selected the "Greensward" plan by the English-born architect Calvert Vaux and Park Superintendent Frederick Law Olmsted on political as well as aesthetic grounds. Olmsted was a Republican who could be trusted to keep the park's management out of the hands of popularly elected Democrats, and Vaux's prior association with the country's leading Romantic landscape gardener, Andrew Jackson Downing, certified the design's good taste.[10] The Greensward plan, working within the English tradition of landscape design, stressed the visual arrangement of the park's natural features—meadows, lakes, rocky outcroppings, and intricately planted hillsides—to create pastoral and picturesque scenic effects.

The park's unified "aesthetic conception," in turn, implied a particular motive for going to the park and a particular style of recreation. At the heart of the Greensward plan lay the designers' claim that "the popular idea of the park is a beautiful open green space, in which quiet drives, rides and strolls may be had." To establish a "natural" landscape in the midst of an "artificial" cityscape, Vaux and Olmsted sought to insulate the park from both the sights and activities of everyday city life.[11] Indeed, it was only through this clear separation of park and city that the designers and commissioners could establish full control over both the public landscape and the public behavior of those who visited it.

This vision of the city's park explicitly rejected the variety, flexibility, and unpredictability of the eclectic pleasure ground model advocated by the *Irish News* as well as proposals for a more formally designed park with monuments, museums, expositions, and extensive promenades in the continental European tradition. The design-ers' goal was to create a new kind of public space purified of the streets' commercial excesses and social disorders. In a culture that had seen the state's active retreat from economic affairs, such an artistically designed public park offered not only a symbolic statement of the refined tastes of the city's leading citizens but also a controlled set-ting for rituals of social decorum that reinforced elite New Yorkers' claims to cultural as well as political authority.

When Central Park opened in 1859, newspapers celebrated its "democratic" character, stressing the mixed class composition of crowds. Journalists had a particular penchant for representing park-goers' social diversity through figures of duality, noting the presence of "hard-handed labor" and "soft-palmed wealth," the "millionaire" and the "humble shop girl."[12] Yet we should not mistake nineteenth century journalism for twentieth century sociology. The insistence of newspapers on broad public use reflected the civic boosterism that motivated the park movement as well as the democratic ideology that underlay the willingness of taxpayers to expend millions of dollars to create this public institution. But journalistic conventions also masked the more complex and changing social realities of who used the park and in what ways.

The new park *was* enormously popular, attracting two and one-half million visitors annually in the early 1860s and more than eight and one-half million people at the decade's end. Yet despite its popularity, the park was far from democratic in the early decades of its use. In the 1860s, for example, more than half the park's visitors arrived in carriages—costly vehicles that only the wealthiest 3 percent of the city's 800,000 residents could afford to own.[13]

Particularly in the spring and fall, afternoon drives through the park offered elite New Yorkers a new ritual for socializing. On the surface, the parade of carriages winding through the park to admire pastoral scenery neatly conformed to the narrowed definition of the park as a public space that testified to the moral refinement and elevated tastes of the city's leading citizens. Yet the carriage parade also offered a more direct and less morally edifying statement of the accomplish-ment of the city's elite—their capacity to make and spend money. Newspapers devoted columns of print to covering the "fashionable" carriage scene, which became more lavish as railroads, finance, and Civil War profiteering expanded the ranks and the bank accounts of New York's merchant class. For wealthy women deeply invested in managing the local marriage market, Central Park became a new arena in which to arbitrate who was in and who was out of "Society." If participation was structured by access to carriages (the production of which became a major New York trade in this period) as well as by park rules that restricted commercial vehicles from the drives, elite parkgoers themselves introduced informal codes that determined the appropriate season, hours for a drive, and proper dress and decorum.

Declaring Central Park the "great rendezvous of the polite world," the *Herald* readily recognized the intimate connection among wealth, carriage ownership, and the social symbolism of the park itself. In effect, driving through the park had become part of the cultural definition of membership in the city's upper classes, which claimed to be the "best" public. In a rapidly growing city with an elite increasingly divided by the sources of wealth, religion, politics, and ethnicity, the park became a central institution for affirming shared class values, which to wealthy New Yorkers represented the aspirations of all the city's residents.[14]

Even as commentators sought to decode the "circles within circles" of the carriage parade, the park's accessibility to the rich promoted money as the criterion of cultural power and subverted the authority of earlier elite values of ancestry, taste, the work ethic, and rational leisure. Though newspapers proposed that the "hard working mechanic sees the handsome carriage and envies him who has such abundant wealth," at least some middling and working-class New Yorkers expressed ambivalence or even contempt for the park's display of conspicuous consumption. German immigrant children were reported to have thrown rocks at passing carriages, and one reporter warned that "humble" pedestrians should avoid the park altogether for fear of receiving the "cold shoulder" or even being run over.[15] But in the late nineteenth century, rich New Yorkers went to the park to see and be seen by other rich New Yorkers. In doing so they engaged in an internal class dialogue that affirmed money as a standard of value and display of wealth as a claim on public esteem. Wealth was, of course, an inherently unstable standard and new money continually undermined old. Rich New Yorkers circling the park simultaneously marked out the outer boundaries of their class and jockeyed for the best position on the inside.

Despite its close association with the city's "Society," the park was not an exclusive preserve of the elite. Middle-class and skilled working-class New Yorkers, who constituted from one-fourth to one-third of the city's population, were among the three million annual pedestrian visitors to the park in its first decade. Making their way to the park by foot or horse railway, crowds of 50–100,000 gathered at the Mall for Saturday afternoon band concerts or at the Lake for ice skating. Pedestrian visitors promenaded down the Mall, boated across the lakes, and strolled through the Ramble. The band concert pro-

115

grams reflected the park commissioners' own expectations for these crowds. Carefully mixing light classical pieces by Mendelssohn and Verdi with a "Teutonic" polka and sentimental songs, the concerts were, the commissioners noted, "so constructed as to give each class a fair share of its favorite music without admitting anything not in keeping with the standard of all the surroundings of the park. The aim is, on the whole, to be a little in advance of the average taste." Crowds of clerks, young professionals, skilled tradesmen, and especially their daughters and wives were, one newspaper reported, "orderly, well conducted and respectable in the full sense of the word."[16]

This middling constituency generally embraced the definition of the park as a controlled public space which, unlike the streets, required parlor manners. Still, the open air permitted some departures from those manners. In the winter, for example, both male and female ice skaters could loosen the constraints of "proper" decorum and indulge in boisterous play that was sanctioned by its value as healthy exercise and good clean fun. As ready as wealthy New Yorkers to display what means they had, New York's largely native-born (and often nativist) middle-class public was perhaps most constrained in their style of park use by their own investment in the genteel codes of respectability.

By the end of the park's first decade, observers declared the park's triumph as a democratic public space. Yet this success as a new kind of public institution rested largely on its selectivity. If rich and middle-class New Yorkers found that Central Park accommodated their own manners of sociability and recreation, the city's working people, the families of mechanics and laborers (the least affluent three-quarters of the city's population), discovered little to welcome them. Constrained by time and money from using the park except on Sundays, the city's working class also rejected the park for cultural reasons. In their limited free time, Irish and German immigrant families preferred the resources of the Jones Wood and other pleasure gardens where they could picnic in family groups, dance to lively band music, watch gymnastic exhibitions, play at sports, and drink beer. Through the second half of the nineteenth century, Jones Wood's music festivals, balloon ascensions, sports matches, and carnival atmosphere of sword swallowers, merry-go-rounds, and shooting galleries attracted immigrant choral, sports, temperance, literary, and church groups, as well as young couples out for a good time.[17]

German and Irish immigrants often organized summer excursions and outdoor festivals to raise money for their own churches and benevolent associations. Some working-class New Yorkers' preference for the Jones Wood pleasure garden or for neighborhood saloons as leisure centers may have rested on the desire to maintain their distance from Anglo-American codes of personal restraint in socializing. Furthermore, many young immigrant men enjoyed boisterous recreational pursuits that the native-born Protestant elite and middling classes disapproved—Sunday sports, heavy drinking, gambling, and prize-fighting.[18] Such differences help explain the informal cultural constraints which, alongside of the structural determinants of time and money, restricted access to Central Park and defined it narrowly as a public institution molded in the cultural image of the city's most powerful class.

In addition to structural constraints and informal cultural codes, park administrators devised policies and formal rules that reinforced Central Park's early exclusivity. The park's superintendent (and co-designer), Frederick Law Olmsted, saw the regulation of proper park use as his most important responsibility. Committed to a unitary conception of a public park as rural scenery, Olmsted told the commissioners in 1857: "A large part of the people of New York are ignorant of a park, properly so-called. They will need to be trained in the proper use of it, to be restrained in the abuse of it."[19]

Toward the end of training the "public" in the gentlemanly tastes and manners of his own class, Olmsted relied on a rigid set of rules and a special park police force. Rules prohibited, for example, fast driving and walking or sitting on the grass as well as concerts, boating, and drinking beer on Sunday. By excluding a particular class of activity, some park regulations implicitly excluded a particular class of people. By prohibiting gambling, gaming, fortune telling, hawking, peddling, or any unlicensed commercial activity, the park board sought to insulate the park from the city's lively street culture. By banning group picnics and excursions, the commissioners excluded the outings of churches and such ethnic organizations as the German Turn-verein and the Irish Ancient Order of Hibernians that were such a prominent feature of Jones Wood and other commercial pleasure grounds. By forbidding commercial wagons, they prevented the families of butchers and bakers from joining those of bankers and brokers on the park's drives. And by limiting the park's playing fields to schoolboys (with notes from their principals), they kept out adult teams and their accompanying crowds of spectators and gamblers, as well as working-class youths—few of whom were in school in this period.[20]

To be sure, aspects of the city's popular and working-class cultures seeped through the gates as did working people themselves: the antics of working-class youths upset middle-class ice skaters; flask-carrying visitors defied the liquor bans; German families set out picnics on park lawns; elderly women sold tea and cakes without licenses. In addition, the commission was never able to enforce entirely its regime of order and decorum: park keepers occasionally had to arrest parkgoers for drunkenness; some visitors ignored the rules against walking on the grass; others flaunted the carriage drive speed limits, littered the lawns, or picked park flowers. Yet, to contemporaries, what seemed most striking about the park in the 1860s was how it *differed* from the rest of New York City, how it presented "the very antipode of the city," as the *Times* put it in 1865. In effect, Central Park's initial success as a public park in the 1860s rested on narrow political and cultural definitions of the public.[21]

The next four decades, however, saw an opening up of the political public that controlled the park and the cultural public that used it. The political shift was sharper and is easier to discern. In 1870, Democrats, who now controlled the state legislature, won a new charter for the City of New York, which took power over Central Park away from the (Republican-dominated) park commission and gave it to a new board appointed directly by the city's (Democratic) mayor. Although the new charter arrived under the aegis of political boss William Tweed, the change in park administration lasted well beyond his brief reign. Indeed, even in 1898, when the creation of Greater New York fundamentally reorganized city government, mayors continued to appoint the park board, although they named commissioners by borough.[22]

As a result of these changes in administration, the park commission after 1870 reflected city politics much more directly than during Central Park's first thirteen years. Between 1870 and 1914, active Democrats dominated the park board, holding about four-fifths of the board seats—hardly surprising given that party's general dominance within the city. The post-1870 park boards also included more Irish Americans, the city's largest ethnic group. Still, Democratic commissioners were far from a proletarian lot; only once (in 1905) did a representative of the labor movement win a seat on the park board. Commissioners were more likely to have made their fortunes in real estate, contracting, or business. Attacking the park board's identification with party politics and local economic interests, the *Tribune* urged a return to an earlier era and suggested in 1882 that "the Commissioners should be selected from the list of citizens of recognized public spirit," the sort of men who "take delight in tastefully planted country places of their own." Yet, despite the *Tribune*'s celebration of the disinterestedness of the elite, Central Park's management was now controlled by the party that had the support of the majority of the city's voters, even if that party only imperfectly and indirectly reflected the interests of those voters. And party politics made the commissioners more responsive to pressure from a broader political constituency.[23]

There was one additional way that the new park board more closely mirrored the city than had the old. Under the 1870 charter, the park commission gained control of the city's smaller downtown parks as well as Central Park. Even more dramatically, after 1898 Central Park became part of a five-borough (county) park system that included almost 7,000 acres of parkland. These new administrative arrangements literally "de-centered" Central Park as the city's most important cultural institution; it now had to compete for resources with these other public places. One increasingly prominent source of competition for public funds came from the movement to create children's playgrounds and small parks throughout the city—a movement that gained momentum following the labor movement's mobilization in the early 1880s, Henry George's 1886 campaign for mayor on the United Labor Party ticket, and the rise of progressive reform in the 1890s and early 1900s.[24]

Although more responsive than the first park commission to the political public of voters and taxpayers, Democratic party administration of the park was still a far cry from democratic control. Rather, commissioners weighed and brokered the interests and influence, not only of voters and taxpayers, but of real estate developers, landscape architects, public employees, civil service advocates, progressive reformers, and different groups of park users. New Yorkers' participation in the decision-making that governed park policies often depended on organizational abilities and access to newspapers that readily claimed to speak for "the public interest" while taking widely different positions on proposed changes in Central Park.

Moving from the political public to the cultural public of park users disturbs the precise chronology that generally marks political history. Nevertheless, broad structural changes in population, neighborhoods, transportation, leisure time, and disposable income gradually, but dramatically, expanded Central Park's constituency between 1870 and 1910. During these years, Manhattan's population more than doubled and the population of the wards immediately surrounding the park multiplied about seven times. Even those New Yorkers who did not live within walking distance to the park had increased access to it, as electrified streetcars, elevated railways, and finally subways shortened their "journey to leisure." At the same time, rising real wages, which went up by 50 percent between 1870 and 1900, and declining working hours, which averaged 50 hours per week by 1910, meant that the city's working people were more likely to have money and time to spend on recreational excursions. Still, even after fifty years of such incremental changes, Central Park's resources were not equally available to all New Yorkers. Asked by a reporter in 1902 why she had never visited Central Park in her thirty years in New York, an Irish immigrant maid, who lived downtown and supported a family of seven, explained: "I have never seen ten cents for carfare that wasn't needed some other way more—that's why."[25]

Thus, although more and more working-class New Yorkers were able to get to Central Park, access remained constrained by long work hours and limited purses. Except for those who lived in the immediate vicinity, Sunday was most New Yorkers' only day in the park. Indeed, by the late 1870s, journalists increasingly headlined articles on Sunday in the park, "The People's Day," "The People's Great Playground," and "The Poor's Holiday." "It is chiefly the poor," went a typical article from the spring of 1877, "who escaping from the cages in which they have been imprisoned for a week, most enjoy God's holiday on the broad walks and among the flower-fringed rambles of our beautiful Park."[26]

The ethnic and working-class character of Sundays in the park became increasingly noticeable (and irritating to some elite observers) as Italians and East European Jews joined Germans and Irish in the burgeoning neighborhoods around Central Park. "At the northern end of the Park an immense population has grown up, which is using the park more and more," Park Commissioner Charles Stover noted in 1910. "Yesterday," he commented after a weekend visit, "I was up at the north end, and visitors were simply swarming over [the] lawns. They had passed beyond those [meadows] which have always been in use and had spread on to others on which no man had ever trod unless to mow the grass or sow seed."[27]

The increased ethnic working-class presence in the park was not simply the result of shifts in such structural factors as wages, income, neighborhood location, and transportation. In the 1870s and 1880s, the park became more appealing to these New Yorkers, as some of the earliest rules and regulations were loosened and the range of activities that could be pursued increased. Altered rules and new activities attracted new users, and those new users in turn pressed for further changes. As the expanded political public represented on the park *board* and the expanded visiting public represented on the park *paths* together made new claims, Central Park became a more democratic public space.

One example of the mutually reinforcing process of opening up the park's political and cultural publics was the resolution of the long-standing controversy over Sunday concerts in the park. When the park had first opened in 1859, well-organized Sabbatarians had successfully lobbied the park commission to prevent boat rentals or concerts on Sundays. But twenty-five years later, the board overruled these religious groups. The decision reflected both the waning power of Sabbatarians in New York and the altered politics of the board and the city. On the park commission, the push for Sunday concerts came largely from a Democratic commissioner who was preparing to make a successful run for Congress. Supporting him was an Irish American commissioner, the contractor John D. Crimmins, who had close ties to the Democratic party and to the building trades. "As a contractor," he noted, "I employ large numbers of men. . . . These are some of the men who will be attracted Sundays," since they "have not time" to attend concerts on Saturday.[28]

With the Central Labor Union and Clothing Cutters' Union passing resolutions, local cigar factories circulating petitions, and Catholic priests preaching sermons for Sunday concerts, these more politically engaged commissioners weighed the consequences of their policies against the votes rather than the prestige of the people on the two sides of what the *Times* called "The Sunday Concert War." German Americans, a growing voting bloc that included Protestants, Catholics, and Jews, denounced Sabbatarians as "fanatics" and "hypocrites." When sixty thousand people showed up for the first concert on a Sunday afternoon in July, the park board was deeply impressed.[29]

The *Times* wrote approvingly of the commissioners' decision to permit Sunday concerts as showing a "proper appreciation of the needs of the general public." Yet what was really at stake was an expanded definition of the meaning of the "general public" as it applied to the park. The *Times* itself participated in that process of redefinition when it sent reporters to interview Catholic priests and labor leaders on the issue. Twenty-five years earlier, such voices had been ignored during the debates over the park's management. Back then, the *Times* had explicitly warned the commissioners not to listen to the counsel of unnamed and unquoted "vulgar agitators."[30]

The inauguration of the Sunday concerts not only reflected an expanded political public that exerted pressure on the commissioners, it also expanded the public that used the park. The first Sunday concert looked like "a great big labor-union picnic," the *Times* reported; such scenes offered, the *Staats-Zeitung* observed, a "completely different picture" than the "better society . . . in their velvet and silk that had dominated on Saturdays." After the first month of Sunday concerts, the *World* noted that "the crowds have learned more about the Park, and instead of remaining as heretofore close to the [bandstand] . . . they scattered all over the great pleasure ground, every seat from the ramble to the reservoir harboring at least one couple."[31]

121

As these new working-class visitors informally contested rules, they won other concessions from the park board. Walking on the grass, for example, had long been a source of contention between park administrators and users. As early as 1875, a newspaper editorial had complained that rules keeping visitors off the lawns "are now enforced so rigidly that sending children to the Park is rather a punishment for them than a treat." By the late 1890s, however, commissioners bowed to the force of popular refusal to obey the rules. In 1897, when the president of the park board "called in or overruled every 'Keep Off the Grass' sign in the city," one newspaper approvingly quoted a "philosophical park policeman" who commented: "This may offend artists and landscape architects but, after all, it is the way all parks should be used."[32]

Other rules remained in place but were less vigorously enforced, particularly after 1898 when the parks department lost its own police force. Although in the 1880s and 1890s the commission began to allow archery and tennis on the lawns, regulations continued to limit ball playing in the park to schoolboys. But not everyone followed the rules. In the mid-1870s Olmsted was greatly distressed to find between fifty and two hundred "rude fellows," who were "beyond the school age" playing ball in the park. And in 1895 the *Times* complained of young women whose "sport" involved tossing around "handkerchief balls" stuffed with grass "obtained by tearing it up by the roots from the lawns." Such breakdowns in park discipline also afflicted the heart of the elite park—the carriage parade. Formal rules continued to exclude business wagons throughout the late nineteenth century, but after 1879 newspaper accounts of Sundays in the park included descriptions of butchers' and bakers' wagons on the park drives.[33]

The weakening and uneven enforcement of rigid park rules permitted the appearance in the park of what Olmsted called "customs suitable to paved streets or commons" and undermined the sharp distinction between the park and the city that he and so many commentators had initially celebrated. For the city's elite the appearance of immigrant working-class families in Central Park was already subverting the park's cultural value as a setting for display; the further broadening of the park's public to include the nineteenth century equivalent of "street people"—tramps, beggars, and prostitutes—was even more unsettling. "Tramps and other unpleasant people," the *Tribune* commented with disdain in May 1877, have "quit their Winter quarters for the benches in the Park. These persons are often an annoyance and prevent much enjoyment in the secluded walks." Seventeen years later, during another major depression, the same newspaper complained that the "proletarian class or rough and dirty boys monopolized" park benches, displacing respectable New Yorkers from their rightful seats. Indeed, Oscar Spate defended his 1901 chair rental enterprise as offering an alternative for "decent people" faced with the "idler [who] monopolizes all the choice benches."[34]

At the same time that the park came to resemble the city in its mix of visitors, it also started to look more like the city in its mix of attractions, particularly as it became more of a place to pursue amusement and less a place to retreat from the city's entertainments and commercialism. The strongest indication of this shift can be seen in the rise of the zoo as the park's most popular attraction.

The Greensward plan did not provide space for a zoo. But other contest entrants favored the idea, and it lingered in the air. In early 1863, the park commission acknowledged "that such an establishment is demanded, both for popular amusement and instruction." Indeed, menageries had been a popular feature of the commercial culture of New York's Bowery since at least the 1830s. The nation's leading amusement impresario, P. T. Barnum, displayed animal collections at his American Museum and toured his "Great Asiatic Caravan, Museum, and Menagerie" in the early 1850s. The *Irish News*, one of the most enthusiastic promoters of a park zoo, summoned up this Barnumesque heritage when it proposed that a menagerie "would certainly be the most delightful and instructive addition to the Central Park." Such a zoo, it thought, should include "monkeys chattering in a row to please the nurses and children, and huge black bears performing gymnastic exercises on long poles to keep the cramp out of their legs."[35]

While park officials in the 1860s debated the desirability and location of a zoo, one actually started to emerge under their very noses. Almost from its opening, people had donated to the park a strange mixture of historical relics, "art" objects, and especially animals. Olmsted later recalled that most of the first animals received were "pets of children who had died" or left town. If true, New York children kept a rather weird assortment of pets in the 1860s. Among the animals presented to the park, for example, were a deer, an alligator, a peacock, a porcupine, a prairie wolf, a silver gray fox, and a boa constrictor.[36]

Already by the summer of 1863, the park commission had placed this growing and motley collection of animals in a wire-enclosed space near the Mall. As mounting donations built the collection in 1864 and 1865, it was transferred to temporary quarters at the Arsenal—an inherited building situated at the park's southeast edge. Despite continuing complaints about the need for "better lodgement," the "nucleus of a zoological collection," as the *Times* called it, exerted a "magnetic influence on visitors." In 1870 the new Democratic park board acknowledged the zoo's popularity by constructing five new buildings for it, despite Olmsted's bitter opposition.[37]

Even as successive park commissions wrestled with the thorny question of how to situate a permanent zoo within the pastoral landscape, visitors streamed in to visit the "temporary" zoo created by the Democratic board in 1870. According to the estimate of its director, William Conklin, the zoo attracted more than two and one-half million visitors in 1873, or about one-quarter of all those who came to the park. "No feature of the Park," he argued with justification, "has thus far proved so attractive to the multitudes of visitors, who daily throng its walks." By 1888 Conklin was claiming that "nine out of every ten persons who enter the Park by the lower entrances wend their way to the menagerie."[38]

Whatever the precise attendance figures, the zoo was particularly popular on Sunday and among the working classes.[39] Children made up the largest group among those admirers, and the growing popularity of the zoo coincided with the emergence of children (although generally accompanied by parents) as one of the most important constituencies for the park. Yet particularly on Sunday, the audience was defined by class as well as age, in part because working-class families dominated the park on that day and in part because this was one of the few *free* attractions to which such families could bring their children.

Even during the week, the zoo attracted immigrant New Yorkers. Lower East Side Jews who went to visit sick relatives or get treatment at Mount Sinai Hospital (located two blocks from the park at 67th Street) often stopped at the nearby zoo. Indeed, the *Jewish Daily Forward* joked that "the only thing that interested Jews in Central Park was the zoo. They were afraid to venture farther into the park lest they get lost." At the turn of the century the zoo director reported that "Italian laborers—as many as twenty together—not finding work in the early morning, come to the menagerie with their shovels under their arms and spend an hour or two looking at the animals." And as more and more Eastern and Southern European immigrants settled east of the park in the years after 1890, they became regular patrons of the zoo. A settlement house worker living in that neighborhood noted in 1909 that the local children talked incessantly about the zoo's animals: "They can tell you what each one of them likes and how he eats it." The zoo's distinctly "democratic air" disturbed wealthy residents of Fifth Avenue who repeatedly and unsuccessfully campaigned to move it to a different location.[40]

As the zoo's attendance grew, it became part of the city's popular culture and further subverted the elite conception of Central Park as an exclusive arena of decorum and order. Indeed, the line between the park's zoo and commercially organized entertainment centers blurred as both the people and the animals moved back and forth between them. P. T. Barnum and other circus operators, for example, loaned animals to the zoo during the winter and, in turn, used the zoo's collection as a resource for their own extravaganzas. The popular press, another feature of the city's commercial culture, also developed a reciprocal relationship with the zoo. Journalists' unusually detailed coverage of the zoo and its animals entertained readers and promoted the zoo, as readers turned out to look at the new kangaroos or see how much "Murphy, the Hippo" had grown.[41]

The zoo's appeal as a center of amusement grew in the mid-1880s. Overflow crowds packed the Monkey House to see the first chimpanzee ever exhibited in the United States. When "Mr. Crowley" took ill, the zoo had to issue regular bulletins about his condition, which were printed daily in the newspapers. Letters poured in offering sympathy and every sort of popular health remedy. Faith healers showed up to pray for him and prohibitionists protested against the use of ardent spirits as a medication. After he recovered, a thirty-cent paperback book recounted the chimp's exploits. Controversy even flared over whether the name given to the chimp—"Mike Crowley"—was an insult to the Irish.[42]

Such a popular sensation could not escape the notice of Barnum, who wanted the chimp as a leading attraction of his "Greatest Show on Earth." When the park board rejected his initial bid of $5,000, he offered the largest elephant in his collection, which he valued at $10,000. "All these propositions being declined," Mr. Crowley's biographer reported, "the great showman departed, with some vexation on his usually cheerful features."[43]

For rather different reasons, such goings on also brought "some vexation" to Frederick Law Olmsted. That the park's zoo could have a bigger attraction than Barnum no doubt pleased those park officials who turned down the showman's offer, but for Olmsted such popular attractions had nothing to do with "the leading purpose for which the land of the Park as a whole was bought by the city." Asked by the park commission in 1890 to review the still disputed question of the best permanent location for the zoo, Olmsted readily conceded that there was no "portion of the Park that is more crowded, or in which the people, and especially the children find more amusement." But, he argued, "the leading purpose of the Park is not the amusement of the People," particularly the sort of amusement provided by a Punch and Judy performance, a "negro minstrel show," a theater, or a menagerie. Quite the contrary, the "proper and only justifying purpose of so large a park" was to provide "great numbers of people living in a compactly built town . . . with an opportunity to get quickly out of the scenery of buildings, streets and yards into scenery to be formed with a view of supplying a refreshing contrast with it."[44]

Sadly for Olmsted, most New Yorkers did not share his vision of the park as a tranquil retreat from the city. Between 1870 and 1910 they expressed their preferences, through political pressure and patterns of use, for a park that was more amenable to the excitement of the city's commercial culture. The scenic vistas did not disappear, but they sometimes took a back seat to the more novel and gregarious pleasures of city life.

From the opening of the park, the commission had received—and generally rejected—numerous petitions from entrepreneurs who wished to introduce commercial attractions into the park, from weighing machines to a miniature railroad. Between 1870 and 1910, with the waning influence of the park's old cultural guard, the barriers to such amusements were lowered slightly. Some of the changes began even before the Democratic park board took power. At the end of the 1860s, the commission had sought to control and regulate what it regarded as legitimate accommodations for the parkgoing public by giving out licenses to operators of boats, two restaurants, a carriage service, a wheel chair rental business, a photo house, and a children's goat cart. Both before and after 1870, the park commission tended to be more indulgent of commercial "intrusions" in the park if children were to be the primary audience, and they licensed a carousel and donkey and pony rides.[45]

To some degree, the appearance of these commercial amusements in the park emphasized the class distinctions that existed within the cultural public by basing access on the ability to pay. The charges for "the go-carts, the ponies, the hobby horses, and the boats," a reporter noted in 1877, "are above a poor man's means. . . . Ten cents is asked a child for a ride . . . in a go-cart, while many of the fathers of the children . . . are glad during the week to get work at 12 cents an hour." Actually, poor children were more likely to be the purveyors of commercial goods and services than their consumers. Children were employed to operate the rides, and in the 1890s, immigrant youths (including future movie mogul William Fox and future senator Robert Wagner) regularly sold candy in the park despite the long-standing ban on peddling and hawking.[46]

Although the park's commercial amusements were not equally available to all its visitors, their presence expanded the range of people attracted to the park and introduced new patterns of segregated use. The exclusive restaurants—the Casino and Mount St. Vincent—provided a place for affluent New Yorkers to retreat to in a park that they no longer dominated. At the same time, the availability of lager beer for five cents at the Terrace brought in some visitors who might have instead spent their Sunday at a commercial beer garden. And while ten cents for a goat-cart ride probably stretched the pocketbook of unskilled laboring families, it was not out of the reach of skilled workers' families, particularly by the 1880s. Moreover, in 1877, the park's Tammany-allied president, William R. Martin, cut the fee on the carousel from ten to five cents. Even for laboring families, then, visiting the park with its free zoo and its modest rides was one of the cheapest ways to enter the world of commercial entertainment on a special occasion. "A trip to Central Park, with a ride in the goat wagon, was something that came to you on your birthday if you were lucky," Al Smith recalled of his childhood on the Lower East Side in the 1880s.[47]

The park concerts also partook of aspects of the city's commercial culture and helped transform the Mall into what one observer described as the "headquarters" of "cosmopolitanism." The 1884 Sunday concert crowd that vigorously cheered for *both* the Catholic "Ave Maria" and the Protestant "Nearer My God to Thee" revealed a degree of cultural interaction and mutual tolerance that would have been surprising in New York a decade earlier. The eighties, moreover, seem to have brought a "popularization" of the music along with a popularization of the concert crowds. One critic complained that whereas in the 1860s, programs had offered "the cream of musical composition," later programs were "saturated with the skimmed milk of frivolity, adapted only to the minimum capabilities of the audience." Yet growing numbers of immigrant concertgoers themselves helped "popularize" the classical works of European composers. And by the 1890s musical entrepreneurs from Tin Pan Alley were using park concerts as a venue for promoting their new tunes. "The man who went to hear 'A Trip to Coney Island' enjoyed the concert as much as the man who went to hear a work of Wagner or Verdi or Beethoven," one music lover recalled of eclectic park concerts at the turn of the century.[48]

As Central Park appealed to a broader cultural public, the overall direction of change could be glimpsed in park guidebooks, which increasingly emphasized the novel and entertaining features of the park rather than lyrically describing its scenic landscape. As the new guidebooks testified, the park was becoming a place to seek lively amusement rather than repose and escape. "The Sunday excursionist," a *Herald* reporter suggested in 1881, "is not in quest of quiet pleasures, as a rule: it is a sensation he or she is looking for. To gaze at the [Egyptian] obelisk was regarded as a far greater treat by the majority of the Park visitors than to watch the wondrous developments of nature as set forth in tree or shrub."[49]

Such analyses probably understated working-class visitors' appreciation of the park's natural charms, but they still testified to a changed park and a changed public of parkgoers. If nothing else, the sheer numbers of people on the paths made it an increasingly intense urban experience of social and visual interaction. "The Mall, Terrace, and all the favorite promenades were as crowded as Broadway on a gala day," the *Herald* noted in a typical Sunday report. "As one progressed to the southern centre of the garden," the same paper reported of another Sunday, "every seat, every rail, every wayside rock, every arbor, every nook was occupied, and the music of human voices and laughter drowned and silenced the precocious chirping and whistling of insects and birds. In these crowded centres the illusion of country was completely lost." Yet the throngs of immigrants themselves proved a compelling attraction to visitors like William Dean Howells. The "foreigners on the Mall," he wrote, "all unite to form a spectacle I never cease to marvel at, with a perpetual hunger of conjecture as to what they really think of one another."[50]

For Olmsted, contemplating people did not serve the same purpose as contemplating nature, and he bemoaned the loss of the "illusion of country" in Central Park. Denouncing party politicians for mismanaging the park and neglecting its landscape, he warned of an observable trend. "I tell you," he wrote to a friend, "that I think the park is going to the devil and have grave doubt whether the undertakings to provide a *rural* recreation ground upon such a site in the midst of a city like this was not a mistake, was not doomed to failure because of the general ignorance of the conditions of success and the impossibility of getting proper care taken of it."[51]

Despite Olmsted's jeremiads, the park's natural attractions did not disappear. Each spring, the grass turned green and the shrubs and trees bloomed. And throughout the year, thousands if not millions came to enjoy nature, to wander through the Ramble, to contemplate the vistas. In the 1870s and 1880s, classical school principal James Herbert Morse regularly walked in the park, writing poems in his head, and noting "signs . . . of the coming season of flowers." Morse was living out Olmsted's prescription of the park as an "agreeable contrast to the confinement, bustle, and monotonous street-division of the city." "After three weeks of hard work and dissipation, parties, theaters, dinners, and clubs," Morse wrote in his diary in March 1881, "I am in the park, alone, with a joyous spring sunshine pounding down upon the world."[52]

But Morse saw and experienced more than nature in his rambles through the park: panhandlers approached him for pennies; children ran across the lawns; men sat on the lawns smoking pipes and reading scandal sheets; an elderly woman in a "shabby grey shawl" and with "ill-shod feet" gathered dandelions to sell; his own children fed the animals at the zoo. The experience of the park had never been a unified one despite the designers' and the first park commission's best efforts. And as time went on, Central Park became more eclectic, just as the crowds of visitors become more diverse—and more democratic. Some people went there to commune with nature; others went to ride the carousel. On the carriage drives were some of the city's richest people, on the pedestrian walks were some of the poorest.

It was not an experience of democratic social mixing, however. New Yorkers choreographed who went where, who did what, and when they did it. The *bon ton* frequented the East Drive on a fall afternoon or sipped wine at the Mount St. Vincent restaurant after a winter sleigh ride through the park. But they shunned the lines of shouting children waiting to ride the carousel and the sweaty crowds squeezed together on the Mall for the free Sunday afternoon concert.

Central Park's transformation in the late nineteenth and early twentieth centuries resided not simply in the variety of the crowds and activities; it also came from the ability of people to interpret the same experiences of the park in *different* ways. One day in the 1890s, Annie Nathan Meyer, scion of a wealthy Sephardic Jewish family, rode through the park, looking at the Sheep Meadow and thinking about the "calming touch, the healing power that seems to reach out from these scenes." Then she turned to look at the other women in her carriage: "Have they seen the sheep, I wonder? One of the ladies opposite to me did bend forward, I remember, but merely to see a cape that was more elegant than hers flash by in a noiseless victoria."[53]

Vaux and Olmsted had envisioned a public park as a beautiful pastoral landscape that could be appreciated by men like James Herbert Morse and women like Annie Nathan Meyer, not as a common ground for the old woman collecting dandelions to sell or as a fashionable parade for the young woman surveying the latest fashions. But the vision of the park as a unified work of landscape art, defined in opposition to the city, could not be sustained. Like the city, the park had become multivocal, incorporating people of different backgrounds and experiences who used this public space in different ways. In claiming access to the park, in pressing for new policies in its governance, and in themselves contributing to the park's attractions, working-class New Yorkers had transformed the genteel and, in practice, exclusive Central Park of the 1860s into a more open public space, one that accommodated a wider range of tastes, manners, amusements, and needs.

It was to preserve this openness, to defend their common rights to enjoy parks equally with all other members of the public, however heterogeneous and divided that public might be, that protesters attacked a chair rental policy that implied that the city's parks had become too open and too popular. The triumph of Vaux and Olmsted had been to turn a swampy and rocky "wasteland" into a beautifully designed natural landscape in the largest city in the nation. The triumph of the New Yorkers who visited Central Park was not only to turn it into a more democratic public space but also to contest and negotiate the meaning of that ambiguous term.

This chapter draws on the research for our recently published book, *The Park and the People: A History of Central Park* (Ithaca, 1992), in which further documentation can be found.

Notes

1. *New York Times* (June 23, 24, 25, 1901); *New York Tribune* (June 25, 26, 1901); *New York Journal and Advertiser* (July 2, 3 (quot.), 4–10, 1901); *Sun* (July 8, 1901). The *Journal*, owned by William Randolph Hearst, made the chair controversy into its particular crusade. See also *Tribune* (July 2, 3, 7–11, 1901), for incidents in Central Park and Madison Square Park, and *Tribune* (July 11–14, 1901), on legal efforts to overturn the chair rental policy.
2. *Times* (July 10, 1901). For additional coverage, see *Times* (July 2–14, 1901); *Journal* (July 2–16, 19, 20, 24, 30, 1901).
3. For definitions of public, private, and common property rights, see C. B. Macpherson, *Property: Mainstream and Critical Positions* (Toronto, 1973), 4–6. For the legal status and exclusive property rights of the municipal corporation and its relation to state sovereignty, see Hendrik Hartog, *Public Property and Private Power: The Corporation of the City of New York in American Law, 1730–1870* (Chapel Hill, 1983).
4. *Journal* (July 2, 1901).
5. *Times* (July 5, 1901). One newspaper claimed that it was a cable from the vacationing Democratic political boss Richard Croker that finally ended the "undemocratic" chair rental scheme. *Journal* (July 10, 1901).
6. *Staats-Zeitung* (July 15, 1853; Apr. 21, 1854). See also *Staats-Zeitung* (Aug. 1, 1851; Apr. 1, 1853; Apr. 1, 1854).
7. The northern boundary was extended to 110th Street in 1863.
8. On the retreat of New York patricians from office holding, see Amy

Bridges, *A City in the Republic: Antebellum New York and the Origins of the Machine Politics* (Ithaca, 1984), 72–74, 127–128; on appointment of the Metropolitan Police Commission, see Edward Spann, *The New Metropolis: New York City, 1840–1857* (New York, 1981), 386–388; on the state-appointed fire and health commissions, see James C. Mohr, *The Radical Republicans and Reform in New York During Reconstruction* (Ithaca, 1973), 19–60, 86–114.

9. *Herald* (June 15, 1856); *Tribune* (June 28, 1853); *Irish News* (Jan. 29, 1859).

10. Descriptions of the entries to the design competition are found in Board of Commissioners of the Central Park [hereafter BCCP], *Catalogue of Plans for the Improvement of Central Park* (New York, 1858), copy available at New York Public Library. On the politics of the selection of the park plan, see Charles E. Beveridge and David Schuyler, eds., *Creating Central Park, 1857–1861* (Baltimore, 1983), 26–27; BCCP, *Minutes*, Apr. 28, 1858.

11. "Description of a Plan for the Improvement of Central Park: Greensward" in Beveridge and Schuyler, eds., *Creating Central Park*, 118–177; for elaboration of the designers' intentions, see Vaux's court testimony, "Defense of Central Park Plan," Mar. 1864 in Frederick Law Olmsted Papers, Box 38, File 32, Library of Congress; for perspectives on nineteenth century landscape ideas, see Thomas Bender, *Toward an Urban Vision: Ideas and Institutions in Nineteenth Century America* (Lexington, 1975); David Schuyler, *The New Urban Landscape* (Baltimore, 1986); Galen Cranz, *The Politics of Park Design: A History of Urban Parks* (Cambridge, 1982).

12. *Tribune* (Sept. 3, 1860); *Times* (Aug. 13, 1865). See similarly, *Times* (Dec. 27, 1859); *Herald* (June 9, 1867).

13. Ezra M. Stratton, *The World on Wheels* (New York, 1878), 458. Attendance figures can be found in the BCCP Annual Reports, 1861–1873.

14. *Herald* (May 5, 1860). Guidebooks and newspapers that covered the carriage scene extended the reach of this "public space" and the visibility of new levels of prosperity. Here, we encounter a third meaning of public—its sense of openness to view—embodied in the term "publicity." Newspapers were crucial in creating and disseminating this "public" park.

15. *Times* (Mar. 13, 1870); *Leader* (June 30, 1860).

16. BCCP, *Ninth Annual Report, for Year Ending December 31, 1865* (New York, 1866), 33 [hereafter the park reports are cited by year]; *Times* (July 31, 1859).

17. For descriptions of festivals and amusements at Jones Wood, see, for example, *Times* (June 24, 1859); *Tribune* (July 6, 16, 1859, July 4, 1866); *World* (May 26, 1863); *Herald* (July 6, 1866).

18. On styles of working-class recreation, see, for example, Elliot J. Gorn, *The Manly Art: Bare-Knuckle Prize Fighting in America* (Ithaca, 1986); Roy Rosenzweig, *Eight Hours for What We Will: Workers and Leisure in an Industrial City* (New York, 1983).

19. Frederick Law Olmsted, Jr., and Theodora Kimball, eds., *Forty Years of Landscape Architecture: Frederick Law Olmsted, Sr.* Reprint, 1973; New York, 1928, 58–59.

20. BCCP, *Minutes*, July 31, Sept. 23, Dec. 29, 1859; "Regulations of the

Use of the Central Park," Nov. 3, 1860, in Beveridge and Schuyler, *Creating Central Park*, 279.

21. *Times* (Aug. 13, 1865); see also *Herald* (July 31, 1859).

22. On politics behind the 1870 charter, see Seymour J. Mandelbaum, *Boss Tweed's New York* (New York, 1965), 66–75; and for park boards after consolidation, Department of Parks, City of New York [hereafter Parks Department], *Annual Report* (1893), 3–4, (1903), 7–8. A single commissioner covered Manhattan and Staten Island; another represented Brooklyn and Queens. After 1911, Queens had its own commissioner.

23. *Tribune* (Mar. 19, 1982). The Democratic party in this period was highly factionalized, as was the park board. On New York political alignments, see David C. Hammack, *Power and Society: Greater New York at the Turn of the Century* (New York, 1982), 99–181 and *passim*; and Martin Shefter, "The Emergence of the Political Machine: An Alternative View," in *Theoretical Perspectives on Urban Politics*, Willis Hawley, ed. (Englewood Cliffs, N.J., 1976), 14–44; and "The Electoral Foundations of City Machines: New York City, 1884–1897," in *American Electoral History: Quantitative Studies in Popular Voting Behavior*, Joel Silbey et al., eds. (Princeton, N.J., 1978), 263–298.

24. For New York City park acreage, see Lee F. Hammer, *Public Recreation: A Study of Parks, Playgrounds, and Other Outdoor Recreation Facilities* (New York, 1928), 39. On the 1886 election, see David Scobey, "Boycotting the Politics Factory: Labor Radicalism and the New York City Mayoral Election of 1886," *Radical History Review* 28–30 (Sept. 1984): 280–325; on the small parks and playground movement, see Richard Knapp, "Parks and Politics: The Rise of Municipal Responsibility for Playgrounds in New York City, 1887–1905." M.A. Thesis, Duke University, 1968; Rosenzweig, *Eight Hours*, Chap. 5.

25. Rosenzweig, *Eight Hours*, 179–180; *New York World* (Aug. 18, 1902); see also *Times* (July 3, 1910). A social reform study of the "Middle West Side" (the West 40s and 50s) concluded in 1914 that Central Park was "too inaccessible" to be the "regular playground" for that district's working-class boys, who were "often needed at home after school hours to run errands and make [themselves] generally useful. Moreover to go any distance involves a question of food and transportation." *Boyhood and Lawlessness* (New York, 1914), 10–11.

26. *Herald* (May 14, 21, June 4, 18, 25, Aug. 20, 1877).

27. *Times* (July 4, 1910). On the development of these uptown neighborhoods, see Jeffrey S. Gurock, *When Harlem Was Jewish, 1870–1930* (New York, 1979). It seems likely that neighborhood residents treated parks differently from those who came from more distant locales. For them, Central Park was more like their "front yard."

28. *Times* (July 15, 1884).

29. *Staats-Zeitung* (July 3, 7, 1884); *Times* (July 15, 1884). On the campaign for concerts, see also *Times* (July 7, 8, 14–16, 21, 23, 25, 1884); *Herald* (July 7, 8, 14, 16, 17, 20–22, 1884).

30. *Times* (Sept. 3, 1859, July 4, 1884).

31. *Times* (July 7, 1884); *Staats-Zeitung* (July 7, 1884); *World* (Aug. 4, 1884).

32. *Times* (Nov. 15, 1875, July 11, 1897). The new park board that arrived with the consolidation of Greater New York decided to reimpose some of the "keep-off-the-grass" rules in 1898, but apparently had only mixed

success in enforcing the rule. At around the same time, the park board also became increasingly willing to offer permits for the use of the lawns for children's picnics. In 1898, for example, 2,500 permits allowed the lawns to be used by 250,000 people. Parks Department, *Annual Report* (1898), 11, 13, (1901), 16; *Times* (July 8, 1901). By the early twentieth century, Tammany politicians were organizing large-scale children's picnics in the park. See, for example, *World* (June 1, 1902); *American* (June 18, 1905).

33. Frederick Law Olmsted to Henry G. Stebbins, May 18, 1875, Box 14, Folder 739, Olmsted Papers, Library of Congress, Washington, DC; *Times* (May 27, 1895); on wagons, see, e.g., *Times* (Aug. 7, 1871); *Herald* (July 23, 1877); *Tribune* (May 6, 1894). The parks department regained partial control of the park police in 1908; *Times* (Feb. 18, 1908); Parks Department, *Annual Report* (1908), 113.

34. *Tribune* (May 12, 1877, June 30, 1893); *Journal* (July 6, 11, 1901). See also *Appleton's Journal* (Sept. 11, 1875); *Times* (May 14, 1873, May 24, Nov. 7, 1875, July 2, 1888, May 14, 1894); *Tribune* (May 24, 1873, Sept. 7, 1884, Mar. 20, 1882).

35. BCCP, *Sixth Annual Report* (1862), 15; Peter G. Buckley, "To the Opera House: Culture and Society in New York City, 1820–1860." Ph.D. Diss., State University of New York at Stony Brook, 1984, 31; Neil Harris, *Humbug: The Art of P. T. Barnum* (Chicago, 1973), 146, 166; *Irish News* (Feb. 11, 1860). See also Helen Horowitz, "The National Zoological Park: 'City of Refuge' or Zoo?" *Records of the Columbia Historical Society* (1973), 405–429.

36. Olmsted, Jr., and Kimball, ed., *Forty Years of Landscape Architecture*, 512; BCCP, *Ninth Annual Report* (1865), 72–80.

37. *Times* (July 25, 1863); Board of Commissioners of the Department of Public Parks [hereafter, BDPP], *Annual Report* (1871), 20–21.

38. BDPP, *Annual Report* (1873), 196; *Times* (July 4, 1888). On the further expansion of the zoo in the 1890s, see *Times* (May 19, 1901).

39. See, for example, *Herald* (June 7, 1875); *Times* (May 20, 1878); *Tribune* (Mar. 20, 1882); Parks Department, *Annual Report* (1903), 52.

40. *Forward* quoted in Irving Howe, *World of Our Fathers* (New York, 1976), 131; John W. Smith, "Central Park Animals as Their Keepers Know Them," *Outing* (May 1903): 248; *Times* (March 19, 1909); on Fifth Avenue residents, see, e.g., *Times* (Dec. 24, 1885, Mar. 18, 1887, Apr. 11, 1890, May 4, 1890).

41. On the exchange of animals, see, e.g., BDPP, *Annual Report* (1872), 165, 200; *Herald* (June 25, 1877); *Tribune* (May 9, 1890); BDPP, *Minutes*, July 3, 1874, Apr. 5, 1875; on newspaper coverage, *Star* (Oct. 19, Nov. 6, 27, 1886). On November 9, 1874, the *Herald* devoted its entire front page to a story describing in grizzly detail the escape of the zoo's animals. The hoax threw many New Yorkers into a panic and showed not only the close relationship between the popular press and the zoo but also how centrally the zoo had come to figure in the imagination of the general public; Steven D. Lyons, "James Gordon Bennett, Jr." in Peter J. Ashley, ed., *American Newspaper Journalists, 1873–1900* (Detroit, 1983), 12; *Sun* (Nov. 12, 1874).

42. Henry S. Fuller, *Mr. Crowley of Central Park: A Historie* (New York, 1888), 89 (controversy over name), 148–149; *Herald* (June 8, 1885). In

the 1890s Irish Americans again complained that the zoo's animals were habitually called "Patsy, Mike, Biddy, or Teddy, or by some other name unmistakably Irish"—a practice that disturbed Irish-American children who regularly visited the zoo with their families on Sundays; *Times* (Apr. 11, 1893).

43. Fuller, *Mr. Crowley*, 111–112. Significantly, elite organizers of the New York Zoological Park (Bronx Zoo), which opened in 1899, acted to keep it out of the hands of the "public." Although the zoo was built on city land with city funds, a private board controlled the zoo's management; Helen L. Horowitz, "Animal and Man in the New York Zoological Park," *New York History* 46 (Oct. 1975): 427–455.

44. Olmsted, Jr., and Kimball, *Forty Years of Landscape Architecture*, 511–517.

45. See, e.g., BCCP, *Thirteenth Annual Report* (1869), 47–48; BDPP, *Minutes*, June 17, 1874; and *City Record*, Aug. 12, 1875.

46. *Times* (June 4, 1877); *Herald* (May 6, 1895); Neal Gabler, *An Empire of Their Own: How the Jews Invented Hollywood* (New York, 1988), 65; Joseph Huthmacher, *Senator Robert F. Wagner and the Rise of Urban Liberalism* (New York, 1968), 13.

47. *Herald* (May 28, 1877); Alfred E. Smith, *Up to Now: An Autobiography* (New York, 1929), 18.

48. J. Crawford Hamilton, "Snap Shots in Central Park," *Munsey's Magazine* (Sept. 1895): 576–577; *Herald* (July 7, 1884); *Times* (Aug. 22, 1883) (July 28, 1900). On the Tin Pan Alley promoters and debates over popular music at park concerts, see Ben Mutschler, "Let the Twelve Apostles of the Chromatic Scale Preach to the People in the Park: Public Concerts in Central Park, 1859–1910." M.A. Thesis, Columbia University, 1992.

49. *Complete Guide to Central Park with Map* (New York, 1877); cf. Clarence Cook, *A Description of the New York Central Park* (New York, 1869); *Herald* (May 13, 1881).

50. *Herald* (June 26, 1871, Aug. 20, 1877); William Dean Howells, "Glimpses of New York," in *Impressions and Experiences* (1896; Reprint, Freeport, N.Y., 1972), 131–132. Daniel Bluestone discusses the "gregarious" and urbane character of parks in "From Promenade to Park: The Gregarious Origins of Brooklyn's Park Movement," *American Quarterly* 39 (Winter 1987): 529–550.

51. Quoted in Laura Wood Roper, *FLO: A Biography of Frederick Law Olmsted* (Baltimore, 1973), 351.

52. James Herbert Morse, Diary, June 28, 1875, Mar. 2, 8, 1881, New-York Historical Society; Beveridge and Schuyler, *Creating Central Park*, 212–213.

53. Annie Nathan Meyer, *My Park Book* (New York, 1898), 32.

Part III

NEIGHBORHOODS: CLASS AND ETHNICITY

*A*LTHOUGH the image of the metropolis as a city of strangers in public captures a fundamental truth, it is incomplete. Public life in the metropolis is a world of difference, but much of it is lived in smaller, more homogeneous contexts. The peoples who represent difference in public come from those smaller units of the city that are typically defined by ethnocultural and class values. István Teplán describes such a community of ethnic Hungarians, most of whom were former officials in parts of Hungary severed from the nation by the Trianon Treaty. They constructed and settled in the quite homogeneous St. Imre Garden City. Deborah Dash Moore extends the terrain of analysis, providing a map of the remarkable variety of ethnic neighborhoods in New York. She emphasizes the neighborhoods in which the foreign-born and their children lived. But others, too, lived in homogeneous neighborhoods. There were insulated upper-class districts, but a place like Sunnyside Gardens in Queens, a planned community built about the same time as St. Imre, might reasonably be compared with the Hungarian garden city. Sunnyside was not populated by repatriated officials, but it was very much a favored place of residence for New Yorkers of roughly the same economic level and occupational type: native-stock writers, teachers, service professionals, and government employees.

Middle-class New Yorkers—ranging from the residents of Sunnyside to those of commercial and cooperative apartment complexes built in the 1920s by developers, to the trade-union-sponsored and state-assisted Amalgamated Houses (1927) in the Bronx and the Amalgamated Dwellings (1930) in Manhattan—were more clearly committed than their Hungarian social counterparts to modern architectural style and amenities in their domestic environments, though Tudor Revivals were popular, too, in New York during the 1920s. A portion of Budapest's middle classes embraced Bauhaus modernism in the 1920s, but that was a rather specific and limited group. A more loosely defined commitment to modernity appealed to a broader spectrum of New Yorkers.

The traditionalism of the St. Imre development gives concrete expression to the demographic distinction of Budapest: its inmigrants, including 300,000 ethnic Hungarians repatriated after Trianon, made the city more, not less, Hungarian. Like the St. Imre group, many of these inmigrants were skeptical of metropolitan modernity. Having lost homes and jobs and more in those regions of larger Hungary that became new, successor states after the war, these middle-class inmigrants were drawn to Budapest by their commitment to their Hungarian identity. They clung tightly to that identity, and expressed it in traditional stylistic symbols, as Teplán shows. But this commitment to a traditional Hungarian identity also found political expression. The postwar migration to the metropolis nourished a traditional, militant nationalism, which helped to sustain an ethnocentric political antimodernism in the interwar years.

Whatever the character of the particular units of residential and social life, in each city various particularistic groups—whether native or immigrant—had to participate in the more general society. They were brought into contact with others through common institutions (schools), public places, and popular culture. This complex pattern of interaction apparently pulled people in opposite directions, at once heightening particularistic identities and promoting familiarity with others. Such an experience *could* encourage enough tolerance to enhance the possibility of metropolitan comity, and this happened in New York. But it did not occur nearly so much in Budapest.

Ethnic identity is a historical construction. It is not fixed—identity is partly a matter of descent, but it is also partly freely chosen, a matter of consent. Moore makes the important point that the identities of particular groups in New York City were constantly undergoing modification through various modes of mobility—geographical and social. If ethnic identity was inscribed in the map of the metropolis, it was also dynamic, constantly being reconstructed. Teplán tells us less about the persistence of the particular culture he describes. Yet it seems safe to propose that the identity of the group he studied was more stable, more fixed. Moreover, the common identity of New Yorkers was more limited than that of Budapesters. While immigrant

New Yorkers were often determined Americans, the meaning of "American" was filtered through the lens of particular ethnic aspirations. Nationalism may have inhibited such fragmentation of a common identity in Budapest, but perhaps at the cost of severe limits on the development of an autonomous metropolitan culture.

Chapter 5

Class and Ethnicity in the Creation of New York City Neighborhoods: 1900–1930

DEBORAH DASH MOORE

*F*OR A CENTURY New York City, the immigrant entrepôt of the United States, has fascinated journalists, social scientists, and historians writing on ethnicity.[1] They have discovered on the streets of Manhattan the materials with which to build their models of ethnic residential patterns, including the imagery and concept of the ghetto in America.[2] The physical proximity of the Lower East Side to the financial and commercial center of New York at the turn of the century, coupled with its aggressively foreign character, drew observers who interpreted its significance for other Americans. The attention directed at New York prior to 1900 increased in subsequent years. The city's continuing prominence as the home of the foreign-born and their children distinguished it from other large American cities, in which the major population trends after 1900 indicated an increase of native-born and a corresponding decline of foreign-born and their children. In New York, by contrast, from 1900 to 1930 the number of household heads who were native-born of native parents (at a minimum, third-generation Americans) scarcely increased. The slight change from 16 percent to 18 percent of all white heads of households reflected the impact of the mass immigration of Italians and Jews as well as a constant, albeit drastically curtailed, immigration in the 1920s. Despite greatly reduced numbers, a larger percentage of immigrants to the United States in the 1920s chose to settle in New York City. As a result, in 1930 as in 1900, over 80 percent of all white household heads in New York were immigrants and their children, the second generation.[3]

New York City differed from other large American cities because of the size of its varied immigrant groups. The sheer numbers of immigrants in each group provided a critical mass, which encouraged distinctive residential patterns and allowed for class variations to develop both within and without the constraints of ethnic group boundaries. In 1900, before the impact of the mass migration of Italians and Jews was felt, the city's two major ethnic groups were German and Irish, with populations of 785,000 and 710,000, respectively. In both cases, the majority were second-generation children of immigrants, or, in the language of the census, native-born of foreign or mixed parentage. The next two largest ethnic groups in 1900, Russians (largely Jews) and Italians, had 251,000 and 220,000, respectively, with immigrants outnumbering the second generation. In 1900 there were also substantial numbers of other ethnic groups, including 210,000 from Great Britain, 134,000 from Austria (mostly Jews from Galicia), 55,000 from Poland, 54,000 from Hungary, and 45,000 from Sweden.[4] Cutting across the varied national origins of these census figures is the fact that by 1900 over 500,000 Jews, from Eastern Europe and Germany, made their home in New York City.[5] By 1930 the two leading ethnic groups had exchanged places, with Jews and Italians accounting for approximately 42 percent of the New York City population and Germans and Irish following with 18 percent. Several other ethnic groups also appeared in significant numbers for the first time, including Romanians, Norwegians, and Czechoslovakians.

These figures demonstrate the ethnic complexity of New York City, the relative position of each major group, and the notable absence of any majority population. In fact, the largest single ethnic group in the city in 1930, the Jews, conservatively estimated at 1,830,000, or 26 percent of the population, contained significant internal divisions based upon class, time of arrival in America, and cultural traditions derived from country of origin.[6]

New Yorkers reckoned their ethnicity as part of the common coin of urban discourse and as a feature of the urban landscape. They understood the relativity of ethnicity: it depended upon the angle of vision. Immigrants served as reference groups for each other, helping to define what they shared as New Yorkers and where they differed. Thus, for the children of Jewish immigrants attending public schools in the first decades of the century, Irish school teachers represented the epitome of the genuine American.[7] By contrast, second- and third-generation New Yorkers recognized these same teachers as Irish, members of an ethnic world composed of second-generation Irish civil servants. When a later generation of Jewish children studied under Jewish public school teachers, the teachers' Jewish identity subtly modified the meaning attached to their symbolic American position.[8] Similarly, where each group chose to settle inevitably influenced its comparative perceptions. The enormous mobility of the New York population during the first three decades of the century constantly reshuffled the ethnic composition of the city's neighborhoods, requiring that residents continually renegotiate their ethnic identity.[9]

The diversity of immigrant behavior in the city spawned not only the theory of the immigrant ghetto as an agent of assimilation but subsequent interpretive revisions. Scholars have contrasted data from New York with that of other, more representative, cities in the debate over the importance of residential concentration for immigrant mobility and acculturation.[10] New York has been considered an exception to general trends throughout the United States because its immigrant slums housed members drawn almost exclusively from one ethnic group. Yet, viewing New York City from such a perspective does not do justice to the enormous influence its experience has exerted upon the meaning and content of ethnicity in America. In the popular imagination, New York City came to embody the ethnic and the foreign, providing a yardstick with which to measure either the authentic ethnicity or, alternatively, the genuine Americanness of other cities. Jewish expressions of ethnicity especially shaped the city's image of itself and the nation's perception of New York.

To understand the significance of residential patterns for the transformation of ethnicity from an immigrant to an American culture, we need to see New York first as the immigrant city it was in 1900. The visible concentration of immigrants south of 14th Street in lower Manhattan and the high population densities heralded its foreign character. In the 1890s approximately 75 percent of New York's Jews lived on the Lower East Side, and 52 percent of the city's Italians lived below 14th Street in the area that came to be known as Little Italy. Before the influx of new immigrants in the 1890s, the older German and Irish immigrants moved north. The Irish dispersed throughout the West Side and Harlem while the Germans established new concentrations in Yorkville on the Upper East Side and in Harlem. These alternative patterns of dispersal without concentration for the Irish and concentrated dispersal for the Germans reappear in the residential strategies of other ethnic groups. For example, 50 percent of the Hungarians and 65 percent of the Bohemians clustered on the Upper East Side near the German settlement.[11] Germans and Irish also followed the elevated transit lines beyond Harlem to the South Bronx. There they settled in new tenements and two-family dwellings, swelling earlier immigrant clusters. Unlike Harlem, the Bronx offered employment in metal and wood factories, food processing, and piano manufacture.[12] The visible concentrations of immigrant groups prompted Jacob Riis, an urban reformer and journalist, to write about the "other half" who lived in the tenements in 1890. His map of Manhattan, "colored to designate nationalities," was divided "into two great halves, green for the Irish prevailing in the West Side tenement districts, and blue for the Germans on the East Side. But intermingled with these ground colors would be an odd variety of tints that would give the whole the appearance of an extraordinary crazy-quilt."[13] Riis's rhetoric suggested how the external signs of immigrant culture on the city's streets dominated the outsider's impressions.

Insiders discovered a more complex reality. When the sympathetic journalist Hutchins Hapgood penned his remarkable portrait of the Jewish Lower East Side in 1902, he recognized the diversity of immigrant settlement patterns. Although Jews shared a common religious culture and language that drew them to settle initially on the Lower East Side, their different European backgrounds led them to cluster on certain streets. Moses Rischin, the leading historian of the Lower East Side, called the section "an immigrant Jewish cosmopolis" by the first decade of the twentieth century.[14] Five major groups of Jews lived in the area: Hungarians in the northern portion above Houston Street in the section that had previously been known as *Kleindeutschland*; Galicians south of Houston; Romanians in the western section east of the Bowery, south of Houston, and north of Grand Street; a small cluster of Levantine Jews near the Romanians; and the largest group of all, Russians from Grand Street south, including the main street of East Broadway. Most of the major immigrant institutions were located in the Russian area.[15] The large Italian immigrant district similarly contained subdivisions based upon the immigrants' Italian provenance. Sicilians, Calabrians, Genoese, and Neapolitans discovered their common Italian ethnicity on the streets of New York, in no small measure aided by other immigrants who failed to distinguish their separate traditions. But inside the immigrant neighborhood, the pull of village and family ties sorted Italians into different clusters.[16] When Italians and Jews moved away from these large, heterogeneous immigrant enclaves—a process they initiated as early as 1900—they began to erase the significance of internal ethnic divisions. In Harlem, where Jews and Italians lived near Irish and Germans, the differences between Russians and Galicians or between Sicilians and Neapolitans faded from the urban geography.[17]

The 1898 consolidation of New York and Brooklyn marked the end of Brooklyn's political distinctiveness as a separate city. Building the bridges linking Manhattan and Brooklyn—the Brooklyn Bridge (1883), followed by the Williamsburg Bridge (1903), and the Manhattan Bridge

(1909)—remade Brooklyn in the image of Manhattan by initiating a process of intracity migration. In 1900 there were only 344,000 immigrants in Brooklyn, approximately 30 percent of its population. Brooklyn was the home of native Americans, the "city of churches." Within ten years of the bridge construction, Brooklyn experienced a 61 percent increase in its foreign-born, changing its ethnic profile to correspond to that of New York.[18] By 1930 Brooklyn's population had more than doubled, and 50 percent of its adult residents were immigrants.[19] The influx of immigrants transformed Brooklyn's urban geography. From a ring of middle-class neighborhoods surrounding the urban core near the waterfront that housed the rich, the poor, and the working classes, Brooklyn developed a scattered pattern of ethnic neighborhoods segregated by class.[20] Although the older areas of Williamsburg, Greenpoint, and South Brooklyn resembled Manhattan's immigrant districts, an alternative ethnic geography also emerged. Such Brooklyn neighborhoods as Brownsville, Ridgewood, Sunset Park, and Borough Park grew out of an interaction of ethnicity and class that encouraged the creation of new neighborhoods far more homogeneous than those of Manhattan and the Bronx. In addition, such resort areas as Coney Island and Far Rockaway in Brooklyn and Queens were developed into permanent residential communities.

Unlike Brooklyn and the Bronx, Queens experienced a decline in immigrant population from 1900 to 1930. In 1900 its 45,000 immigrants made up only 29 percent of the population; thirty years later the percentage declined to 25 percent.[21] This pattern resembles that of most other large American cities, although it diverges from the New York City norm. At the turn of the century Queens comprised scattered clustered settlements of formerly separate villages that often contained factories as well as residences. Half of the workers in Queens lived in the borough, many of them within walking distance of their workplaces. Germans constituted the largest ethnic group with concentrations in such sections as Astoria, Steinway (around the piano factories), Ridgewood, and Jamaica.[22] The Irish also found their way to Queens, but in smaller numbers. During the first decades of the twentieth century the borough's population quadrupled, and a number of model urban communities were constructed, including Sunnyside Gardens, Forest Hills, and Jackson Heights. These planned communities chose their residents carefully, excluding immigrants and middle-class Jews, both deemed undesirable neighbors. Builders covered other sections of Queens with rows of tract houses, modest one-family dwellings for the middle class.[23] Native-born Americans, second- and third-generation young families, settled in these areas and commuted to work in Manhattan. By 1930, Queens had acquired

Brooklyn's earlier reputation as a bedroom community, despite the substantial number of industrial and commercial enterprises located along its East River waterfront.

The transformation of New York from immigrant city to ethnic metropolis occurred during a period of enormous growth in population and physical expansion. The doubling of New York's population catapulted it into the forefront of the great cities of the world. Boosters of Brooklyn and the Bronx, not to be outdone by New Yorkers who were identified with Manhattan, claimed fourth and sixth places for their boroughs, respectively, among the nation's cities in terms of population. Brooklyn, containing 80 square miles, exceeded many American cities in size as well. The New York of 1930 was a city of cities, including ethnic cities. The *Jewish Daily Forward*, a mass circulation Yiddish Socialist newspaper, claimed that the Jews of New York were "the fourth American city."[24] As early as 1920 there were 1,640,000 New York Jews (10 percent of the total world Jewish population), and the next largest city offering any competition, Warsaw, had only 300,000 Jews (2 percent of the world population).[25] This boosterism especially influenced the culture of builders who sought to leave their mark on the city's streets.

Builders etched the familiar skyline of New York upon the horizon in these years, making it the symbol of the "city of opportunity." Thomas Kessner, in his study of social mobility in New York, argued persuasively for the reality behind the image of opportunity. Italian and Jewish immigrants experienced substantial gains in their socio-economic position by 1915.[26] These achievements were inscribed on the city's physical face as immigrants moved out of the downtown districts, sometimes following in the footsteps of the Germans and Irish who had preceded them and at other times charting new directions in virgin territory. But significant continuities masked the changes taking place. Immigrants crowded into the city in such numbers that New York's population doubled from 3,437,000 to 6,930,000 between 1900 and 1930.[27] Their presence insured that a gradual decline of the immigrant areas would accompany the rapid growth of new neighborhoods.

For the newcomers, New York offered two major models of immigrant settlement: the German and the Irish (see Table 5.1). East European Jews usually chose to follow the German pattern, influenced by the German Jews who had immigrated in the nineteenth century. Italians often followed the Irish alternative, sharing a common Catholic faith and similar immigrant occupational patterns.[28] German immigrants settled in sections of the city near industries established by the German entrepreneurs who employed them. The neighborhoods that developed contained a high proportion of Germans. They constructed a fairly complete ethnic economy that included workers as well as a range of mercantile establishments that catered to ethnic tastes and, in the process, perpetuated ethnic culture. The residential concentration also sustained diverse ethnic organizational activities. Thus, German ethnicity permeated the urban class culture of the neighborhood. For example, the thriving Brooklyn working-class neighborhood of Bushwick grew around the breweries as Williamsburg developed around the German tailor shops.[29] Irish immigrants also chose to live close to their employment, but they were influenced as well by the siting of a church. The Irish rarely concentrated in such numbers throughout a neighborhood that they created a complete local ethnic economy. Instead they fashioned an ethnic network through politics and the church which did not require significant residential concentration. The power of this network to influence residential patterns can be seen in decisions of the Brooklyn diocese. The diocese bought land for a church and established parishes in undeveloped areas, thus stimulating Irish settlement. Irish residents moved to Sunset Park and built homes there after St. Michael's Church had been established.[30] Most other groups built churches and other ethnic institutions after they had settled in a neighborhood. Polish immigrants drawn to Sunset Park by jobs controlled by Polish foremen at the Greenwood Cemetery and the Ansonia Clock Company (in South Brooklyn, north of Sunset Park) did not organize the parish of Our Lady of Czenstochowa until after a decade of living in the area and walking to St. Casimir's in downtown Brooklyn.[31]

Both models of immigrant behavior indicated the importance of ethnicity in the city's economy.[32] Ethnic bonds guided immigrant decisions of where to work and live. Individual immigrant groups parceled out the city's economic opportunities, adopting several strategies. Some groups concentrated in certain industries, forming the majority of owners and workers. Jewish distribution in the garment trades provides the best example. Here, as in the residence patterns on the Lower East Side, Jews from specific towns or districts in Europe clustered in certain branches of the industry. Rischin noted that Romanians controlled the production of pants, Jews from Puchevitz went into the fur industry, Warsaw *landslayt* dominated the pursemakers, while vestmakers were divided between skilled Hungarians and semiskilled Russians.[33] Specialization also existed in some areas of commerce. As early as 1910 Italians were a majority of the city's barbers and controlled many of its shoe repair shops.[34] Other occu-

Table 5.1   1920 Residential Distribution of Immigrant Groups, by Neighborhood

Manhattan

	Ireland	Germany	Italy	Russia	Poland	Austria	Hungary	Sweden
Lower East Side	2,000	4,000	35,000	99,000	41,000	32,000	9,000	3,000
Mid-East Side	21,000	9,000	22,000	6,000	4,000	4,000	4,000	2,000
Yorkville	22,000	19,000	23,000	37,000	7,000	11,000	16,000	1,000
Harlem	10,000	7,000	27,000	31,000	5,000	8,000	5,000	
Greenwich Village	8,000	2,000	51,000	1,000	1,000	1,000		
Mid-West Side	21,000	6,000	16,000	4,000	2,000	2,000	1,000	2,000
Upper West Side	20,000	11,000	5,000	5,000	1,000	3,000	3,000	
Washington Heights	7,000	4,000	1,000	6,000	1,000	1,000	1,000	
Inwood	3,000	4,000	2,000	5,000	1,000	2,000	2,000	
Total *	117,000	71,000	185,000	194,000	64,000	66,000	41,000	

Brooklyn

	Ireland	Germany	Italy	Russia	Poland	Austria	Hungary	Norway
Brooklyn Heights	4,000	2,000	9,000	9,000	1,000			4,000
Red Hook	5,000	1,000	20,000	1,000				2,000
South Brooklyn	8,000	4,000	15,000	3,000	5,000			
Bedford	6,000	2,000	8,000	1,000				
Crown Heights	6,000	6,000	12,000	37,000	8,000	6,000	2,000	
Bushwick	4,000	18,000	15,000	6,000	2,000	3,000	1,000	
Williamsburg	3,000	5,000	23,000	43,000	15,000	8,000	2,000	
Greenpoint	4,000	2,000	1,000	2,000	5,000			
Bay Ridge	5,000	4,000	5,000	2,000		4,000	1,000	8,000
Borough Park	2,000	3,000	17,000	18,000	2,000			1,000
Flatbush	4,000	5,000	4,000	4,000		3,000		
Brownsville			2,000	42,000	5,000	4,000		
East New York	1,000	5,000	6,000	29,000	5,000			
Total *	54,000	57,000	138,000	189,000	51,000	32,000	9,000	17,000

Bronx

	Ireland	Germany	Italy	Russia	Poland	Austria	Hungary	Romania
South Bronx	8,000	10,000	11,000	26,000	7,000	8,000	4,000	3,000
Morrisania	3,000	8,000	3,000	44,000	8,000	11,000	4,000	4,000
Grand Concourse	2,000	3,000	1,000	3,000				
Riverdale								
Pelham	4,000	5,000	17,000	13,000	2,000	3,000	1,000	
East Bronx	1,000	2,000	3,000					
North Bronx		1,000	3,000					
City Island								
Total*	19,000	30,000	40,000	87,000	19,000	24,000	11,000	9,000

SOURCE: Walter Laidlaw, *Population of the City of New York, 1890–1930* (New York, 1932), 85, 95, 110, 256–257.†

*Total exceeds table columns because it includes those neighborhoods with less than 1,000 immigrants. Figures rounded to nearest thousand.

†The table can offer only a pattern of settlement. Laidlaw's figures do not include children of immigrants, and his neighborhood boundaries, even in Manhattan, are much broader than those drawn by local patterns of living (e.g., Harlem includes a section of the Upper West Side along Central Park West). I did not include Queens because Laidlaw divided the borough into only five sections. Despite the smaller number of immigrant groups, the gross pattern resembles the other boroughs.

pations were divided along ethnic lines, including fruit and vegetable businesses and construction. Of the multiethnic industries, the building industry most influenced the city's residential growth.

Virtually all immigrant groups worked in construction, albeit not all in the same occupations. The Irish and the Italians, working as laborers building the city's streets and transit lines, discovered new neighborhoods through their work. Norwegian, Swedish, and Finnish carpenters plied their crafts for fellow immigrants and often built their own houses. Jewish immigrants in the building trades, excluded from the Irish-controlled unions, found themselves confined to alteration work—altering existing buildings for multifamily residences. Because of their jobs, many moved to the neighborhood of Harlem where they established their own alteration unions. But the ethnic division of the construction industry did more than introduce workers to areas of the city they previously had not known; it also fostered ethnically distinct housing markets. In the first decades of the century immigrant and second-generation Germans, Irish, Italians, Norwegians, Finns, and Jews embraced the city's boom psychology and entered the construction industry by becoming builders. Knowing what their fellow ethnics deemed desirable in housing, they built for an ethnically segregated market. In the early 1900s Finns pioneered in constructing cooperative apartments in Sunset Park and Bay Ridge for fellow workers.[35] Later, in the 1920s, Jews in the garment industry built several cooperative apartment projects in the Bronx. In the Jackson Heights section of Queens, Edward MacDougall constructed "the largest community of cooperatively owned garden apartment homes under single management."[36] Other workers rejected the cooperative model. Italians built modest one- and two-family houses in Canarsie in the 1920s within working-class financial constraints, as the Germans had done earlier in Bushwick.[37] Although most immigrants lived in tenements they had neither built nor altered, New York's ethnic residential distribution cannot be understood without examining the role of immigrant and second-generation builders. These individuals, and their fellow ethnics in real estate, created most of the new city neighborhoods in the years of New York's building booms before and after World War I.[38]

To speak of ethnic construction markets is not to deny the importance of such universal urban trends as the extension of rapid transit facilities, the introduction of zoning regulations in 1916, the tax abatement laws passed in the 1920s, and fluctuations in the economy and real estate market. Nor is the focus on ethnicity meant to suggest that a simple correlation exists between the ethnic group membership of a group of builders and the character of a city neighborhood.

148

There were wide variations within ethnic groups in residence choices as well as significant differences among ethnic groups. However, the position of ethnic builders within the chain of migration that peopled large sections of the city contributed significantly to the complexity of urban residential growth. The broad theories of immigrant concentration yielding to more acculturated patterns of dispersed settlement cannot account for all of the specific historic configurations that produced discrete neighborhoods in New York City.[39] Only through an exploration of a number of alternative types of neighborhoods—immigrant and second-generation; working-class, middle-class, and upper-class; religious, nationalist, secular, and radical—can the significance of ethnicity to the process of urban growth be charted.[40] Given the size and ethnic diversity of New York, such an analysis of ethnicity, class, and ideology in the creation of urban neighborhoods can best be accomplished by examining one ethnic group. The prominence of Jews—the largest single ethnic group in the city by 1910, the influence they exerted on the city, and their extraordinary diversity—make them an ideal group to examine in detail.

The intense concentration of East European Jewish immigrants on the Lower East Side at the turn of the century and the smaller settlement of native-born Jews of German background on the Upper East Side produced an enduring geographic metaphor for Jewish ethnicity. Speaking of uptown and downtown, Jews from both sections soon transformed these geographic designations into code words for entire cultural outlooks. Uptown Jews were assimilated, wealthy bankers or merchants, American or German, religiously Reform and politically Progressive (that is, supporters of the Progressive wing of the Republican party). Downtown Jews, by contrast, were unassimilated, Yiddish-speaking, poor garment workers or pushcart peddlers, East European, religiously Orthodox or politically radical. So powerful were the geographic metaphors that Jews of both areas came to accept the notion that where you lived told the world who you were.[41] To move to a new neighborhood meant to exchange an old ethnic identity for a new one. Although hundreds of thousands of Jews left the Lower East Side from 1900 to 1930 (the area contained 50 percent of the city's Jews in 1905 and only 25 percent by 1915), the imagery of downtown Jews versus uptown Jews persisted.[42] Even institutions acquired the reputation of their locale in the eyes of their supporters. When Orthodox Jews sought to change the image of the Rabbi Isaac Elhanan Theological Seminary from an immigrant to an American one, they moved their school uptown to Washington Heights in upper Manhattan.[43] Synagogues also relocated, following their more successful members. B'nai Jeshurun, the oldest Ashkenazic congregation in New

149

York, left the Lower East Side for 34th Street, then moved up to 65th Street and Madison Avenue in 1884, then relocated to 88th Street and West End Avenue on the Upper West Side in 1918, where it finally settled.[44] Conversely, those organizations that remained rooted on the Lower East Side retained an unmatched Jewish authenticity in the eyes of their members. Jews who left the area returned regularly for lodge meetings, Yiddish theater, and other cultural activities.

Yet even in its heyday as the Yiddish cosmopolis, the Lower East Side coexisted with alternative immigrant sections. As early as 1890 Jewish immigrants began to move across the East River to Williamsburg, uptown to Harlem, and even into the South Bronx. After construction of the approaches to the Williamsburg bridge displaced 10,000 Lower East Side residents, the migration took on substantial proportions. Jews shared similar reasons for wanting to leave the Lower East Side, "to get away from the congestion, filth and lack of open space," but their paths took them to three different types of immigrant neighborhoods.[45] Harlem, Williamsburg, and Brownsville represented alternative immigrant Jewish sections, and their individual histories suggest the complex ethnic dimensions of residential migration and urban growth. Harlem in Manhattan was the most ethnically diverse neighborhood; Brownsville in Brooklyn stood at the opposite extreme. Williamsburg, initially resembling Harlem, gradually grew closer to Brownsville.

Harlem first attracted German Jews and successful East European immigrants who had arrived in the 1880s.[46] They moved to Harlem prior to 1900 and settled in middle-class housing, six- and seven-story apartment buildings, along Fifth and Lenox avenues. Jeffrey Gurock, the historian of Jewish Harlem, observed that "Harlem's limited employment opportunities undoubtedly restricted uptown settlement."[47] Only those who could afford to travel to work—successful manufacturers and a handful of skilled workers—or men who found jobs in the area—peddlers and small shopkeepers and a few building trades workers, moved up to Harlem before its real estate boom after 1905. These two groups of Jews established the two nuclei of the community along class lines, a working-class settlement below 110th Street west of Third Avenue and a middle-class enclave north of Central Park along the large avenues.

Advertisements in the Yiddish press extolling the attractions of Harlem's housing enticed residents. "The Voice of Joy, the Voice of Gladness, The Voice of the Bridegroom, the Voice of the Bride. Young couples and growing families can receive a practical, decorated three-room apartment for $8.50–$9.50 in the great new Steinway Apartment House," read one ad. "Do you want an elegant place for cheap rent?" it queried.[48] Indeed, many did. They moved up to Harlem without delay and with little knowledge of the neighborhood. Occasionally, a Jewish immigrant discovered that he had settled on the wrong side of the street—on the east side of Park Avenue where the Irish lived instead of the west side—and had to move again onto a Jewish block.[49]

The decision of so many immigrants to move, the dislocation of urban development on the Lower East Side, and construction of a subway through Harlem triggered a mass migration that stimulated a building boom in Harlem. Jewish building trades workers flocked to the area, as did workers in the cigar factories, which had also migrated uptown on the east side. Jews eagerly bought and sold Harlem real estate at a curbside market established on the corner of 116th Street and Fifth Avenue. The speculators' rapid turnover of remodeled tenements produced rising rents and ignited a rent strike by Jewish tenants in 1904 and again in 1908. By 1910 over 100,000 Jews lived in Harlem, an impressive increase over the 17,000 who had come prior to 1900. Almost 60 percent resided in the working-class area below 110th Street. Of these, 60 percent were skilled laborers, with the building trades, needle trades, and cigar-making accounting for 87 percent of them. Another 26 percent worked as petty proprietors. By contrast, of the 40 percent of Harlem's Jews who lived dispersed in the northern and western sections, only 26 percent were skilled workers and 75 percent were in white collar jobs, many of them clerks or proprietors. Most of the Germans and Irish began to leave Harlem as the Jews moved in, but a compact settlement of Italians flourished in the district east of Third Avenue, and a small cluster of African Americans developed in the area north of 135th Street.

Brownsville grew during the same years as Harlem but in a different fashion.[50] In 1884 Gilbert Thatford, a large property owner in the area, convinced Aaron Kaplan, a Jewish real estate agent who summered in Brownsville, to buy 13 lots. It took another decade, however, before he, in turn, persuaded his fellow vacationer, Elias Kaplan, to move his garment factory out to Brownsville. The garment factory's relocation awaited the provision of mass transit facilities but not such other urban amenities as paved streets, lighting, gas, and electricity. In the early days Brownsville residents who ventured out at night ran the risk of falling into unfinished cellars, and when it rained, residents claimed that there were puddles large enough to drown a horse. The first houses clustered near the early factories. The most popular structures built by Jewish builders were small multifamily dwellings, many with commercial space on the ground floor. Despite the individuality and diversity of Brownsville builders—64 percent of them constructed only one to four houses—the neighborhood developed a homogeneity that reflected the tastes and pocketbooks of its future residents.[51] Like their Harlem counterparts, the builders and real estate speculators promoted Brownsville in the Yiddish press. However, rather than stressing modern housing, they advertised the "fresh open spaces of the suburbs."[52] By 1905, with paved streets, water, electricity, sewage, and rapid transit to Manhattan, Brownsville's Jewish population soared. But so did its non-Jewish population. In 1905 approximately 49,000 Jews lived in Brownsville, roughly 80 percent of the neighborhood's residents. By 1925 over 250,000 Jews lived in Brownsville, but their proportion of the district remained a constant 80 percent of the total.

Unlike Harlem, Brownsville developed into an exclusively working-class section. The successful entrepreneurs who owned the many stores on Pitkin Avenue, the main shopping street, and the manufacturers who profited from Brownsville's garment shops lived in the adjacent neighborhood of Eastern Parkway. Although a 1925 survey of housing costs in Brownsville disclosed some new postwar buildings renting for as much as $19 per room—significantly higher than the older houses which rented for $5–$6 per room, prices competitive with or lower than the Lower East Side—the families paid the higher rents by pooling the income of three or four members.[53] Brownsville's occupational distribution also differed from that of Harlem. The majority of Brownsville's Jewish immigrants were skilled workers, with the largest percentage employed in the needle trades, most of them in local garment shops. These included a larger proportion of men's relative to women's clothing factories than existed in Manhattan, suggesting that the decision to relocate was made selectively by firms following Kaplan's lead. The building trades employed the second largest number of Brownsville's immigrant workers, followed by the printing trades. Brownsville's immigrant population included many more recent arrivals than did Harlem's; by 1910 Jews leaving Ellis Island often came directly to Brownsville without tarrying for several years on the Lower East Side. Of the males in Brownsville in 1910, 43 percent had lived in the United States less than five years.[54] Brownsville lacked not only Harlem's socioeconomic diversity but its ethnic variety. The majority of Brownsville's Jews came from Russia. Few Galicians, Romanians, or Hungarians settled in the neighborhood.

Williamsburg presented a third alternative located between the working-class immigrant homogeneity of Brownsville and the socioeconomic and ethnic heterogeneity of Harlem.[55] If religious Jewish immigrants considered Brownsville a "Jerusalem" prior to World War I, they thought of Williamsburg as a "midbar," a desert. Both neighborhoods included densely populated sections, but Williamsburg was a mixed ethnic neighborhood. Attracted by its garment shops, bakeries, and other industries, immigrant Jews moved from the Lower East Side to the German sections of Williamsburg as Italian and Polish immigrants moved to the Irish areas. Those middle-class German Jews, who had lived in Williamsburg at the turn of the century and established its first synagogues, gradually left the neighborhood for such new districts as Park Slope. But unlike Harlem, where the Jewish population declined dramatically after World War I as blacks moved into the northern section above 125th Street, Williamsburg witnessed a form of Jewish ethnic succession. This process registered in the transference of institutional buildings. In 1921, the year after Temple Israel of Harlem sold its Lenox Avenue synagogue to a congregation of Seventh Day Adventists, the Reform Temple Beth Elohim in Williamsburg sold its Keap Street building to a group of Orthodox East European Jews. Other congregations purchased former churches, turning them into Orthodox synagogues. During the 1920s Jewish Williamsburg contracted, lost its socioeconomic and ethnic diversity, and became a neighborhood of Russian and Polish immigrant workers and petty proprietors. These Jews established several major Orthodox institutions, forging an alternative to those seeking an American locale for orthodoxy.

These middle-class Orthodox Jews rejected Williamsburg's immigrant and lower middle-class, densely populated urban milieu in favor of a neighborhood that blended American affluence with traditional Judaism. During the same years that Russian Jews filled up Brownsville's drab brick multifamily dwellings, these successful immigrants and their children moved into single-family homes in Borough Park along tree-lined streets.[56] Borough Park, initially developed by the politician William Reynolds and the builder Edward Johnson, grew along the streetcar lines. By the first decades of the twentieth century Jewish builders had discovered the area, and in the 1920s extensive construction occurred. The Jewish novelist Michael Gold sharply portrayed the real estate fever and temptation that building offered Jews in his autobiographical novel, *Jews Without Money*:

> We traveled to Borough Park to see the house and lot Zechariah was persuading my father to buy. It was a dreary day of fall. The suburb was a place of half-finished skeleton houses and piles of lumber and brick. Paved streets ran in rows between empty fields where only the weeds rattled. Real estate signs were stuck everywhere. In the midst of some rusty cans and muck would be a sign shouting "This Wonderful Apartment House Site for Sale!" In a muddy pool where ducks paddled, another sign read: "Why Pay Rent? Build Your House in God's Country."[57]

The 60,000 Jews who settled in Borough Park by 1925 also built houses to God. Egon Mayer, a sociologist who analyzed the Jewish community of Borough Park, observed that "there were no structures built by competing religions or secular organizations to detract from the impressive shadow cast over the community by these early Jewish organizations."[58] Although the Jews of Borough Park made up only half of the total local population, they quickly established the religious parameters of the neighborhood. Their need to walk to the synagogue on the Sabbath and its accessibility for weekday morning and evening prayers reinforced the compactness of the Orthodox neighborhood. The synagogue buildings attested to the prosperity of the residents; many required their officers and clergy to wear formal dress on the Sabbath and holidays. Israel Schorr, rabbi of the Orthodox Temple Beth El, recalled that the members were not interested in *"arbeiter yidn"* (working-class Jews). Indeed, few Jewish workers could afford to live in the neighborhood above 46th Street, which boasted a median annual family income of $4,000 in 1930. But less religious Jews also avoided Borough Park. The shadow cast by the impressive synagogues and large communal religious schools discouraged the aggressively secular from settling in the district, although a handful of Yiddish schools were established in the lower-middle-class section. Borough Park represented not only a middle-class, second-generation Jewish neighborhood but a religious one. More homogeneous than Brownsville, which housed synagogues as well as many radical groups, Borough Park catered largely to one ideological segment of New York Jews. The rapid growth of new areas encouraged segregation along class, ethnic, and ideological lines in place of concentration based on national origins.

Religious Jews were not alone in building new neighborhoods. Radical Jews used their garment unions and fraternal organizations to acquire some of the perquisites of light, air, trees, and gardens found in the unbuilt sections of the city that attracted the middle class.[59] However, they turned to the Bronx, rather than Brooklyn, to realize their dreams of a better life. Jewish workers employed in the garment and fur industries moved to the Bronx in the decade preceding World War I. The Bronx was "the country." In fact, the Bronx contained more parkland than any other borough, although it also housed a variety of industries along its southern waterfront. Radical Jewish immigrants first moved to the East Bronx, an ideologically and socioeconomically diverse neighborhood that held approximately 130,000 Jews by 1930. From the immigrant East Bronx a smaller number moved into the Pelham Parkway section; some residents came from Harlem or even directly from the Lower East Side. Yiddishists, Socialist Zionists, Communists, and the Socialist Amalgamated Clothing Workers union each built large cooperative apartment houses in the 1920s. Most were located near the parks, either the eastern edge of Bronx Park or the southern rim of Van Cortlandt Park.

Jewish builders, committed to some form of socialism and believers in the virtues of consumer cooperatives, constructed these apartment houses and tailored them to the desires of their future tenants. To provide light and air, each room contained a window and the apartments had two exposures. The centrally heated buildings offered the latest plumbing advances. In addition, the houses contained several community rooms for meetings, social gatherings, a cooperative library, and a kindergarten. However, the six-story buildings did not have elevators, distinguishing them from the "ritzy" elevator apartment buildings in the West Bronx. The Jews who moved into the cooperatives found that their new environment nourished an intense ideological fervor that spilled over into the neighborhood. In the Communist Workers Cooperative Colony, "the most important day of the year was neither Yom Kippur nor Christmas but May Day," recalled one resident.[60] The cooperative's spirit permeated the neighborhood, giving it a distinct character, set apart from other lower-middle-class districts. With a population of 29,000 by 1930, Pelham Parkway represented a radical and secular Jewish alternative to both the immigrant and the diverse middle-class Jewish sections.

Not only did working-class and middle-class, immigrant and second-generation Jews create new ethnic neighborhoods in New York City, even upper-class Jews chose to settle in their own district. On the Upper West Side of Manhattan, from 79th Street north to 110th Street west of Central Park, wealthy East European and upper-middle-class German Jews fashioned yet another type of ethnic urban neighborhood.[61] Unsympathetic observers labeled it "the gilded ghetto" and mocked the "alrightniks" who chose to live in its fancy, massive apartment houses.[62] In fact, the Upper West Side represented less of a "ghetto" in terms of the proportion of its residents who were Jewish than did its middle-class version on the Grand Concourse. Despite its reputation, the Upper West Side did not contain a substantial Jewish residential concentration; even by 1930 only a third of its population was Jewish.

The physical character of the Upper West Side, a blend of large elevator apartment buildings along Central Park West, West End Avenue, and Broadway, with brownstones on the side streets and tenements beside the elevated train on Columbus Avenue, contributed to the perception of Jewish ethnic concentration. Jews lived almost exclusively in the luxury apartment buildings, especially those built after

World War I, Irish lived in the tenements, and a mixed population of native-born white Protestants and second-generation Germans lived in the brownstones. Although Jews shared the streets with other ethnics on the Upper West Side, and their synagogues stood opposite an array of Protestant and Catholic churches, they less often shared their lobbies. Of the seventeen largest apartment houses in 1930, Jews were 100 percent of the tenants in one building, 75 percent of the tenants in two, half of the tenants of four more, and a third of the remaining ten. The historian Selma Berrol noted that "the most homogeneously Jewish buildings were tenanted by East European Jews and located furthest north on West End Avenue."[63] Second-generation German Jews more often lived dispersed along Central Park West. In fact, the Upper West Side resembled the ethnic and socioeconomic diversity of the western part of Harlem, reflecting its previous residential history.

Jews first moved across Central Park in the years before World War I, at a time when the Upper West Side had already grown through the two previous building booms that set the pattern of its housing. Although Jewish builders tore down a number of the private homes to construct apartment buildings after the war, they did not change the mixed character of the neighborhood. The pioneers of the Jewish neighborhood had been wealthy East European garment manufacturers and successful American Jewish professionals. They were followed after the war by the more successful Russian, German, and Hungarian Jews who abandoned Harlem as its black population grew and expanded. Attracted by the extension of the subway down the West Side to the new heart of the garment center on Seventh Avenue in the Thirties, garment manufacturers found homes in the area in large numbers. By 1925 a sample of Jewish neighborhood households revealed that over half were clothing manufacturers, a remarkable increase over the 3 percent in this occupation in 1915. Rents of $100–$200 per month attested to the affluence of the Jewish tenants who chose to rent apartments in a densely populated urban district rather than to buy single-family homes in the suburbs. The physical attributes of the upper-class neighborhood they fashioned catered to their sense of urbanity and style, while its ethnicity, visible in the solid synagogues, kosher butcher shops, bookstores, delicatessens, and bakeries, nourished a sense of cohesion and security.

Despite the diversity of Jewish ethnic neighborhoods, they shared some common attributes, as did the Jewish garment manufacturers and their Jewish workers. Most contained multifamily dwellings and in many, these dominated not merely the corner plots but the large avenues. The evolution of the apartment house, from its tenement origins to the height of art deco luxury, suggests a persistent affection for multifamily living by most Jewish immigrants and their children. The sociologist Marshall Sklare has called the apartment house "the emblem of the Jews' love affair with the city."[64] Jews also retained a common vision of the ideal urban neighborhood that permeates the various imperfect manifestations constructed on the streets of New York City. This improved urban environment included wide, preferably tree-lined, streets and access to parks—public spaces to allow for the easy intercourse that sustained a sense of neighborhood and community. New York Jews did not abandon the city streets for private pleasures even when they acquired the affluence to support such privacy. In fact, they continued to endow the streets with ethnic attributes, even boldly claiming a whole neighborhood like the Upper West Side as their own when they constituted only a sizable fraction of its population.

Jews were not alone, of course, in their ability to transform the gridiron into an ethnic mosaic. Italians, Germans, Hungarians, Norwegians, as well as smaller ethnic groups placed their stamp upon the city. But Jewish immigrants and their children developed a remarkable array of urban choices that encouraged physical mobility not only as an expression of social mobility and acculturation, but of ideological preference. There were many paths leading from the Lower East Side. For most Jews, they led toward New York and America through alternative ethnic neighborhoods.

Notes

1. There is an extensive literature on ethnicity in America. For an excellent discussion, see Werner Sollors, *Beyond Ethnicity: Consent and Descent in American Culture* (New York, 1986).
2. See Moses Rischin's persuasive introduction to Hutchins Hapgood, *The Spirit of the Ghetto* (Cambridge, Mass., 1967), especially xxi–xxx, where he traces the intellectual history of the concept of the immigrant ghetto and the significance of the Lower East Side.
3. Ira Rosenwaike, *Population History of New York City* (Syracuse, 1972), 90–92. In the late 1920s New York City drew almost one out of four immigrants entering the country compared to less than one out of five in the preceding decade.
4. Ira Rosenwaike, *Population History of New York City*, Table C-1, 202. I have rounded the numbers since I am less interested in statistical precision than in the historical interpretation.
5. Jewish population figures in the United States are estimates derived from a variety of sources: death records, Yiddish mother-tongue, public school records, communal estimates. The data are much less accurate than

census materials and therefore will be presented in grosser form. For a detailed discussion of the problems of estimating Jewish population of New York City, see the Appendix to my book, Deborah Dash Moore, *At Home in America: Second Generation New York Jews* (New York, 1981), 243–245. A good overview of the history of New York Jews, including its demographic dimensions, appears in the *Encyclopedia Judaica*, 1062–1124. See tables on p. 1078 for figures.

6. Moore, *At Home*, 21. In 1900 German Jews were 20 percent of the New York Jewish population, but fifteen years later they were only 10 percent of the total.

7. Stephen Brumberg, *Going to America, Going to School* (New York, 1986), *passim*.

8. Deborah Dash Moore, *At Home in America*, Chap. 4.

9. Thomas Kessner, *The Golden Door: Italian and Jewish Immigrant Mobility in New York City 1880–1915* (New York, 1977), 140–141, 143–156, documents the mobility of Irish and German immigrants in the decades before the turn of the century as well as the physical mobility of Italians and Jews.

10. Sam Bass Warner, Jr., and Colin B. Burke, "Cultural Change and the Ghetto," *Journal of Contemporary History* 4, 4 (1969): 172–174, 182–183. For a good response, see Kathleen Neils Conzen, "Immigrants, Immigrant Neighborhoods, and Ethnic Identity: Historical Issues," *Journal of American History* 68, 3 (December 1979): 603–608.

11. Ira Rosenwaike, *Population History of New York City*, 84–85; Thomas Kessner, *The Golden Door*, 153–155.

12. Bronx Council of Social Agencies, *A Study of the Lower Bronx* (New York, 1939), 85–86.

13. Jacob A. Riis, *How the Other Half Lives* (1890; Reprint, New York, 1957), 18–19.

14. Moses Rischin, *The Promised City: New York Jews, 1870–1914* (Cambridge, Mass., 1962), 76.

15. Moses Rischin, *The Promised City*, 76–78.

16. Kate Claghorn, "Foreign Immigrant in New York City," *Industrial Commission on Immigration* XV: 474, quoted in Ira Rosenwaike, *Population History of New York*, 84.

17. Thomas Kessner, *The Golden Door*, 147–154.

18. Eleanora W. Schoenebaum, "Emerging Neighborhoods: The Development of Brooklyn's Fringe Areas, 1850–1930," Ph.D. Dissertation, Columbia University (1977), 81–82.

19. David Ment, *The Shaping of a City: A Brief History of Brooklyn* (New York, 1979), 70.

20. Eleanora W. Schoenebaum, "Emerging Neighborhoods," 12, 77–78.

21. Computed from Ira Rosenwaike, *Population History of New York City*, 133.

22. *New York Panorama: A Companion Guide to the WPA Guide to New York City*, Federal Writers Project of the Works Progress Administration (1938; Reprint, New York, 1984), 100–101.

23. *The WPA Guide to New York City*, Federal Writers Project of the Works Progress Administration (1939; Reprint, New York, 1982), chapters on Queens, especially 566–567, 578–579, 581–582.

24. *The Fourth American City—The Jewish Community of New York*,

A Book of Facts About the Jewish Field, New York, Chicago, and National (New York, 1927), n.p., in YIVO Institute for Jewish Research.

25. Arthur Ruppin, "The Jewish Population of the World," *The Jewish People, Past and Present* I (New York, 1948) 357.
26. Thomas Kessner, *The Golden Door*, 176.
27. Ira Rosenwaike, *Population History of New York City*, 141.
28. For a comparison of Italian, Jewish, German, and Irish occupational and residential patterns, see Ronald Bayor, *Neighbors in Conflict: The Irish, Germans, Jews, and Italians of New York City, 1929–1941* (Baltimore, 1978), 14–24, 150–155, 159–160.
29. Eleanora W. Schoenebaum, "Emerging Neighborhoods," 84–88.
30. David Ment and Mary Donovan, *The People of Brooklyn: A History of Two Neighborhoods* (Brooklyn Education and Cultural Alliance, 1980), 55.
31. David Ment and Mary Donovan, *The People of Brooklyn*, 59.
32. Nathan Glazer and Daniel Patrick Moynihan emphasized this in their study, *Beyond the Melting Pot: The Negroes, Puerto Ricans, Jews, Italians, and Irish of New York City* (Cambridge, Mass., 1963), which contributed to a renewed interest in ethnicity.
33. Moses Rischin, *The Promised City*, 183.
34. Ronald Bayor, *Neighbors in Conflict*, 14.
35. David Ment and Mary Donovan, *The People of Brooklyn*, 67–68. On the Norwegians, see Christen T. Jonassen, "Cultural Variables in the Ecology of an Ethnic Group," *American Sociological Review* 14, 1 (February 1949): 32–42.
36. Barbara Flanagan, "Gracious, Spacious and Old: Garden Apartments in Queens," *New York Times* (September 10, 1987): C1.
37. Eleanora W. Schoenebaum, "Emerging Neighborhoods," 292; Jonathan Rieder, *Canarsie: The Jews and Italians of Brooklyn Against Liberalism* (Cambridge, Mass., 1985), 15.
38. *Population, Land Values and Government: Studies of the Growth and Distribution of Population and Land Values; and of Problems of Government*, Regional Survey of New York and Its Environs, Vol. 2 (New York, 1929), 64.
39. Paul Frederick Cressey, "Population Succession in Chicago: 1898–1930," *American Journal of Sociology* LXIV (July 1938): 59–69; and Louis Wirth, *The Ghetto* (Chicago, 1928) provide the major statements of these theories.
40. The experience of African Americans in New York City cannot be considered comparable to that of the immigrant groups despite some activity by African Americans in real estate. The housing discrimination against African Americans—exceeding substantially that experienced by any other group—greatly limited their mobility. The growth of Harlem as the "black metropolis" in the 1920s followed a different pattern than the one presented here. See Gilbert Osofsky, *Harlem: The Making of a Ghetto* (New York, 1963).
41. For a more extended discussion of geography and metaphor, see Deborah Dash Moore, "The Construction of Community: Jewish Migration and Ethnicity in the United States," in *The Jews of North America*, Moses Rischin, ed. (Detroit, 1987), 105–117.

42. *Studies in the New York Jewish Population,* Jewish Communal Survey of Greater New York (New York, 1928), 5.
43. Jeffrey S. Gurock, *The Men and Women of Yeshiva: Higher Education, Orthodoxy, and American Judaism* (New York, 1988), 82–94.
44. *Encyclopedia Judaica,* 1080.
45. Leo Grebler, *Housing Market Behavior in a Declining Area,* quoted in Thomas Kessner, *The Golden Door,* 152.
46. The following account draws on the history of Jewish Harlem by Jeffrey S. Gurock, *When Harlem Was Jewish: 1870–1930* (New York, 1979).
47. Jeffrey S. Gurock, *When Harlem Was Jewish,* 29.
48. Quoted in Jeffrey S. Gurock, *When Harlem Was Jewish,* 32.
49. Samuel Golden, "Some Days Are More Important," in *Jewish Settlement and Community in the Modern Western World,* Ronald Dötterer, Deborah Dash Moore, and Steven M. Cohen, eds. *Susquehanna University Studies,* Vol. 14 (1991), 178–179.
50. The account of Brownsville draws on Alter Landesman, *Brownsville: The Birth, Development and Passing of a Jewish Community* (New York, 1969); the statistics derive from Max Halpert, "Jews of Brownsville 1880–1925." Ph.D. Dissertation, Yeshiva University (1958).
51. Eleanora W. Schoenebaum, "Emerging Neighborhoods," 141.
52. Quoted in Max Halpert, "The Jews of Brownsville," 15.
53. Alter F. Landesman, "A Neighborhood Survey of Brownsville," Report for Members of the Society. Brooklyn, n.d., 4a.
54. Eleanora W. Schoenebaum, "Emerging Neighborhoods," 153.
55. The account of Williamsburg draws on George Kranzler, *Williamsburg: A Jewish Community in Transition* (New York, 1961).
56. The account of Borough Park draws on Egon Mayer, *From Suburb to Shtetl: The Jews of Borough Park* (Philadelphia, 1979).
57. Michael Gold, *Jews Without Money* (1930; Reprint, New York, 1965), 155.
58. Egon Mayer, *From Suburb to Shtetl,* 27.
59. There are no studies of Jewish neighborhoods of the Bronx. For documentation and sources, see Moore, *At Home in America,* Chaps. 2 and 3.
60. Quoted in Calvin Trillin, "U.S. Journal: The Bronx," *The New Yorker* (August 1, 1977): 50.
61. This account draws on Selma Berrol, "The Jewish West Side of New York City 1920–1970," *Journal of Ethnic Studies* 13, 4: 21–45.
62. Aaron M. Frankel, "Back to Eighty-sixth Street," *Commentary* (August 1946): 169–170.
63. Selma Berrol, "The Jewish West Side of New York City," 31.
64. Marshall Sklare, "Jews, Ethnics, and the American City," *Commentary* (April 1972): 72.

Chapter 6

St. Imre Garden City:
An Urban Community

ISTVÁN TEPLÁN

*I*N THE BOOK, *Five Spirits*, Béla Hamvas writes with remarkable
lucidity about the "spirit of a location" that captivates people,
about that strange impression certain places make on the observer: ". . . a place has metaphysical, as well as physical presence
and, as such, is both a spirit and a spectacle. That is why one cannot
define it, but merely describe it, because it is not calculable, because
it is a face."[1] For quite some time now I have been pondering the
question of whether this face can be reconstructed. "Place" and "spirit"
have a peculiar interrelation, claims Hamvas, they mutually determine each other. That traditions, customs, and spiritual factors in
general are important in forming the profile of a city does not need
proving. For me, the Chinatowns of North American cities, or Williamsburg in New York, give the most striking demonstration of
that phenomenon. However, I am not so certain of the proposition
that the description of a segregated district is possible beyond the literary approach, in some kind of "scientific" manner; still, this is precisely what I intend to try in the following.

My studies are based on the assumption that the one-time spirit of
a place leaves the most telling evidence on the material culture it
once created, and of all these, the architectural objects are the most
accessible. These are objectifications that carry connotative meaning
apart from their functional use, and from these connotative signs we
are able to infer such spiritual phenomena as "awareness of life" and
"lifestyle," as Huizinga calls them. In the case of a Gothic cathedral,
for example, no one doubts that a cornice or a pediment is a communicative artifact, which carries a connotative meaning. In earlier

times one was able to deduce from the outside appearance of a building not only its function (religious, military, administrative, industrial, etc.), but in the case of a dwelling place, for example, the social standing, religion, and perhaps even the ethnic origin of its inhabitants. The international style that after World War II has defined modern urbanism has tended to produce a situation in which cities in all corners of the world resemble each other. Naturally, even the urban environment of today cannot do without symbols, but this system of symbols coupled with abstract ornamentation is banal and unrefined by comparison with the Gothic Age, for example. Yet as the work of Marshall Berman and Roland Barthes demonstrates, it is possible to analyze urban systems of symbols in modernity.[2]

There is another important assumption; namely, that when analyzing a cultural fact or object one has to consider what its creators thought about it. One must reconstruct the object in question the way they saw it and used it. To analyze a building, a garden, or even just an architectural column one has to examine the parental "worldview" of the objects since these objects are the communicative signs of that world-view. "Every cultural phenomenon is a system of symbols; in other words, culture is essentially communication," declares Umberto Eco, a pioneer of the subject.[3] Every building, even the simplest one, carries with it communicative, connotative signs beyond the primary, denotative (functional) meaning. By analyzing these signs we can tap a pool of information which could provide important additional data and complement the traditional analysis of urban studies and historical economy. Naturally, to understand the social content of a given architectonic vocabulary, a great deal of other information is necessary.

The area to be studied here, St. Imre Garden City, is a quite distinctive region of Budapest, one largely unknown to the public. It is visually striking, appearing very homogeneous. One immediately feels its boundaries in both space and time. Although it had no two identical buildings, a homogeneous intent and spirit were apparent—the manifestation of some kind of a style that is not merely architectural. The signs of a past existence are still visible on the often dilapidated houses and the overgrown gardens, the weed-covered bowers, small pools, and statues.

This milieu appeals to me. I am in agreement with Jane Jacobs, who claims that we can become familiar with a district only if we identify with it and try to understand the way of life of its inhabitants, in the same way anthropologists have to in order to understand, say, a tribal society.[4] But documentary sources, other than the major physical source of St. Imre itself, were rather sparse. Yet that physicality is a source of considerable usefulness, and we can usefully build our analysis upon it.

The Origin of Garden City

The colony of St. Imre Garden City came into being under historic circumstances. It was created in 1929 to provide a locus for the resettlement of Hungarians uprooted from Transylvania and the other annexed territories. From the beginning, the charter residents of St. Imre planned it as a settlement along distinct cultural lines: their vision reflected the residential character of the secure, tradition-bound communities they were forced to abandon. (The colony was named after Prince Imre, the son of Hungary's first king, (St.) István I. The crown prince was twenty-four years old in 1031, when he died in a hunting accident. He was canonized in 1083.)

The area in question was initially called St. Imre Colony; later it was known as the Officials' Colony. Now its inhabitants mostly refer to it as Garden City. Geographically, it is located on the outskirts of Budapest, in the suburb of Pestlőrinc. It has a history of a mere sixty years, that is to say, sixty years ago there was nothing but ploughland there. It comprises about 170 acres, with approximately 300–400 properties.

Several documents were useful in my investigations: "Pestszentlőrinci Kertotthon és Házépítő Fogyasztási, Termelő és Értékesítő Szövetkezet Hivatalos Értesítője" (the official gazette of the Consuming, Producing and Marketing Society of Pestszentlőrinc Home Garden Property Development, initially called "Home Garden," then the "Saint Imre Colony Journal," and from 1936 "Saint Imre Garden City Journal"); the entries of the "Országos Földbirtokrendező Bíróság," or O.F.B. (National Court of Land-Registry); and the contemporary land registrations. But I relied mostly on interviews.

Although the archives of the Pestvidéki Törvényszék Cégbírósága (Pest County Court Jury of Company-Law), where the Building Society had been registered, were destroyed, we are able to draw a picture, admittedly incomplete, of the Society's dealings from their Gazette, since it usually published the minutes of the general meetings. Apart from documents concerning Society matters, the Gazette often published news and articles about the everyday life of the colony. Unfortunately, several issues of the Gazette were lost.

I also made use of a questionnaire which I mailed to 300 addresses, as well as interviews and conversations that I held with the older members of the community. Despite their initial reserve, these inhabitants, who had lived through some turbulent times, provided extremely valuable information about the former way of life in the community.

The idea of building the settlement was introduced in 1920. At that time, those government officials who fled from the lost territories in the south and north of Hungary and Transylvania lived with their families in freight cars in the railway stations of Budapest. According to contemporary newspapers, they included high court judges, mayors, army officers, and even a land-steward.

By the end of World War I the population of Budapest increased far beyond its natural growth and had swelled well beyond its supply of housing. Refugees were arriving from all parts of the dismembered empire, and among the largest groups arriving in the capital were those from Transylvania. In an article discussing the refugee problem Endre Liber wrote that

> following the Rumanian occupation of Transylvania in 1916 nearly half-a-million people were forced to leave their homes and at that time, too, Budapest was the centre of the exodus. The same thing happened after the revolution in 1918, when, again, people came to Budapest from the occupied territories in great numbers as a consequence of the occupation of parts of the country. Understandably, the expelled government officials almost exclusively gravitated towards Budapest.[5]

Although there had been many vacant apartments in 1914, by 1918 there was a great shortage of accommodations. In 1921, 60,000 refugees were registered in Budapest and of these, 755 families lived in freight cars. In 1910 there were 175,000 apartments in Budapest. From then until 1920, only 19,000 new ones were built and most of those had been built in the prewar years. In the years following the war, a large middle-class immigrant population settled in and around Budapest. With the aim of solving the refugee problem, a sum of 300 million Koronas was allocated in the budget of 1921 for the building of houses; on top of this, building societies, mainly drawing their membership from public employees, were able to purchase land on government subsidy. All this was made possible by the Land-Law Reform Bill of 1921. That was how the Producing, Consuming and Marketing Society of Pestlőrinc Home Garden and Property Development managed to acquire approximately 310 acres. The Treasury had taken this land away from Miklós Szemere's estate as indemnity. In 1920, some of the civil servants who had previously fled from Transylvania formed the Közalkalmazottak Kispesti Beszerzési Csoportja (Supply Co-Operative of Kispest Public Employees) and, led by the parish priest of Szentlőrinc, Béla Wimmerth, they turned to the president of the National Assembly with a request for a suitable plot of land for the purpose of the garden city, in accordance with the Landed Property Act. Their petition was passed on to the Országos Földbirtokrendező Bíróság (National Landed Property Court) within the Ministry of Agriculture by the president of the National Assembly, together with his positive recommendation.

The Köztisztviselők Kertgazdasági Otthona Pestszentlőrinc (Petszentlőrinc Garden Estate Home of Civil Servants) was founded in October, 1920, with 250 members, a number that later grew to 800, settling finally (around 1930) at about 280–300. The fluctuation was as great then as it was later. A number of nonrefugee officials joined the originally mostly Transylvanian and north- and south-Hungarian members. There were an ex-minister, several secretaries of state, and junior secretaries of state among the 36 elected members of the board. The 310 acres taken from the 2,400-acre estate of the late Miklós Szemere (on whom, incidentally, the novelist Gyula Krúdy modelled the well-known Hungarian literary character Eduard Alvinczi) gave rise to a dispute between the legal heirs and the Society that was to last several years. The conflict was about both the amount of land sought and the price per *négyszögöl* (1 négyszögöl = 3.57 square meters), which was fixed in grain rather than money because of inflation (about 10 kilos of grain per négyszögöl). Finally, in 1925, the Society acquired about 170 acres at 1.7 Pengős per négyszögöl, which at that time was considered extremely cheap. That was when the Society was officially transformed into a cooperative. The area was finally parceled out and allocated to members in 1929, following a few years of wrangling over the allotment maps.

The colony was soon given a streetcar service, electricity, and telephone lines. The planning of the area, the roads and pavements, as well as the construction of the waterworks, were managed entirely from the community's own resources. The waterworks was a particularly impressive achievement. Its cost (400,000 Pengő) was raised almost entirely by the community, with only a 10,000 Pengő government subsidy. The ideal "garden city" was taken into consideration at the time of the parceling of the land; at the center of the colony there was a main square of about 4,000 négyszögöl.

Each of the two main roads of the garden city is 25 meters wide, including the pavements. The rest of the streets are all 18 meters wide, which is well above the average width of a street. A "green strip" of ornamental plants and shrubbery separates the pavements from the roads. The size of an individual plot was between 200 and 600 négyszögöl. According to the original plan only 25 percent of the total land was to be used for the erection of buildings. Areas were generously set aside for public purposes: 1,200 négyszögöl for the waterworks (the garden of which later became one of the centers of social life with tennis courts, dance floors for garden parties, bowling lanes, etc.); 1,500 négyszögöl for schools; 1,200 négyszögöl for the National Scout Association (the Scout House that was built here became the other social center); and 1,000 négyszögöl for the Roman Catholic church and presbytery. Apart from this, there were further areas reserved for the Protestant church and parsonage, the cooperative offices, business premises, and the casino, as well as other cultural and sporting institutions.

The streets and the squares were named after Transylvanian towns and regions. These street names have survived, apart from those few which were judged to have too strong connotations, like Hargitha Square, and such streets as Királyhágó, Fogaras, and Kolozsvár, which, to the genuine sorrow of the locals, were renamed Tatabanya Square, Vörös Fény, Dugó, and Tarkő, respectively, after 1945.

The Society's regulation aiming to secure the "garden city character" of the colony states that

> . . . buildings can be erected no less than 5 meters away from the edge of the road, and in the forecourts gardens must be cultivated. Only gable-roofed or flat-roofed, villa-style houses with at least two rooms may be built in St. Imre Colony, the appearance of which serve to emphasize the garden city character . . . only such stone, iron, wire or lath fences can be erected—to a minimum height of 170 cm—which are pleasing to the observer.

Raising animals—with the exception of poultry—was forbidden. The planting of the green strips along the pavements with flowers and trees was obligatory, the same species to be used in the whole street. Otherwise the owners were at liberty to choose any type of building; architectural constructions and dimensions were to be according to individual taste and financial situation.

The majority of the 200 buildings were constructed during the Depression, between 1930 and 1936. With one or two exceptions, people lived on tight budgets. The stratum of the so-called Christian middle class—most of the colony's population, since the precondition for acquiring a plot was either to have public employee status or to have a pension—was severely hurt by the Depression. Further research of the records concerning the individual applications for plots and mortgages will likely reveal more about their finances. People could also claim plots in their parents' right.

And it was not uncommon for officials to pass on the subsidized plots to their sons, daughters, or in-laws. There were also a considerable number of young couples just starting out independently.

The breakdown by occupation of the 274 people who owned villas in 1936 is as follows:

81 government, municipal, local officials (secretary of state, counsellor, notary, clerk, etc.)

16 private officials (factory director, manager, engineer, bank clerk)

8 medical and veterinary doctors (state-employed)

2 solicitors

76 teachers (university lecturer, schoolmaster, secondary, elementary, and nursery school)

16 post office employees (counsellor, supervisor, officer)

5 public transport employees

16 railway employees (supervisor, officer)

1 boat captain

11 judicial employees (judge, official)

19 military personnel (the widow of a lieutenant general, colonel, retired lieutenant colonel, major, captain, lieutenant, second lieutenant)

5 vicars, religious instructors (Roman Catholic, Protestant)

1 museum officer

1 agronomist

1 sculptor

1 movie director

1 fencing instructor

People often took out mortgages to build their houses, and most of them opted for the so-called L.A.B. mortgage, which had favorable terms. It was provided by the Lakásépítési Állandó Bizottság (Permanent Homebuilding Committee) to public employees and to people with state pensions. These home-building loans were at 7 percent interest, with a 20-year payment schedule. One could finance up to 60 percent of the overall cost of building. Borrowers put up their property for security with first right of land registration, together with the rent allowances given to public employees and pensioners. Others borrowed money privately, and some private officials took out an M.A.B.I. mortgage (provided by the Magán Alkalmazottak Biztosítási Intézete/ Private Employees' Insurance Company/ through the L.A.B.). The average 5,000–6,000 Pengő mortgage meant a severe financial strain for the members, since many of them were paying the arrears of the cost of the land and the installments of the waterworks. Several public schemes proposed by the Society could not be realized for the same reason.

The idea of a cooperative business was abandoned for financial reasons. Fortunately, there was no real need for it, since the new colony attracted tradesmen. Grocery shops (among them the No. 111 branch of the "Public Employees' Store"), needlework, hairdressing salons and fashion shops, ironmongers, paint stores, drugstores, tobacco shops, butchers, and workshops of upholsterers and watchmakers stood along the edge of the colony on the other side of Üllői Út. In 1932 the state police set up their 110th patrol room in the colony, and the post office established a branch in the same year. The four-form elementary school for boys and girls opened in 1933, together with the Divine Providence Apothecary. The B.Sz.K.R.T. (Budapest Public Transport Service) even ran a night service for theatergoers. The fact that the community lobbied the authorities for years to drop the 10 fillér fare supplement, charged because the colony was beyond Határ út (the city boundary road), shed light on its members' general financial situation. Scores of people walked to the Roman Catholic Church of Lőrinc on Sundays rather than pay the extra fare of 10 fillérs. The pride of the colony was the so-called Fogadalmi Kereszt (Cross of the Pledge), a monument done by János Fadrusz, which was paid for from private donations of sums of between 50 fillérs and 10 Pengős and from money raised at various social functions. The Society's Gazette and its minutes of general meetings are filled with complaints about financial problems and high overheads.

The charter residents of St. Imre were a Christian, middle-class group. Their colony was a special phenomenon of Hungarian suburbanization because it was generally the lower classes who moved to the residential outskirts of the cities. The middle and upper classes usually stayed inside the urban centers. In the outer ring of the Pest side, there were a few similar residential settlements of the lower middle class (like Mátyásföld, Rákosliget, and Sashalom) with the same family homes but, generally, working-class neighborhoods dominated the cities' outlying areas. St. Imre is a special case. Because of the forced migration of a society of administrators, bureaucrats, and intelligentsia from the annexed territories, a homogeneous group of the Christian middle class settled in the same place, and their world-view left its mark on the newly established neighborhood. It is not by chance that Hungarian public buildings after the Treaty of Trianon were designed in a baroque style. The post–Trianon Hungarian society, according to Gyula Szekfű, was a neo-baroque society, and the neo-baroque architectural style corresponded to the style of the society.[6] Contrary to other new middle-class quarters that had already been built in the Bauhaus style by the Jewish middle class in other parts of Budapest, here we find a *"ressentiment-neighborhood,"* on the edge of the growing capital.

It mirrors the "persisting old regime," as Arno Mayer calls it. In the small world of this garden city, we see an almost urban life with a mixture of bourgeois and gentry elements. The residents, wishing to defend their lost world in their new neighborhood, reestablished their beloved but sometimes old-fashioned society based on values that they cherished but which were fast disappearing. This settlement was on the edge of the modern city in both time and space, and it represents the contradictory social development of interwar Hungary.

The Social Life of Garden City

Although people living in the colony were far from being well-off, they modeled their lifestyle on that of the bourgeoisie, often stretching their budgets beyond their means. Almost everyone considered themselves part of the middle class. Heads of families for several generations back had pursued middle-class professions. The prevalent lifestyle of the colony reflects this, and the still existing examples of its material culture testify to the same effect. But this bourgeois model still carries many rural elements, and it is mixed with the remnants of an earlier lifestyle modeled after the nobility. Although the modernism of the Bauhaus had captivated the professional classes elsewhere in Budapest, here the majority of the villas looked like country houses.

During the summer the intensive social life of St. Imre was centered on the waterworks garden and the open areas surrounding the main square. Here, tennis courts and bowling lanes had been laid down and garden parties were frequently held. The Scout House—which was handed over to the community by Count Pál Teleki upon its completion—became home to the major social events: to the balls, the various performances, concerts, and exhibitions. The Gazette was the main organ of communal life in the colony; apart from briefing people on the news of the cooperative and the daily life of the colony, it also organized such events as the tree and flower planting project. It also took sides in such political issues as the peace plan of Flandin, the

French foreign minister, against which the community unanimously protested through the Magyar Revizios Liga (Hungarian Revisionist League). Irredentism was, understandably, very strong in Garden City. Campfires were regularly held by the Cross of the Pledge and in the garden of the Scout House, commemorating the lost "Transylvanian Homeland."

There was a strong St. Imre cult in the colony. Almost the whole population of Garden City took part in the annual Emerican Ball (Emericus is the Latin version of the name Imre), organized by the Emericana Group, which was the culmination of the colony's social life. Besides the social occasions affecting the whole of the community, gatherings involving sometimes as many as 25–30 people were frequently held in private homes. These gatherings played an important role in the life of the community. They provided the opportunities for young people to meet, meetings that led to tennis games and, quite often, marriages. Marriages within the colony were relatively frequent. Since the world of the population was regarded as belonging to the "genteel" class, there were no special social barriers and the closest-knit circles were based primarily on mutual affinities.

The majority of women were not employed outside of the home. They ran the households, typically with the help of a least one servant. "Good" housewives who ran the households themselves enjoyed a very high esteem in the colony. The organizing of cooking, washing, and perhaps preserving took up their mornings. Explicitly female gatherings were held in the afternoons. They included tea parties, "at homes," and even card games, although playing cards was regarded as improper behavior for a "Hungarian lady." Quite a number of women took part in the so-called needlework afternoons, where they embroidered tablecloths and even dresses, using the motifs of Sárköz, Buzsák, Matyó, Torockó, Kalotaszeg, and Rábaköz. These dresses were worn only on special occasions. A number of houses had a "Hungarian corner" where these embroideries and other rustic objects were displayed. Mainly, however, it was the porch of the house where these objects were placed. The often rustic appearance of the porch stood in sharp contrast with the otherwise bourgeois taste of the furniture in the rest of the rooms. The best embroideries were put on display in the Scout House every year. The magazines that women subscribed to corresponded to the bourgeois taste of the period, and the novels of Hercegh and Harsányi were featured most frequently on their bookshelves. Specifically male parties were less frequent and took place in smaller circles. Young people mostly met on the sports fields.

The squares that provided a stage for communal life, indeed, the whole environment, reflected the community's past way of life. Each member of the colony used and looked upon the communal spaces as his own property, since these had been designed by public consent, according to communal requirements.

Public areas were developed for recreational and cultural purposes, not for business and transport functions. Business premises were deliberately kept out of the street image; they were restricted to the boundaries of the colony, where a shopping lane grew up over the years. A busy, noisy, and crowded shopping street did not fit into the community's sense of a smart residential district.

Although similar colonies exist (for example in Mátyásföld, Rákosliget), St. Imre Garden City represents a particular type of suburb. In some Western European and North American metropolises the rich middle class moved to the elegant green suburbs, leaving the crowded inner areas for the poorer people, but it was the other way around in Budapest, especially on the Pest side. The well-to-do bourgeoisie lived in the elegant apartment buildings and the inner residential areas that were surrounded by a ring of poorer suburbs. Erzsébet, Kispest, Kőbánya, Csepel, Angyalföld, Újpest, etc. can be regarded as examples of these suburbs. The less well-to-do middle class moved to such areas that were developed still further outside this ring, in the place of earlier summer residential areas (Pestszentlőrinc, Parkváros, Rákosliget, Mátyásföld). These were entirely residential districts: inhabitants here commuted to the city every day, often spending one to two hours on the journey.

The Scenes of Family Life

The family home was the most important center of social life; this was true even in the case of modern dwellings. On the whole, the houses were built according to the conceptions of the creators of the community, leaving the professional architect little room for innovation. The majority of the houses were one- or two-story buildings, with an occasional attic. Usually they consisted of one or two bedrooms plus, perhaps, a guest room on the first floor, a dining room, a sitting room and/or parlor, the servant's room by the kitchen, a bathroom and toilet by the hall, and a porch or veranda. The latter served as one of the most important areas of family life from spring to autumn. The houses frequently had two (front and back) entrances (see Figure 6.1). The way to the sitting room and the dining room usually led through the spacious hall. The bedrooms either faced the garden or were upstairs. The large glassed-in porches and the terraces also looked on to the gardens. Quite often, the porch served as the main entrance. The kitchen and the servant's room were frequently put in

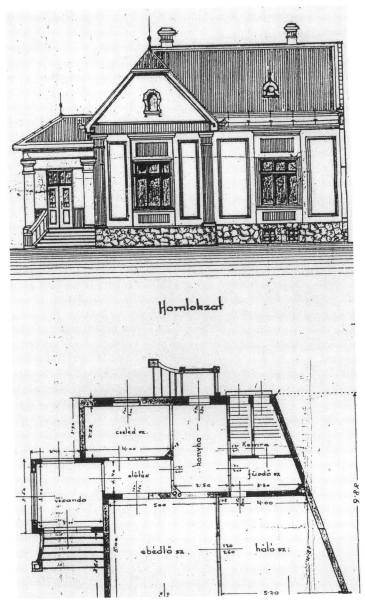

Figure 6.1 House Plan, St. Imre Gardens, ca. 1929.

Figure 6.2   House, St. Imre Gardens. Photograph by author.

the basement, or sometimes the servant and his or her family were moved to the small building at the bottom of the garden. The rooms that were used by the whole family (dining room, parlor, porch) were generally very large (5×5, 5×6 meters). In Figure 6.2 a house is shown with a porch. The hall, the dining room, and the parlor were separated by disproportionately large double doors, which were left open during family and social gatherings, thus achieving a space of considerable size spreading over three to four rooms. The kitchens were usually placed out of the way, and not even in the smallest houses were they used for dining or sleeping. Food was served in the dining room, and on festive occasions the table was set in almost every household with the highly cherished family silverware. Often in the dining room there was a glass cabinet used for storing the silver plates and cutlery. The piano was a compulsory feature of the parlor. The tables, shelves, and cabinets were crowded with lace covers, as were the walls with pictures. Although the furnishing of particular rooms varied from one household to the other according to individual taste, the layout and the use of space of the house as a whole was almost identical throughout the colony.

During the week, the family gathered together for supper every day,

173

since the majority of the officials worked in Budapest and arrived home late in the evening. Large family gatherings were frequent on holidays. Families spent a lot of time sitting in the glassed-in porches, on the terraces, and in the garden when the weather permitted. Eating outside in the garden in the bower designated for this purpose, or in the small, open-sided summer house, was common practice. The garden was usually split into two parts: first there was a grassy area around the house decorated with flower beds, featuring miniature pools, rose arbors, pine trees and other evergreens, and perhaps small statues. Fruit trees, vines, and perhaps a smaller vegetable plot made up the other half. The small barns and storehouses stood in the back of the garden, together with the servants' accommodations. Almost nobody had garages, since—even as late as in the 1940s—cars were rare. Often the original larger plots were divided up into smaller parcels of land, frequently resulting in the loss of character in house and garden alike.

The population of Garden City was significantly altered after World War II. With the evacuation of 1944 and the deportation and forced migration of the 1950s, as well as the severe drop in living standards following the war (one of the most frequent occupations in Garden City during the 1950s was night porter), the society of the colony declined. That left a mark on its external appearance, too. Houses were split into smaller flats, gardens into smaller parcels. Many buildings were damaged or destroyed in the war, since some heavy fighting took place in the area. The condition of the houses deteriorated greatly, and the original ornamentation can be spotted only occasionally. Very few buildings have been restored to their past condition; generally the original stuccoes have been removed and the houses have been renovated in contemporary styles.

Connotational Signs in the Architecture of Garden City

I have studied the architectonic connotations of the colony, which I assumed to be characteristic of its population, but if one were to share Umberto Eco's opinion and regard every aspect of culture as communicational artifact, then one could just as well investigate the components of the behavior, the fashion, or even the diet of this group. Since ornamentation was only occasionally visible, only the frontal designs of the buildings were examined. Naturally, all this is based on the assumption that an architectonic system of signs exists and has a sociological interpretation.

Since Charles Morris published his classic *Foundations of the General Theory of Signs*, semiotics—which had earlier been limited to the field of linguistics—has become a truly interdisciplinary science, making headway in several other areas of social sciences.[7] The historical disciplines—with the sole exception of ethnography—have made little use of this method, although it is well suited to complement other research methods. In semiotics the point of departure is that every aspect of culture is a system of signs, or communication. Although a historical analysis of semiotics from Peirce to Derrida to Gadamer is not possible in this short chapter, it is necessary to define a few categories which I believe to be also applicable in historical investigations.

It was Roland Barthes who worked out the denotation-connotation antithesis and applied it to several fields. According to this, for every notion there is a simple notation (denotation) and a superimposed notation (connotation). Umberto Eco looks upon the whole world as a "semiotic apparatus" and interprets architecture as one of the most important communicative facts.[8] In the case of architecture, denotative and connotative functions mingle, since architectural objects are primarily designed to function, and their communicative function is only secondary. According to Eco, however, practical objects also belong to the "facts of culture," and sooner or later every practice gets transformed into the symbol of this very practice, and itself advances and denotes a particular *mode* of practice; i.e., it communicates the way it is used.[9] In the case of architecture Gábor Hajnóczy distinguishes between a functional level and a communicative level that has cultural, ideological, artistic, etc., meaning.[10] What an architectural object communicates is not the function it fulfills, but the way in which this function is fulfilled. Naturally, an architectural object cannot be treated in a homogeneous fashion, since some of its parts pertain more to its functional level, while others—groups of certain architectonic forms (the so-called morphemes)—carry connotative meanings. An architectural object is studied first of all on a semantic level, although its syntactic and pragmatic dimensions can also be investigated. It was Eco who distinguished between purely architectonic, sociohistorical, and aesthetic connotations.

Can such sociohistorical connotations be discovered in the architecture of the St. Imre Colony, and do they really characterize its inhabitants? In the next few examples I shall address this question.

Since such unambiguous signs as the stuccoed coats of arms and the original ornamentations have already disappeared from the fronts of the houses, we have to rely on the architectonic design of the buildings. These houses are not particularly beautiful, nor architectonically particularly interesting; still, together they represent something. They reflect the aesthetic world and the "world-view" of their

Figure 6.3 House, St. Imre Gardens. Photograph by author.

original builders. It is important, therefore, that one should examine how they saw these buildings, what effects they hoped to achieve with them, what aspirations and what "meaning" these houses expressed. We can trace a number of signs, paraphrases of earlier architectural styles, analogies of former traditions that specifically characterized this social group and set these buildings apart from the houses built in other suburbs of Budapest by other social strata. In the following list of architectonic symbols the above characteristics and analogies are apparent.

The symbol of the "family home" has in itself an added meaning (both linguistically and architectonically) beyond its function. This was stated in the Gazette of Garden City almost in the form of a manifesto. Starting a family house with a little land that was to be a home for several generations was the primary intention of all the members of the Society from the beginning. They wanted to create a home that would give lasting protection to a group of genteel officials suddenly snatched from the security of a feudal state, battered by the storms of history and the crises of capitalism. They built family "fortresses." These "fortresses"—and that was explicitly stated—took their pattern from the old family mansions or country houses, following

Figure 6.4 House, St. Imre Garden City. Photograph by author.

them both conceptually and in their outside appearance. We can see in Figure 6.3 the symmetry of the houses, as well as the middle room that protrudes like a steeple or a dome, radiating strength. The frontal design that is often indented with projections, the triple, sometimes arched windows, the ornamented pediments, and the gables strive after elegance. The aesthetic world of the builders is expressed in the design of the mansard roofs and attics, the roof terraces and loggias. This aesthetic world also differed from that of merchants, tradesmen, and workers in its architectural manifestations. The disproportionate height of the rooms, or of the floor level, the extravagance of the frequent steeples and domes, all meant to illustrate the grandness, the grace, and the social standing of the family. The domed structure of the house shown in Figure 6.4 seems to imitate—perhaps the analogy is not stretched too far—that of the baroque palace of Gernyeszeg.

The terraced house seen in Figure 6.2 can be regarded as a characteristic, rural, architectural analogy. The evidences of palace-type construction are even more striking, with variously shaped turrets. Some building pinnacles seem to have been patterned after the Bethlen castle of Küküllő, but imitations of Gothic and Renaissance turrets can also be found. The height of the occasional upper level in

Figure 6.5   House, St. Imre Garden City. Photograph by author.

these turrets is often so minimal that it is impossible to stand up, making these spaces practically unusable. They are just as out of proportion and useless (from the practical point of view) as are the grand stairways which were added to the front of often quite small buildings.

In some cases the steeple of a small Transylvanian church has been transplanted to domestic architecture. The arched or geometrical pediments and frontispieces often seen in the Renaissance and Baroque castles of Transylvania have similar connotative functions, even on very simple little houses. The mansard roofs, roof terraces, balconies, and loggias reflect a little more urban influence. But the balconies and loggias shown in Figure 6.5 are also so small that they still could have no use, only a symbolic function. Similar phenomena can be observed in the gardens, especially in the case of the small parks surrounding the houses. The tiny graveled garden paths, small pools and ponds, rock gardens, the circular- and oval-shaped flower beds screened off by trimmed hedges also imitate the parks.

The design and the use of streets and squares, again, followed rural residential patterns. Continuous rows of houses along the street front were not planned nor permitted in the colony. Shopping lanes were moved outside the boundaries of the settlement. The putting up of any kinds of advertisements or signs was firmly controlled.

Naturally, the above-mentioned architectonic motifs cannot be generalized and can be used only in conjunction with other information. Their meanings are not nearly as varied and specific as, for example, that of the folk costume (one classic example of ethnosemiotic descriptions was given about Moravian folk costumes).[11] Despite the imperfect reading of architectural motifs, I still believe that we can find motifs that can characterize a given social stratum in a given period. The simple semiotic analysis of the architecture of a typical "small-town" district such as the St. Imre Colony, built in the vicinity of a metropolis, can provide source material to a sociohistoric study of social history. It might also open up new possibilities in comparative studies, since it facilitates the comparison of different material cultures of the same social group in various countries of the region. From these comparisons we can infer important factors of social life that would not result from other historicoeconomic analyses.

I believe the above architectural examples faithfully characterize certain Weltanschauung-type messages of a social group when they are looked upon as cultural objects of this group. Almost all the buildings suggest the mixing of a former lifestyle with the partially accepted bourgeois models. These messages are what even today make the profile of the former St. Imre Garden City both different and homogeneous.

Notes

1. Béla Hamvas, *The Five Spirits* (Bern, 1985).
2. Marshall Berman, *All That Is Solid Melts into Air* (New York, 1982); Roland Barthes, *The Eiffel Tower and Other Mythologies.*
3. Umberto Eco, "Social Life as a Sign System," in *Structuralism* (Oxford, 1973).
4. Jane Jacobs, *The Death and Life of Great American Cities* (New York, 1961).
5. Endre Liber, "Budapest a Menekültügy Szolgálatában" (Budapest in the service of the refugee problem), in *A Nagy Vihar Hajótöröttei* (Shipwrecked people of the great storm) (Budapest, 1927); "Vagonlakók a Pályaudvarokon" (Freight-car people in the railway stations), *Népszava* (November 23, 1919); "Ahol a Menekültek Városa Épül" (Where the refugee city is built), *Virradat* (March 22, 1922).
6. Gyula Szekfű, *Három Nemzedék és Ami Utána Következik (Three generations and what follows afterwards)* (Budapest, 1934), 404.
7. Charles Morris, *Foundations of the General Theory of Signs* (Chicago, 1938).

8. Umberto Eco, "Theory of Semiotics," in Thomas Sebeok, ed., *Architecture and Communication* (Bloomington, Ind., 1975).

9. Vilmos Voigt, *Bevezetés a Szemiotikába (Introduction to semiotics)* (Budapest, 1975).

10. Gábor Hajnóczy, *Építészet-Szemiotikai Vizsgálódások* (Studies in architectural semiotics) (Epiteszettudomany, 1972).

11. Peter Bogatyrev, *The Functions of Folk Costumes in Moravian Slovakia* (The Hague-Paris, 1971).

Part IV

POPULAR CULTURE: HETEROGENEITY AND INTEGRATION

*I*N THE TURBULENT half-century after 1880, Budapest and New York cobbled together populations of the most diverse cultures into metropolitan entities of enormous political and economic power. Could they, out of polyglot masses, create a community identity? And what, if such were achieved, would be its relationship to the nations in which each would have to define its collective future? The very process by which the several subcultures, both ethnic and class, would modify their particularity to find a common consciousness as New Yorkers or Budapesters would inevitably separate them in a new and often more defined way from their respective national contexts. Construction of a common city culture out of its different, often uprooted human components involved a partial deconstruction and transformation of the prevenient and still powerful traditional cultural system.

Urban integration and a fraying of the ties of the city to the nation were part of a single process. Despite New York's greater size and cultural complexity, it developed a strikingly autonomous metropolitan identity by the 1920s. New Yorkers high and low began to conceive of their creation of a new multiethnic culture as a model for a cosmopolitan America that would in many ways transcend traditional Anglo-Saxon Protestant culture. Briefly put, New York—multicultural, energetic, modern, hedonistic—began to be seen by many New Yorkers as what America should be. In Budapest, by contrast, the persistent social power of the landed elite, reenforcing and reenforced by bourgeois nationalism, imposed Magyar language and culture as a virtually absolute condition of the city's acceptance and the economic and social assimilation of the ethnic groups that composed it. This policy of Magyar primacy inhibited the development of an urban self-image in which Budapest's ethnic pluralism could be embraced as a civic principle, or be asserted without the shame of foreignness or the taint of infidelity. To be sure, the intellectuals sought to redefine "Hungarianness" in ways consistent with modernity, democracy, and ethnic tolerance. The common man's cosmopolitanism, however, had to take the form of a universalism of creed, such as Marxism or Catholicism, rather than one of cultural pluralism or metropolitan worldliness. Moreover, the traumatic experience of defeat and dismemberment after World War I dealt a crippling blow to Budapest's development of a cosmopolitan urban identity in the 1920s, the very time when New York, sustained by its vigorous culture industry, consolidated its urban self-image as America's model of modernity and as a smart megalopolitan village: Gotham.

Of all the problems raised in this book, the construction of modern metropolitan culture is perhaps the most complex. It is also the most recent to be explored by historians. Since modern culture is strongly defined by class, we have addressed popular and high culture in two separate sections, although their interpenetration will emerge in both cities as an important subtheme. In the present section on popular culture, the four authors have chosen to sink shafts in the areas of entertainment and commercial journalism. There they explore within a feasible scope important institutional vehicles by means of which the disparate and often contending ethnic and class components of each metropolitan society became integrated on a platform of a shared expressive and informational culture. The materials for building that platform came largely from below, from the several ethnic communities, in their autochthonous arts, such as neighborhood theater, pub, and street entertainment. But the organization, integration, and distribution of these came from above, from entrepreneurs and educated authors or artists.

For New York, Robert Snyder has chosen to illuminate the process through the vastly popular art of vaudeville. He shows how entrepreneurs, eager to exploit a citywide market, brought originally distinct ethnic theatrical acts onto a common stage. Through chain theaters, all New Yorkers assembled as one public to enjoy their own cultural variety. Snyder records the loss as well as the gain from this centripetal process. On the one hand, the new, common entertainment culture bonded New Yorkers of every sort, with the Irish enjoying the

Jewish comedians, the Germans the Italian singers, etc. On the other, the standarization of stock types blanched out the richness and candor of each ethnic group's expressive culture, along with the national or religious aggressivity that could no longer be tolerated on a democratized metropolitan stage. The blacks, however, remained the butt of hostile stereotypes—in theater as elsewhere the permanent underclass of the emergent multicultural society. Black actors and musicians too were long banned from careers in commercial entertainment. Here the capitalist entrepreneurs of show biz and their allegedly cosmopolitan consumers combined to sustain and reenforce America's deepest social prejudice.

New York vaudeville had no exact analogue in Budapest. Yet Péter Hanák demonstrates that operetta, the most popular theatrical form of the Hungarian middle class, performed similar integrative functions for the multinational Habsburg Empire that vaudeville fulfilled in multiethnic America. The gently spoofing wit of operetta's social satire blunted the edge of class and ethnic antagonism—and also of the war between the sexes—in a pleasure-oriented synthesis of different national cultural elements. But the ideological center of operetta's cultural collage is imperial, not, as in New York, metropolitan. While middle-class publics high and low from all the nationalities of the Habsburg Empire delighted in the operetta's sprightly suprapolitical, ironic play, Hanák shows that many nationalist critics in Budapest deplored the inadequate presence of Magyar virtue in the mix. In operetta as in so much else in Budapest history, the guardians of national purity identified cosmopolitanism as an alien product of which both city and nation must be suspicious. That there were such voices in America goes without saying, but they had no comparable importance in New York itself.

Journalism too played its part in the development of a unified metropolitan consciousness, often with the comic spirit as its medium. Géza Buzinkay, tracing the use of the joke in Budapest's popular comic weeklies, finds the same tendency toward multiethnic variety that we have seen in New York's vaudeville. Both genres employ ethnic stereotyping. In Budapest, as in New York, there were comic weeklies that blanched the stereotypes into the same unaggressive cheerfulness found in New York's apolitical commercial entertainment. But with the rise of anti-Semitism, some comic weeklies were hardened by Magyar hegemonic culture, within whose confining frame the more liberal urban forces had to proceed with circumspection in their struggle for influence. The cultural pluralism that was fostered by both democracy and the capitalist entertainment industry in New York was somewhat stunted by nationalist politics in Budapest.

Neil Harris's chapter, "Covering New York," analyzes another agency of integration of the culture of New York: the press. His perspective on his subject may be fruitfully contrasted with Snyder's treatment of vaudeville. Snyder writes his history from the bottom, Harris from the top. Snyder, exploring the roots of his genre in particularized ethnic communities, shows how they were synthesized through the metropolitanwide cultural medium, in part through the careers of actors. In the process of their own assimilation through their profession, actors became the agents of the substantive transformation of their ethnic heritages. In the case of the press, Harris stresses more strongly the role of the press lord as integrating agent. In his narrative too we see the patchwork quilt of the metropolitan population stitched together by the press lord's interest in creating, through puzzles, comics, scandals, and urban news, a consumer public whose tastes would be diverse but not divisive. Eroding the local community press by providing urban news and entertainment in vivid, basically simplified English, the mass dailies molded a public whose sense of metropolitan and personal identity could bracket and transcend allegiance to any exclusive subculture, whether class or ethnic. Celebrity culture, with its heroes created on hedonistic rather than political premises, was a further instrument of the press in reshaping immigrants into American urbanists.

The power of the mass press in modern New York was symbolized by the crucial placement of its proud buildings—the *New York World*'s early skyscraper at the city's political center, near City Hall; the *Herald* on the square that bears its name beside the great department stores that gathered around it in a prime locus of the new consumerism; and finally, the *Times* on the square where journalism, commerce, and theater converged as New York became the culture capital of the nation in the new century. In exposing the role of the great journals in the city's transmutation of an apparently intractable social multiplicity into a loose-jointed, polymorphous culture of the new, Harris's essay provides a strong foundation for the meaning given to New York by its artists and writers which, in the final section of this volume, will be seen in strongest contrast to Budapest.

Chapter 7

Immigrants, Ethnicity, and Mass Culture: The Vaudeville Stage in New York City: 1880–1930

ROBERT W. SNYDER

*I*N EVERY SENSE of the term, vaudeville was the most popular form of theater in turn-of-the-century New York. Its form—separate acts strung together to make a complete bill—was the direct descendant of the mid-nineteenth century variety theater, which had catered to carousing working-class and middle-class men in saloons and music halls. But vaudeville was variety in a new context. Beginning in the 1880s, showmen seeking to attract the wives and families of male variety fans, and so to create a wider and more lucrative audience, banned liquor from their houses and censored some of their bawdy acts. They jettisoned the older name, "variety," with its stigma of vice and alcohol, and adopted the classier-sounding name, "vaudeville." The result was a significantly broader audience.

Vaudeville's generous reach placed it at the center of popular culture in New York City, where it fostered communication across the lines of ethnicity, class, gender, and geography. Vaudeville became an arena for circularity, the reciprocal exchange of cultural influences. In the middle of a modern metropolis, it fostered a cultural dialogue between native and immigrant, working class, middle class, and upper class, Jews and Gentiles. The result was a many-sided conversation, in a context midway between the street culture of the Bowery and the motion picture companies of the twentieth century. Vaudeville combined nationwide theater chains and intimate contact between artist and audience, old staples like blackface comedy and new elements like movies.

Among the most important participants in this dialogue were the newest arrivals in the city, first- and second-generation ethnics and blacks, who were strongly represented among New York's vaudevillians. Maggie Cline, the lusty-voiced "Irish Queen" and darling of the gallery gods at Tony Pastor's 14th Street Theatre, was the daughter of a shoe factory foreman. James "Jimmy Vee" Bevacqua, a blackface singer and dancer from Mount Vernon, New York, was the American-born son of immigrants from Calabria, Italy. Eddie Cantor, an immigrant's son from the Lower East Side, grew up "on the sidewalks of New York with an occasional fall into the gutter." Eubie Blake—pianist, composer, and son of former slaves—started out by playing ragtime piano in a Baltimore brothel.[1]

All of them performed on the New York vaudeville stage between 1900 and 1925. Their backgrounds make an important point: vaudeville and related twentieth century cultural forms—movies, Tin Pan Alley, and radio—were not simply imposed on blacks and ethnics. Instead, they often supplied both the talent and audiences for vaudeville and its successors.[2]

In the process, they participated in a series of cultural transformations. They helped fashion new ethnic identities that were formed more from American popular culture than from Old World ways. They contributed to a new urban language and style of popular culture that drew on both nineteenth century working-class egalitarianism and the newer, hedonistic self-expression of consumerism. Their vitality and energy challenged and subverted the Victorianism of middle-class, native-born Americans.

But there was an irony to this: despite their immigrant background, many vaudevillians' portrayal of ethnic culture was two-dimensional, concocted more from stock characters than from any serious exploration of ethnic realities. The explanations for this phenomenon lie in the context in which immigrants and their children took to the vaudeville stage. If our analysis is confined to who appeared onstage, vaudeville appears to be the domain of the sons and daughters of immigrant New York. But if we examine the conditions under which they performed, a far more complicated picture emerges.

Although vaudeville's creative roots lay in a world of tenements, immigrants, saloon singers, cheap theaters, and streetcorner wiseguys, the vaudevillians disseminated a commercial ethnic culture that was more concerned with mass-market appeal than with the fullest possible exploration of ethnic life. The result was that vaudeville portrayed ethnic groups and racial minorities, the most traduced of all, in an oversimplified manner. Nuances were boiled down to a few basic stereotypes with just enough reality to be plausible, but too little to provide a full portrait.

Such portrayals—whether in song, comedy, or sketches—could be mined for more complex meanings than appeared on the surface. And representations of ethnics were bound to be problematic at a time when the stresses of immigration and acculturation left many in a continual state of upheaval. Still, vaudeville was not as generous as it might have been to ethnic culture, and at its worst it set a precedent for the simplistic portrayals of racial and ethnic groups found in movies and television.[3]

Despite these problems, the mainstream of popular culture clearly had its lures for the vaudevillians. Vaudeville—even its very form of separate acts—was a capacious arena, capable of accommodating and rewarding a diverse collection of performers.

The road from streetcorner hoofing in hard-pressed immigrant neighborhoods to bigtime vaudeville and national stardom could take years, and it frequently passed through rough and confusing cultural terrain. The hardships of show business life and the challenge of performing before diverse and demanding audiences all took their toll. The path was blazed largely by the Irish, who appeared on the variety stage in the 1880s and 1890s.[4] These Irish acts, performed either by Irish people or people pretending to be Irish according to the conventions of the nineteenth century theater, predominated on the vaudeville stage. They were followed in prominence by blackface and Dutch (meaning German) dialect comics, reflecting all three groups' visibility in American society.[5] Tony Pastor featured Kitty O'Neill, a jig dancer, and John W. Kelly, "The Rolling Mill Man" who told humorous stories of his days working in the sheet metal mills.[6] Maggie Cline, "the Irish Queen," rocked Pastor's audiences with "Throw Him Down, McCloskey," an epic ballad of a boxing match. In the 1880s, the Jerry Cohan family, including young George M., toured presenting sketches that included "The Irish Hibernia" or "Hibernicon."[7] All pioneered the path from ethnic origins to national stardom that would become so important in vaudeville.[8]

Succeeding generations of ethnic vaudevillians followed in a continuum. The Jews, who arrived later than the Irish, gained sway in the early twentieth century. Black artists established a beachhead in vaudeville, which helped make their profound contribution to twentieth century popular culture possible.

Such vaudevillians and their successors learned their craft in countless settings. Growing up in the Yorkville section of Manhattan, Jimmy Cagney learned his first moves from a boy at the Lenox Hill

Settlement House.[9] Growing up in Philadelphia, Honi Coles, a black dancer, witnessed scenes that were repeated many times on the streets of New York.

> We used to dance on the street corners in the summertime, 'cause this was our real form of entertainment. We had no playgrounds or . . . other facilities in which to entertain ourselves. And it became highly competitive. Other neighborhoods would send guys over and . . . we would all compete with each other . . . on the street corner, until somebody late at night would say, "Get off that corner!" and they'd throw some water on us.[10]

The candy stores of the turn-of-the-century Lower East Side nurtured abundant talent, as a University Settlement House report observed in 1899.

> Occasionally a dozen or more youngsters are entertained here by a team of aspiring amateur comedians of the ages of sixteen or seventeen, whose sole ambition is to shine on the stage of some Bowery variety theater. The comedian or comedians will try their new "hits" on their critical audiences (and a more critical one can not be found), dance, jig, and re-tell the jokes heard by them in the continuous performance or vaudeville theatres.[11]

From such settings came Jewish Eddie Cantor, who followed vaudeville from the streets to stardom. His memoirs convey a sense of rising like Horatio Alger from rags to riches, of literally moving from one world to another. He interpreted the changes he passed through as living five different lives.[12] However you count them, they show how the promises and possibilities of popular culture—both true and false—lit up the streets of the Lower East Side.

Born on Eldridge Street in 1892, Cantor was orphaned at the age of two and then cared for by his grandmother. His childhood saw frequent moves from one overcrowded apartment to another, tight money, street life, gang fights, petty crime, strike breaking, short-term employment as a clerk, and nights spent sleeping on the roof.[13] His autobiography, complete with regrettable racial stereotyping, captures his drive:

> I grew up lean, big-eyed, eager, eating from grocery barrels, singing in back yards, playing in gutters and on the roofs of houses, and combining with it all the smattering of a public school education. I was not introspective—whatever that is. I simply took to life as a darky takes to rhythms, and vibrated with it. In short, I was a typi-

cal New York street boy who, by a peculiar and deft twist of fortune, eventually lands either in the Bowery Mission or in a bower of roses.[14]

He first appeared on what he called the "regular" stage in 1908, broke and in borrowed pants, at an amateur night show at Miner's Bowery Theatre. The audience was rowdy, and unpopular performers were being given the hook. Cantor took the stage and impersonated vaudeville stars, in itself a testimony to how bigtime vaudeville had permeated the Lower East Side. When he won the contest and a prize of five dollars, he celebrated with a meal in Chinatown. But that night he again slept on a roof.[15]

For the next nine years, Cantor worked his way to the heights of vaudeville. His itinerary reads like a catalogue of vaudeville and related forms of popular culture: more amateur contests; a job in a touring burlesque revue, alternately playing a tramp, a Hebrew comic, and a bootblack; a summer in Coney Island working as a singing waiter in a saloon and as a boardwalk shill; and appearances as a master of ceremonies at Lower East Side wedding halls, in what was apparently an American application of the traditional European Jewish role of *badkhn,* or wedding jester. An apprenticeship in a bigtime act finally paid off in 1917, when he joined the popular and lucrative Ziegfeld Follies.[16]

Cantor's stardom was singular, but his general path was typical. Oral histories, newspaper accounts, and performers' memoirs hint at thousands of others who followed the same route—a few to fame, most to the endless grind of the smalltime theaters and an eventual shift into another career.

Despite the odds against success, vaudeville was egalitarian in a selective, competitive way. It was far more open than formal professions. The start-up costs were minimal, and the key to success was the ability to put an act over by singing, dancing, joking, or doing somersaults in midair. Their capital was in their bodies and their craftsmanship. Family lineage or formal education meant little. As the 1915 *Billboard* noted under its reviews of acts at the Palace, "here genius not birth your rank insures."[17]

So the outsiders trying to become insiders flocked to vaudeville. However hard and precarious such a life might be, it offered unique opportunities for one group—women. Whatever the obstacles facing working-class or immigrant men, women faced all of these *and* the restrictions of sex discrimination. In vaudeville they could see the possibility of an independent career and wages virtually closed to them in other fields.

Dancer Frances Poplawski recognized vaudeville's offer of economic opportunity, security, and cultural expression. Poplawski, the Massachusetts-born daughter of a Polish longshoreman, studied ballet as a girl. But she saw that there was little work for her there.

> Most people who belonged to ballet companies were children of rich people. I could not afford ballet. In other words, my love for vaudeville was for the lucrative place where you knew for a year where you were going to be and you worked all year long and you prayed for a layoff so you could have a rest.[18]

Like Poplawski, Sophie Tucker also found a living in vaudeville. But where Poplawski left the ballet, Tucker left the Yiddish theater. As a woman, Tucker found money and independence virtually closed to her elsewhere. As a Jew, she followed earlier artists who used vaudeville to achieve stardom far beyond their original communities without entirely erasing their older ethnic identification.

Tucker grew up in Hartford, Connecticut, where her immigrant parents ran a delicatessen restaurant with a rooming house upstairs.[19] Most of their patrons were workingmen. Occasionally Jewish theater companies stopped in Hartford and visited her parents' establishment. Sophie, who sang to attract customers, waited on stars of the Yiddish stage, such as Jacob Adler and Boris Thomashefsky. She was thrilled to take an order from Bertha Kalich. But when Adler and Thomashefsky asked Tucker's family to allow Sophie to tour with them, she was against it. "I wasn't keen for it," she recalled in her memoir.

> I had seen how hard it was to make the Jewish plays a success even for one night. It used to be up to Papa to sell the tickets. Many times he was left, holding the bag, with hundreds of seats, meals, and sleeping rooms given free because of no business. I had noticed that this sort of thing didn't happen with the regular American shows.[20]

Despite her love for the Yiddish theater, Tucker was also at home with the "American shows" that outdrew Yiddish productions. She sang Tin Pan Alley hits to attract customers into her parents' establishment and performed at amateur concerts at Hartford's Riverside Park. No stranger to mainstream show business, she visited Saturday matinees at Poli's Vaudeville Theatre and Hartford Opera House, where her favorite performers were "American" musical comedy acts.[21]

Tucker married in her teens, but the marriage soon failed amidst financial troubles, leaving her with a child to support. She left Hartford in 1906 to find work in New York City. In New York she did not go to the Yiddish stage of her youth, but to the Von Tilzer songwriting house of Tin Pan Alley, armed with a reference from vaudevillian Willie Howard. (The sequence was not a testament to Jewish assimilation, but to the increasing Jewish presence in American popular music.) Soon she was singing at Manhattan beer gardens and cafés, avoiding the prostitution that tempted similarly struggling women, and earning $15 a week plus tips singing 50–100 songs nightly at the German Village beer garden on 40th Street off Broadway.[22] It was the beginning of an international career. And it was a long way from being thrilled at waiting on Yiddish players like Bertha Kalich.

Belle Baker (originally Bella Becker) also performed in the Yiddish theater as a child and then crossed over into vaudeville. Her rendition of "Eli, Eli" had great meaning for Jewish audience members, but she was also fluent in other styles. In an interview, she described Sarah Bernhardt as her "inspiration" and asserted that she worked at using melody to "portray pathos and drama" like Bernhardt. A vaudeville program of 1915 called her "The Bernhardt of Songs."[23]

From Bella Becker to Belle Baker to "The Bernhardt of Songs" was a journey followed in some form by every performer who moved from an immigrant neighborhood to bigtime vaudeville. Those who made the trek did not necessarily lose the mark of their origins. But as performers, they drew more and more of their goals, expressions, and identity from the heterogeneous world of popular culture, where ethnicity, class, gender, and mainstream star status combined in complex ways.

Vaudeville stardom did not mean a denial of ethnic identification. Ethnic New Yorkers embraced vaudeville because it presented enough of their culture onstage to affirm their presence in the theater and the metropolis. This affirmation, however, was intimately bound up with the new categories of popular culture stardom.

So it appeared when the Jewish Ross Brothers of Cherry Street on the Lower East Side played Keith's Jefferson on 14th Street under their slogan, "hitting home runs on the fields of song." They drew crowds of people from their old neighborhood—so many that they received top billing over the better-known Belle Baker, to her displeasure.[24] They were Lower East Siders who had made good in the outside world, and their old neighbors loved them for it. The aura of bigtime vaudeville made them something special.

Such performers rarely offered their diverse audiences pure Old World culture. Instead, they expressed a synthetic ethnicity, a blend of immigrant experiences, new forms of popular culture, and the stereotyped national and racial characters of the American theater.[25]

As it emerged in vaudeville, early twentieth century popular culture could speak *to* many different New Yorkers, but only intermittently could it speak *for* them. The process and products were similar to those which Stuart Hall has observed in British journalism.

> The language of the *Daily Mirror* is neither a pure construction of Fleet Street "newspeak" nor is it the language which its working-class readers actually speak. It is a highly complex species of linguistic *ventriloquism* in which the debased brutalism of popular journalism is skillfully combined . . . with some elements of the directness and vivid particularity of working-class language. It cannot get by without preserving some element of its roots in a real vernacular—in "the popular." It wouldn't get very far unless it were capable of reshaping popular elements into a species of canned and neutralised demotic populism.[26]

In an article written in 1924, journalist Marian Spitzer recognized that legitimate theater audiences were "pretty much alike."

> Things that get a laugh are likely to get a laugh tomorrow night as well. But vaudeville audiences are different all the time. It's almost impossible to set a performance and then play it that way forever. Each town seems to be different; every neighborhood in the city needs different handling. So a vaudevillian has to be forever on the alert, to feel out his audience and work accordingly.[27]

Performers based such appeals on a close analysis of the audience. They learned to tailor their presentations to the specific crowd before them. As a fledgling performer, Eddie Cantor flopped when he presented an English language act in a theater where most of the patrons apparently spoke Yiddish. He translated the act into Yiddish and scored a hit:

> We had simply talked to them in the wrong language, and this in a way is every actor's problem in adapting himself to his audience. Drifting as I did into every conceivable type of crowd, I trained myself to the fact that "the audience is never wrong," and if a performance failed to go across it was either the fault of the material or the manner of presentation. By carefully correcting the one or the other or both with an eye to the peculiarities of the audience I could never fail a second time. I proved this to myself on many occasions later on, when in the same night I'd perform at the Vanderbilt home and then rush down to Loew's Avenue B and be a hit in both places.[28]

Cantor appealed to Jews by speaking Yiddish. Yossele Rosenblatt, a renowned cantor who toured in vaudeville in the 1920s after his financial support of an Orthodox Jewish newspaper drove him into bankruptcy, typically sang one song in English and two in Hebrew. For the Irish, Pat Rooney commented on the Land League and Maggie Cline tossed barbs at the Queen of England.[29]

But vaudeville's relationship to ethnic culture was not always so sympathetic. Vaudevillians also traded heavily in the stereotyped national and racial characters which dated to the mid-nineteenth century American theater.[30] In cities whose size and diversity made their inhabitants strangers, vaudeville introduced urbanites to each other through stereotypical characters which would, in Raymond Williams's words, "simulate but not affirm human identity."[31]

Stereotypes provided simple characteristics which roughly explained immigrants to native-born Americans and introduced immigrant Americans to each other. They were identifying markers on a bewildering cityscape of races, nationalities and cultures. They were also sometimes bigoted and racist, a trait which occasionally roused the aggrieved to protest portrayals of black chicken thieves, Jewish cheapskates, and drunk Irishmen. Sometimes the complaint was as subtle as a rabbi's backstage visit to a Jewish comedian who lampooned his own people; sometimes it was as shrewd as a threat of a boycott; sometimes it was as smashing as the boos, hisses, and vegetable matter that the Ancient Order of Hibernians used to silence the Russell Brothers' spoof of two Irish servant girls. Vaudeville booking office files contain repeated references to cuts of both jokes about ethnic characters and nastier expressions such as "kike," "wop," and "dirty little Greek."[32]

According to the conventions of the period, a vaudevillian could play any nationality. All that was required was a convincing presentation of stock traits. The Jewish Ross Brothers of New York City did Italian dialect impersonations. Lee Barth advertised himself as "the man with many dialects/ I please all nationalities and cater to originality." In 1920 and 1921 a Californian of Spanish descent, Leo Carillo, performed Chinese and Italian dialect stories on the Keith circuit. Certainly one of the most bizarre, to late twentieth century eyes, appeared in 1911 under the name of Morris and Allen. "Two Jews singing Irish songs with a little talk and some bag pipe playing," noted a New York vaudeville theater manager. "This act is a find for any house and is as good an act of the Hebrew brand as has been around in many a day."[33]

Stereotypes were effective and durable because they were simple to understand and because they evolved over time as their real-life counterparts changed. Acts which used them claimed to base their routines on close, careful observation of their subjects.[34] As Jewish Belle Baker asserted in 1919:

> You see, a comic song to be truly comic ought to have a true-to-nature touch. If you don't understand the people you are characterizing, your impersonation is just a burlesque and not real at all. Well, I don't have to make a sightseeing tour to get my types. I was born in New York right among them. . . . All my impersonations are real. When I sing an Italian or Irish or Yiddish song, I have a definite character in mind that I've known for years. I present the character from that point of view—not the outsider's.[35]

Baker, a plump woman with large eyes and a strong rich voice, worked a variety of ethnic characters into her act. A typical performance could begin with an imaginary plea from 43-year-old Sadie Cohen that her beau Jacob should not let her remain single much longer, and then launch into "Come Back Antonio," an Italian-style dialect plea from a wife whose husband "taka the gun, maka the run to Mexico." The woman's chief worry is that if he loses a hand in the fighting he will be unable to work shining shoes. Next would be "My Mother's Rosary," a piece of Tin Pan Alley bathos calculated to appeal to at least some of the Catholics in the audience. Then, "Robinson Crusoe," which musically asks where Robinson Crusoe went with Friday on Saturday night, and concludes that, "Where there are wild men, there must be wild women." Baker might conclude with her signature tune, "Eli, Eli," a passionate, wailing Hebrew lament that always stirred the Jews in the audience.[36]

"Eli, Eli" aside, performers like Baker presented caricatures. But their portrayals were rooted in reality, and they evolved over time as the immigrants and their children changed. Without an element of truth—however thinly stretched—their acts would have appeared totally implausible. Without an element of simplicity and standardization, their acts would have lacked their requisite mass appeal. Without broad satire, they would not have been funny.

The typical Irish character of the late nineteenth century appeared in a takeoff on an immigrant workingman's garb: a plaid suit, green stockings and corduroy breeches, a square-tailed coat, a battered stovepipe hat with a pipe stuck in the band, a hod carrier's rig, and chin whiskers. His stage voice was frequently that of Pat Rooney, who expressed class consciousness and racism in his 1880s song, "Is that Mr. Riley?"

194

. . . now if they'd let me be, I'd set Ireland free;
On the railway you'd never pay fare.
I'd have the United States under my thumb,
And sleep in the president's chair.
I'd have nothing but Irishmen on the police.
Patrick's day would be Fourth of July.
I'd get me a thousand infernal machines
To teach the Chinese how to die.
Help the working man's cause, manufacture the laws;
New York would be swimming in wine.
A hundred a day would be very small pay,
If the White House and Capital were mine.[37]

Yet the Irish characters changed. An observer noted in 1902 how they followed the development of Irish status in America.

There was a sudden transition from the Castle Garden greenhorn to the East Side "Mick." This is the Irishman who is either a contractor, a politician or a policeman, and a wonderful amount of cleverness has been expended in impersonating him by hundreds of performers, scores of whom have become famous in that line.[38]

The dislocation that surrounded Irish immigrants' social climbing was captured by Mike Haggerty, who appeared in a formal frock coat and a laborer's hobnailed boots. Their triumph rang out in songs such as "Irish Jubilee," which chronicles a huge party given to celebrate Doherty's election to the Senate. The hallmarks include "invitations in twenty different languages," dancing, "a thousand kegs of lager-beer" for the poor, and a surreal menu of "pigs-head and gold-fish, mockingbirds and ostriches, ice cream and cold cream, vaseline and sandwiches."[39]

The characters also gained credibility because they were multi-sided, capable of meaning different things to different people. Consider the following exchange between Pat Rooney, son of the man who sang "Is that Mr. Riley?" and Marion Bent:

Rooney: What's your favorite stone?
Bent: Turquoise.
Rooney: Mine's a brick.[40]

For a working-class Irishman, it is a wry confirmation of working life; for others, the difference between a hard-working laborer and an acquisitive woman; for non-Irishmen, a humorous look at how the other half lives.

Such characters were often placed in an urban context that brought the verve of street life to the stage. This attempt at urban realism drew on the legacy of nineteenth century "sunlight and shadow" books, which had introduced middle-class people and outsiders to city life and the underworld. Rooney and Bent, for example, performed an act called "At the News Stand." In 1912, Charles E. Lawlor and his daughters presented a series of Irish and Italian characters in a routine called "Night and Day on the Sidewalks of New York."[41]

In New York, such efforts led vaudevillians to express a distinctly urban language and stance that could appeal to many different people. (Jimmy Cagney's persona, born on the vaudeville stage, is a good example.) Maggie Cline made much of her Irishness, but she had a broader New York style as well. Once, when she finished the song "Don't Let Me Die Till I See Ireland," a man in the gallery shouted, "Well, why don't you go there?" "Nit!" Cline called back. "It's too far from the Bowery." She swaggered off a stage awash in cheers.[42]

Such appeals also served the Jewish artists who followed the path-breaking Irish onto the vaudeville stage. When Jews appeared in vaudeville, they rarely performed their European folk songs and dances. The audience that vaudeville entrepreneurs were cultivating was too broad to accommodate many acts with a strictly Jewish appeal. Few could become American entertainers by narrowly following the precedents set in the Old World by cantors, wedding jesters, and itinerant musicians.[43]

The Jewish performers who surfaced in the late nineteenth century usually appeared as Dutch (meaning German) characters because many thought that their Yiddish accents sounded German. The Dutch and Jewish stereotypes were otherwise different, but their similar sound provided Jews with an entry point. As Jews became a more visible urban presence in the years after 1900, a full-fledged Jewish character appeared, often a peddler or a confused immigrant.[44]

Julian Rose was one of the earliest and most successful performers in this drama. A Jewish accountant from Philadelphia, Rose appeared widely during the early 1900s and on through the twenties. His most famous monologue was "Levinsky at the Wedding," first formulated in 1899, which explored the confusions and conflicts of immigrants.

First we had menu, but I didn't get any of that. I guess they ran out of it early.

. . . The janitor of the apartment, Mickey McCann, calls himself the Superintendent, and he was there too. He gets forty-five dollars a month wages and the neighbors' milk. He got noisy and hit Cone with a bottle. It was a good thing Cone got in the way, or the bottle would have broken a window. . . . A cop walking by called Mickey over to the window and asked what's going on in there. Mickey told him he was cleaning up a Jewish wedding, and the cop shook hands with Mickey and lent him his club.[45]

As with the Irish who preceded them, the Jewish position on the vaudeville stage evolved to reflect Jews' adaptation to the American environment. Jewish artists who succeeded the first generation in the decades after 1900 aimed at an ever-larger audience and cast off European traits in their encounter with American culture.[46] Al Jolson, Sophie Tucker, Eddie Cantor, Belle Baker, and others explored the tensions, transitions, and possibilities that flowed from the meeting of a European heritage and the new ways of America. Some of their acts were distinctly Jewish, but they were also as likely to be influenced by popular music and jazz. Many of them started out in blackface.

When she sang her hit "My Yiddisha Mama," Sophie Tucker relied on the song's multiple meanings to reach Jews and non-Jews.

"My Yiddisha Mama" was written for me by Jack Yellen and Lou Pollack. I introduced it at the Palace Theatre in New York in 1925 and after that in the key cities of the U.S.A. where there were many Jews. Even though I loved the song, and it was a sensational hit every time I sang it, I was always careful to use it only when I knew the majority of the house would understand the Yiddish. However, I have found whenever I have sung "My Yiddisha Mama" in the U.S.A. or in Europe, Gentiles have loved the song and have called for it. They didn't need to understand the Yiddish words. They knew, by instinct, what I was saying, and their hearts responded just as the hearts of Jews and Gentiles of every nationality responded when John McCormack sang "Mother Machree." You didn't have to have an old mother in Ireland to feel "Mother Machree," and you didn't have to be a Jew to be moved by "My Yiddisha Mama." Mother in any language means the same thing.[47]

"My Yiddisha Mama," which Tucker sang in both Yiddish and English, was the classic statement of a performer with one foot in the immigrant Jewish community and another in twentieth century American popular music. Introduced in 1925, the English language version used the conventions of Victorian sentiment and Tin Pan Alley. The song, as Mark Slobin has noted, was simultaneously a statement on Jewish Americanization and a sentimental "mother" song for the mainstream American audience.

The song's melody was not genuinely foreign, but its minor mode and tango-style rhythm gave it an exotic flavor. Tucker sang the English version without accent. In the language of the Victorian parlor songs, the piece assumed the stance of a comfortable, assimilated Jew longing for a special person on the East Side, "the sweetest angel," her Yiddisha Mama. The Yiddish version spoke more directly about assimilation and guilt at leaving aged parents. It romanticized ghetto life, evoking a poverty-stricken kitchen that still smelled of roast dumplings, a home where there was always enough for the children. It sobbed at the mother's impending death, and wailed at the tragedy of losing her.[48]

"My Yiddisha Mama" addressed Jewish concerns, but the motherhood motif also had appeal for non-Jews. And the theme of a Jewish child's love for its mother portrayed Jews in a more positive light than the stereotypes of befuddled immigrants or sharp businessmen.

If such representations of white ethnic groups offered considerable cultural latitude, the blackface image of African Americans was far more restrictive and negative. First developed in antebellum minstrelsy, blackface carried over into vaudeville as minstrel shows declined in the 1890s.

Much of an entire generation of vaudevillians, who started out from the 1890s well into the twentieth century, broke into showbusiness behind burnt cork.[49] For performers from immigrant backgrounds, blackface was a theatrical convention that offered a way of becoming American—at least in appearance. Audiences knew that white performers in blackface—who made up the majority of blackface performers—were not really black. But they associated blackface performers with a uniquely freer, more expressive style—a stage convention that expressed the racist belief that blacks were less cerebral than whites, and therefore more emotional. "They were loose in their emotions," recalled audience member Norman Steinberg. "It was a free thing, they had voices, they could deliver the song." As blackface singer and dancer Jimmy Vee put it, they would "bang the song out."[50]

If white performers found a liberating mask in blackface, black performers found a straitjacket. No one knew this better than Bert Williams, the black dancer, singer, and comedian and star of vaudeville and musical comedy. Williams, a West Indian, was compelled to wear blackface makeup so the reality of his face would fit the stage stereotype. He was well aware of the way that stage conventions limited his portrayal of black Americans. "If I were free to *do as I like*," he noted, "I would give both sides of the shiftless darky—the pathos as well as the fun. But the public knows me for certain things. If I attempt anything outside of those things I am not Bert Williams."[51]

The best that can be said for blackface characters is that occasionally they displayed pathos, or a folksy, sly humor. At their worst, they show an awful process of black characters—often actually whites wearing makeup—being made to conform to racist white expectations. In blackface, popular culture expressed the hierarchy that prevailed outside the theater: whatever the preceived deficiencies of white immigrants, all were superior to blacks, who were enshrined as the butt of everyone's jokes, hostility, and disrespect.

"McMahon's Water-melon Girls," a holdover hit at Hyde and Behman's in Brooklyn in 1903, mixed blackface and Indian characters in a Dixieland setting. The theater's manager enthusiastically captured its details in a report to the Keith booking offices.

> This is a new act, it opens with . . . two girls in Indian costume, singing chorus, and McMahon and Nevins, dressed in handsome black suits, following with song and dance assisted by the girls, then (sic) stage opens in full, girls in watermelon suits, standing on each side of the stage, a large drop curtain in rear representing a steamboat all lighted, coming up to dock. On the dock is an immense water-melon filled with electric lights, which opens and shows McMahon and Nevins, in black face, reclining inside. They come out and sing and dance, assisted by the chorus. It is one of the prettiest and best acts, in that line, ever seen on our stage. It is a great hit, they are encored four and five times, after each song and dance.[52]

A more vicious example of blackface was captured in Nat Wills's 1915 recording "Two Negro Stories." The short bit is set in a hotel in Canada that employs black waiters. A rich Georgia planter walks into the dining room shortly before meal time and asks,

> "I want to find out who's the head nigger here."
> A black waiter replies, "Nigger. You're mistaken, sir, ain't no niggers here. You're up in Canada now, under the English flag. You ain't down South. So you see all them men standing around by those tables? Well, them is all colored gentlemen. No niggers." The planter replies that he is a guest and that he has a $20 bill for the "head nigger" to ensure good service.
> "I'm the head nigger, boss, yassuh," the waiter replies. "And if you don't believe me ask any of those niggers standing over there and they'll tell you I am."[53]

Jazz and ragtime pianist Eubie Blake also understood the insidiousness of blackface, and how it shrouded his entry into vaudeville.

> We were supposed to shuffle on stage in blackface and patched-up overalls. In the middle of the stage there is this big box with a piano

on it. The idea was to look as if it were from the *moon* and I'd say, "What's dat?" and Noble would say, "Dat's a py-anner!" And then we'd do our act. Well, Pat Casey would have none of that. He told the agents that Sissle and Blake had played in the houses of millionaires and the social elite and they dressed in tuxedos and he'd be *damned* if he'd let us go on the stage and act like a couple of ignoramuses.

As "The Dixie Duo," Sissle and Blake went on to be bigtime stars. They were one of the first black acts to appear without blackface makeup: when they played the Palace, they wore Palm Beach suits at matinees and dinner jackets in the evening.[54]

When blackface characters articulated eroticized coon songs or the sensual strut of the cakewalk, as they often did in vaudeville, they served another function—to undermine Victorianism by portraying titillating characters who did not share in the precepts of restrained, sober, middle-class Victorian culture—characters on whom audiences could project their own fantasies, anger, and desires. This culturally subversive role was also assigned to ethnic characters.

Irving Berlin used an immigrant theme to explore sexual relations in two songs copyrighted in 1910, "Sweet Italian Love" and "Oh How that German Could Love."

> Sweet Italian love,
> Nice Italian love, . . .
>
> When you squeeze your gal
> And she no say "Please stop-a!"
> When you got twenty kids what call you "Papa!"
> Dat's Italian love, . . .[55]

Or:

> Ach my, what a German when she kissed her Herman,
> It stayed on my cheek for a week.[56]

"The Art of Flirtation" and "The German Senator," used the dialect device to disguise characters who revelled in sexuality. In "The Art of Flirtation," a straight man uses a guidebook to teach his comical friend how to flirt.

> Straight: Ven you flirt, you meet a pretty woman in a shady spot.
> Comedian: Oh, you met a shady woman in a pretty spot.
> Straight: Not a shady woman. A pretty woman in a shady spot . . .

200

The lesson covers the proper use of a handkerchief to attract and communicate with members of the opposite sex. It concludes with advice on what to do when seated arm in arm on a couch, with the gas lamp turned down low.

> Straight: Dat's the end of the book.
> Comedian: Is dat all?
> Straight: Sure. What do you want for ten cents?
> Comedian: But vat do you do after you turn down the gas?
> Straight: Do you expect the book to tell you everything? [57]

The popular "German Senator" combined this immigrant mask and a kind of laughing cynicism. After satire and wordplay on everything from the Statue of Liberty to Andrew Carnegie to socialists to crooked politicians, the monologue concludes with recognition of conflicts between men and women:

> And that's why the women suffering gents have gotten together
>   and are fighting for their rights.
> And you can't blame them.
> Now I see where one married woman has hit on a great idea.
> She says there's only one protection for the wives.
> And that's a wive's union.
> Imagine a union for wives.
> A couple gets married.
> And as soon as they get settled, along comes the walking delegate
>   and orders a strike.
> Then imagine thousands and thousands of wives walking up and
>   down the street on strike, and scabs taking their places. [58]

The meeting and mixing process where different cultures were introduced to each other in vaudeville was hardly a model of pluralism or cultural democracy. The prevailing values of the vaudeville entrepreneurs were the values of the marketplace, and whatever failed to meet the test of the box office was rejected. Only those performers with a wide appeal were marketable. Sophie Tucker was a deservedly popular Jewish singer, but her style was very different from that of the singers of the shtetl. Her enormous commercial success guaranteed that singers who performed in older styles would sound archaic, odd, and foreign. In the aftermath of such developments, Americans of all backgrounds who chose to create musically would find themselves measured against arbitrary commercial standards. Music, "the soul of man expressed in sound," would be measured by the standards of the marketplace. [59]

The images that immigrant, black, and ethnic New Yorkers portrayed on the vaudeville stage were filtered and circumscribed by commercial priorities. Yet one of those commercial priorities was to attract the different peoples of New York City. Because entrepreneurs sought an ethnically diverse audience, they were compelled to make at least a token representation of ethnic culture.

After vaudeville, increasing numbers of ethnic Americans would express part of their identity through popular culture.[60] If creating a culture is partly accomplished by choosing among symbols and resources, then when vaudeville and its successors displaced some foreign ethnic cultures, they reduced the number and variety of cultural resources available to Americans.

It would be historically unfair, however, to expect the New Yorkers of the late nineteenth and early twentieth centuries to be aware of all the cultural consequences of the vaudeville era. As long as the ethnic theaters and lodges remained viable, people could define and explore their ethnicity through songs, stories, plays, and poems produced for that purpose. After ethnic cultural institutions were displaced, people would face the problem of trying to construct a particular identity from mass culture.

And many of the negative aspects of modern popular culture, such as the growth in the power of huge, hierarchical electronic entertainment industries, became apparent only after vaudeville died in the 1930s. Although vaudeville helped pave the way for these, much of what was best about it looked back to the nineteenth century—the vitality of street life, and the accessibility, immediacy, and human intimacy of live theater.

There were real gratifications to be found in vaudeville. Eddie Cantor was a very funny man; Maggie Cline touched a genuine chord in the New York Irish when she belted out "Throw Him Down, McCloskey"; Belle Baker clearly sang to Jewish emotions and experiences when she performed "Eli, Eli"; Bill "Bojangles" Robinson was a great African American dancer.

The hybrids that flowered in vaudeville—Sophie Tucker singing with a jazz band about her "Yiddisha Mama"—were attuned to the emergent realities of city life in all its diversity and complexity. They did not mean the end of ethnic identity, but the beginning of new forms of expression.

In the twentieth century, much of America's most important and exciting music, dance, acting, and comedy have roots in the vaudeville stage, where they were presented by immigrants, immigrants' children, and blacks. But our applause for their achievements should be tempered by a knowledge of their shortcomings. Vaudeville's drive for a broad audience led it to avoid complexities and conflicts that might limit audiences, but many of the complexities and conflicts which they avoided were part of ethnic culture. In the films, recordings, radio, and television that evolved out of vaudeville, the strengths—and limitations—of their creations remain with us.

Portions of this chapter appeared earlier in *The Voice of the City: Vaudeville and Popular Culture in New York* (Oxford, 1989). In my revisions, I found the suggestions of William Taylor, Daniel Czitrom, and Peter Eisenstadt particularly helpful. Unless noted otherwise, all interviews cited in this essay were conducted by the author.

Notes

Abbreviations

NYPL-LC: New York Public Library at Lincoln Center

FTC 128: Federal Trade Commission 128, Federal Archives, Suitland, Maryland

Iowa Collection: Keith/Albee Collection, Special Collections Department, University of Iowa Libraries, Iowa City, Iowa

HTC: Harvard Theater Collection

1. On Cline, see "Maggie Cline Rites Planned," New York *Sun*, June 12, 1934, 25; on Bevacqua, see interview with Robert W. Snyder in Mount Vernon, New York, November 1, 1983; on Cantor, see Eddie Cantor, as told to David Freedman, *My Life Is in Your Hands* (New York, 1932), 6–9, 11, 14–17 and quote from 18; on Blake, see Robert Kimball and William Bolcom, *Reminiscences with Sissle and Blake* (New York, 1973), 36–37, 42.
2. On vaudevillians' social origins, see John Dimeglio, *Vaudeville U.S.A.* (Bowling Green, Ohio, 1973), 197; Bill Smith, "Vaudeville: Entertainment of the Masses," in Myron Matlaw, ed., *American Popular Entertainment* (Westport, Conn., 1979), 13; on the important immigrant influence on vaudeville, see "American Entertainment: An Immigrant Domain," by Carl H. Scheele, in *A Nation of Nations*, Peter C. Marzio, ed. (New York, 1976), 410–450, esp. 425–434 on vaudeville. Also see census data in appendix in Robert William Snyder, "The Voice of the City: Vaudeville and the Formation of Mass Culture in New York

Neighborhoods, 1880–1930." Ph.D. Diss., New York University, 1985. On immigrants and their children in vaudeville as entrepreneurs, performers, and audience members, see Frederick Edward Snyder, "American Vaudeville—Theatre in a Package: The Origins of Mass Entertainment." Ph.D. Diss., Yale University, 1970, 61.

3. On inadequate treatments of race and ethnicity in contemporary television, see Todd Gitlin, *Inside Prime Time* (New York, 1983), 179–187.

4. On this trend, see Felix Isman, *Weber and Fields: Their Tribulations, Triumphs, and Their Associates* (New York, 1924), 183. About half or more of the founders of the White Rats in 1900 were of Irish background. See advertisements and business cards listed in George Fuller Golden, *My Lady Vaudeville and Her White Rats* (New York, 1909).

5. On the predominance of different acts, see Douglas Gilbert, *American Vaudeville: Its Life and Times* (New York, 1940, 1968), 62; on who performed ethnic comedy, see Paul Antonie Distler, "The Rise and Fall of the Racial Comics in American Vaudeville." Ph.D. Diss., Tulane University, 1963, Chaps. V and VI.

6. See "The Variety Stage: Early Creators of a Renumerative Vogue," *Harper's Weekly* 46 (March 29, 1902): 414.

7. Laurence Senelick, "Variety into Vaudeville, the Process Observed in Two Manuscript Gagbooks," *Theatre Survey* 19 (May 1978): 11.

8. On the origins of the Irish performers, see Distler, "The Rise and Fall . . . ," Chap. V, *passim*, especially 112–113, 117–118, 127–130, 131–135.

9. On Cagney, see James Cagney, *Cagney* (New York, 1976), 26–27.

10. See Honi Coles interview with Charlayne Hunter-Gault, McNeil-Lehrer Newshour, June 15, 1984.

11. On Lower East Side street life and candy stores, see *Yearbook of the University Settlement Society of New York, 1899*, John W. Martin, "Social Life in the Street," 22–23; and Benjamin Reich, "A New Social Center. The Candy Store as a Social Influence," 32. On streetcorner dancing in Philadelphia in a slightly later period, see Coles interview with Hunter-Gault.

12. Eddie Cantor, *My Life*, 1–5.

13. Eddie Cantor, *My Life*, 6–9, 11, 14–17, 66–68, 19, 21, 40–41.

14. Eddie Cantor, *My Life*, 23.

15. Eddie Cantor, *My Life*, 77–86.

16. Eddie Cantor, *My Life*, 75–76, 88–89, 92, 96–102, 112–127, 129–133, 142, 148–149, 151, 153, 156.

17. Robert Lipsyte makes this point with regard to professional sports in his introduction to C. L. R. James, *Beyond a Boundary* (New York, 1983), xi–xii; "here genius . . ." appeared repeatedly in the 1915 *Billboard*; otherwise, on this general theme, see Irving Howe, *World of Our Fathers* (New York, 1976), 556–566.

18. Interview with Frances Poplawski, New York City, January 28, 1984. On the attractions of a vaudeville career for women, see Albert Auster, *Actresses and Suffragists: Women in the American Theater, 1890–1920* (New York, 1984); interview with Ethel Hardey, February 23, 1984.

19. On Tucker's age, see her obituary, *New York Times* (February 10, 1961): 1; also "Sophie Tucker," *Variety* (February 16, 1966): 4. Tucker's memoir is vague on whether the establishment was a restaurant or delicates-

sen, rooming house or hotel, but a basic description of her years there is found in Sophie Tucker, in collaboration with Dorothy Giles, *Some of These Days: The Autobiography of Sophie Tucker* (Garden City, N.Y., 1945), 1–7, 10.

20. Sophie Tucker, *Some of These Days*, 10–11.

21. Sophie Tucker, *Some of These Days*, 10–11.

22. Sophie Tucker, *Some of These Days*, 10, 32. Dates in *New York Times* obituary (February 10, 1966): 1. On the Howard Brothers and the Empire City Quartette, see Edward B. Marks, as told to Abbott J. Liebling, *They All Sang: From Tony Pastor to Rudy Vallee* (New York, 1935), 283, 286.

23. For the story of Belle Baker, see *Dramatic Mirror*, n.d., clippings, and Keith program for the week of April 12, 1915, all in Baker clipping file, NYPL-LC.

24. See interview with Mike Ross, New York City, December 19, 1983.

25. In vaudeville's biggest years, from roughly 1890–1920, more than three-quarters of New York City's population were immigrants and their children. See Niles Carpenter, *Immigrants and their Children 1920* (Washington, D.C., U.S. Government Printing Office, 1927), 27; their presence in vaudeville as entrepreneurs, performers, and audience members is discussed in Snyder, "American Vaudeville," 61; Francis G. Couvares, "The Triumph of Commerce: Class Culture and Mass Culture in Pittsburgh," in *Working-Class America: Essays on Labor, Community, and American Society*, Michael H. Frisch and Daniel J. Walkowitz, eds. (Urbana, Ill., 1986), 147. On race and ethnicity in minstrelsy, variety, and vaudeville, see David Grimsted, *Melodrama Unveiled: American Theatre and Culture, 1800–1850* (Chicago, 1974), 37, 42–43, 185–187; on racial and ethnic stereotypes and the comedy of early variety, see Douglas Gilbert, *American Vaudeville*, 61–62; on the element of exaggeration in stereotypes, see Distler, "The Rise and Fall of the Racial Comics," 67.

26. Stuart Hall, "Notes on Deconstructing 'the Popular,' " in *People's History and Socialist Theory*, Raphael Samuel, ed. (London, 1981), 232.

27. Marian Spitzer, "The People of Vaudeville," *Saturday Evening Post*, July 12, 1924, 6.

28. Eddie Cantor, *My Life*, 76.

29. On Rosenblatt, see Dr. Samuel Rosenblatt, *Yossele Rosenblatt: A Biography* (New York, 1954), 223–234, 252–255, 258–261, 270. On Rooney, see Jennings, *Theatrical and Circus Life*, 429; on Cline, April 10, 1909, clipping, Cline clipping file, NYPL-LC.

30. On stereotypes, see David Grimsted, *Melodrama Unveiled*, 189–192, 194; on blackface minstrelsy, see Toll, *Blacking Up*, 37, 42–43, 185–187; on early variety comedy's ethnic and racial stereotypes, see Douglas Gilbert, *American Vaudeville*, 61–62; on the element of exaggeration in these stereotypes, see Distler, "The Rise and Fall of the Racial Comics," 67.

31. Raymond Williams, *Drama in a Dramatised Society* (Cambridge, England, 1975), 9.

32. Irving Howe, *World of Our Fathers*, 401–405. The backstage visit from the rabbi was described for me in 1984 by a Jewish man who toured with his vaudevillian father. On the boycotts and Hibernian protests, see Distler, "The Rise and Fall of the Racial Comics," 187–194. For

examples of cuts, see the following from the the the U.B.O. report books in the Iowa Collection: "Kike," Keith's Boston, September 16, 1907, Report Book 6, p. 241; references to a "Jew Boat" and "Jews Running Away from a Sale," Keith's Boston, July 22, 1918, Report Book 20, p. 85; "Wops," Keith's Providence, Rhode Island Theatre, December 29, 1919, report book 21, p. 123; "Dirty Little Greek," Keith's Boston, August 22, 1921, Report Book 22, p. 203.

33. For examples of jokes involving ethnic stereotypes, see *McNally's Bulletin* (New York, 1916–1932), *passim.* For a list of the wide variety of types which could be impersonated by one performer, see FTC 128, March 28, 1919, box 73, 1127–1131. On the Ross Brothers, see interview with Michael Ross, New York City, December 19, 1983. On Lee Barth, see *The Player,* December 31, 1909, 29. On Leo Carillo, see Leo Carillo scrapbook, NYPL-LC; on Morris and Allen's appearance at the Fifth Avenue Theatre in 1911, see Report Book 12, 105.

34. On this point, see Carillo in March 2, 1921, clipping, n.p., NYPL-LC; remarks by David Warfield in Marks, *They All Sang,* 14–15; interview with John T. Kelly in Cleveland *Leader,* June 17, 1906, cited in Distler, "The Rise and Fall of the Racial Comics in American Vaudeville," 116–117.

35. Interview with Belle Baker, n.p., October 24, 1919, Belle Baker clipping file, NYPL-LC.

36. The description of Baker's performances is derived mainly from the following articles in the Belle Baker clipping file, NYPL-LC: on Baker at the Palace, see *New York Dramatic Mirror,* July 15, 1914, 17 and clipping, c. 1916, Belle Baker clipping file, NYPL-LC. For examples of audience reaction to a Baker performance, in particular, "Eli, Eli," see the following in her clipping file, NYPL-LC: an account from an unidentified publication of her appearance at Henderson's Music Hall, Coney Island, for the week ending June 22, 1919; a clipping from the New York *Star,* n.d.; on other Baker appearances, see the Brooklyn *Daily Eagle,* c. July 1914; clipping without date or name of newspaper of origin; and, for her appearance, a picture of her from the New York *Star,* c. June 1916.

37. The description of the Irish character is derived from Jennings, *Theatrical and Circus Life,* 420–422; and Charles R. Sherlock, "Where Vaudeville Holds the Boards," *The Cosmopolitan* 32 (February 1902): 33–34. The lyrics for "Is that Mr. Riley?" are from Gilbert, *American Vaudeville,* 68.

38. Charles R. Sherlock, "Where Vaudeville Holds the Boards," 33–34.

39. On the Haggerty character, popular from the 1880s to the mid-teens, see Distler, "The Rise and Fall of the Racial Comics," 124–126; see also "Irish Jubilee," words by J. Thornton and music by Charles Lawlor, © M. Whitmore and Sons, 1890.

40. Reprinted in Anthony Slide, *The Vaudevillians: A Dictionary of Vaudeville Performers* (Westport, Conn., 1981), 128.

41. For Rooney and Bent, see Report Book 14, 117; on Charles Lawlor and daughters, see Report Book 13, 86. Also see review on Joe Welch "In a Study from Life," Report Book 7, 157; review of "A Congressman at Large," week of September 29, 1902, undated report book, 12. All report books from Iowa collection.

42. For the Bowery anecdote, see *New York Herald Tribune* (June 12, 1934): 21; for an anecdote on Cline's Irish appeal, see *Dramatic News*, n.d., c. April 1907; clipping, n.p., April 10, 1909, both in Cline clipping file, NYPL-LC. Collection, NYPL-LC.
43. See Irving Howe, *World of Our Fathers*, 556–566.
44. See Douglas Gilbert, *American Vaudeville*, 72, 287–292; Irving Howe, *World of Our Fathers*, 401–405.
45. Paul Antonie Distler, "The Rise and Fall of the Racial Comics," 165–167; monologue, 208–209. For a Julian Rose recording which is very close to the version cited by Distler, see Rose, "Levinsky at the Wedding, Parts 3 and 4," Columbia A-2366, March 16, 1917. Carl H. Scheele generously introduced me to this recording and provided me with background information on it.
46. Mark Slobin, *Tenement Songs*, 2.
47. Sophie Tucker, *Some of These Days*, 260.
48. Mark Slobin, *Tenement Songs*, 203–205; version of song cited is from a 2-sided English and Yiddish 78 rpm recording, Decca 23902.
49. See Sophie Tucker, *Some of These Days*, 33; Jessel, *So Help Me*, photograph of Jessel and Cantor; Mark Slobin, "Some Intersections of Jews, Music, and Theater," in Cohen, *From Hester Street to Hollywood*, 36; interview with Lloyd Pickard, Englewood, N.J., February 7, 1984; and Bevacqua.
50. See interviews with Norman Steinberg, Schwartz, New York City, December 7, 1983; Jack Gross, New York City, 1984; Howard Basler, New York City, January 13, 1984; Harold Applebaum, New York City, January 18, 1984; and Bevacqua.
51. Quoted in William S. Holler, "Apart but not Alien," W.P.A. "Negro New York" file, Schomburg Center for Research in Black Culture, NYPL.
52. See report on May 11, 1903, show at Hyde and Behman's, Brooklyn, NY, undated report book, Iowa Collection, 267.
53. All material cited is from Nat Wills, "Two Darkey Stories" ("Colored Social Club" and "The Headwaiter"), Columbia A-1765, March 29, 1915. I thank Carl H. Scheele for introducing me to this recording.
54. See Kimball and Bolcom, *Reminiscing With Sissle and Blake*, 52, 81.
55. "Sweet Italian Love," words by Irving Berlin, music by Ted Snyder, © 1910 by Ted Snyder Co., Inc., reprinted in Brett Page, *Writing for Vaudeville* (Springfield, Mass., 1915), 339–340.
56. "Oh How that German Could Love," Berlin and Snyder, © 1910, Ted Snyder Co., Inc., reprinted in Page, *Writing for Vaudeville*, 341–342.
57. "The Art of Flirtation," by Aaron Hoffman, © 1910, reprinted in Page, *Writing for Vaudeville*, 447–456, quotes from 450, 456.
58. "The German Senator," by Aaron Hoffman, © March 3, 1914, class D. XXC, 36,300, reprinted in Page, *Writing for Vaudeville*, 435–443, quotes from 443.
59. The definition of music as "the soul of man expressed in sound" was offered by a traditional folk singer whose name I have unfortunately forgotten. On the marketplace and culture, see T. J. Jackson Lears, "Some Versions of Fantasy: Toward a Cultural History of American Advertising, 1880–1930," *Perspectives* 9 (1984): 387.
60. On March 16, 1984, the night before Saint Patrick's Day, I was at the Eagle Tavern in New York City, one of America's foremost centers of

Irish music. Onstage were Greg Daly and Bryan Conway, two accomplished musicians, playing traditional Irish songs and dance tunes. The audience was friendly but only mildly receptive. Daly and Conway then played a medley of George M. Cohan songs. The audience sang along on every number and cheered loudly.

Chapter 8

The Cultural Role
of the Vienna-Budapest Operetta

PÉTER HANÁK

O PERETTA IS ONE of the most rewarding topics of cultural history. Imagine a performance in an average musical theater. Its libretto is primitive and silly (if not idiotic), unbelievable and ridiculous. Its music is a mélange of cheap opera arias and fashionable dance music full of sentimental commonplaces and a few melodious hits for everybody's home whistling. In most cases, operettas cannot be measured by high aesthetic or dramatic values. Yet, despite all deficiencies, operetta always was and is very popular, particularly in Central Europe, the old Habsburg Monarchy and its successors; not only with ordinary people and the lower middle classes but also with the educated upper classes, creative intellectuals, musicians, and writers. Operetta effortlessly cuts across regions, countries, and nations, and across social strata; it is interregional, international, and transpersonal. Its success is really an intriguing question for cultural historians.[1]

Answering the question requires a short historical overview of its genesis. The mixed ancestry of the operetta ranges from such elegant forms as opera buffa, through the specifically German *Singspiel*, down to the knockabout farce of the fairground. Included among its precursors are a few glittering names (Pergolesi, Mozart, Donizetti) and many more that are dimly remembered or simply lost in the passage of time (Schenk, Dittersdorf, John Gay, and Papusch).[2] Operetta that is merely elevated *Singspiel*, or debased opera, however, belongs to the infancy of the genre. Operetta proper arose in the Paris of the 1850s and represented the most conspicuous cultural product of the emerging middle classes. Its creator, who brought it to a high state of perfection, was Jacques Offenbach.[3]

The overwhelming success of the Parisian operetta (and shortly afterward the English and Viennese offerings in the same genre) may be attributed to three principal factors: First, it was the freshness and wit of the music, which drew inspiration from the most melodious elements of opera but which avoided opera's sententiousness and melodrama. (Indeed, these aspects of opera were frequently mocked in operetta.) Its music was also sufficiently uncomplicated to make it suitable for home rendition and to supply amateur musicians with a ready-made repertoire of dance music and stylized "folk music."

Second, plots of operettas dexterously combined escapism with gentle political and/or social satire. Thus, they pandered to the sentimentality while exposing the hypocrisy of the audience and that of the ruling classes.

Third, operetta provided its audience with spectacle on a grand scale—glittering costumes, elaborate scenery, slick choreography—theatrical elements that are nowadays known as lavish production values. In operetta, the formerly exclusive hybrid art of opera broadened its appeal and was transformed into a medium of metropolitan mass entertainment. Clearly, the one indispensable prerequisite of the birth and development of the operetta was the *metropolis.* Each form and genre of public entertainment had its social setting and spatial environment, from the antique *polis* and the Renaissance princely court to the modern city. The nineteenth century metropolis developed a massive need for typically urban forms of entertainment and professional groups of unhindered critics, writers, composers, and actors. In the second half of the nineteenth century, traditional opera became increasingly a minority interest whose elite audience of connoisseurs was able to follow it into the abstract and intellectual realm of Wagner and of post-Wagnerian music. Belles-lettres, theater, and music of the urban high culture segregated rather than integrated the society of the metropolis. But operetta constituted popular culture, appealing equally to the upper and middle classes and even more to those down the social scale.

In Vienna, specifically advantageous circumstances came together for the new genre. Vienna was the European city whose multiethnic society had always inclined to cosmopolitanism; its loyal subjects admired but at the same time ridiculed the aristocracy and the absolutist bureaucracy. The Baroque and Biedermeier traditions of the city complemented each other: piety and sensuality, loyalty and ironic skepticism—all brought music and humor together at the same time in the operetta.

The genre had deep roots in the country. The Old Viennese Folk Comedy, with its hundreds of well-known roles, goes back to the eighteenth century.[4] So do the dance musics of the Empire in the first half of the nineteenth century (the Austrian and German waltz, Ländler, the Czech and Polish polka and mazurka, and the Hungarian csárdás). The play known as *Singspiel*, however, influenced by the Parisian operetta, received a new name and new sense in the second half of the century. It was shown by the stormy success of Offenbach and the French operetta and its quick adoption by Suppé, Millöcker, and above all, in Johann Strauss's works.[5] However, Viennese operetta conspicuously differed from its Parisian model from the very beginning: it was not so relentlessly ironical. In its music it did not adopt an acrid, playful humor, but rather a daydream melody, a sweetness, a sentimentality, as its *leitmotif.* This is what audiences liked so much in Suppé's *Die Schöne Galathée* and *Bocaccio,* and especially in Strauss's great operettas.

I shall not analyze Strauss's oeuvre here.[6] But I do want to introduce *The Gypsy Baron,* which I regard as the most representative of his works, from the cultural historian's point of view.

Strauss was close to sixty when he started work on *The Gypsy Baron.* He himself, just like the genre, seemed to be tiring out. Oh, those 1880s! The exceptional decade when peace and quiet reigned in the Habsburg empire. The Compromise of 1867 between Austria and Hungary had created a climate of political stability in which a Central European version of constitutional liberalism could exist, underpinned by a period of economic prosperity and international security. In this climate Strauss, as well as the public, desired something entirely new. His Hungarian friends—who constituted a specific bilingual channel between Vienna and Budapest—had been suggesting for some time that he pick a Hungarian subject and that he turn to the famous writer, Mór Jókai. The summit between the King of the Waltz and the Hungarian Prince of Writers took place at the beginning of September 1883.[7]

Jókai offered a ready-made formula for a romantic play by turning to a topic of the past in the Hungary recovered from the Turks. There you will find wasteland, swamp, and burnt-out villages wherever you look. He populated this romantic landscape with romantic people, in this case with Gypsies: "This nice, vagrant people will automatically bring success on the stage of the opera house."[8] The formula also called for some treasure to be found in the play. Operettas where the hero has scraped together his fortune, however, by hacking and grubbing the soil for thirty years have hardly any impact. The public would say, we can also gather together a little fortune penny by penny ourselves. More effectively, money should fall from heaven, or it should emerge suddenly from the belly of the earth. And in this romantic landscape, lovers should find each other while looking for buried treasure; they should not be married by a priest. The lawful wedding can come only at the end of the play. The music to accompany the wedding of Jókai's lovers will be supplied by birds and crickets.

Strauss immediately liked the subject, especially when Joseph Schnitzer presented him with the libretto translated into German and improved by witty lyrics. However, he took his time: he worked on the operetta (which, incidentally, found its way to the opera house, too, at the end of the century) for almost two years.[9] In *The Gypsy Baron* that opened in October 1885, all the ingredients of a romantic musical play are brought together. There is Barinkay, the Hungarian nobleman in exile, who will be pardoned by the kind Empress (Maria Theresa) and who will also recover his lands; the upstart pig dealer, who will allow only a baron to marry his daughter; honest, kind-hearted Gypsies; and Saffi, the beautiful Gypsy girl, who turns out to be a princess, the daughter of the last Pascha in Temesvár. There is also some hidden treasure in the play that the lovers will find. The Austrian bureaucracy is duly mocked, yet the Hungarians' patriotism will protect the Monarchy and its young Empress from the Spanish. The final product is an ingeniously composed music extracted from the musical treasury of almost all the peoples in the Monarchy. We can hear polkas, recruiting music (the verbunk), and Gypsy songs, with the waltz binding them all together.[10] At the end of the second act, a recruitment song is heard that had been composed by a genuine Gypsy musician in 1848.[11] At the seventy-fifth performance in 1886, even the Rákóczi March, which had been strictly banned, rang out for the first time on stage in Vienna. Again, the ingeniously constructed finale is bound together by Viennese music.[12]

The piquancy of the story is that the operetta was constructed of elements rooted in real life. The original model of Barinkay was an actual man (Botsinkay), an *artiste* in a circus touring abroad before he was given back his land.[13] The romantic story pieced together of romantic fragments and Strauss's well-spiced, Hungarianized, sweetly plaintive Viennese music brought him a worldwide success that reverberates even today.

It was a sweeping success. Up to the end of the last century there had been more than three hundred performances in Vienna, and over a hundred in Budapest; it was translated into seventeen languages and performed in several dozen cities ranging from New York to St. Petersburg. Theater critics received it with praise, even with adulation at times, although there were some critical remarks as well.[14] Critics of the Budapest press disapproved of the fact that Barinkay was played (in the absence of a tenor) by a pretty prima donna, Ilka Pálmay, with a boyish grace. But gone was the projection of Hungarian manly strength.[15] The press objected most of all to the fact that Schnitzer, who adapted the story written by Jókai, had changed the essence to suit Viennese taste. Jókai's compliance with the change was deemed a mistake. "If somebody is a big enough star to illuminate all of Hungary, why does he want to be a tallow candle on the music-stand of a Viennese musician?" wrote one of the comic papers.[16] Some praised him, saying that "the alliance between the Viennese waltz and the Hungarian csárdás is piquante and new," while others protested against the "waltzification" of the patriotic Hungarian world of music.[17] There were also critics who considered this romantic idyll to be outdated: "waltzes do nothing but thump emptily" wrote a critic in the Viennese *Extrablatt*.[18] This type of cultural criticism was expressed most sharply by Hermann Broch.

Broch compared three types of operettas: one by Offenbach, one by Sullivan, and one by Strauss. Even the best of the satirical tendencies is lost in Strauss's operetta. The ironic notes in Raimund and Nestroy "have disappeared, too, without any trace and nothing remained but a copy of the comic opera simplified to idiocy . . . this is how the operetta form founded by Strauss has become a specific vacuum-product: it is only as a vacuum-decoration that it has proved to become maintainable."[19]

There is some truth in the contemporary criticism and in Broch's views. In Strauss's operettas, social criticism was milder, the irony more sugary; and there were more sentimentalism and drive for reconciliation than in operettas staged in Paris or London. Nevertheless, we would be unfair not to appreciate the softer ironies of the Jókai-Schnitzer-Strauss trio. On the stages of Vienna and Budapest, it was not outdated at the time to mock the extremely formal and old-fashioned bureaucracy and the hypocritical "Commission of Morals" *(Sittenkommission)*, and it was very much in vogue to praise the freedom of love and even the legality of marriage without the clergy's blessing—especially in the years of frustrated clerical reforms. In *kaiserlich-königlich* Vienna, even at the end of the century, it took considerable courage to play a Hungarian military song of the 1848 Revolution, especially the Rákóczi March. The fact that this piece of music was oppositionist and critical is made manifest by the disapproval of the authorities and its success with the people.

It would be unfair on our part, however, to measure the Viennese-Budapest operetta by the scale of London or Paris. In those two cities, characterized by a relatively homogenous national atmosphere and a

strong middle class, the critical function of the operetta was to provide a social and political satire. In the Dual Monarchy, however, other
priorities prevailed. It had been only one and a half decades earlier
that the Compromise was signed; the grudge was still vividly alive
both in Budapest and in Vienna. It was very much up-to-date to pacify
the grudges and hurt feelings created by the absolutist retaliation of
1869. Franz Jauner, director of the Theater an der Wien, who was
among the really well informed, said after the premiere,

> The performance of the Gypsy Baron has been the greatest theatri-
> cal experience in my life. . . . The Gypsy Baron is a victory: a dem-
> onstration for the Hungarians, for democracy. A wonderful manifes-
> tation of fellow-feelings which has been glowing in the air for more
> than half a century but only exploded now . . . this operetta has
> been due to come on the scene since July 3rd, 1866, when Benedek
> lost the battle of Königgrätz. After the catastrophe, the thought oc-
> curred to many responsible: the Hungarians must be conciliated.
> . . . Consequently they were happy that someone at last stepped
> out in front of the Hungarian audience, made Barinkay a hero and
> laughed loudly at the caricature of Metternich censorship."[20]

By the way, the Hungarian verse to the song mocking the Commission of Morals was written by Jókai himself. Hence, it is not an exaggeration to say that *The Gypsy Baron* itself was also a part of the
compromise process, *the reconciliation of the hearts*, a political
agreement narrated in words and music. Its integrating effect was not
confined to the Austrian and Hungarian public. In the Monarchy, fad-
ing state patriotism, history, and belles-lettres proved incapable of
creating a common civic ethos, which could be accomplished only
through music and the arts. In the Empire, it was only within the
army that German prevailed as the language of service. In public and
private life, a dozen languages, idioms, national feelings competed with
each other. Only Mozart, Haydn, Schubert, Brahms, Liszt, Smetana,
Dvořák, Goldmark, Strauss, Lehár, and Kálmán were able to create a
language commonly understood by all peoples, lands, and cities, a kind
of community of cultural identity. Accordingly, we agree less with
Hermann Broch than with Franz Werfel: "In this banal form of art
the old Austria is reflected with all her rhythm, all her wit." Moreover, "the whole old opera form could keep itself cleaner here and
this way survive in the people's minds."[21]
   In the Monarchy, the integrating function played by operetta did
not confine itself to the creation of a city culture or the integration
of multicolored group cultures: it had a wider scope—a role that was

much more important from a cultural-historical point of view. The Viennese and the Budapest operetta gathered something from the music and dances, the characteristic figures, and mentalities of all the peoples living in the Monarchy; it had an overall "monarchic" character. In this way it related to every nation. The vacuum that Hermann Broch had shrunk back from in horror perhaps did exist in the aesthetical and philosophical sense. But in everyday life, although very faintly, only as a second theme, a realistic value existed. This was the coexistence and peaceful cultural interaction of the nations and peoples in Central Europe. The Viennese-Budapest operetta definitely contributed to the formation of a common mass culture in the Monarchy, thereby contributing to cultural integration.

Operetta was able to enjoy a new lease on life at the beginning of the twentieth century, when a fundamental shift took place in historical and cultural attitudes. National and social tensions accumulated within the Empire along with diplomatic conflicts abroad. Romanticism lost its attraction, and styles of historicism and naturalism also became outdated. The primary source of the operetta form, the Viennese *Singspiel* and the Budapest play about the idealized peasant, dried up, and the operetta of "the golden age" fell into a crisis. It is enough to say that the home of the musical theater, the Theater an der Wien, was closed down at the beginning of the century, and all other theaters also had to struggle.[22] In the turbulent and decadent fin-de-siècle atmosphere, the question was raised as to whether the Viennese-Budapest operetta could be rejuvenated and adjusted to the sentiments and expressions of the new age.

Just at this time of crisis, signs of a real rejuvenation appeared on the stage. In Vienna it was mostly Leo Fall's modernized operettas that became popular; in Budapest it was the work of Jenő Huszka, whose *Prince Bob (The Vagabond Prince* in the United States) was the first hit of the new century, in both city and countryside. Referring to the amazing success of *Prince Bob*, a young journalist of *Nagyvárad* pointed out how misguided it would be to despise operetta as a naive and foolish genre. As a matter of fact, "the operetta is a most serious theatrical genre. It is the one with which we can freely strike out kings without danger. . . . It can destroy more of this rotten world and better prepare the future than five protests in Parliament."[23] The young journalist was Endré Ady, Hungary's greatest poet of this century.

Yet another Hungarian poet, Gyula Juhász, wrote with good reason several years later that "the center of the European operetta had shifted into the Austro-Hungarian Monarchy, and it is slowly but surely coming to Hungary." Juhász attempted to explain the reason for this successful shifting of the genre toward the East. The drama had not yet found its new form, he argued; it does not correspond to the requirements of the age of the newspaper and the movie. The operetta, however, "is a quickly moving story with much easy lyricism and music, much decoration and little earnestness." These are just what the audience is longing for, particularly in East Central Europe which is not mature enough for Ibsen and Hauptmann.[24]

The most representative figure of the rejuvenation, "the silver age" of the operetta, is Franz Lehár, and his most representative play is *The Merry Widow*. Lehár was a characteristic figure of the Old Empire: a man of a "Habsburg nationality."[25] The family came from Moravia; they were probably the descendants of Germanized Slavic peasants and craftsmen. (According to family legend, however, a French officer of the name of Le Harde stayed in Austria during the Napoleonic wars; his descendant would be the military musician Lehár.) What we know for certain is that the composer's father was the conductor of a military band and that he traveled throughout the Empire with his family, from his birthplace Komárom to Kolozsvár (Cluj), from Prague to Sarajevo. The young man had a promising musical talent and attended the conservatory in Prague. He was a great admirer of Antonin Dvořák. He was studying to become a violinist but decided to follow his father's path; he became the leader of a military band for twelve years and toured the Empire from Losonc to Vienna. The long time he spent in the military band had two advantages. This institution which was so popular in the Monarchy also had an integrative role. Its conductor was expected to know all musical genres, the novelties of Vienna, the local folklore, and the changes in taste of the mass culture. It was in this atmosphere that Lehár's musical talent unfolded, together with his sensitivity towards the public. The new director of the Theater an der Wien, Vilmos Karczag, a Hungarian theater entrepreneur, made the right choice when he offered the young Lehár a position as a composer by the side of two talented librettists.

The two librettists, Victor Leon and Leo Stein, discovered a work gathering dust among secondhand librettos, written by the witty playwright, Henri Meilhac, entitled *L'Attaché*. They made some cosmetic changes and placed the locale of the story in a small state in the Balkans, which they called Pontevedro. The embassy of this small state was commissioned to save Hanna Glavari, the immensely rich widow from Pontevedro, for her homeland, together with her millions, of course. To achieve this, the handsome attaché of the embassy had to win Hanna to his side. However, Hanna was afraid of dowry-hunters, while Danilo was afraid of being taken for one. A passionate breakup was followed by an equally passionate reconciliation and a most passionate embrace. Boy wins girl and the Fatherland is saved.

What is so new, so fascinating about this story? In the storyline, nothing, but there are significant innovations in the lyrics. Gone is the Biedermeier sentimentality: frivolous city humor, criticism of capitalism, bourgeois morals, marriage, and diplomacy take its place. "We widows are in demand. . . . But when we poor widows are rich, why then, our value is doubled," sings Hanna in her entrance. Marriage, Danilo retorts, is like a Dual Alliance in the beginning, "but soon the league's increased to three (Triple Alliance). . . . Madame too readily adopts the policy of open doors!" For these new cavaliers even the Fatherland is not sacred any more. What do we hear in Danilo's famous Maxim song? "And then the champagne flows, and often can-can goes. And there's fondling, kissing, with all these charmers . . . they make me forget, then, the dear Fatherland!"[26]

The real novelty and attraction, however, lay not in the lyrics but in Lehár's music. When he finished the first song, he called his librettist well after midnight and played "Dummer, dummer Reitersmann" (Foolish, foolish knight) to him, and though Mr. Stein was sleepy and irritated, he had to admit that "the waltz had a strict but flexible rhythm, it was seductive, and explicitly erotic."[27] In describing Lehár's music, Bernard Grun holds that the absolute novelty of the piece lies in the ingenuous boldness by which the plot musically interprets the ever-vibrating sensuality. The melodies speak about nothing but desire, passion, instinct, embrace, lovemaking. "Libido has dominated there where pure love, . . . psychology where simpleness once prevailed." But their interpretation is new, breaking all conventions; it freely alters major keys with minor keys and uses different musical elements. Hanna's entry begins with a mazurka and ends with a Parisian slow waltz, her Vilia song. A soft and sentimental romance is finished off with a fast and sarcastic polka rhythm played by the orchestra. No doubt Lehár uses musical colors and harmonies which he must have heard in the works of Debussy, Richard Strauss, and Mahler.[28]

The operetta takes place in Paris, with Parisian scenery. This local color is, however, merely a façade behind which the story resembles Vienna and East Central Europe. Both the mocking spirit that makes fun of the aristocracy, the nouveaux riches, the ardent patriotism, and the heroine, Hanna, who may be from Budapest, Prague, or Zagreb, are first and foremost Viennese.

With *The Merry Widow*, *The Count of Luxemburg*, and some other works, Lehár performed a real feat of daring. With his remarkable compositions of rejuvenated operetta he managed to reintegrate a very differentiated city culture where the more and more esoteric and alienated high culture was sharply segregated from the mass productions of the entertainment industry. Lehár's operettas spoke about the city to the people of all strata and kinds living in the city; even the people of the nightclubs in working-class neighborhoods danced to the new and refreshing sounds of the dance music seeping out of the upper-middle-class saloons.

The Merry Widow opened in Vienna on December 30, 1905. During the first ten years it was performed four hundred times there and one hundred fifty times in Budapest. The fact that Budapest accepted and became enamored of the lovely, sensual widow with the wonderful voice shows that the capital had truly become a metropolis. On the other hand, the other half of Budapest's heart was still drawn towards modernized national romanticism represented by János Vitéz (John the Hero), composed by Pongrác Kacsóh. The enormous success of this musical play surpassed even that of Lehár and Strauss, testifying that the new metropolis was strongly attached to the glorious past, a national nostalgia which inundated the East Central European mentality.[29]

Together with Lehár, the independent Budapest operetta blossomed in the first decade of our century. What were the main features of its spectacular rise in popularity?

As we saw in Lehár's The Merry Widow, some Budapest operettas also became more "democratic"; they were imbued by a strong antifeudal and anticapitalist spirit. This meant at first a more explicit ironical criticism of the "feudal-capitalistic" society, and a growing importance of popular figures. Not only attractive actresses and music hall girls advanced into the ranks of higher society, but also common people, waiters, and stableboys played protagonist roles, as in Albert Szirmai's play, the Mágnás Miska.

Together with "democratization," structural changes also took place in the librettos. Beside the usual couple who embodied great romantic love, a second couple appeared in the new librettos: the soubrette and the comic dancer. They counterbalanced and made fun of the first, often boring couple: they brought humor and nonconformity onto the stage.[30]

Finally, the rising Budapest operetta rejuvenated the world of music, too. Beyond traditional waltz and csárdás, it adopted more popular elements and later incorporated modern ragtime rhythms. Outstanding composers like Jacobi, Huszka, Kacsóh, and Szirmai were not ingenuous amateurs but musicians who had graduated from music academies, who had learned composition and orchestration.

Claim to the most vigorous talent could be made by Imre Kálmán, who was born on the shores of Lake Balaton, in Siófok, in 1882.[31] The family consisted of rich bourgeois entrepreneurs who went bankrupt when Kálmán was only a child. Like Lehár, who had wanted to become a violinist, Kálmán longed to be a pianist, but his chronic myositis was a deterrent. What was left was composition—and operetta. His operettas represent an overall Monarchic identity: they are set in the Empire, the protagonists are the aristocracy, the army, soldiers, Gypsies, and citizens. The music of the *Tatárjárás (The Autumn Maneuver)* and the *Gypsy Primás* (the leading violinist in a Gypsy band) embodies Viennese waltzes, military marches, couplets, and Gypsy music like that of his greatest "hit," *The Csárdás Princess.*[32]

The subject of the libretto is banal hackwork—the romantic love story of a Budapest music hall prima donna, Sylvia Vereczki, and Prince Edwin Lippert-Weilersheim. Their love is so strong and pure that it overcomes all obstacles—the resistance of aristocratic parents and all the machinations of high society. The libretto, a buffoonery of the Golden Age, was born in the cloudless spring of 1914. When war broke out, Kálmán lapsed into silence. It took him a year of solitude in a villa in Bad Ischl to compose the operetta, perhaps as a protest against the worldwide massacre.[33] *The Csárdás Princess* opened in Vienna on November 17, 1915, during the fourth Isonzo offensive in northern Italy. That prolonged attack resulted in 440,000 deaths and more than double that number of casualties.

In spite of daily tragedies, the new operetta had startling success. By April, 1917, there were five hundred performances in Vienna, two hundred in both Berlin and Budapest, and in Stockholm, Gothenburg, Hamburg, Cologne, Munich, Hanover, Leipzig, and Frankfurt over a hundred performances.[34]

The people, heavily weighed down by the calamities of war, misery, and death, wanted to forget: they delighted in the operetta that evoked the world of the music hall, in which love and song, not lords and death, prevailed. And in *The Csárdás Princess,* Kálmán crystallized all the inventions, tricks, and accomplishments of the Budapest operetta. He created a stylistic mélange out of the piquant wit of the Parisian operetta, the sweetness of Viennese music, and stylized Hungarian gypsy music, blending them with the typical figures, jokes, and musical expressions of the opera buffa and the Budapest-Berlin cabaret. In his fairy tale, dreams of the glittering marriage of a poor girl symbolizing the triumph of love were intertwined with a satire on the idiotic conventions of the nobility. This ambivalence can be seen in the main characters of *The Csárdás Princess*—Prince Edwin and the prima donna Sylvia. He is a handsome, pleasing man infatuated with Sylvia, and his love seems sincere and serious. But he possesses neither a strong moral character nor even a mediocre intelligence. Sylvia provokes admiration. She comes from a small, distant village on the banks of the river Tisza—achieves a miraculous career evolving from a village elf to a music hall angel and finally to a real court princess—without losing her innocence. Because of the absurdity of such a character in twentieth century Central Europe the libretto relativizes her genuine chastity. In the opening song she declares: "If you only want to have fun, keep away from me, darling!" And for the sake of unequivocal understanding, her partner adds the warning: "You cannot get Sylvia for 'something' (for a conventional relationship). She does not permit stupidity. Here one must make an offer of marriage or go away."[35]

Characteristic of the operetta is the unexpected unmasking of Prince Edwin's mother, who firmly resisted the planned misalliance. At the end of the play, however, it is revealed that the mother once had been a music hall performer too, and had preserved her reputation only by marrying each lover in turn. Having thus been unveiled, she succumbs and gives her blessing.

Finally, we have to mention an important ingredient of the operetta's success—lyrics that greatly contributed to keeping an ironical distance from the fairy tale. The lyrics and the Hungarian translation were written by a talented humorist—an expert of the theater and the music hall—Andor Gábor. His sparkling lyrics are witty couplets mixing up folklore and metropolitan elements, creating an unmistakably Pest-slang of aristocratic, Jewish, German, and other idioms. Gábor's text is parody at its best.

The deepest secret of *The Csárdás Princess*, however, lies in its fascinating music. "Melodies that go on playing in our hearts entwine our souls like the odor of wonderful flowers," wrote a viewer in the magazine *Szinházi Élet (Theater Life)*. "Imre Kálmán is a magician. . . . His music drives all sorrow away and tells about a wonderful love. . . . We believe him as the little child believes his mother when she relates to him a fairy tale."[36] "Bubbling over with blood-boiling Hungarian rhythm, Hungarian songs, brilliant orchestration," said a Budapest daily, the *Budapesti Hírlap*.[37] "His greatest merit is that he refreshes the operetta with the enchanting aura and pulsating vitality of the Hungarian folk song, whose ability to get the blood circulating had already been slackening . . . because of sugary Viennese sentimentalism." The reviewer of the *Pesti Hírlap* was not enchanted. Kálmán has sacrificed his art for "cheap effects . . . regarding popularity that brings happiness as the only major objective." There are many lovesick Viennese waltzes in his work, too; "they were written by Emmerich, but there is also a lot of interesting atmospheric Hungarian music in it as well: they are the works of Imre Kálmán." The Hungarian translator, Andor Gábor, however, spiced the dialogues with a lot of ideas and good humor.[38] The text is parody at its best.

Perhaps the secret of the integrative power and world success of the operetta lies in this ambivalence of interpretation. It could be taken literally as a fairy tale: within the magical world of the stage the everyday laws of bourgeois reality are suspended; or it could be perceived as a parody of the evils of militarism and bureaucracy, of all the faults of the Establishment. One could even discreetly buy the sheet music of the operetta—just as Gustav Mahler bought *The Merry Widow*—and enjoy playing and humming it in the privacy of one's home.[39]

This view may be supported by the worldwide success of *The Csárdás Princess* during World War I. It was first performed in Vienna in the autumn of 1915, a year later in Budapest, then in Paris, St. Petersburg, and Moscow in 1917. The operetta penetrated the trenches, the minefields, and all frontiers. A Viennese critic could write in 1917: "The whole world resounds with two things: the roar of the cannon and the success of *The Csárdás Princess.*"[40]

The power of the operetta to effect social integration on both an internal and international level prevailed during World War I and World War II, between the wars, and in spite of the wars in our century. This genre is part of mass culture. Its standards may vary, but it opens the way to higher musical education. Surely this is what gives it its broad cultural and historical significance.

I would like to refer the reader to the archives of the *Hungarian Institute for Theater*, where I found valuable data relating to the librettos, performances, and reviews of operettas discussed in this chapter.

Notes

1. It is not by chance that an outstanding monographer of the operetta regarded his work as a kind of "cultural history." Bernard Grun, *Kulturgeschichte der Operette* (Munich, 1961); see also Martin Lichtfuss, *Operette im Ausverkauf (Wien-Köln, 1989)*; Otto Schneiderei, *Paul Lincke und die Erstehung der Berliner Operette* (Berlin, 1989).
2. Bernard Grun, *Kulturgeschichte der Operette*, 75–80.

3. Bernard Grun, *Kulturgeschichte der Operette*, 105–106, 115ff; see also Paul Bekker, *Jacques Offenbach* (Berlin, 1909).

4. Otto Brusatti and Wilhelm Deutschmann, eds., *Die Wiener Operette*, Katalog der 91, Sonderausstellung des Historischen Museums der Stadt Wien (Vienna, 1985), 25.

5. *Die Wiener Operette*, 31; see also Franz Hadamowsky and Otto Heinz, *Die Wiener Operette* (Vienna, 1947).

6. With regard to Strauss's oeuvre, see Ignaz Schnitzer, *Meister Johann* (Vienna, 1920); Ernst Decsey, *Johann Strauss* (Stuttgart, 1922); György Sándor Gál and Vilmos Somogyi, *Mesél a Bécsi Erdő* (The Wienerwald talks) (Budapest, 1972).

7. The meeting is depicted in Ignaz Schnitzer, *Meister Johann*; in György Sándor Gál and Vilmos Somogyi, *Mesél a Bécsi Erdő*, 533–537; and in H. E. Jacob, *A Régi Budapest* (The old Budapest) (Budapest, 1938), 261–266.

8. György Sándor Gál and Vilmos Somogyi, *Mesél a Bécsi Erdő*, 538–539.

9. H. E. Jacob, *A Régi Budapest*, 266; Ignaz Schnitzer, *Meister Johann*.

10. "Mit den ersten vier Takten klingt der Akkord der Ungarnwelt, beginnt das Mollreich der Synkopen, beginnt das Czimballhafte, Rhapsodische, wozu als Gegensatz das Wienertum tritt." See Ernst Decsey, *Johann Strauss*.

11. It was the novelist Jókai who recommended the unknown recruiting music to Strauss.

12. H. E. Jacob, *A Régi Budapest*, 269–270.

13. Adolf Bassaraba, "Schweinzuchter mit gräfischer Krone," *Wochenschau*, October 24, 1965.

14. *Pesti Hírlap* (Pest Journal) (October 25, 1885), 7, and (March 27, 1886), 7; *Pesti Napló* (Pest Daily) (October 27, 1885 and March 27, 1886); and *Vasárnapi Ujság* (Sunday Gazette) (April 25, 1886).

15. *Ország-Világ* (Country and World) (April 3, 1886), 228.

16. *Borsszem Jankó* (Johnny the pepper) (November 1, 1885). Cartoon on page 1; text on page 8.

17. *Vasárnapi Ujság* (Sunday Gazette) (November 15, 1885), 742.

18. See the *Extrablatt*, quoted by Bernard Grun in *Kulturgeschichte der Operette*, 232.

19. Hermann Broch, *Hofmannsthal und seine Zeit* (Munich, 1964), 57.

20. György Sándor Gál and Vilmos Somogyi, *Mesél a Bécsi Erdő* (Budapest, 1972), 542–543.

21. Alma Mahler-Werfel, *Mein Leben* (Frankfurt, 1960), 149.

22. Bernard Grun, *Kulturgeschichte der Operette*, 323–324. Curt Riess, "Als die Witwen noch lustig waren," *Du. Kulturelle Monatschrift* (April 1963), 84–86.

23. Erzsébet Vezér, *Publicistical Writings of Endre Ady*, Vol. 1 (Budapest, 1977), 414.

24. Gyula Juhász, "Az Operett," *Nagyvárad* (July 1, 1909).

25. Bernard Grun, *Kulturgeschichte der Operette*, 333–341; Erns Decsey, *Franz Lehár* (Vienna, 1924); Franz Hadamowsky and Heinz Otte, *Die Wiener Operette* (Vienna, 1947).

26. Péter Molnár Gál, *A Víg Özvegy* (The merry widow) *Mozgó Világ* (Moving world) (April 1988), 110–116. I appreciate the kind support of Profes-

sor Moritz Csáky, Graz, Vienna, who allowed me to read his manuscript on the Viennese operetta.

27. Bernard Grun, *Kulturgeschichte der Operette*, 347; Curt Riess, "Als die Witwen noch lustig waren," in *Du.*, 86.

28. Bernard Grun, *Kulturgeschichte der Operette*, 349.

29. With regard to this unique piece of Hungarian operetta based on folklore, see Janos Bókay, *Egy Rózsaszal Szebben Beszél* . . . (One rose speaks sweeter . . .) (Budapest, 1978).

30. István Takács, *A Csárdáskirálynő—Egykor és Most* (The Csárdás Princess—once and now), in *Szinhaz* (Theater) XIII, 5 (May 1980), 19.

31. Julius Bistron, *Emmerich Kálmán* (Vienna, 1932); Rudolf Oesterreicher, *Emmerich Kálmán* (Vienna, 1954); Róbert Rátonyi, *Operett.* I (Budapest, 1984), 160–171.

32. Bernard Grun, *Kulturgeschichte der Operette*, 386–387.

33. The libretto of the play, *Szinházi Élet (Theater life)* VI, 15 (April 1917): 1.

34. Róbert Rátonyi, *Operett.* I: 216–217.

35. *Szinházi Élet* VI, 15 (April 1917): 6–8.

36. *Szinházi Élet* V, 40 (1916).

37. *Budapesti Hirlap* (November 4, 1916).

38. *Pesti Hirlap* (November 4, 1916).

39. Alma Mahler Werfel, *And the Bridge Is Love* (New York, 1958), 32.

40. Róbert Rátonyi, *Operett.* I: 220.

Chapter 9

The Budapest Joke
and Comic Weeklies
as Mirrors of Cultural Assimilation

GÉZA BUZINKAY

*I*N CENTRAL EUROPE, jokes as a new genre appeared with the birth of modern large cities. Their contextual and formal development paralleled the evolution of metropolitan society.

Humor has long been as integral to Hungarian as in the literature of other languages. In fact, humor can be traced back in Hungary to the time before a written literature. Popular anecdote collections from different regions began to appear in the 1840s and 1850s and they resembled collections of folk poetry and tales.[1] The so-called Pest joke first surfaced in the 1860s. What initially appears to be a continuity in development, however, was actually a parallel process, since the newly evolving Pest joke was very much different from traditional Hungarian anecdotes, comic poetry, and tales.

From Anecdotes to Jokes

As far back as antiquity, historical or rhetorical literature used anecdotes as a stylistic tool, but they did not yet constitute an independent literary genre.[2] However, a spoken variation of the anecdote developed at the same time, and it already exhibited distinct properties for entertainment. Anecdotes were meant to characterize real events or people concisely and acutely. Since the middle of the nineteenth century oral anecdotes have been an important part of Hungarian literature because they were adapted by such eminent writers as Mór Jókai or, later, Kálmán Mikszáth. Initially, the comic weeklies that began to appear in the late 1850s lived off this store of anecdotes. For example, for some two decades Jókai's *Üstökös* regularly solicited anecdotes of different regions from its correspondents from outside the capital and its readers. These have since become documents that serve as social historical sources for studying the landed gentry and the world they lived in.[3]

Differences in the social and cultural background of anecdotes and jokes explain basic differences between the two forms of expression.[4] The fact that anecdotes originated in rural society must have been a factor in their acquiring their characteristically elaborate style. In order for an anecdote to seem authentic and for its portrayal to be effective, it required a lot of explanation and interjections, and objects had to be described in detail so that a listener without a similar education or even no previous information at all could understand the story or the punch line. The latter, though, is not an essential part of an anecdote.

But the punch line is the essence of jokes. The verbose quality of the anecdote did not suit the way of life and the tastes of the newly evolving middle class. It lived in cities, the biggest and most important of which was Pest (later Budapest), and city life meant a confined and organized space that supplied a setting for collective information. Because they shared educational and geographic backgrounds, the jokes that the middle class created and enjoyed had to merely hint at a few key circumstances and then focus on the punch line. The jokes were thus much more concise and abstract than anecdotes.

Beyond these general characteristics of urban jokes, the Budapest joke had its own special qualities. It often combined various international motifs, played with words, emphasized puns, and preferred political subjects, conveying the unique outlook of petit bourgeois wisdom. The founder of the cabaret in Budapest, Endre Nagy, summed up poetically the essence of the joke: ". . . like a mischievous whirlwind it stirred up rigidly segregated forms of expression; it threw a questioning smile at inflated pathos, and softened desiccating cynicism with a sprinkle of sentimental tears."[5]

Even if there is no absolutely clear borderline between anecdotes and jokes, the differences are real and they help us grasp the cultural history of the Budapest joke.[6]

Adapting Yiddish-German Anecdotes to the Hungarian Language

The Pest joke originated somewhere around the time of the Austro-Hungarian Compromise of 1867 and the unification of the three independent cities into the single municipality of Budapest in 1872. Adolf Ágai, publisher and editor of the comic weekly *Borsszem Jankó*, which he founded in 1868, adapted the jokes and anecdotes, which were mainly of Yiddish origin from Berlin, later from Vienna or Munich, into Hungarian.

It is not clear, however, who adapted what. The late Chief Rabbi and historian Alexander Scheiber mentioned a Jewish anecdote he considered of Hungarian origin that traveled the world; after several Hungarian and German variations, it finally ended up as the subject of a short story by W. S. Maugham *(The Man Who Made His Mark*, 1929, subsequently entitled: *The Verger).*[7] I have also found a Jewish joke published in Hungarian in *Borsszem Jankó* that Sigmund Freud used in an essay almost thirty years later.[8]

Freud used one joke (it originated as an anecdote) that serves as a good illustration of how a Jewish joke became a Hungarian one. Judging by the names of the locations it cites, the original must have come to Vienna from Galicia. It goes as follows:

> In the temple at Cracow the Great Rabbi N. was sitting and praying with his disciples. Suddenly he uttered a cry, and in reply to his disciples' anxious enquiries, exclaimed: "At this very moment the Great Rabbi L. has died in Lemberg." The community was in mourning for the dead man. In the course of the next few days people arriving from Lemberg were asked how the Rabbi had died and what had been wrong with him; but they knew nothing about it, since they had left him in the best of health. At last it was established with certainty that the Rabbi L. in Lemberg had not died at the moment at which the Rabbi N. had observed his death by telepathy, since he was still alive. A stranger took the opportunity of jeering at one of the Cracow Rabbi's disciples about this occurrence: "Your Rabbi made a great fool of himself that time, when he said the Rabbi L. died in Lemberg. The man's alive to this day." "That makes no difference," replied the disciple. "No matter what you say, the *Kück* from Cracow to Lemberg was a magnificent one."[9] (The *Kück* is a Yiddish word from the German *gucken*, to look or view.)

In a *Borsszemm Jankó* issue of 1878 a decidedly Jewish lower-middle-class figure named Salamon Seiffensteiner, "a chandler on Three Drums Street" in Theresa-Town, tells a variation of this same anecdote. He mentions that he himself read it in the liberal daily *Pester Journal*, which indicates that he read it in German. But in his jumble of Hungarian-German-Yiddish, he ends up with a version adapted to Hungarian in two respects. He replaces the German names of locations with Hungarian ones, and he lends the joke a local political connotation. These are the closing days of the Russian-Turkish War in the Balkans and the time of the occupation of Bosnia-Herzegovina by Austro-Hungarian troops. Furthermore, Salamon Seiffensteiner refers to the foreign minister of the Monarchy, Gyula Andrássy, when he says: "Granted, the Bosnians are not happy with being occupied—but his *kücking* from Vienna all the way to Sarajevo is a great wonder in itself."[10]

No matter how many examples we find to underline the Hungarian origin of anecdotes and jokes, they cannot have been conceived as such either in Hungary, or in Poland, Bohemia, or Germany. Rather, they were born in East and Central Europe's Jewish communities. Jewish intellectuals played a leading role in the creation and development of the German press and later the press of other nations of the region.[11] The ability to make witty leaps with words, a product of their cultural heritage, naturally found its way into publications. Jewish jokes first appeared in German and later in the languages of these other countries.

The appearance of anecdotes and jokes of Jewish origin primarily meant, therefore, that Hungarian culture, which until then was considered ethnically exclusive, homogeneous, and specific, was now incorporating international cultural trends and the motifs that accompanied widespread urbanization.

The Transformation of Comic Weeklies in the Nineteenth Century

Historical research on modern urban humor is aided by the fact that as this type of humor was taking root, it simultaneously created its own genre in the form of comic weeklies. Publications of this type were developed in Western Europe but soon spread to Central and Eastern Europe. While weeklies published in the latter regions looked to Western Europe for their models, they eventually established a comic journal that was different in content and even in character.

Donald J. Gray has convincingly shown how the tone of English comic weeklies evolved in the course of the nineteenth century from crude, unpolished, and impertinent provocation into literary vehicles of gentle irony. They moved from an almost exclusively political orientation to social topics and, finally, to becoming a form of entertainment. And while in the early nineteenth century these papers were mostly textual press, by the end of the century they contained an overwhelming number of illustrations and comic strips. The impetus for this complex development, Gray found, was that "they are popular journals which ride with strongly established opinions and tastes rather than trying to create them."[12] Instead of focusing on moral education or politics, their goal was to sell tens of thousands, later hundreds of thousands, of copies. In this respect, they were early indicators of the direction that the press and popular culture were to take. English comic weeklies like *Punch* or *Ally Sloper's Half-Holiday* divorced themselves from the satirically oriented society papers which contained caricatures and whose low circulations implied that they were elite publications. "Society papers *Vanity Fair* and *Truth* emphasized news, however trivial; comic journals emphasized the amusing ways in which their writers and illustrators played off the news."[13]

Following England, satirical papers sprang up in different parts of the world as organs of leftist social movements and of expressionism, from *Simplicissimus* (1896–1944) in Munich to *The Masses* (1912–1917) in New York. In East Central Europe they never assumed a defined and enduring profile because they were confined to smaller language regions and thus had more limited markets. They were also hampered by an excessive national consciousness. Even among the comic weeklies with a primarily light humor only a few were able to evolve by 1910 into true enterprises with large circulations. But the majority kept a didactically moralizing and politically directed profile, reflecting the satirically oriented publications in England.

The circulation figures of comic weeklies appearing in Budapest and New York present an interesting comparison: In the two decades before 1905, comic weeklies in Budapest had a circulation of 1,200–4,400, with the most popular comic journals published in 1910 having circulations of 12,000–29,000 copies.[14] About this same time, the New York publications *Puck* (1877–1918), *Judge* (1881–1938), and *Life* (1883–1937) had circulations of 80,000–120,000.[15] The Hungarian comic weeklies belonged predominantly to large newspaper publishers and never became independent undertakings. And while the purely business-oriented New York press reflected precise information about the level of education and the tastes of its readership, the Hungarian papers were influenced at least as much by the taste and orientation of their publishers and editors as by their readers. (This must be kept in mind if one relies on comic weeklies to draw up one's conclusions about Hungarian social history!) Thus, with the exception of the appearance of comic strips, the same tendencies which Donald J. Gray observed in the English press are found in the Hungarian comic weeklies as well, only a decade or two later.

The Birth of the Comic Weekly in Budapest

In the history of Hungarian comic papers and jokes the landmark year was 1868, the date of the first issue of *Borsszem Jankó*. Although the previously established comic weeklies, *Üstökös* (1858–1919), *Bolond Miska* (1860–1875), or *Ludas Matyi* (1867–1873) appeared in Pest (later Budapest), they had hardly any ties to the capital. Instead, they served the political interests of the opposition, with an eye to readers who were primarily provincial and to political supporters whom they often called on to relate anecdotes or political conflicts taking place in their areas. *Borsszem Jankó* (1868–1936) was the first comic journal that was truly urban. It was the intellectual product of Budapest's Districts VI and VII (Elizabeth-Town and Theresa-Town), which had a lower-middle-class population. These were the areas where the shops of the small craftsmen and merchants dominated the streets, and where most of the small and middle businessmen and the new generation of self-employed intellectuals lived. Here, the proportion of the Jewish population was the highest, making up some three-quarters of the two districts' inhabitants.[16] It is characteristic of the weekly that its platform was enunciated by a representative of this latter group, Iczig Spitzig, one of the first outstanding comic figures created by the paper's editor, Adolf Ágai. Iczig Spitzig brought into focus the struggle for the social recognition of Jewish emancipation, which had just been passed into law.[17] *Borsszem Jankó* conducted liberal politics in its own way, by doing just what all good and lasting humor does: it presented questions of the gravest importance under the cloak of triviality and added to the impact of this contrast by stunning punch lines.

The journal quickly multiplied the number of its subscribers and became widely respected. The initial 500–600 subscribers grew to 4,000 by its third year in 1870, and sustained that level, running at 4,400 copies in 1889. At the core of its subscribers were clubs, reading circles, coffeehouses, or associations, which created a readership that was multiples of the number of copies printed. Around 1910 Hungarian publishers calculated an average of three readers per newspaper copy.[18] For magazines, that proportion was considerably higher. In short, between 1870 and the early 1890s, *Borsszem Jankó* was Budapest's comic weekly with the highest circulation and a readership of at least 15,000–20,000.

By the middle of the 1870s, *Borsszem Jankó* had made its final breakthrough. By keeping a keen eye on the economic and cultural role of the Jews and on their vocational and religious life, it became the most popular comic journal in Budapest and the major cities.[19] It is highly significant that a paper which did not disguise its affiliation with a minority, which spoke out for the protection of their rights and which, to top it all, was the comic weekly of the ruling party, was the very paper that became the most popular.

What was the reason for *Borsszem Jankó*'s popularity? What made such comic weeklies so popular that they became an accepted genre even though they were introduced into Hungarian society by an ethnic group which was considered alien and which suffered discrimination?

Urban Assimilation and the Budapest Joke

The popularity of *Borsszem Jankó* stemmed from its appearance at the right time and under the right conditions. During the optimistic period that preceded the 1867 Compromise between Austria and Hungary, a liberal and tolerant leadership found important allies in the Jewish intellectuals, especially in the press and the democratic views they propagated. These Jewish intellectuals were quite well educated; their social position and schooling in several languages provided them with a broad outlook. The government that passed the political emancipation of Jews into law found staunch supporters among this minority group, which was seeking assimilation. Thus, they were critical of the government in a positive way and furthered democratization.[20] ". . . I wage a war . . . *against* insolence, frivolity, arrogance and bravado *on the side* of the Hungarian spirit, for the freedom of conscience, and civilization," was Adolf Ágai's apologia in the one thousandth issue of *Borsszem Jankó*.[21]

It was this cultured and broad outlook, as well as the spirit of positive criticism and optimistic belief in the future, that gave importance to *Borsszem Jankó* and its jokes. Moreover, Hungary's prime minister, Gyula Andrássy, was personally involved in its establishment. It was he who outlined its scope, gave it its title, and chose Adolf Ágai as its editor. Accordingly, the launching of *Borsszem Jankó* became a political affair of national significance, in the very year of the Compromise.

It must be remembered that comic weeklies had their golden age in the nineteenth century because of the appearance and propagation of the principles of democracy. Politics was evolving from being the exclusive concern of a cabinet into a more-or-less public affair, and the politicians themselves were becoming more visible. Moreover, their fate depended increasingly on their ability to win the masses. So the appearance of comic journals expressed an exuberance about the spreading of democracy, reflecting most clearly that politics and its practice had become commonplace, and that politicians were to be regarded like any other citizens. This is the main reason why the comic weeklies of the nineteenth century were first and foremost politically oriented.

When democracy passed from a matter of militant politics to becoming an everyday affair, the comic weeklies acquired a more diffuse social content. They became vehicles of entertainment as democracy's political ideal, however limited in effectiveness, grew familiar. It is historically significant, then, that after the mid-1880s frivolous entertainment became a constituent of comic journals, and after 1890 it became an integral part of the comic papers of the Budapest bourgeoisie. Now, politics were pushed into the background. But those comic journals that addressed a readership outside the capital and professed traditional ideals and social concepts kept a political profile.

There was another novelty that *Borsszem Jankó* brought to the press and that was the Budapest joke. It made its appearance either in a literary or in a cruder form—in sketches, parodies, squibs, puns, verses, or illustrations. Nothing had been published before that was so expressively concise and easy to grasp.

Undoubtedly, *Borsszem Jankó* also owed its popularity to Adolf Ágai and his exceptionally talented original staff, including Ludwig Hevesi, Lajos Dóczy, Jenő Rákosi, Árpád Berczik, and cartoonist Karl Klietsch (Karel Klič, Charles Kley).[22] Hevesi became a leading theoretician and critic of art nouveau in Vienna in the beginning of the twentieth century. Dóczy was a popular Austro-Hungarian poet and librettist of operettas at the end of the nineteenth century as well as the press chief of the foreign ministry; he was awarded the title of baron by the emperor. Rákosi first gained popularity in Budapest as a playwright. In the 1880s, he became a major media magnate as owner and editor of the newspaper *Budapesti Hírlap* and was later rewarded for his nationalistic propaganda with a seat in the Upper House. Berczik earned a name for himself as a playwright, and gained influence through his position as head of the press office of the prime ministry. Klietsch was a well-known caricaturist and inventor of a printing technique; after leaving Budapest he lived first in Vienna and later in England.[23]

That *Borsszem Jankó* was essentially a Budapest journal was evident from the first page of its first number. Its illustrations and texts were inspired by the city's leading figures and events. The range of its topics spanned everything from city traffic, sanitation, public management, and public safety, to prostitution and fashion, or the unveiling of a statue. The paper knew and loved the rapidly growing city and its people, popularizing its way of life and civilization teasingly or satirically, but always from the perspective of an active participant.

This was before the 1880s, a time when all other comic weeklies spoke derisively of Budapest as a place that should be revitalized by people of the countryside; it was "a Sodom," as one of *Borsszem Jankó's* gentry figures liked to call it.

Borsszem Jankó continued to be recognized for its uniqueness as an urban comic weekly. Only after the early 1880s, when political anti-Semitism became the platform of a party, did it launch its attack against that line of thinking. After that, Ágai became the man who "perhaps had the greatest number of enemies in old Hungary," meaning the provinces, as an influential Hungarian writer recalled decades later.[24] Such judgment is not surprising, considering that Ágai's paper displayed not a trace of submission or fear; indeed, it reflected confidence and pride in dealing with the ethnically and religiously multi-faceted capital. An expression of this attitude is seen in a joke it published in 1892 entitled "Foreigners in Budapest." (As there were no tourist guides yet, the commentator role was taken on by baggage carriers or porters:)

> Porter: "Back on Calvin Square I already had the honor of showing you the church of the Calvinists, and on the Danube shore the Greek Orthodox church. Now, that one over there, that crumbled one, belongs to the Lutherans, and the one with the big dome there, that's the Basilica of the Catholics.'
> Lord Somebody: "And that one with the twin towers?"
> Porter: "That, my Lord, that's the synagogue of the population of Budapest."[25]

In this world of diverse and opposed religions and ethnic groups there was a part of the middle class whose intellectual representatives were able to formulate what their more advanced state of bourgeois development actually meant to society as a whole. To general society this came as a revelation. Articulating it also contributed to *Borsszem Jankó's* popularity and provided the right atmosphere in which the new genre of the joke could take root.

Jokes, Nationalities, and Ethnic Minorities

The genre that *Borsszem Jankó* had made popular was put to use in the very criticism it inspired. The new style it had introduced could not be circumvented even by its opponents. The jokes it had popularized and the figures it had created dominated comic weeklies for decades. As a consequence, even the simple imitation of its jokes was used as a tool of attack against the paper. Either the style of its jokes was employed to dress up some derisive comment, or the content of its jokes was turned inside out. For example, beginning in January 1895 *Herkó Páter*, a comic weekly with a People's Party orientation, launched a series of anti-Semitic attacks against Adolf Ágai under the title "The Good Wishes of Hepp (Kike) Cziczesz Dr. Ágai," a crudely revamped version of *Borsszem Jankó*'s regular column "The Terrible Curses of Reb Menachem Cziczesbeiszer."

Some extreme leftist and rightist groups, ultramontanes, and, in the 1890s, the sympathizers with the People's Party, lumped all their enemies together by calling them "Jewish/Free-Masonic/Liberals." At the same time jokes conquered the public mind as reflected in the press and feuilletons, in the short stories and sketches that were being newly created in Budapest, in social comedies and popular plays, in operettas, the cabaret and stage troop performances, and in the programs of literary circles. And yet there were accusations that comic criticism represented a foreign spirit, was superficial, frivolous, or downright immoral, and corrupted the language. Even rigid Protestant criticism appeared with admonitions on moral grounds, speaking out as early as 1874 against all comic literature and its critics for a licentiousness that ridiculed and mocked everything without respecting "the borderline between sacredness and sacrilege."[26]

By the end of the 1870s, the social atmosphere around *Borsszem Jankó* had changed considerably. Anti-Semitism appeared in politics, and, later on, became the platform of a political party.[27] Formally carrying the marks of jokes of Jewish origin, yet entirely different in their content, offensive anti-Semitic jokes began to gain ground. By then jokes had become an inherent part of Hungarian language culture. It must have been the realization that the joke as a form could be used for criticism of the most diverse sorts that also contributed to its ever-spreading popularity, especially in the countryside. Just as *Borsszem Jankó* had manufactured and propagated jokes that looked down on the nationalities, the anti-Semitic jokes now multiplied according to the same pattern.[28] By this time, the question of nationalities and of ethnic minorities had evolved into two distinct problems within Hungarian society. Comic journals, though treating nationalities and ethnic minorities differently, consciously never made a distinction between them.

Borsszem Jankó treated the matter more selectively, printing Gypsy jokes under the same criterion as it published Jewish jokes. It spoke out against the discrimination or derision of Gypsies only when they—and Gypsy musicians in particular—had crossed the threshold of bourgeois society through their way of life and reputation.[29] There is no Gypsy among the many permanent figures in *Borsszem Jankó*. The paper regarded national minorities as political enemies of the Hungarian state, and fought against them with irony, caricatures, and all the tools it had available. But in Slovakian, German, or Croatian nationalities it discovered some social or cultural traits which were to be valued, like diligence or a striving for education, and held these up as examples to be followed.

The other comic weeklies of the 1860s to 1880s looked down on nationalities and minorities, but in a different way. More than once they attempted to form a united front with the nationalities politically—against the Habsburg court, against the government, against the aristocracy, the Jews, or the Church, but they remained anti-Semitic throughout. Since Gypsies were never regarded as full-fledged members of society, these comic journals dealt with them only rarely, but then always discriminately and derisively, as people who had nothing to do with the Hungarian nation. More sharply than all other groups, however, these papers opposed the Jews (in the first half of the 1880s).

For decades after it was launched, *Borsszem Jankó*'s jokes were highly defensive. To those who attacked it out of anti-Semitism, it responded by stressing a need for levelheadedness in the interest of progress for the whole country; to those who mistakenly accused it of anti-Semitism, only because it dared to address a taboo, it did not cease to stress that it had been the paper itself that had popularized Jewish jokes in Hungary. It held that those jokes which most offended the Jews of Pest were just those favored by Viennese and Berlin Jews.[30]

"The brain's the hat—the joke's the flower atop it!" Adolf Ágai said.[31] How bourgeois such levelheadedness was, how it contrasted with the dominant gentry concept of life, is best illustrated by Salamon Seiffensteiner's joke entitled "Economy." "What a strange way to speculate!" says the *Borsszem Jankó* figure. "His lordship acquires an *eight*penny rabbit with a *hundred*-forint greyhound and riding a *thousand*-forint stallion (i.e., on a hunt)! . . . Sami Gerstschleim is a lot smarter: He buys a rabbit skin for *thirty* pennies and with it acquires a *thousand*-forint horse, two three-storey houses and a four-thousand-acre estate![32]

In launching *Borsszem Jankó*, Ágai was always aware of the fact that he was accomplishing a mission, no matter how unrestrained the jokes in his paper were. A literary historian acknowledged Ágai's goal when he wrote that "Spitzig acquaints Hungarian society with his race, because while evoking laughter with his witticisms, he becomes less and less a stranger."[33]

The wave of anti-Semitism running through the first half of the 1880s, its failure, and finally, in the middle of the decade, the dissolution of the Anti-Semite Party resulted in *Borsszem Jankó* taking on a more inflexible tone. Completely different from Ágai's defensive and militant style was the cheerfully self-confident and entertainment-oriented humor of Jenő Heltai and Ferenc Molnár, which became dominant at the turn of the century. Characteristic for the comic weekly *Fidibusz* were jokes like the one entitled "Philosophy":

> "You're getting baptized? What for?"
> "Well . . . the people forget, God forgives. . . ."
> "But the nose, it remains unchanged!"[34]

A Social Spectrum to Budapest Jokes

The contents of the jokes provide an unusual sociography of Hungarian society, which can be illustrated with the weeklies' permanent comic figures.[35] They existed already in the mid-nineteenth century in the comic journals of Vienna and Berlin, but there they were not at all as striking as in the weeklies of Budapest. The figures that Ágai created and which *Borsszem Jankó* popularized also had their precursors in the German periodicals, but only insofar as they provided the idea for the creation of such figures. Their actual roots were in the Hungarian comedies and literary genre pictures of the Age of Reform in the second quarter of the century. These were figures with almost no individual characteristics, and even their names indicated that they represented stereotypes. The innovation of *Borsszem Jankó*—which all the other comic weeklies took up—was to give its permanent figures specific caricature traits and manners of speech that emphasized local accents or jargons, or else the excessive use of certain specialty words. Such character marks were only superficial tools, however. What made the figures interesting was not how they appeared, but the social position that they represented.

In Hungarian society of the late nineteenth century, a stratum of the population that represented a vestige of feudalism and a newly evolving bourgeoisie that was rapidly gaining power existed simultaneously.[36] It was this latter group which the comic figures were able to portray most colorfully. The makeup of the readership and staff of the comic weeklies explains why this was so. There were figures from the upper and middle bourgeoisie, from Kobi Blau of the 1870s to Hadi Márton (Martin Military) of the World War I period; middle-class women; men of the world and playboys; Lengenádfalvay Kotlik Zirzabella (which translates into something like Zirzabella Clucking of Reedshire), who flirted with emancipation from the 1860s on for more than half a century; the turn-of-the-century feminists like

235

Emanczi Paula; lawyers like Nyúzó Boldizsár (Balthasar Skinner); doctors like Dr. Baczillus; scientists; teachers like Péter Éhös (Peter Hungry); journalists; several artists; then the horde of the lower middle class, including the small bureaucrat Vendel Sanyaró (Lowly); excisemen; shopkeepers like Iczig Spitzig or Salomon Seiffensteiner; traveling salesmen; concierges with characteristically Czech names; mailmen; hairdressers; train conductors like Ádám Pokrócz (Rough Blanket); baggagemen; servants; policemen like András Mihaszna (Goodfornothing); and, finally, soldiers.

The Middle Classes in Caricature Figures

Along with the development of the middle class, the Jewish question in its broadest sense was a central topic in Hungarian comic weeklies. Many of the figures were born because of the importance of this problem. Based on the Jewish figures in the comic papers, a detailed social-historical study can be made of the stratification of the middle class in Budapest. Those Jewish figures that stressed their Jewishness were created mainly for the purpose of formulating in Hungarian the Yiddish types of jokes (like Salamon Seiffensteiner); Borzeviczy W. M., a pun with the stock exchange; and Reb Menachem Cziczesbeiszer. They did so either in self-abasement, self-defensiveness, or attack. They appeared in all social strata, from the upper middle class to the shopkeepers or small businessmen like Jakó Vigécz (Drummer); from elegant ladies to journalists like Kobi Federvich.

One of the most significant figures of comic weeklies was Iczig Spitzig, the "well-known patriot and paterfamilias." Adolf Ágai created the figure in 1865, when he was still on the staff of the comic journal *Bolond Miska.* With his characteristically Jewish-German name, Spitzig was a lower-middle-class character from Theresa-Town. He was a devoted Hungarian but had difficulty stripping himself of his German-Yiddish traditions. He was a determined liberal fighting any kind of orthodoxy, be it political or religious. He spoke out tirelessly in favor of political equality; when that was realized his goal was achieving social recognition. He was sensitive about any kind of discrimination but just as militant in opposing isolation and the slightest appearance of the ghetto spirit. He spoke up in favor of the governmental party, but he was a democrat at heart and never ceased to condemn the spectacle of aggressive Jews climbing the social ladder toward the high bourgeoisie, or the bankers and industrialists in their fashionable struggle for gaining titles, or nobility, or otherwise. "Dear Mr. Editor, sir, I am a Jew, a Hungarian Israelite, and I am proud of that, because even if I weren't proud, I would still be a Jew," is the way Spitzig introduced himself in late 1865.[37]

Iczig Spitzig also was serenely enthusiastic. Only when political anti-Semitism came out in the open did it become evident how naive his longing for assimilation had been. And when in the summer of 1878 the later head of the Anti-Semite Party spoke up in Parliament in favor of resettling the Jews, it became impossible to go on joking about emancipation as before. Iczig Spitzig offered one more exasperated rebuke, and was never heard of again.

It was only the gentry, the actual ruling class of the time, and one of the remnants of feudalism, that was portrayed colorfully: its conditions of ownership and employment, its political leanings, and its preferred pastimes were alloted equal interest. To this group belonged the legendary Berczi Mokány (Berti Spunky), several bankrupt estate-holders, members of the governing party and the opposition, apprentices of law, and impoverished gentry figures who took on employment as stewards on the estate of newly rich Jews like Dániel Tojás (Egg) who was portrayed as the steward of Dávid Vöröshegyi (Rotberger).

Berczi Mokány was also Adolf Ágai's creation, first appearing in *Borsszem Jankó* in 1873. In sketching his major social opponent, Ágai did not restrain his satire and sarcasm; he was able to bring to life a figure that came to play a role in countless calendars, some comedies, and several voluminous collections. He was still in existence in the 1910s. Berczi Mokány expressed the leading—if contradictory—ideals of the time; he called himself a liberal while being a feudalist to the marrow; and he was portrayed as a pushy and unkempt provincial noble, a member of the opposition, resorting to slogans like "the nation" and "the right to independence." He wittily used these nationalistic slogans to achieve his own aims. He was also a devoted card-player, a capacious drinker, and the hero of nighttime music-making. Staunchly proud of his noble birth, he practiced a manner of speech full of the pathos and declamations that characterized the county lords. He shed tears for lost "Hungarian valor," and knew that "we are perishing, done for." He looked on women as toys, and he looked down on all ethnic and national minorities. With time, his anti-Semitism became an increasingly strong characteristic.

Among the dozens of gentry types projected in comic weeklies, Berczi Mokány's figure was the most successful. In 1891 *Borsszem Jankó* gave him as background an imaginary backward Hungarian village where, with the involvement of the local lords, national events took place in a grotesque, scaled-down form, down to a parody of the millenary celebration of the conquest of Hungary. With this background, feudal provincialism was provided with symbols (like Mucsa, the village name that to this day survives in the Hungarian language).

Churches and their priests were rarely portrayed through comic figures; the few that were were always Catholic. This omission owed less to reverence than to the fact that the new secular thinking was not much concerned with priests. Disputes about state policies concerning the Church were not conducted through comic figures but were treated more directly in jokes and caricatures.

It is surprising how few comic figures were modeled after aristocrats, even though the aristocracy played an active role in public life and there were numerous jokes concerning this class. This may have been due to the respect of the Jewish middle-class papers and their contributors for the tolerant, liberal aristocrats. Yet, such figures were also missing from other comic weeklies that fed traditional anti-aristocratic sentiments. (Future scholarship should shed more light on this topic.)

The other end of the social spectrum is missing as well; there were no workers' figures. They were simply beyond the scope of interest of the middle class at large.

The countless figures of soldiers and policemen must also be mentioned. These two groups did not play an equal role in comic weeklies. Soldiers' figures were actually no more than tools for presenting military jokes, and the figures of military officers were primarily for purposes of political mockery leveled at the supranational officers' corps of the Austro-Hungarian army. A unique figure was the common soldier Demeter Peczek in the paper *Üstökös*, but his role was later taken up by *Bolond Istók*. Peczek was born in 1876, when the Balkan crisis reached its height. He was a country boy who sent letters to his parents and his fiancée from the Serbian front. Writing in a mixed Austrian-Hungarian soldier's jargon about life, battles, and routine at camp, the peasant boy, unaccustomed to writing, was clumsy in his use of the language. His funniness stems mainly from the clash between different linguistic strata, but he was exceptional in that he got married and had a family after the end of the war.

Among the policemen figures András Mihaszna came to fame. His purpose was not only to serve as a tool for presenting jokes about policemen; he embodied the awkward constable with his sense of omnipotence, a representative of official arrogance and conceit, the officer whose duty it is to keep order in the chaos of the metropolis but who is, of course, always clumsy, always in the wrong place at the wrong time. He opens his "Observations" with the phrase: "Here's a man of brains!" and always ends them with what became a household phrase at that time: "There's got to be order!" For almost two decades after 1882, András Mihaszna was a regular in *Borsszem Jankó*, and even after the turn of the century he appeared occasionally.

Though there were many figures representing nationalities, most of these also appeared only once or twice. Hungarian Swabians or Saxons, Slovakians, Romanians, or Serbs and Croats were usually portrayed in a demeaning and crude way—and all papers adhered to that.[38] Tobiás Kraxelhuber, the "Pressburg landlord" stood out among them. He represented the German burgher who had not been assimilated and who, moreover, flaunting "grossdeutsch" confidence, wished to civilize the "barbarian" Hungarians.

There was only one section of society that initially was not treated in the comic papers, but eventually it became a significant component—the village, or peasant figures, who appeared in countless personifications in the early 1890s. Their emergence must have been due to the new agrarian movement of this decade along with the forming of the People's Party; there was also a rising interest in populist history as a result of the preparations for the country's millenium celebrations. One such figure, published in *Kakas Márton*, was especially successful: the village mayor Gábor Göre. He shows how these figures were looked down on, or at least treated in a patronizing tone. Again, this was a result of the middle-class sense of superiority that was prevalent in the capital.

Progressing Toward a Metropolitan Society

The more famous comic figures, existing for several decades, became an integral part of urban folklore. By 1890 Ágai had become acutely aware that his paper's ". . . 33 figures were intermittently paraded across the stage of theaters in the country and the capital alike. The acute authors are of course perplexed at the thought that . . . (the figures) have become common property just like folk songs, whose writers no one cares about either." In the most recent short stories, editorials, feuilletons, and shorter articles these 33 appear quite frequently. Even Lajos Kossuth refers to them in his writings and letters.[39]

The largest number of comic figures existed side by side in the 1890s. The urban variety which *Borsszem Jankó* reflected was supplemented by numerous figures mirroring agrarian society. After the turn of the century, representatives of new professions and movements emerged. Newsboys, drivers, movie owners, tourists, prohibitionists, matchmakers, pilots, and feminists were inseparably connected with metropolitan life. Their names would reveal more about them than the texts set underneath. Such short sentences or jokes only remotely sought to impose on the figures the function of social caricature, an indication that the type of joke represented by a comic figure was on the decline. With the 1910s it had disappeared almost completely and did not reemerge until after the end of World War I.

The reasons for the emergence of jokes based on figures of society, and their gradual disappearance half a century later, are to be found not in literature but rather in social history. The mid-1860s, when the first comic figures were created in Budapest, marked a time when a social structure that had developed over a long period of time was beginning to decay. At the beginning of this transformation, the old guard, as representative of permanence, and the new guard, which was moving into the ranks of the old, were both recognizably present. Despite the dynamic changes taking place, it was clear who and what belonged where. Both the simultaneous existence of old and new social types and their subsequent fusion were new social phenomena, and this was what gave rise to these comic figures. But by the turn of the century the transformation brought to life ever newer incidents and types in quick succession. This caused the waning of those types that had emerged not so long before. Metropolitan life came to mean incessant and quick change, and a broader readership could no longer be supplied with facile, superficial types that it might recognize. By the time the figures would have become broadly recognizable, they would already have been transformed.

The Shift to Light Humor

In the early 1890s, a few important political comic weeklies were created. They were like volunteers entering the service of one or the other party, without consideration of whether they were acceptable to that party. Such weeklies included the Independent Party's *Mátyás Diák* (1888–1921) and *Kakas Márton* (1894–1914), or the Catholic People's Party's *Herkó Páter* (1893–1933). In a few years' time, however, even these papers, like their earlier counterparts, dealt less directly with politics: social tensions, distortions, and movements were becoming the dominating subjects in *Borsszem Jankó*. Most of the newer weeklies were piquant boulevardiers, with juicy and frivolous topics and tone. Most significant among these were *Magyar Figaró* (1886–1918) and *Fidibusz* (1905–1927). The latter was published in the largest number of copies by far, with a circulation of 29,000 by 1910. Its publication policies and business concepts were more in line with the penny press, though it employed the best journalists, writers, poets, and graphic artists, including eminent personalities like Ferenc Molnár.

The tendencies in the development of comic papers, outlined by Donald J. Gray, who traced these weeklies from a political orientation towards the suggestive and the sensational, was true for Hungarian comic journals just as much as for their otherwise completely different English counterparts. There are some explanations for the similarity. For one, the laws that govern the business and the policies of publication are applicable everywhere. For another, the New York publication *Puck*, which established a new type of English-language comic weekly, was founded by Joseph Keppler, who came from Vienna.[40]

Light humor did not solve any problems, but it bridged them, or at least made them bearable for a time by taking the edge off the opposing parties. Such humor found a common denominator for social extremes without creating a compromise between them; it no doubt came about and flourished in the Austro-Hungarian Monarchy just as did the operetta.

The transformation of Budapest comic journals at the end of the nineteenth century indicates that the public it addressed had changed as well. The circulation of the still primarily politically oriented comic weeklies *(Bolond Istók, Üstökös,* and *Herkó Páter)* depended mostly on regular subscribers who were provincials, judging from their letters to the editors, their comic figures, and the tone of their jokes. Addressing a general readership in the entire country, these papers, with their circulation of several thousand, were far behind their increasingly suggestive and sensation-oriented metropolitan counterparts. The latters' readership was Budapest's middle class, and their papers were sold mostly by street vendors. They included *Fidibusz*, and to some degree, *Magyar Figaró* and *Mátyás Diák;* only *Borsszem Jankó* was still sold mostly through subscription. Traditional political comic weeklies sought confrontation, which surfaced mostly in their political orientation and their anti-Semitism. That, however, was never as much of central concern after the turn of the century as it had been in the 1880s—which did not mean that they were approaching a solution to this conflict: it was merely suppressed.

The new type of comic weeklies characterized by light humor displayed an increasing number of Jewish jokes replete with self-irony, and the weeklies became more relaxed, even carefree. They were intended for a readership from the assimilating middle classes of Budapest, and the first generation of middle-class readers and intellectuals "assimilating" to them. Thus, they were socially more exclusive than the political comic journals, a condition resulting from being more open, more interested, modern, cultured, and metropolitan. All of these qualities point toward a socially and culturally higher level of openness and inclusivity than the traditional political comic journals which, purportedly "addressing the people," were politically narrowminded and prejudiced.

The Coffeehouse and the Turf

Reflections on one's life and career in Budapest became characteristic grist for anecdotes and jokes by the turn of the century. There were countless memoirs by artists, journalists, and writers, which portrayed the lives of their authors in an easygoing tone.[41] The situations, characters, and dialogues in these memoirs seem to come right out of *Borsszem Jankó* or *Fidibusz*. The prevalent style was lightly humorous: the authors telling the readers of their life struggles, their cleverness, their sweeping business ideas, and their persistence (i.e., their bourgeois virtues). They joked about their own virtues and successes because they knew from experience that the collapsing, degenerate old order was still present and that its still influential adherents stood guard against them. While the turf became the symbol of the irrevocably declining gentry, that of the artist and intellectual middle class became the coffeehouse, where new ideas and whole works were born.

Newly born ideas played a key role in a society where rules and norms still prevailed that had lost most of their significance. No longer effective, they were nevertheless sustained. But there were no workable norms or rules that could accommodate a middle class facing the whole new range of possibilities provided by a new age. In such a world, the man of ideas has an advantage and a chance for success; one such kind of man is a man with humor. In this respect, Budapest was developing into a metropolis that could be characterized as a city of jokes and ideas.

Fading Beliefs and Comic Weeklies after World War I

The trauma that Budapest and all of Hungary suffered at the end of World War I, as well as during the ensuing revolution, transformed the character of comic journals and the basic tone of many of the jokes. In 1919 the Hungarian Soviet Republic closed all comic journals as intellectual products of the bourgeoisie. After it was over, only a few came to life again; those that were revived were no longer the same. The journals that favored social disintegration were becoming louder and cruder, and with that the middle-class comic journals also lost much of their confidence in integration. The comic weeklies lost their significance as vehicles of Pest humor because jokes and caricatures were now offered as supplements to the dailies and weeklies like *Szinházi Élet* (Theater World). The exclusively comic weeklies were much less attractive to the public than they had been earlier.

In the jokes, many extant until today, the outlook of the more and more distilled, generalized, and more abstractly presented "burgher of Pest" continued to dominate. German-Jewish and Polish-Jewish names were common now (like Kohn and Grün, Little Moritz, Moskovic, Leibovic, and others), as well as German names translated literally into Hungarian. On the other hand, characters and locations from the turn of the century were brought up-to-date and used again in the political jokes. By the 1920s and 1930s, it became evident that the joke was not just a comic genre based on international models and motifs but one that could be continually updated by each generation.[42] With this the jokes' social-historical significance sank sharply.

In metropolitan society, jokes became a public treasure, and the journals and literature created in the city spread them all over the country. The joke became a literary tool for fine writers who addressed an intellectual readership, from Frigyes Karinthy (1887–1938) to our contemporary Péter Esterházy. To the rural intellectuals, the jokes usually exemplified the loss of national roots, the impoverishment of language, and something that was alien to the Hungarian character. The populist ideology considered the joke as it did the slang it employed as a disdainful urban product ". . . which is not a dialect of Hungarian, as some have asserted, but of Yiddish . . . ," as one of its otherwise highly educated and relatively tolerant representatives rebuked.[43] Employing jokes in literary works was indignantly rejected by the traditionalists, even if the authors were writers recognized for the outstanding quality of their works; what is more, their literary talent was called into question.[44]

The Budapest joke, and the comic weeklies that served as its autonomous organs, were born in the 1860s. They were products of the process of the cultural assimilation of members of the urban Jewish lower middle class, who adapted jokes of German-Yiddish origin. The outlook on life of the middle-class residents of Theresa-Town and Elizabeth-Town—their eternal wisdoms, social experiences, and goals—determined the joke's tone. An attitude that came from the experience of political emancipation, which was militant but nevertheless optimistic, characterized the jokes and the figures of comic weeklies. It was an attitude that changed direction for the first time in the 1880s, with the rise of anti-Semitism. After that, two kinds of comic journals existed side by side. The first consisted of those based on piquant light humor, which were optimistic in spite of the difficulties of social integration and which found their own audience in the growing metropolis of Budapest. Their aim was to relieve through humor the taboos and complexes in areas of sex in society at large. The second category consisted of those journals that propagated and practiced the exclusion of all minorities; they claimed to be in the majority but in fact had a lower circulation than the first type. The quality and popularity of the former pointed to the long-term victory of the metropolitan, middle-class attitude and the speeding up of social unification and cultural modernization. With the end of World War I, the process came to a halt and Hungarian society—as embodied both in the jokes and in their consumers—fractured.

I wish to thank the Soros Foundation for granting me a scholarship, which made the writing of this chapter possible.

Notes

1. Several humor writers and journalists of the mid-nineteenth century considered it their duty to collect anecdotes; they then used them as their own literary sources. To our knowledge, Ignac Nagy published the first Hungarian collection of anecdotes in the 1840s, before the Revolution of 1848. Interestingly, it was in the 1850s that many collections appeared, such as those by Gusztáv Lauka, Gereben Vas, Viktor Szokoly, the Transylvanian László Kővári, and others. In the 1860s, a collection of Gypsy anecdotes was published as well.
2. For details about the origins and basic types of literary anecdotes, see Alfons Lhotsky, "Über das anekdotische in spätmittelalterlichen Geschichtswerken Österreichs," in *Historiographie, Quellenkunde, Wissenschaftsgeschichte* (Munchen, 1972), 117–137.
3. For the *Üstökös*'s social-historically noteworthy anecdotes and literary material, see Géza Buzinkay, *Borsszem Jankó és Társai. Magyar Élclapok és Karikatúráik a XIX. Század Második Felében* (Borsszem Jankó and its companion. Hungarian comic journals and their caricatures in the second half of the 19th century) (Budapest, 1983), 25, 75–76. For a detailed history of comic papers, see this author's chapters in Domokos Kosary and G. Béla Németh, eds., *A Magyar Sajtó Története 1867–1892.* (History of the Hungarian press), Vol. II/1 (Budapest, 1985), 169–206, 393–431.
4. For a more complete comparison between the anecdote and the joke, see Buzinkay, *Borsszem Jankó*, 115–116.
5. Endre Nagy, "A Kabaré Regénye" (History of the cabaret), 1935, in *Várad - Pest - Párizs* (Budapest, 1958), 154.
6. The purpose of this chapter is not to deal with questions of content or genre, not with how jokes are created, or what their effects are with respect to individual psychology, which Sigmund Freud has already analyzed in depth. (Sigmund Freud, *Jokes and Their Relation to the Unconscious*, trans. and ed. James Strachey [New York, 1963].) Nor do I want

to discuss the absurd contradictions between the joke's ease of form and seriousness of content, which have already been covered brilliantly in Elemer Hankiss: "A Komikus Határhelyzet"; "Donald Kacsa es a Szemiotika" (A comic borderline situation; Donald Duck and semiotics), in *Érték és társadalom* (Values and society) (Budapest, 1977), 31–78.

7. Sándor Scheiber, "Világjáró Magyar-Zsidó Anekdota" (A world-traveling Hungarian-Jewish anecdote), *Folklór és Tárgytörténet* (Folklore and motif history), Vol. 2 (Budapest, 1974), 435–437.

8. "Seiffensteiner Salamon tünődései" (The reflections of Salamon Seiffensteiner), *Borsszem Jankó* (Oct. 27, 1878); Sigmund Freud, *Jokes and Their Relation to the Unconscious*, 63.

9. Sigmund Freud, *Jokes and Their Relation to the Unconscious*, 63.

10. The joke version published in *Borsszem Jankó* can be found in Geza Buzinkay, ed., *Mokány Berczi és Spitzig Iczig, Göre Gábor mög a Többiek. A Magyar Társadalom Figurái az Élclapokban 1860 és 1918 Között* (Berczi Mokány and Iczic Spitzig, Gábor Göre and others: Figures of Hungarian society in comic journals between 1860 and 1918) (Budapest, 1988), 660–662.

11. On the role of Jewry in the development of the Central European press and its Jewish press, see Jacob Toury, *Die Judische Presse im Österreichischen Kaiserreich: Ein Beitrag zur Problematik der Akkulturation 1802–1918* (Tübingen, 1983).

12. Donald J. Gray, "List of Comic Periodicals Published in Great Britain, 1800–1900, With a Prefatory Essay," *Victorian Periodicals Newsletter* 15 (March 1972): 3.

13. Donald J. Gray, "List of Comic Periodicals: 5.

14. *A Magyar Sajtó Története 1867–1892* (History of the Hungarian press), Vol. II/2, 169–172, 193–394; Julius Leopold, *Katalog, Annonzen-Expedition* (Budapest, 1910).

15. John Tebbel, *The American Magazine: A Compact History* (New York, 1969), 151–155.

16. In detail, see Károly Vörös, *Budapest Története a Márciusi Forradalomtól az Öszirózsás Forradalomig* (History of Budapest 1848–1918), Vol. IV (Budapest, 1978), 456; Péter Hanák, "Verbürgerlichung und Urbanisierung. Ein Vergleich der Stadtentwicklung Wiens und Budapests," in *Gesellschaft, Politik und Verwaltung in der Habsburger-monarchie 1830–1918*, F. Glatz and R. Melville, eds. (Wiesbaden-Stuttgart, 1987), 203–235.

17. Iczig Spitzig's most characteristic "Letters from Király Street" can be found in Buzinkay, *Mokány Berczi*, 517–532.

18. *Újságkiadók Lapja* (Journal of Newspaper Publishers) 102 (February 1910): 6.

19. For a detailed history of the *Borsszem Jankó*, see Buzinkay, *Borsszem Jankó*, 34–71.

20. On the cultural role of the Hungarian Jewry, see Lajos Venetianer, *A magyar zsidóság története* (History of Hungarian Jewry) (Budapest, 1922, 1986), 242–271; Péter Hanák, "A Lezáratlan Per" (The undetermined trial) in *Zsidókérdés, asszimiláció, antiszemitizmus* (The Jewish question, assimilation, anti-Semitism) (Budapest, 1984), 357–375.

21. *Borsszem Jankó* (March 13, 1887): 8.

22. On Adolf Ágai and his literary circle, see G. Béla Németh, "Fejezetek az

Irodalomkritika Történetéből a Kiegyezés Után" (Chapters from the history of literary criticism after the Austro-Hungarian compromise), in *Létharc és Nemzetiség* (Struggle for life and national Consciousness) (Budapest, 1976), 268–272.

23. Géza Buzinkay, "A Challenge for Intellectuals: Austro-Hungarians with Two Languages," in *Hungary and European Civilization*, György Ránki and Attila Pók, eds. (Budapest, 1989), 321–329.

24. Gyula Krúdy, *A Tegnapok Ködlovagjai* (Riders in the fog yesterday) (Budapest, 1925), 184.

25. *Borsszem Jankó* (Sept. 11, 1892): 7.

26. Cited in Ferenc Baráth, "A Magyar Élczlapokról" (On Hungarian comic journals) *Budapesti Szemle* (Budapest Revue) 4 (1874): 396.

27. Judit Kubinszky, *Politikai Antiszemitizmus Magyarorszagon 1875–1890* (Political anti-Semitism in Hungary 1875–1890) (Budapest, 1976).

28. For the relationship between ethnic groups and the jokes, see Péter Hanák, "A Másokról Alkotott Kép" (The image of the others) in *A Kert és a Műhely* (The garden and the workshop) (Budapest, 1988 and Princeton [forthcoming, in English]), 81–111.

29. *Borsszem Jankó* (April 1, 1877): 10.

30. *Borsszem Jankó* (January 19, 1879): 10.

31. Berczi Mokány (Adolf Ágai), "Epigraph," in *Abrincs! 150 Jordány Vicc* (150 Jewish jokes) (Budapest, 1879).

32. *Borsszem Jankó* (November 13, 1887): 7.

33. Gyula Romhányi, "A Magyar Politikai Vigjáték Fejlődése" (The evolution of the Hungarian political comedy), *Irodalomtörténeti Közlemények* (1930), 423.

34. *Fidibusz*, 3 (1905): 8.

35. For the figures, selected texts, and the society reflected by the figures, see Buzinkay, *Mokány Berczi.*

36. For the best analysis of the social structure in the Age of Dualism, see Péter Hanák, "Magyarország Társadalma a Századforduló Idején" (The social structure of Hungary at the turn of the century), in *Magyarország Története 1890–1918* (History of Hungary 1890–1918), Vol. 7/1, Péter Hanák and Ferenc Mucsi, eds. (Budapest, 1978), 403–415.

37. *Bolond Miska* (November 5, 1865).

38. For an analysis of the relationship between various ethnic groups, see Hanák, "A Másokról Alkotott Kép."

39. Quotation from *Borsszem Jankó* (January 12, 1890): 10.

40. John Tebbel, *The American Magazine: A Compact History*, 151–152.

41. E.g., Ödon Bárdi, *A Régi Vígszínház* (The old comedy theater) (Budapest, 1957); Sándor Incze, *Színházi Életeim. Egy Újságíró karrierregénye* (My "theater lives," a career story of a journalist) (Budapest, 1987); Zsigmond Lenkei, *A Mosolygó Mozi. Emlékezések, Anekdóták* (Smiling movie. Memoirs, anecdotes) (Budapest, 1930); Vilmos Tarján, *Riporteri Titkaimat nem Viszem Sírba* (My reporter's secrets don't die with me) (Budapest, 1943).

42. The most useful joke anthologies for a comparison are Imre Nagy's and Gyula Galántai's numerous booklets and books from the 1920s and 1930s, as well as István Beke's two comprehensive volumes (*Új Magyar Anekdótakincs a Századfordulótól a Felszabadulásig* [New Hungarian treasure of anecdotes from the turn of the century to 1945]) (Budapest, 1962);

(Legújabb Magyar Anekdótakincs [Newest Hungarian treasure of anecdotes] (Budapest, 1966]). For a good typology of political jokes, see Imre Katona, *Mi a Különbség? Közéleti Vicceinkről* (What's the difference? On Hungarian political jokes) (Budapest, 1980).

43. Lajos Fülep to Milán Füst, April 20, 1942, *Kortárs* (Contemporary) 10 (1987): 100.

44. See, for example, Károly Szalay, *Minden Másképpen Van. Karinthy Frigyes Munkássága Viták és Vélemények Tükrében* (Everything is different: The work of Frigyes Karinthy in discussions and thoughts) (Budapest, 1987), 61–62.

Chapter 10

Covering New York:
Journalism and Civic Identity
in the Twentieth Century

NEIL HARRIS

*O*LD NEWSPAPERS are as difficult to interpret as they are stimulating to read. Their capacity to shed light on almost every question of form and content inevitably hinders efforts to limit discussion. There is hardly any set of attitudes, practices, or values that American newspapers have not in some way either reflected or helped to shape.

This chapter will not focus upon any single event, group of people, or set of opinions. Rather, it suggests that, in their modes of presentation and systems of coverage, the city's newspapers of the early twentieth century helped define the self-consciousness of New Yorkers about their city, specifying a new meaning for urbanity. Once newspapers had succeeded in adapting their readers to the pace of life in a great industrial city, a task largely accomplished by 1900 or so, they faced the task of helping to shape that civic personality itself. In the teens and twenties they did so.

My procedure will be straightforward. First, I will summarize the history of New York City's newspapers between the end of the Civil War and the coming of World War I. Second, I will draw on the existing secondary literature and highlight the major generalizations that seem in current use. Finally, I will focus upon a specific period, the years between 1915 and 1930, in order to evaluate the contributions made by the press to civic identity and the larger social life. Although New York's newspapers are sometimes displayed at their peak of influence (and notoriety) in the era of Hearst and Pulitzer—the most dramatic period of foreign immigration and Americanization—they played an equally significant role exploring and defining the popular culture of the city between 1910 and 1930. To a large extent they contributed to a self-image that remains powerful even today. It is that aspect of New York's journalistic history which will occupy my major attention.

During the 1870s the population of Manhattan Island first reached the million mark. The size of the other four boroughs which would come together to form Greater New York in 1898 was still relatively insignificant, with the exception of Brooklyn, which added 50 percent again to New York's size and was itself counted as one of the largest cities in the country.

New York newspapers of the 1870s were dominated by five dailies, some of them extremely venerable by American standards, and a Tammany penny sheet which specialized in reporting on lottery drawings. This was the *New York Daily News,* and it managed to sell as many as 175,000 copies a day. It was not, however, a major journalistic influence.[1]

All the others had recently enjoyed the services of colorful and powerful editors, representing vital political, social, or literary interests. No established paper of the decade enjoyed a daily circulation much over 150,000, a figure that the two leaders, the *Herald* and the *Sun,* reached only upon occasion. James Gordon Bennett, Sr., the Scottish-born founder of the *Herald,* had helped create the independent American newspaper four decades earlier. Published not in the interests of a political party or ideology, a traditional newspaper purpose, but to carry timely, exciting, and highly eventful stories, the *Herald* became the liveliest and most popular paper in the country in the antebellum period, during the 1840s and 1850s. Upon Bennett's death in 1872 control passed to a son and namesake who, despite rather luxurious and self-indulgent personal tastes, managed to assemble an extraordinary corps of international reporters. Covering wars, revolutions, coups d'état, and electoral campaigns, they were continually coming up with electrifying scoops, the most sensational being the successful (if lengthy) quest of *Herald* reporter Henry M. Stanley for the Scottish missionary and explorer David Livingstone.

Charles A. Dana's *Sun,* principal rival to the *Herald,* resembled it in style and coverage. Dana's own life was tied to major currents of national thought and opinion. After spending five years at Brook Farm, an associate of reformers like Thomas Wentworth Higginson, Margaret Fuller, and novelist Nathaniel Hawthorne, Dana worked fifteen years more on Horace Greeley's *Tribune*, during which time he emerged as a master of compressed prose. He became publisher and editor of the *Sun* in 1868, with the objective of presenting a "daily photograph of the whole world's doings in the most luminous and lively manner." Like the *Herald* the *Sun* featured crime, society gossip, interviews, and human interest stories which focused upon colorful local types. In general, more tightly edited and more "literary" than the *Herald*, the *Sun* was to a large extent Dana's personal shadow.

The three other major papers had much smaller circulations but enjoyed great influence in local civic and literary life. The *Evening Post*, long edited by poet William Cullen Bryant, endured a variety of changes of ownership and management in the 1870s, but the new editors helped maintain its status as the most intellectual, refined, and gentlemanly of the daily papers. The *Tribune*, which had enjoyed its glory years under Horace Greeley, when it had become synonymous with the great cause of the Union and antislavery, suffered a decline after Greeley's death in 1872, as did the *New York Times* after the 1869 death of its great editor, Henry J. Raymond. But this trio, despite their avoidance of the sensationalism that characterized the *Herald* and the *Sun*, managed to survive, even to turn a profit, and enjoyed special relationships with their host city even before the Pulitzer revolution of the 1880s.[2]

There were several features of the New York press connection that deserve attention, and they were in place as early as the 1870s. One was the proclivity of newspapers to monitor the character of local government and, in the case of New York at least, to criticize, lampoon, and protest the political excesses that seemed so pervasive. Cartoonists (like the *Tribune*'s Thomas Nast), editorial writers, and persistent reporters combined to bring down the local machine on several occasions. It was somehow assumed that the independent press of New York, free from the close party positions of an earlier day, could act to promote the interests of the community as a whole, particularly by speaking out in the name of good government. The press presented itself as an avenging force, fearless of control or persecution, exposing corruption and incompetence wherever they lay.

A second feature, established before the 1880s but much expanded in that decade, was the stimulation by local newspapers of municipal crusades that went beyond issues of politics and government. As a self-proclaimed civic conscience, the newspaper could take up reforms that aimed at redressing the abuses of urban life or enhancing its amenities. Thus, the *Evening Post* in the 1870s undertook a campaign to popularize the virtues of flat living, in a culture that continued to suspect the advantages of multifamily housing. The *Tribune* began its fresh air fund in 1876, making an annual appeal for funds to send slum children out of the city into the country for several weeks each summer. The *Times* spearheaded a crusade against the abuses of the New York Life Insurance Company, which led to an extensive and elaborate series of legislative enactments. And, under Pulitzer's leadership in the 1880s, the *World* underwrote an unending series of civic campaigns: free coal and ice deliveries, free Christmas dinners for the poor, fundraising to complete the pedestal for the Statue of Liberty, and protests against dangerous tenement houses, telephone and oil monopolies, railroad rates and lobbyists, the white slave traffic, and police brutality. In all these carefully orchestrated combinations of news stories, features, and editorial essays, the New York newspapers struck a pose of public involvement, serving as grievance clearing-houses. Their goal was not simply to bring the news to the public but to improve, as they saw it, the life of the larger community.

Finally, newspapers of the seventies and eighties became much involved with stunts, well-publicized reportorial feats of disguise, endurance, or legerdemain, which transformed staff members into public actors. Reporters disguised themselves as criminals or lunatics to uncover conditions in jails and asylums; they undertook trips around the world to set speed records; they arranged for sensational interviews. While some of the subject matter, as in Henry Stanley's case, could be international in scope, there was inevitably a flirtation with the immediate scene and its special mysteries.

By the mid-1880s then, New York possessed half a dozen newspapers with personalized editing, sensational news coverage, basic independence of party, broad readership, and competitive scooping. They identified themselves, moreover, with civic progress and good government. In the late eighties and nineties, however, this press tradition would undergo further elaboration with the entry of two major publishing personalities. The first was Joseph Pulitzer, a Hungarian émigré. And the second was the wealthy heir to a western mining fortune, William Randolph Hearst. Between them they transformed the scale and expanded the presence of the American newspaper.

Pulitzer got his publishing start in St. Louis, but achieved his great fame only after buying, in 1883, a declining New York newspaper called the *World*.[3] Estimates vary, but according to some sources, the *World* had only 20,000 readers when Pulitzer took over. Within five years he had multiplied them more than twelvefold to a quarter of a million and made his the largest newspaper in the city. By 1892, with its sister, the *Evening World*, which Pulitzer had established four years earlier, the combined circulation approached 400,000, larger than the next two New York papers reached together; the Sunday edition added another 250,000 readers.

Such extraordinary success provoked analysis and, rather quickly, imitation. Many of Pulitzer's contemporaries in the 1880s and 1890s found his practices new and original. The *World* became synonymous with what was labeled the New Journalism, an evocative symbol not only of newspapers as such, but of the American Melting Pot's success in absorbing immense numbers of foreign immigrants and reshaping them as modern urbanites.

The techniques can be easily summarized. Frank Luther Mott, dean of American journalist historians, divided the Pulitzer contribution into six major sectors: unusual and sensational as well as serious news coverage; frequent crusades and stunts; an editorial page of high character; large size; lavish use of illustrations; and extensive promotion.[4] Although a few of these elements were novel, others represented extensions of existing practices. Some historians, like Gunther Barth, argue that Pulitzer's methods simply built on extant traditions.[5]

Just as interesting and fundamental to the *World* was Pulitzer's clear identification of his newspaper with the cause of the urban masses. His calls for taxation of inheritances and large incomes and for punishing politically intimidating employers seemed radical to some propertied interests. While he declined to give labor or any special group carte blanche, he displayed broad sympathy with the underdog, with the poor, the oppressed, the victimized. Some of this was rhetorical, but the *World* did act for the next several decades of its existence as a social gadfly. And its actual success, particularly after Pulitzer withdrew from close, formal supervision, rested on a corps of skillful editors, reporters, and cartoonists.

The basis of the *World*'s appeal was an unlikely combination of civic responsibility and sensation mongering, still another fulfillment of Tocqueville's analysis of the American democracy more than half a century earlier. The claims of the *World* to public significance came not only in the credos issued by Pulitzer and the tone of the editorial page. They were stated by the elaborate structure Pulitzer had built for his newspaper, the highest building in New York, its gilded dome a feature of the city's skyline. Earlier newspaper buildings had occasionally been lofty—for a while the *Tribune* building was the city's highest—but the *World* projected a presence that was meant to be culturally significant as well as massive, an emblem of metropolitan ambitions. The *World* intended to become a feature, not simply of New York City's skyline, but of its daily life.

In his broad and exciting news coverage Pulitzer could be accused of merely extending borders that had been explored by great editors before him, like Greeley, Dana, Raymond, and Bennett, sustaining what Gunther Barth has labeled the "metropolitan press." By this phrase Barth defined a kind of newspaper in place since the 1830s or 1840s, a "mirror of urban affairs," satisfying "people's need for information about the bewildering place they found themselves in, the other inhabitants, and themselves." These journalistic practices spoke of "their hope and despair, honesty and corruption, success and failure, and virtue and sin." Being informed, Barth concluded, "was a substitute for the visible order of people by appearance or location that in earlier centuries had allowed throngs of strangers to live city lives."[6] The plain, colloquial English of the papers helped newcomers from abroad learn the language: it introduced them to economic activities, to appropriate social behavior, to American food and dress patterns, to leisure and recreational activities. Barth has argued that Pulitzer's success with the *World* merely climaxed the earlier initiatives.

From this point of view, by the mid-1890s the New York press had developed, perhaps even perfected, an array of techniques designed to ease and structure the lives of their mass readership, a readership consisting largely of strangers to city life and standards, recent migrants from abroad or from the American countryside. Although the *World* was a bit more aggressive in identifying itself with the aspirations of the masses and the fate of the city they lived in, several other papers of the era, particularly the *Herald* and the *Times,* also emphasized their sense of civic identity by building for themselves splendid new buildings, clear symbols of the role they expected to play in the larger life of the great city.[7]

But Pulitzer's specific methods were not imitated and exploited by everyone in the 1890s and after. The *New York Times* pursued a very different policy under publisher Adolph S. Ochs, who took it over shortly before the turn of the century. Ochs, who reinvested his growing profits in his staff and physical plant, sought accurate and nonsensational news coverage, and refused to identify his paper with the cause of the working classes. He did lower its three cent price to a penny, but that was the extent of his pandering. Instead he slowly put together, through a well-supported staff, a reputation for precision and completeness, particularly when it came to financial and commercial reporting.[8] The *Times* appealed increasingly, as Michael Schudson has argued, to a sense of seriousness and a desire for public respectability, particularly among the propertied and socially aspiring classes.[9] It did not incorporate the cartoons, stunts, lurid stories, and challenging interviews featured by the more sensational papers (although it had a notable sports section and an elaborate Sunday magazine), but made up in comprehensiveness and balance for its absence of brilliance. The older papers, like the *Herald*, the *Sun*, the *Tribune*, the *Evening Post*, clung to their traditional characters before 1910 or so, not from any clear sense of strategy like the *Times*, but because it was easier to do this than anything else. Their circulations remained stable or went into decline.

But in the 1890s at least, the city's journalism was dominated by warfare between Pulitzer's *World*, and an upstart rival who, by imitating Pulitzer's methods, hoped to outdistance him. In terms of circulation, he soon did so. This newcomer was the young millionaire, William Randolph Hearst, and his vehicle was, initially, the New York *Journal*. Hearst's purse was larger than Pulitzer's. Pouring immense quantities of money into his paper, Hearst's challenge (and Pulitzer's response to it) made the late 1890s the heyday of yellow journalism in the city.[10]

The Hearst technique involved hiring away the *World*'s best writers, cartoonists, and editors. The prize of Hearst's catch was a veteran reporter named Arthur Brisbane, son of a utopian reformer who had known Goethe, Hegel, Michelet, and Heine.[11] His travels abroad brought son Arthur the advantages of several languages and a high degree of urbanity. The young Brisbane persuaded the New York *Sun* to hire him as a foreign correspondent: in that role he managed several scoops, including an interview with the Pope. After a brief stint editing the *Evening Sun* Brisbane moved to Pulitzer's *World* in 1890.

While working for Pulitzer Brisbane showed his real talents. He was not only a clever interviewer and zealous reporter but a master of newspaper prose with its short sentences, brief paragraphs, and creative repetitions. He also demonstrated his grip on mass taste by skillfully blending crime, sex, and what has been termed "weird science" in the Sunday paper that he edited for Pulitzer. But he was never able to break into the *World*'s tightly guarded editorial columns, and this proved a source of frustration.

Brisbane did not stay with the *Sunday World* for long. In 1897 he was lured to Hearst's employ (along with a number of colleagues) and given broad new responsibilities. Hearst, like Pulitzer, combined crusades with broad coverage, sensational stories, and appealing formats. He actively embraced the new technology, purchasing special presses to promote his large comic sections, and vigorously denouncing a range of economic and political abuses. Like Pulitzer again he declared himself the friend of the working classes, but unlike Pulitzer he had strong political ambitions of his own. He used his newspapers, and editors such as Brisbane, to promote his candidacy for several offices, including the governorship of New York, the mayoralty of New York City, and congressman. He achieved only the last.

Brisbane arrived on the *Journal* just in time to participate in the epochal promotion of the Spanish-American War. Tempted by a contract that gave him salary increases for every thousand new readers he added, he moved circulation of the *Journal* explosively higher. Brisbane soon became rich, rich enough to invest heavily in suburban real estate and to live in baronial splendor. His reputation for energy, efficiency, and journalistic genius made Brisbane a celebrity of the newspaper world in the early twentieth century. Innovations large and small—from the huge, special type he devised for the foot-high headlines screaming the latest sensations to his positioning comics, editorials, and sermonettes on the back page where they could be more easily seen by the casual reader—helped make the *Evening Journal* and later the *American* the best-selling newspapers in the country. When Brisbane died in 1936 he was called by the *Daily News* "the greatest newspaperman of our time."[12]

It is here, with the struggle between the *World* and the *Journal* and the slow emergence of Ochs's *Times* that many journalist historians pause. After all, these newspaper leviathans had apparently perfected their winning formulas. Their vast readerships, many of them foreign-born, preferred English-language dailies to their own German, Yiddish, or Italian papers and used them to master American living styles and examine the nature of civic loyalty. Immigrants and native-born found stereotypes plentiful in their pages, but the largest newspapers sought exclusion not inclusion and tried to avoid giving offense to any ethnic group. Troubles for the press did lie ahead, particularly the technologies of radio and the motion pictures, which would challenge newspaper primacy. But that made for a different story.

In fact, as early as the first decade of the twentieth century, the New York press began to endure another set of changes, well before the triumph of the electronic media. These changes reflected a new kind of urban world. And ironically enough, some of the changes were forced by the very success so recently attained.

The most obvious paradox involved the simple expansion of coverage. At one time the urban newspaper could concentrate its attention on the immediate area, serving up the winning combinations of sex, violence, gossip, and society revelations. But the growing scope of national power, previewed in the Spanish-American War and the imperial commitments that came along with it, put some of the local interests in the shade. The changing national role in world affairs, Gunther Barth observes, "disrupted the symbiotic relationship between the metropolitan press and the modern city. It made city news just another topic, like events in Europe and Africa, Asia and Latin America."[13] Fomenting conflict in Cuba proved a double-edged weapon to the newspaper magnates. Their sensational stories brought them new readers, but readers who were now taught to look beyond the city for their daily diet of information, Through the subverting impact of world news coverage, newspapers faced the loss of their special monopoly on local attention. Journalistic traditions would face changes, in the teens and twenties, in part from an attempt to catch and define the new character of New York as the centerpiece of an innovative blend of popular and high cultures and as an ambitious claimant to world urban leadership.

World War I can be said to have intensified the dilemma posed by the Spanish-American War. The story of the war was so large, of such length, and of such broad interest, even before American involvement, that coverage requirements tested the commitments of the major newspapers and helped shape their long-term strategies. The *New York Times* was in an enviable position because of its existing reputation for accuracy and completeness. Investment in a large and distinguished staff of foreign correspondents helped solidify the newspaper's position. Carl T. Van Anda, the managing editor, oversaw a 50 percent circulation growth during the war years. After the war ended Ochs spent still more money to sustain the size of his reportorial staff and to maintain the newspaper's reputation for comprehensiveness and depth.[14]

The *Times* was able to follow a consistent strategy for several decades. Its international coverage could be defined as a response to New York's new identity, because it demonstrated the worldwide interests and influence of the metropolis. If New York City stood at the center of world thought and action, as postwar New Yorkers liked to think, then their greatest newspaper dignified the city by bringing to its attention, in encyclopedic detail, happenings elsewhere, no matter how far away. And when its pages juxtaposed with great events like treaty signings, foreign panics, assassinations, wars, the homely details of local life, college commencements, banquets, parades, traffic accidents, all of which the *Times* carefully followed, the dignity of city life gained even further. The coverage of the *Times* along with its generally judicious and restrained tone proved to be a flattering method for expanding readership. Entry into its pages constituted more than mere publicity; it was in itself a form of legitimation.

Most other New York newspapers, however, had neither the resources of the *Times* nor the patience to grow slowly. They moved ahead in concentrated dramatic gestures, and they were then faced with the task of retaining readers attracted by diets of sensationalism.

This had been the pattern for the Hearst press, but it, and several competitors, had begun to add a new strategy. Some of this was already evident in the work of Arthur Brisbane.

For Brisbane had already demonstrated his sense of the new need by turning the editorial page and his own columns into an extraordinarily various but self-assured fountainhead of advice for overcoming the complexities of the modern world. Although the notion of structuring life through information might have made sense for the new urban masses of the middle and late nineteenth century, twentieth century New Yorkers increasingly required more active attention to decision-making. The advice column and the letters to the editor were already features of the immigrant press, and what Brisbane and some of his colleagues helped do was transfer this function to the more sensational English language papers. In the course of so doing he, and many of the columnists and editorialists who followed him, soon became celebrities in their own right.

Brisbane's eclectic late nineteenth century reading, some of it an inheritance from his idealistic father, now stood him in good stead. Its broadly synthetic outlook on history, art, religion, and the progress of civilization offered him a platform from which he could announce position papers on child rearing, marriage, trusts, politics, indeed on practically anything requiring a choice of some sort. As he catalogued, categorized, and translated the new achievements of science to a mass public, Brisbane invoked the great names of western civilization. Metropolitan status here meant not the encyclopedic coverage and depth of the *Times* but the easy if superficial invocation of a vast range of historical personages, and the flattering assumption that guides could lead the reader through the complex contemporary world. Brisbane's mind, noted a muckraking biographer, mirrored "the mind of the average man," being "a jungle of half-digested and half-remembered fact and fiction. Brisbane's editorials were like the conversation carried on by an average group of persons who, in the space of a few minutes, have covered personal feelings, business affairs, problems of the day, sex, crime, and politics."[15] This paternalistic and personalized vision of reality, a tailoring of complexity to suit popular tastes and needs, emerged to shape one kind of New York newspaper in the early twentieth century.

However, Brisbane did not stand alone. Other newspapers produced editors whose celebrity rivaled the most famous figures covered by their reporters. And they also began to feature columnists whose viewpoints, as well as advice, were enjoyed avidly by readers. In the years just after World War I the old Hearst-Pulitzer duel was continued through the presence of Brisbane's counterpart on the New York

World, the equally fabled Herbert Bayard Swope, a considerable contrast in personality, political position, and lifestyle, but another example of the new celebrity editor.[16]

Like Brisbane, Swope had worked as a reporter (in Chicago), before
being hired by the New York *Herald*. His ambition was to work on
the *World*, and in 1909 he was offered a reporting job there. Exuberant
and debonair, Swope made friends easily among theater and sporting
people like Irving Berlin, John Barrymore, and George M. Cohan. His
early reporting beats included the Triangle Fire, the sinking of the
Titanic, and a 1912 New York police scandal. These successes led to
fame and to political friendships also, the most notable being with
Woodrow Wilson and Bernard Baruch. Swope continued to report as
well as to advise and to speak; he won the first Pulitzer Prize awarded
in journalism for his series on Germany. Heading the United States
press delegation to the Peace Conference, Swope was an actor as well
as a reporter in the larger diplomatic process.

Returning home, Swope became a special assistant to Ralph Pulitzer, Joseph Pulitzer's son and the publisher of the *World*. While
Frank Cobb remained editor-in-chief until his death in 1923, Swope
became executive editor of the paper and chief spirit of the council
that met daily to discuss the newspaper's policies. He helped bring
Walter Lippmann and Arthur Krock to the editorial page after Cobb's
death. But his special achievement was to develop the page opposite
the editorial page into a series of columns of opinion. Previously it
had been a mélange of obituaries, community service announce-
ments, and releases on the doings of society. Swope transformed the
page into a home for the most famous columnists in America, including Heywood Broun, Franklin P. Adams (known as F.P.A.), Robert
Benchley (briefly), Alexander Woollcott, Deems Taylor, and others of
similar distinction who covered music, theater, books, radio, vaudeville, films, and the cultural life of the city more generally. Those
contributing to the *World* in this period, either through columns of
their own or through F.P.A.'s famous "Conning Tower," included Ring
Lardner, John O'Hara, Dorothy Parker, Russel Crouse, Marc Connelly, Elinor Wylie, George S. Kaufman, Allan Nevins, James M. Cain,
Maxwell Anderson, among the best known essayists, poets, historians, playwrights, and novelists of the interwar years.[17]

But Swope was more than simply an influential editor. His energy
and gift for friendship were legendary. The Swope circle included a
heady mixture of the wealthy, the literati, high society, and free spirits. George Gershwin, John Hay Whitney, Marjorie Merriweather Post,
Fanny Brice, Harpo Marx, William Paley, Will Rogers, George Jean
Nathan, Noel Coward, Gene Tunney, Jack Dempsey, Floyd Dell, Scott

Fitzgerald, made up part of a fabled social set who enjoyed an apparently unending round of weekend parties, dinners, croquet games, and similar gambols. In the twenties they were centered around Swope's Long Island homes, one in Great Neck and its successor, purchased late in the decade, on the Island's very tip. Their ranks included some of the wittiest, richest, most famous, and most successful people in the city, and Swope's fame as reporter and editor was complemented by his celebrity status as a member of this group. He was simultaneously the subject of some newspaper stories and the initiator of others, adviser to political figures like Al Smith and Franklin D. Roosevelt, chum of prizefighters, financiers, artists, and gamblers. He even managed to adorn the cover of *Time* during the decade, epitomizing the ubiquitous presence of his great newspaper. And day after day the *World* focused on events taking place in its home city.[18]

Swope was both participant and witness to a new, more extroverted form of metropolitan culture, New York's special blend of the popular and the performing arts, a flamboyant, commercialized, highly publicized mixture shaped by playwrights, producers, actors and actresses, musicians, gossip columnists, songwriters, critics, publishers, some of whom now began to move back and forth between Broadway and Hollywood or to create new opportunities for themselves on the radio. Despite occasional skepticism and some snobbishness as well, several took the aesthetic claims of the new mass media seriously. Their escapades, tastes, rivalries, witty exchanges, excesses, drinking habits, and amours codified a style of living for a group of sophisticates who identified this style with urbanity and with New York. Such self-absorption, however extreme or unpleasant it may seem in retrospect, fueled continuing public attention.

The new celebrities, moreover, had an appeal that went far beyond elite intellectual circles. Precisely because of their involvement with films, music, shows, radio, sports, and much publicized patterns of personal consumption, the group also gained the attention of a far broader audience, less attracted by specific literary and artistic attainments than by the gossip, high living, and accessible sophistication so presented. New York culture now increasingly identified itself with a novel blending of high and low; its modernism had a broad embrace.[19] Some of this was mere slumming; patronizing and often superficial scouting parties led into various local subcultures. But other aspects were serious, respectful, analytical, and evocative explorations of both the pluralism of city life and the art forms developing around it.

A barrage of books, memoirs, autobiographies, and essays have combined to immortalize the era and several of these figures. The nearest thing to a New York public salon was now presented in the dining room of the Algonquin Hotel.[20] The Round Table emerged as an appropriate symbol of this new urbanity—profane, colloquial, bitter, self-destructive, frequently alcoholic, sexually promiscuous, anti-philistine, broadly though not traditionally educated—finding an audience not only among residents of New York but also among Americans who identified with the city's cosmopolitanism during a decade when rural ideals had apparently captured the nation. This was a different kind of big city than its prewar ancestor, even if many of the roots of its bohemianism could be dated to the first years of the new century, with their increasing emphasis on nightlife, greater sexual freedom, and leisure time pursuits.

Another monument to these values was not a physical object but a periodical. It was, however, a magazine rather than a newspaper, and its attempt to combine humor, elegance, city life, traditional literary aspirations, and popular culture mirrored what was happening in some newspapers of the decade, like the *World* and the *Tribune*. This was, of course, the *New Yorker*. As Harold Ross envisioned it at the time, his new magazine intended to counter a deficit in New York journalism. "There was no magazine—neither weekly nor monthly—for the metropolitan reader."[21] Magazines featuring humor, news, and fiction, filled with expensive advertising and good art, were national in their orientation. Ross, who had come from a newspaper background and had successfully edited the *Stars and Stripes,* an American military newspaper during World War I, was, like Swope, friendly with a broad range of New York celebrities, including newspaper people like Grantland Rice, Ralph Pulitzer, writers like Ring Lardner, Robert Benchley, Marc Connelly, theater people and musicians like Ethel Barrymore, Jascha Heifetz, and Irving Berlin, athletes like Gene Tunney and Jack Dempsey, as well as some businessmen and financiers. He sought to create an attractive, informative, and New York-oriented journal that would feature good criticism, fiction, and sophisticated art.[22]

The *New Yorker* premiered in February 1925. After some difficult months it proved itself within a year. Ross managed to bring together a brilliant staff of writers and artists, many of whom, like Alexander Woollcott, Dorothy Parker, Frank Sullivan, and F.P.A., were already veteran newspaper critics. Part of the magazine's early success built on ways of linking consumption and celebrity. Ads for haberdashers brandished testimonials by writers, artists, actors, and actresses; hotels, theaters, and specialty shops soon followed. Caught up in the period's fascination with itself and the new blend of high and popular art, promoting a sophisticated blend of wit, elegance, and superb editing, the magazine prospered. And so did several other locally edited versions of urbanity, notably the Condé Nast publications of *Vogue* and *Vanity Fair*, although some of them had earlier origins.[23]

But, in fact, the journals were recognizing the same conditions that the New York newspapers had already acknowledged in their criticism, fiction, carricature, columns of opinion, and cartoons. It was not only Swope's *World* and Brisbane's *American* offering such variety. Most of the New York press had responded to their readers by remaking themselves over in the image of the magazine, daily as well as Sunday.

And this included still another innovation of the decade, the tabloid. For much of the nineteenth century, with the exception of an odd experiment here and there, major American newspapers had avoided the small page size common in the eighteenth century. There were a few illustrated papers which used the format, like the *Daily Graphic*, but the increase of business and improved technologies sustained the taste for the larger size. Typographic conventions, which added to the attractiveness of many newspapers, also nourished the preference. Despite some American convictions that a pictorial tabloid would succeed here, it was an Englishman, not an American, who took the first big chance. And that was Lord Northcliffe. His *Daily Mirror*, published in London, had become a huge success, selling as many as a million daily copies before 1920.

The Northcliffe example and the personal ambitions of Joseph M. Patterson, member of a prominent Chicago publishing family and closely connected to the *Chicago Tribune*, led to the creation of New York's first twentieth century tabloid, the *New York Daily News*.[24] The first issue appeared (as the *Illustrated Daily News*) on June 26, 1919, featuring a full page photograph of the Prince of Wales on horseback. Above it were two headlines: "Germans Block Signing of Treaty" and "Newport to Entertain Prince of Wales in August." The second headline was the kind of story that this paper favored. In six months the *News* reached a daily circulation of 100,000; in eight months, 200,000; in fifteen months, 300,000. By its fourth year of operation the *News* had achieved the largest daily circulation in New York, and three years later, the largest Sunday circulation. In the spring of 1926 the *Daily News* was selling 1 million copies of its daily paper, and 1¼ million copies of its Sunday version. It had become, in fact, the most popular newspaper in the United States and soon spawned a series of local imitators. Its unprecedented success further shaped the city's brand of journalism.

Again, the techniques were not entirely new. Patterson was an admirer of Arthur Brisbane; as a college student he had been an avid

reader of Pulitzer's *World.* The *News* emphasized pictorialism, simplicity, brevity, and personalized reader participation. It did this last
not through assembly of a stable of eminent columnists, the technique employed by the *World,* the *Tribune,* and other long-established
papers, but by a series of prize contests which offered cash to winners,
and by other devices that incorporated reader opinion into the pages
of the paper. It proffered beauty contests, picture puzzles, popularity
polls; it sponsored athletic meets, dinners for celebrities, vacation trips
for poor children. Indeed, the first critical growth period for the paper
was built around a fabulously successful limerick contest. Four lines
of a limerick were published, and a daily prize of $100 was promised
for the best last line. The contest ran 100 days and produced 1,203,278
responses, this when the newspaper was only a few months old. According to one of its veteran employees the contest established clearly
the value and timing of circulation stimulants. The monetary prizes
themselves sold extra copies of the paper, and it soon became apparent that a three-week format was sufficient to produce permanent
readers.

Contests themselves were nothing new. Small-town newspapers had
been running versions of them for a long time, although not necessarily with cash prizes. But the success of the contest feature revealed
the changing personality of the New York press in the 1920s, the
reinsertion of something besides mere information to appeal to the
urban audience. The contest was just one of the many things which
suggested that to *News* readers at least, New York was a "big town,"
as well as a "big city," and that village values of personal curiosity
and human interest remained powerful despite the city's growth. This
was the popular counterpart of the celebrity culture that the *World*
and *Tribune* columns were honoring with their gossip-filled exploits
of an extended family of entertainers, artists, writers, playwrights,
composers, actors, and athletes.

Along with extensive coverage of murders, disasters, screen ro-
mances, and celebrity divorces, the *News* emphasized the drama of
neighbors' lives. The inside pages were filled with three or four paragraph stories on local tragedies or trysts, with an occasional national
reference thrown in. The tone of many was caught by the heading,
"Smiles Her Lips Can't Fashion Flash In Eyes," the story of a young
high school student who suffered "nerve paralysis" as a result of an
automobile accident, and could no longer smile.[25] Local news could
be very slight indeed. On March 21, 1925, "Her Felt Chapeau Saves
Girl Wedged In By Subway Train," described the escape of a Brooklyn
girl from serious injury. A Miss Celia Klick of Brooklyn was pushed
by a subway crowd against a waiting train, and fell onto the concrete

floor. But "for her hat, she might have sustained serious injury."[26] This was not really a news story but a family incident. The *News* was filled with them, along with photographed vignettes of daily life— roller-skating, children playing, evidence of seasonal changes, dramatic sports moments, wreckages of fire damage. The names and addresses of the subjects of these stories were every bit as important as they would have been in a small-town newspaper.

Chances for more name-dropping were available in features like The Inquiring Photographer, who interviewed within the city on a daily basis and then published the names, streets of residence, opinions, and pictures of the participants. The questions asked were often domestic and personal, permitting respondents an expression of sentiment or morality. In April, 1925, he quoted Dr. Eugene Fisk who declared that "a nagging wife is the greatest blessing in the life of her husband. Do you agree?" The following day he asked if a special school for "bad boys" would benefit other children. "Is a girl of sixteen too young to have her own latch key?" the Inquiring Photographer wondered shortly thereafter. Was the boxing commission right in barring Jack Dempsey from boxing in New York State, and did the presence of children make married women better wives?[27]

There was also The Voice of the People, an arena for letters to the editor which appeared on the editorial page, often far more interesting, in the twenties at least, than the rather tepid statements of newspaper opinion. And there were the columns. "Dear Roxy," wrote one reader to the author of a daily column on radio, "if you could have seen the happy tears on mother's face as she read my letter to you in Monday's *News*. She smiled and said it would surely place your name with Abu Ben Adhem."[28]

Literal participation through letters, puzzles (the newspaper crossword was an innovation of the decade), contests, was a feature of many New York papers during the twenties, as it had been earlier. What the *News* did was to accentuate this relationship, organizing its readers for their eventual inclusion in one of its news or feature stories. Ethnic festivals, religious feasts, weddings, funerals—these were part of the coverage, and the focus was latitudinarian. Most faiths and national groupings received some representation. The urban village existed for ordinary people as well as for celebrities. And the superb photography and brilliantly controlled prose, always clear, succinct, appealing, iced the cake. "Silver Spoon? No, Rabbit's Foot," headlined a story about a little girl who fell from a fourth story window and emerged unhurt.[29] "Another Broadway butterfly was crushed and bruised yesterday," began the description of a jewel robbery.[30]

Just as Hearst (or Brisbane) had imitated Pulitzer, now he aped the

News. There were actually two major impersonations during the decade, one the relatively short-lived but vivid creation of Bernarr McFadden, the *Evening Graphic,* the other Hearst's *Daily Mirror,* a compound of sex, crime, and sensational stories that came close to parodying its model. Both first appeared in 1924. Within a year the *Mirror* had reached a circulation of 300,000, indicating the success of the tabloid formula and the emphasis on entertainment. The *Graphic* did almost as well, but more quickly crossed the line into blatant sexuality, trumped-up stories, and composite photographs.

The *Mirror* was less sharply edited than the *News,* its typographical and pictorial appearance more crowded and inchoate, its national and international coverage even skimpier.[31] Like the *News,* it ran a serial story and a Daily True Story each day, offering a quota of fiction to its readers. It also featured prize contests, crosswords, puzzles of various kinds, and, by the late 1920s, a columnist exemplifying New York's increasing identity with the gossipy world of entertainment and café society—Walter Winchell.

If Lardner, Woollcott, Swope, F.P.A., Broun, Deems Taylor, and their colleagues reflected highbrow New York's cultural appetites, Winchell demonstrated a broader constituency, a lay audience for news about film stars, radio personalities, gangsters, athletes, and socialites, centering on their personal lives and habits. Winchell, noted Stanley Walker, city editor of the *New York Herald Tribune,* represented something new. The columnists of an earlier day, and even contemporaries like Broun and F.P.A., with their "urbane comments on the news and occasional philosophic disquisitions," did not resemble the loud, slangy *Mirror* columnist with the sixth-grade education.[32] Winchell's background was the vaudeville theater, and his first journalistic efforts were columns for *Billboard* entitled "Stage Whispers." Stage whispers continued, under another name. He was, wrote Walker, "the perfect flower of Broadway, the product of his period as surely as prohibition and the night clubs and the tommy-guns." In pursuit of his task Winchell added to the language: "getting storked" or "anticipate a blessed event" seemed so much more pungent than "expecting a baby," while "Renovated" was a way around the ugly word "divorce." Like the tabloids in general, Winchell's prose was breathless, dramatic, easy to absorb, and succinct.

Winchell was not alone. Nor was he literally the first in line. According to at least one memoir, the *Daily News* actually ran the first Broadway column in December, 1924, Bernardine Szold's "About Town." When she left, the column was taken over by the better known Mark Hellinger, who entitled his daily effort, "About Broadway." Hellinger also became a celebrity, as did *News* columnists Sidney

Skolsky and Ed Sullivan. Sullivan later bridged the distance between Broadway gossip and the postwar world of television entertainment. And among other columnists covering the local worlds of entertainment and café society were Karl K. Kitchen's "Up and Down Broadway," for the *Evening World,* and Cholly Knickerbocker, Dorothy Kilgallen, Elsa Maxwell, and Louis Sobol, all Hearst employees.

The tabloids also quickly installed radio columnists and, like the other New York papers, included several pages each day on films, plays, and radio programming. But neither the *News* nor the *Mirror,* in their early days at least, paid the slightest attention to the stock market or any financial news. Patterson had thought briefly of including stock tables to interest Wall Street types, but soon abandoned the practice. Like lengthy obituaries, the stock tables didn't fit the taste of the audience, an audience subjected to relentless economic and demographic study by staff specialists. Applied research into the reading market was used by newspaper publishers decades before their counterparts in the book trade put it to use. "It does not pretend to be a complete newspaper," declared Stanley Walker about the *News.* "It prints what interests the editors and throws the rest away."[33]

The newspaper realm in New York during the twenties was thus basically tripartite. The *Times* emphasized the detailed and encyclopedic coverage properly due a wealthy community whose interests spanned the world. The *Tribune* and the *World* added the cultural sophistication demanded by the brassy, alert, fast-paced life the city epitomized. And the *News* and *Mirror* reasserted older village values in a form that was quick to absorb and easy to remember. Although each element might be typified by a single newspaper, most combined them in one form or another. The *News,* after all, did treat some world events and hosted popular columns. The *Times* possessed extensive arts and leisure sections, supported the most elaborate corps of theater reviewers, and carefully reported on local ceremonies. And the *World* sustained an extensive news department, turning more heavily to features only when it was clear that its news coverage could not match the work of the *Times.* But the newspaper menu offered to readers on a daily basis included very different emphases, and the many failures and newspaper mergers of the 1920s shook out those that had not mastered the new form.

The tripartite scheme survived for many years to come, just as the image of New York that it served continued to flourish. But the end of the decade coincided with an erosion of the newspaper's capacity to shape as well as reflect urban identity. Some of the players began to drop out. In February, 1931, the *World* suddenly stopped independent publication and was purchased by Scripps-Howard, the result of several disastrous decisions made by the Pulitzers.[34] Radio began to emerge as a major competitor rather than as a complement to the newspaper.[35] It had already challenged the function of the newspaper office as the purveyor of the latest excitement in sports and elections, but its power was intensified in the thirties by the extraordinary impact of the new president on the airwaves and the hourly drama of international tensions. Most of all there was the Depression, a catastrophe that clearly threatened the image of invulnerable brassiness which New York as big town had served up in the papers.

If certain monopolies enjoyed by the newspapers would be challenged in the years just ahead, the big city press did seem almost invulnerable in the years surrounding World War I. Never again would so many local reporters, columnists, and editors attain such wide fame or move so easily from their newspaper work to biography, criticism, fiction, script, and history writing. The Roaring Twenties was to a great extent their mythic achievement, and at the center lay the image of The City That Never Sleeps.

Notes

1. For a broad and incisive overview of New York's papers at this time, see Frank Luther Mott, *American Journalism. A History: 1690–1960*, 3rd ed. (New York, 1963), Chaps. XIII, XV, XXV. Other surveys include Frederic Hudson, *Journalism in the United States, from 1690 to 1872* (New York, 1873); Alfred M. Lee, *The Daily Newspaper in America: The Evolution of a Social Instrument* (New York, 1937); Michael Schudson, *Discovering the News. A Social History of American Newspapers* (New York, 1978); and Bernard Weisberger, *The American Newspaperman* (Chicago, 1961). The most recent bibliographical guide is Richard A. Schwarzlose, *Newspapers. A Reference Guide* (New York, Westport, Conn., London, 1987). For Bennett's *Herald*, James L. Crouthamel, "James Gordon Bennett, the New York *Herald*, and the Development of Newspaper Sensationalism," *New York History* LIV (July 1973): 303–307, is very helpful.

2. Richard Kluger, *The Paper. The Life and Death of the New York Herald Tribune* (New York, 1986), Chaps. 2–5, ably reviews the strategies of these papers, and suggests further reading, 753–756.

3. The major modern biography of Pulitzer is W. A. Swanberg, *Pulitzer* (New York, 1967). George Juergens, *Joseph Pulitzer and the New York World* (Princeton, 1966), presents an excellent analysis.

4. Frank Luther Mott, *American Journalism*, 436–439. See also Marion T. Marzolf, "American 'New Journalism' Takes Root in Europe at End of 19th Century," *Journalism Quarterly* 61 (Autumn 1984): 529–536.

5. For Barth's views, see Gunther Barth, *City People. The Rise of Modern City Culture in Nineteenth-Century America* (New York, Oxford, 1980), Chap. III.

6. Gunther Barth, *City People*, 59, 62.

7. The structures and building programs of the *Times* are described in Meyer Berger, *The Story of The New York Times, 1851–1951* (New York, 1951), *passim.* For the actual rechristening of Longacre Square, see *Editor & Publisher* 3 (April 16, 1904): 2. The *World* building is illustrated and described in *Harper's Weekly* 34 (Jan. 18, 1890): 47. For the *Herald,* see Leland M. Roth, *McKim, Mead & White, Architects* (New York, 1983), 171–173. Allen Churchill, *Park Row* (New York, Toronto, 1958), offers a popular history of many of New York's best established papers, along with descriptions of the buildings they occupied near New York's City Hall. And Thomas A. P. van Leeuwen, *The Skyward Trend of Thought* (The Hague, 1986), 93–113, presents a stimulating interpretation of New York's skyscraper newspaper offices.

8. Richard Kluger, *The Paper,* 184–186.

9. Michael Schudson, *Discovering the News,* 106–120.

10. For Hearst, see W. A. Swanberg, *Citizen Hearst. A Biography of William Randolph Hearst* (New York, 1961). For the yellow journals, see Sidney Kobre, *The Yellow Press and Gilded Age Journalism* (Tallahassee, 1964).

11. Much remains to be written about Brisbane. The principal source, at present, aside from memoirs and autobiographies, is Oliver Carlson, *Brisbane. A Candid Biography* (New York, 1937), an entertaining but biased commentary.

12. This was the most elaborate editorial obituary run by the *News.* See John Chapman, *Tell It to Sweeney: The Informal History of the New York Daily News* (Garden City, 1961), 21.

13. Gunther Barth, *City People,* 66.

14. Richard Kluger, *The Paper,* 210–211. See also Benjamin Stolberg, "The Man Behind The 'Times': The Portrait of a Publisher," *Atlantic* 138 (Dec. 1926): 721–731.

15. Oliver Carlson, *Brisbane,* 182.

16. The most recent study of Swope is Alfred Allan Lewis, *Man of the World. Herbert Bayard Swope: A Charmed Life of Pulitzer Prizes* (Indianapolis, 1978). See also E. J. Kahn, Jr., *The World of Swope* (New York, 1965).

17. For more on the *World* and its columnists, see Sally Ashley, *F.P.A. The Life and Times of Franklin Pierce Adams* (New York, 1986). John K. Hutchens and George Oppenheimer, eds., *The Best in the World* (New York, 1973), presents extracts from the newspaper's great days. Richard O'Connor, *Heywood Broun. A Biography* (New York, 1975), Chaps. 6–11, describes Broun's often stormy relationship with the *World.*

18. Analyzing categories of news stories in the *World* during the mid-twenties, I found that New York stories invariably outnumbered stories of every other type—national, international, sports, or financial. Thus, June 2, 1925, The World Today, a column of brief news summaries, listed 2 stories under Nation; 6 under Foreign Affairs; 4 under Washington; 5 under Financial and Business; 7 under Sports; and 19 under New York.

19. This emerging culture is most evocatively described in Lewis A. Erenberg, *Steppin' Out. New York Nightlife and the Transformation of American Culture, 1890–1930* (New York, 1981).

20. The literature on this group is enormous. See, among others, Samuel Hopkins Adams, *A. Woollcott: His Life and Times* (New York, 1945); John Baragwanath, *A Good Time Was Had* (New York, 1962); Nathaniel Benchley, *Robert Benchley: A Biography* (New York, 1945); Brian Gal-

lagher, *Anything Goes. The Jazz Age Adventures of Neysa McMein and Her Extravagant Circle of Friends* (New York, 1987); Margaret Case Harriman, *The Vicious Circle: The Story of the Algonquin Round Table* (New York, 1951); Edna Ferber, *A Peculiar Treasure* (New York, 1939); Gene Fowler, *Skyline* (New York, 1961); Howard Teichmann, *George S. Kaufman: An Intimate Portrait* (New York, 1971); Howard S. Teichmann, *Smart Aleck: The Wit, World, and Life of Alexander Woollcott* (New York, 1976).

21. As quoted in Janet Grant, *Ross, The New Yorker and Me* (New York, 1968), 212.

22. For more on the *New Yorker* and Ross, see Brendan Gill, *Here at the New Yorker* (New York, 1975), and James Thurber, *The Years with Ross* (Boston, Toronto, 1959).

23. In particular see Caroline Seebohm, *The Man Who Was Vogue: The Life and Times of Condé Nast* (New York, 1982).

24. For the history of the *Daily News*, I have relied principally on John Chapman, *Tell It to Sweeney*; and Leo E. McGivena et al., *The News. The First Fifty Years of New York's Picture Newspaper* (New York, 1969).

25. *New York Daily News* (March 18, 1925), 9.

26. *New York Daily News* (March 21, 1925), 10. The story ran on the same page with another about a young girl in hospital after an attempted suicide. "Here is the old, old story of the girl who comes to the big city to win fame in the movies, of failure and a dwindling treasury, of despair and attempted suicide."

27. These questions all were taken from the first week of April, 1925. This feature continues to operate in the *News*.

28. *New York Daily News* (March 20, 1925): 38.

29. *New York Daily News* (March 9, 1925): 1.

30. *New York Daily News* (March 14, 1925): 2.

31. I base this on a comparative reading of both newspapers for parts of March and April 1925.

32. Stanley Walker, "That 'Dreadful' Winchell Man," *The Night Club Era* (New York, 1933), 129. William R. Taylor, "A Place that Words Built: Broadway, Damon Runyon and the Slanguage of Lobster Alley," in *In Pursuit of Gotham: Commerce and Culture in New York* (New York, 1992),163–182, offers a fascinating and important analysis of the role of journalists and the new linguistic conventions they developed.

33. Stanley Walker, "The Quick and the Dead," *City Editor* (New York, 1934), 70.

34. The end of the *World* became a subject of bitter recrimination and extended debate. Some blamed the Pulitzer family, others Joseph Pulitzer's will, and still others, the regime of Herbert Bayard Swope, who had left the paper not long before. See James W. Barrett, ed., *The End of the World: A Post-mortem by Its Intangible Assets* (New York, 1931); and James W. Barrett, *The World, the Flesh, and Messrs. Pulitzer* (New York, 1931).

35. For some journalists the electronic competition was critical in redefining their era. See Gene Fowler, *Skyline*, 247–248.

Part V

THE HIGH ARTS:
METROPOLITAN
AUTONOMY
AND MODERNISM

*T*HE FOUR CHAPTERS that comprise this section reflect themes that have by now become familiar: tension between metropolis and nation; the relation between the city's self-image and commercialism; the search for an integral metropolitan identity. Since we deal here with creative intellectuals, the self-conscious makers of meaning for their societies, we are brought into the most immediate confrontation with the differences between our two cities despite all that unites them. The artist's act of transmuting feeling into form or perception into symbol presents us with radical condensations of historical experience that can never be representative. Yet it is out of such powerful individual reductions that the defining images of cities are constructed.

The authors of the essays on painting in New York and Budapest, Wanda Corn and Éva Forgács, have focused their lenses sharply on a single problem: the city as subject matter. Other issues, such as problems of style or the nature of the values and social functions of the artists, their conceptions of past, present, and future, emanate from the centrality of the image of the city (or its absence) in these explorations. Perhaps nowhere in this volume does the comparative approach produce clearer evidence of what the cultures of our two cities have shared, yet how drastically history parted the paths of development upon which it had once set them both.

In art as in literature, New York and Budapest during the first half of the nineteenth century lived in provincial dependence, residual from the eighteenth century, on London and Vienna. The burst of autochthonous economic and political energy after the Civil War in the United States and after the Austro-Hungarian Compromise *(Ausgleich)* of 1867 was accompanied in both New York and Budapest by a quest for autonomy in culture. At first the modernizing, nonagrarian new elite of the cities on both the Hudson and the Danube and their painters turned for inspiration and schooling in the visual arts from London and Vienna, respectively, to other European centers: Paris, Düsseldorf, and Munich. There, American and Hungarian artists embraced realistic historicism and a new kind of nature painting which, being neither English nor Austrian, fulfilled the aspiration of their publics for a wider cosmopolitanism by attachment to the latest academic traditions of the continent. These rarely included the city or its life as a proper concern of art.

Against this background in nineteenth century academicism, modernism in art in both New York and Budapest emerged under the dual impact of continental innovation and urban modernization. Artists in both cities adopted new painting techniques from European realists and impressionists. But where the innovative painters in New York exploited them to glorify the city, the Budapest avant-garde eschewed their city as subject. The essays of Wanda Corn and Éva Forgács, carefully attuned to each other, show how each group of painters, even as they created national visions of America and "Hungarianness" for the modern age, pursued almost opposite paths. The New York painters of 1900 celebrated the city with images of skyscrapers, the "cathedrals of commerce," in their overwhelming monumentality, much as their preceding generation had glorified America through the majesty of America's mountains. Indeed the urban artists often used perspectives and visual techniques that had been developed to present nature's grandeur. The rushing torrents of urban life too were affirmatively dramatized in images of masses in motion and the faceless vitality of New York's traffic. Power, energy, virility; tension controlled or released, outer or inner—these were the characterizations of New York which, through increasingly abstract visual language, the city's painters projected as the essence of modern America. The break of the metropolis from traditional rural America was decisive in this art, with a visual affirmation of the new city of man vibrant with a confidence that the city showed the nation the way to its future.

As in the cases of the centralizing press or the vaudeville (see Part IV), where the integrating power of commerce transcended cultural divisions derived from separate pasts, so in the paintings of New York it is the buildings and performances of capitalist enterprise that serve as unifying icons. With a notable difference: the multiethnic origins of New York's urbanism, so visible in the mass press, on the stage, and in city politics, appear only rarely in painting until the 1930s. The city as cultural collage, the city of difference, so evident in the popular media, loses its color in the shadow of the dominating monolithic architectural icons of big business and the rush of Manhattan's faceless getters and spenders presented by the painters.

In *fin-de-siècle* Budapest, the revolt of the painters against the academicism of the mid-nineteenth century was as thorough as in New York. Éva Forgács charts the trajectory of stylistic evolution of Hungarian modernist groups in phases that closely parallel those of New York's: from impressionism through Cézanne-like structural vision to cubism and abstraction. Yet in Budapest none of these styles is connected, as they were increasingly in New York, to the image of the city, whether as scene or as a complex fractured metaphor of inner experience. The ideological agenda of the Hungarians was not to define their modern city, but to redefine "Hungarianness" against the regnant bourgeois-gentry nationalists. The artistic modernism and social urbanism that the New Yorkers joined together, the Hungarian painters sundered. To that end, their first generation of modern painters turned away from the capital city. Against official aristocratic-warrior mythology and academic historicism they posited a purified nature painting and a national culture of rural simplicity. From history to ethnography, from elite culture to folk culture: such was a prominent tendency among the pioneer modernists of Hungary. For them, Budapest represented not a brave new world in birth (like New York), but a capital of ruling-class corruption cloaked in the old-world costume of its principal pseudohistorical monuments, the Parliament House or the Fisherman's Bastion. Cézanne's structuralism and cubism, to be sure, came to Budapest as to New York. But where the New York painters connected these styles with objects in the skyscraper city, the Hungarians used them, as Éva Forgács says, to express "human brainwork." The Activists, the most radical Hungarian avant-garde group, embraced abstraction and even the machine aesthetic as revolutionary rationalists with an international cosmopolitan intent, at once political and cultural, that transcended Budapest as well as "Hungarianness" entirely. They viewed the equation of rationalism with architectural modernity as characteristic of New York or Paris but not of their own metropolis, whose cosmopolitan culture in the 1920s was being destroyed by reactionary politics. Too many of Budapest's masters in the visual arts, as in so many other domains of intellectual life, had in the end to seek outlet for their modernist ideas in exile, while the urban culture of Hungary that they had lifted to international stature sank back into provincialism.

The chapters that probe urban cultural life through fiction show that the writers of Budapest and New York underwent parallel changes in their constructions of the city to those of the painters. Once again, the beginnings in the late nineteenth century are similar, but the roads diverge. In both literatures, the point of departure was a moralistic one, a novel of manners anchored in the traditional codes of gentry and bourgeois family structure and provincial social organization. In Hungary and America these values generated ethical resistance to and a reformist critique of the new city. In two texts, one by Ferenc Molnár, the other by William Dean Howells, our two analysts illuminate the strikingly similar effort of their Hungarian and American authors to find the persistent presence of the old way of life in the modern urban scene. Miklós Lackó's writers do not, like the Budapest painters, wholly abandon the city for the purity of the countryside. But their characters often live in the city with a sense of *dépaysement*, of loss. Even writers who embrace cosmopolitan values and combat official nationalism, like the major poet Endré Ady, strive to draw sustenance for a modern, urban "Hungarianness" from rural vernacular cultural roots. Where New York writers often elevate the city's slang to the status of literary language, Ady forms a new poetic language for Hungary out of high modernist abstraction and archaic folk elements, but little urban argot.

In the literature about Budapest, the search for "home" goes on, with urban individualism and liberated hedonism evidently less valued than in New York. Only in the writings of Lajos Kassák, whom we have met as the leader of the radical Activists in painting, do we find the affirmation of urban Budapest as a ground of existence—but in its most universal quarter, the rough and rugged industrial district.

After World War I, when Budapest's fate was determined more than ever by its agrarian reactionary national environment, the writers' long attempt to integrate a Magyar rural culture into a metropolitan identity, so cherished by the creative intelligentsia in the prewar years, receded into the background. As in painting, so in literature, modernism in the end defined itself without reference to the city as symbol.

Not so in New York. Philip Fisher's narrative quickly leaves behind the social and ethical optic that New York's literary naturalists shared with their Budapest colleagues as both came to grips with metropolis in the 1890s. Like the New York painters, with their representations of New York through the denatured symbols of skyscraper and dynamic urban motion, the novelists affirmed the city in its mighty "otherness" in relation to the traditional America around it in space and behind it in time. In its indifferent, fluid energy, New York was construed as at once fatality and opportunity. A cruel human environment which threatened the individual as America's wilderness had done, it was also inviting to the self-determining individual who felt imprisoned in mainstream national life. Destructive to community, the city opened unheard-of possibilities for social bonding. Where Howells, like most Hungarian writers, tried to find continuity in the city, the characters of Dreiser and Dos Passos sought, successfully or otherwise, discontinuity from the small-town conventional lives they had left behind.

By the awesome massivity of the city itself, and by the radical social multiplicity that paradoxically constituted it, the characters of the New York novels are, as Sartre would have said, "condemned to be free." In a multivalent social system, the ethical perspective of Anglo-American literary tradition yielded to a kaleidoscopic aesthetic one, where imaginary form alone unites what the restless metropolis has randomly juxtaposed. The city as killing machine, Fisher suggests, becomes a playground—albeit one where dangerous games of power and eros prevail.

To register the formal changes in the novel produced out of the encounter of his writers with New York, Fisher uses the newspaper as a key. His analysis here attaches, though at a different level of cultural production, to Neil Harris's characterization in Chapter 10 of the commercial press as the instrument of integration of urban society into a metropolitan village with a common fund of information and a shared, simplified discourse. Harris's picture of the emergence in the 1920s of a sophisticated New York "village" ethos among the writers of smart magazines like *The New Yorker* opens our vision to the relation of popular and commercial culture to art-literature in shaping the city's identity. Fisher's men of letters too began their careers as journalists, watching as New York City, joining high and low, foreigner and native, pulled loose from American culture even while it recast its values.

In Budapest too, the theme that dominates Lackó's delineation of the place of the city in literature reenforces for high culture the problematic governing the essays on popular culture. Here as there, the attempt to widen the definition of "Hungarian" in a multicultural way that suited the character of Budapest was inhibited by the persistent power of nationalist tradition. The recourse for Budapest's powerful cosmopolitan impulse was transcendence, be it in the joke, the fantasyland of multinational operetta, the fiction of an alternate archaic past, or the creative rationalism of an abstract art.

In the consciousness of its artists and writers, New York was free to become by the 1920s what its economic and democratic necessities mandated and allowed—multivalent, optimistic, future-oriented, and almost arrogantly autonomous in relation to America's national mainstream culture and even to Europe. In Budapest, similar economic and demographic factors of modernization were prevented by political and social structures and by the debilitating crises of war and revolution from issuing in the kind of metropolitan cultural autonomy that New York achieved and that fueled the imaginations of both its media entrepreneurs and its artists. Budapest continued to live in the shadow of a feudal-agrarian past that the new century's blows soon reenforced, robbing the intellectual modernists it had so richly nurtured into world citizens of a city they could call their own.

Chapter **11**

The Artist's New York: 1900–1930

WANDA M. CORN

IRCA 1900 a few adventuresome artists began to paint and photograph New York City—its skyline, harbor, skyscrapers, and congested street life. Since artists had long lived in Manhattan but rarely depicted it in their art, this sudden attention to the city landscape is an event of note in the history of American culture. In earlier decades, illustrators had produced depictions of the city for magazines, and genre artists had created picturesque paintings of street vendors and barefoot urchins, but none of the country's important landscape artists painted much in the way of city views. While the countryside was respected artistic material, the city was not.

As if a veil had dropped from their eyes, a number of American artists began to "see" and depict the city in which they lived at the beginning of the new century. They were all associated with progressive styles of art, first Realism and Impressionism, then Cubism and Futurism, and in the 1920s, Precisionism, an American style of geometric abstraction. The first of these artists, primarily turn-of-the-century Impressionist painters and pictorialist photographers, were quite literally lured away from the natural landscape to invent a pictorial language for the city's skyline, suspension bridges, and towering skyscrapers. They were joined in the years 1905–1915 by the so-called Ashcan School—artists who depicted the dynamism and crush of human life in city streets, markets, parks, and tenements. By World War I early modernist artists had begun to picture New York as a kaleidoscopic city of towers, bridges, street traffic, and twinkling electric lights. In the 1920s a more stately and sublime view of New York evolved as artists eliminated movement and people and rendered the city as an awesome (sometimes horrific) urbanscape of streamlined skyscrapers.

Even members of the European avant-garde began to interpret Manhattan, the first new world subject to attract foreigners since Niagara Falls and the American Indian. By the end of World War I, Francis Picabia, Albert Gleizes, and Marcel Duchamp had all visited New York and made art about what they found there. Picabia painted abstract "impressions" of New York's fast-paced street life; Gleizes created cubist medleys of New York's Brooklyn Bridge, Broadway, and jazz musicians; and Duchamp declared one of New York's earliest skyscrapers, the Woolworth Building, a Readymade. In latter years Bernard Boutet de Monvel and Maurice Denis, along with many other European and Latin American artists, visited New York and painted its bridges, skyscrapers, and skyline. For Piet Mondrian, it was American jazz and New York's congested streets that inspired his brilliant series of New York abstractions.

Nor was it necessary for European artists to visit Manhattan to be inspired by it. Working entirely from photographs, film footage, and local lore, George Grosz and certain Dadaists as well as Russian Constructivists made paintings, drawings, and collages depicting New York without ever having crossed the Atlantic.

No other city in the world attracted such artistic homage in the early twentieth century—not London, Milan, Venice, Rome, or Budapest. Even Paris, the city that had been of such great interest to late nineteenth century artists, became a minor theme in the avant-garde repertory, glimpsed only occasionally in the Eiffel Tower paintings by Robert Delaunay, in café still lifes by the Cubists, or in paintings of cabaret dancers by Futurists. Only Berlin, a city that like New York was extreme in its modernity, attracted something of the same attention in the postwar period.

To date, much of the scholarship about paintings and photographs of New York City has focused on artists' attitudes toward the city, specifically on the question of whether their works celebrated or critiqued urban life. There have been studies of the debates that flourished in the art press about the relative beauty or ugliness of skyscrapers, of the humanistic content and democratic ideals of the Ashcan School artists, and of the utopian attitudes of machine age enthusiasts after World War I.[1] My interest, however, is in two more basic questions. First, what was so seductive about Manhattan that artists would suddenly turn to it in great numbers while the older and more celebrated cities of Paris or London fell out of favor as subject matter? Second, what did artists choose to "see" in New York City, and what rhetoric or language did they invent to describe this city?

It is remarkable how little of New York the artist elected to represent. To a city dweller, the artist's New York is a strange place, for it generally condenses urban chaos into only a handful of artistic signs—

soaring skyscrapers, frenzied crowds, pincushion skylines, and dazzling electric lights. The selectivity is significant since cities are by
definition complex and eclectic aggregations of myriad things. The
choices artists made in putting particular frames around parts of New
York City, therefore, carry meaning. Deciding what to depict of the
city, and how to render it, takes on even greater interest given that
the first artists to depict New York were primarily trained as landscapists, and they perceived New York primarily through the conventions of nature painting. Only by transforming a preexisting nature
vocabulary did these artists evolve a set of signs for rendering man-
made New York and come up with a schematic definition of "New
Yorkness."

My questions lead us to consider the kind of city New York had
become in the early twentieth century and the artists' desires to create pictures about the uniqueness of their own age. Their compulsion
was to identify and understand those features of life that were not
just modern, but also distinctively American. In trying to uncover
"New Yorkness," artists were groping to understand "Americanness,"
which they sensed to be situated in a new style of twentieth century
urban life.

One imperative that clearly prompted progressive artists to pay attention to the city they lived in was the Realists' call for artists to
shun the classicism of the academy and to depict one's own age, place,
and time. Such a commitment to milieu had led the French Realists
and Impressionists in the 1860s and 1870s to begin to paint and write
about contemporary Paris; about a generation later, novelists and
painters did the same for New York City. In the 1890s, William Dean
Howells in A Hazard of New Fortunes (1889) and American Impressionists like Childe Hassam and Theodore Butler, along with painters
of a more picturesque bent, such as Joseph Pennell and Birge Harrison, and photographers Alfred Stieglitz and Alvin Coburn began to
create art about contemporary New York. They depicted what they
could see of New York from windows high above the city and from
their walks along city streets. Like their European counterparts who
had depicted Paris, these artists were particularly attentive to sensations that were novel and modern: they were the first to paint or
photograph the modern city from the extreme height of a skyscraper;
to picture the looming hulks of individual skyscrapers and the canyons formed between tall buildings; and to convey, by a few sketchy
strokes of paint, a descriptive and sensory impression of a rush hour
crowd. They even documented genre details unique to New York City's
landscape, such as members of the city's sanitation force who, in a

277

Figure 11.1 Alfred Stieglitz, *Spring Flowers—The Street Sweeper*, 1901. Photogravure, 310 mm × 127 mm (12⅛″ × 5″). Alfred Stieglitz Collection, © 1992 National Gallery of Art, Washington, DC.

controversial decision of the mid-1890s, were uniformed in white suits and were known as the "white wings" (Figures 11.1 and 11.4). Painters and photographers were also careful to include the white steam clouds that hung over New York, a detail that tourists always commented upon in Manhattan where so many buildings were centrally heated by steam plants (Figures 11.8 and 11.9). And when they depicted New York by night, their pictures featured the public street lights and windows in skyscrapers that by the turn of the century were lit by electricity rather than by gaslight, a visible sign of New York's up-to-dateness and modernity (Figures 11.6 and 11.7).

278

Figure 11.2 Alfred Stieglitz, *Old and New New York*, 1910. Photogravure, 333 mm × 257 mm (13⅛″ × 10⅛″). Alfred Stieglitz Collection, © 1992 National Gallery of Art, Washington, DC.

Indeed, if we study the first art photographs and paintings of New York purely for documentary information, they tell us about many of the physical and economic changes that took place in New York City in the late nineteenth century. It was in those years that the city metamorphosed from a major port city of middling size to one of the great financial capitals of the world. That change manifested itself in a radically transformed landscape, one often referred to in the early

279

twentieth century as the "new" New York.[2] The old skyline of church spires was replaced by the new skyline of higher and more aggressive skyscraper towers. Once a city of horse-drawn carts and carriages, the city's traffic now included electric streetcars, motorbuses, taxis, and automobiles. By 1900 the Elevated—a highly visible mass transit system—snaked around the city, and the first links of the citywide subway were under construction. At night, New York no longer looked like Whistler's London, lit by the softness of gaslight; it blazed with more electric lighting than any other metropolis in the world.

The city also became infinitely more crowded and congested. Skyscrapers revolutionized not only the scale and form of the city's streets and edges but, along with the new transportation systems, made it possible for thousands of new jobs to be packed into small areas, engendering the new phrase "rush hour." Along with the traditional ferry boats, there were now suspension bridges and tunnels pumping masses of people into and out of the island of Manhattan daily. And along the edges of the island and in various pockets of Manhattan, tenements and densely populated ethnic neighborhoods sprang up to absorb the great swell of immigrants to America at the turn of the century.

After 1900, artist renderings of New York were exceedingly sensitive to this "new" New York that was overtaking the slower-paced, less crowded, more genteel city of mid-century. Indeed, so sensitive were they to the fact that they lived in a city of rapid change, one that had a reputation of tearing down old buildings to make way for the new, that they invented idioms for growth and change. They often pictured construction sites of skyscrapers as huge theaters of scaffolding and self-consciously composed pictures of new buildings towering over old ones (Figures 11.2 and 11.3). But what is perhaps most striking about the first generation of Impressionist and picturesque representations of New York City is the degree to which "old" New York begins to fade from artistic consideration. Although there were in 1900—as there still are today—quiet treelined streets, city squares, churches, brownstones, dressmaker shops, mansions, specialty shops, and streets known for fashionable street life, artists began to ignore them. Increasingly, they turned their back on old, picturesque, and genteel New York and turned to selected features of the burgeoning city.

They began to concentrate on those aspects of New York that were unlike European cities. We can see this best in the work of Childe Hassam. In the 1890s, Hassam's paintings of New York's fashionable streets and avenues might have been taken as views of London or Paris: a few fashionable pedestrians strolling along streets lined with Beaux-arts mansions and churches (Figure 11.4). But in the new cen-

Figure 11.3 Childe Hassam, *The Hovel and the Skyscraper*, 1904. Oil on canvas, 25″ × 31.″ Mr. and Mrs. Meyer Potamkin.

tury, his paintings began to include scenes that were peculiar to New York. He added the Manhattan skyline to his repertoire and put sky-scrapers into his work (Figure 11.5). And instead of always painting from street level, he began to represent the city from the vantage point of a tall building. He also found a way to dramatize the unprece-dented heights of the new skyscrapers by painting buildings soaring up both sides of the canvas to form deep canyons that were then an-chored in dense pedestrian and vehicular traffic below.

We can see a similar development in other artists' work, as Butler, Pennell, Coburn, and Stieglitz all moved away from general city scenes

Figure 11.4 Childe Hassam, *Washington Arch, Spring,* 1890. Oil on canvas, 27⅛" × 22⅛." The Phillips Collection, Washington.

to concentrate on certain key New York experiences. The one that challenged them the most was that of the skyscraper. Artists had no ready vocabulary for these new behemoths, no more so than the architects who designed them, and had to invent ways of describing what these new structures looked and felt like. Their first solutions were to paint or photograph them very much as if they were natural phenomena, bathed in nature's light, and seen through the branches of trees (Figures 11.6 and 11.7). Just as early writers about the skyscraper fell back upon landscape metaphors, calling skyscrapers "stony cliffs" and the streets running between them "canyons," the painters

Figure 11.5 Childe Hassam, *Lower Manhattan View Down Broad Street*, 1907. Oil on canvas, 30⅛″ × 16.″ Herbert F. Johnson Museum of Art, Willard Straight Hall Collection. Gift of Mrs. Leonard K. Elmhirst. Photo by Jon Reis.

relied upon older conventions of landscape painting to describe the new buildings. They depicted skyscrapers as if they were cliffs with a ravine running through them (Figure 11.7) or as great towering peaks or mountain ranges (Figures 11.6 and 11.8). To give some sense of their scale, artists did just as romantic landscapists once did and exaggerated the height of the buildings and depicted them as looming over ant-size people (Figures 11.5 and 11.7). They also used an old convention in painting, the bird's-eye view, picturing the city from the extreme height of the new buildings (Figure 11.9).

These artists softened their images of the brand-new, starkly white skyscrapers by bathing them in light and palpable atmosphere. Indeed they seemed incapable of rendering skyscrapers, the skyline, or the

Figure 11.6 Edward Steichen, *The Flatiron—Evening,* 1909 print from 1904 negative. Photograph, gum-bichromate over gelatine silver, 18¹³⁄₁₆″ × 15⅛″ (478 mm × 384 mm). The Metropolitan Museum of Art, New York, The Alfred Stieglitz Collection, 1923 (33.43.43).

city's new canyons without the comforting presence of mother nature. Marrying nature and skyscrapers was a way of learning how to describe what was novel by using terms that were timeworn and familiar. When Howells described "the moony sheen of the electrics," he was using the same rhetorical strategy as did photographers and painters depicting skyscrapers in mist, snowstorms, and rain, and at dusk and nightfall.[3] While such mixing of nature's light and man's machine-age forms appears incongruous to us today—and perhaps an interpretive strategy for resisting or opposing the new buildings—we

Figure 11.7 Birge Harrison, *Fifth Avenue at Twilight*, n.d. Oil on canvas, 30″ × 23.″ The Detroit Institute of Arts.

need to remember that it was a common perception in the early 1900s that the skyscraper was at its most beautiful in subdued lighting. This cultural taste, one held by both skyscraper enthusiasts and detractors alike, was not just lingering romanticism but an early strategy of accommodation. New Yorkers had to learn how to live with overscaled buildings that appeared unexpectedly like monsters on their skyline. Artists and writers aided in the process by constructing skyscrapers

Figure 11.8 Alfred Stieglitz, *The City of Ambition*, 1910. Photogravure, 340 mm × 260 mm (13⅜″ × 10¼″). Alfred Steiglitz Collection © 1992 National Gallery of Art, Washington, DC.

as magnificent and beautiful when nature intervened to make the new behemoths look most like mountains and cliffs.

These early twentieth century representations are the first attempts to define the skyscraper city and to gain some psychic control over its foreignness. It fell to another group of artists to articulate the skyscraper city's accelerated pace. Early twentieth century visitors to New York were deeply impressed by the crowds, rush-hour traffic,

Figure 11.9 Theodore Earl Butler, *Brooklyn Bridge*, 1900. Oil on canvas, 30" × 40." Private Collection. Photo courtesy of Maxwell Galleries, San Francisco.

fast-paced life, and the relentless energy of New York's streets. They had never felt anything like it. Whether they liked the crush of crowds or not, they perceived such phenomena as one of Manhattan's most peculiar novelties. "The chief impression you get on landing in New York," one visitor characteristically wrote, "is an atmosphere of frightful hurry and restless bustle everywhere. . . . What is there in the air of New York, different to that of other cities, which would explain this headlong stampede of its citizens?"[4] For Henry James, crowds in New York, especially those of businessmen in Wall Street, were so chaotic and disorienting that "relief, detachment, dignity, meaning, perished utterly."[5]

It is in the work of the Ashcan painters—John Sloan, George Luks, Everett Shinn, and George Bellows—that we first find efforts to isolate, construct, and define Manhattan's dense crowds and raucous street life. These artists were not landscapists by training but illustrators and journalists. Their interest was in the human side of city life, in the local color of neighborhoods, and in the wide diversity of people that made up New York's polyglot population. Through their works, we go from broadest avenue to coarsest alley, visiting tenements, street markets, bars, restaurants, Coney Island, and vaudeville theater. We look through windows into shops and backyards, visit rooftops, and look up from street level to the elevated railway. We watch city people doing city jobs and enjoying city leisure: laborers, shoppers, restaurant-goers, slum dwellers, prostitutes, beggars, entertainers, nannies, and bartenders.

These pictures are rich social documents about the "new" New York's changing citizenry—the advent of the working woman, the growth of a new urban middle class, and the newly arrived immigrant cultures. But more to the point of this chapter, many of these paintings are pioneering exercises in giving pictorial definition to New York's fabled energy and busyness. The Ashcan artists invented ways to narrate the sensation of being in a New York crowd. John Sloan's *Fifth Avenue* may at first glance seem a "snapshot" painting of a city street, but if we look again we realize its distortions: superactive cars and pedestrians densely packed like sardines into a ridiculously small space (Figure 11.10). Bodies travel in every possible direction, a randomness repeated in the choppiness and unevenness of Sloan's stroke. In George Bellows's painting of a chaotic traffic jam in *New York*, the eye hardly knows where to light because there is so much brush activity and so many vehicles and pedestrians (Figure 11.11). People are always in movement in these paintings, seemingly filled with inexhaustible energy and life. Their energy is embedded in the sketchiness of paint itself which swirls and darts across the canvas. The Ashcan artists were deliberately rough with their brush, equating the quick stroke, swirling impasto, and sketchiness of contour with the zest, buoyancy, and tactility of New York's crowded streets.

If the Impressionists and Ashcan School artists inaugurated a "new" New York iconography, it was the American Cubo-Futurists who refined, sharpened, and purified it. These artists brought two strong beliefs to the project that earlier artists had not possessed: first, a firm conviction that they lived in a city whose extreme modernity was its most distinctive feature; and second, that modern times demanded a modern art, an art radically different in style from those of the past.

It is in the 1910–1920 city paintings of John Marin, Abraham Walkowitz, Max Weber, and Joseph Stella that we find these convictions first expressed. Here the artists portray exclusively those aspects of New York that were deemed new and modern, and they do so in

Figure 11.10 John Sloan, *Fifth Avenue,* 1909. Oil on canvas, 32″ × 26.″ Private collection. Courtesy of Kraushaar Galleries, New York. Photo by Geoffrey Clements.

Figure 11.11   George Bellows, *New York*, 1911. Oil on canvas, 42" × 60."
Collection of Mr. and Mrs. Paul Mellon, © 1992 National Gallery of Art,
Washington, DC.

cubist-derived styles which self-consciously break with descriptive
modes of the past. In Marin's *Movement, Fifth Avenue* (1912), tall
buildings dance along the avenue, their broken movements and dynamism echoed in the traffic and crowd below (Figure 11.12). In Walkowitz's *Cityscape,* a jumble of skyscrapers are wrapped in a skein of
energetic lines which emanate from the antlike crowds below (Figure
11.13). Repeating vectors and thrusting diagonals represent the crush
of New York traffic in Weber's *Rush Hour,* while thin rectangular
forms of skyscrapers loom above (Figure 11.14). A similar vocabulary
of prismatic forms and dramatic force lines in Stella's *Brooklyn Bridge*
(1917) represents the soaring towers and cables of Brooklyn Bridge,
with skyscrapers beyond (Figure 11.15).

Figure 11.12 John Marin, *Movement, Fifth Avenue*, 1912. Watercolor, 43.3 cm × 35 cm. © The Art Institute of Chicago, Alfred Stieglitz Collection, 1949.554. Photo by Kathleen Culbert-Aguilar, Chicago. All rights reserved.

What strikes us about these works is the narrowness of their urban vision. New York has been reduced to a schema of its own special modernity—skyscrapers, Brooklyn Bridge, energy, and crowds. There are no neighborhoods, no trees, no meandering pedestrians, no parks, no picturesque gestures, or soft veils of atmosphere to diffuse, soften, or humanize the message of the pictures. These are paintings that

291

Figure 11.13 Abraham Walkowitz, *Cityscape,* ca. 1913. Pencil and graphite on paper, 20" × 13." National Museum of American Art, Washington. Gift of the artist in memory of Gertrude Vanderbilt Whitney. Photo courtesy Art Resource, New York.

spell out Manhattan hieroglyphically as an ultramodern city of incessant energy and herculean architectural achievements.

The interpretation is embedded as much in the modern styles of these paintings as in the imagery itself. Fractured forms and independent lines convey frenetic movement; and the repetition of forms and

Figure 11.14 Max Weber, *Rush Hour, New York*, 1915. Oil on canvas, 92 cm × 77.5 cm (36¼″ × 30¼″). Gift of the Avalon Foundation. © 1992 National Gallery of Art, Washington, DC.

jumble of cubist imagery spell out emphatically that New York is a city of superhuman scale and tireless restlessness.

What makes these paintings so radically different from those we have looked at thus far is their use of abstraction, expressive line, and distorted space to create a bewildering psychic experience, an equivalent for how one emotionally feels when experiencing New York's streets. The Impressionist and Ashcan School artist's stance toward the city was always that of a spectator standing outside the sights

Figure 11.15 Joseph Stella, *Brooklyn Bridge*, 1918–1920. Oil on canvas, 214.5 mm × 194 mm (84″ × 76″). Yale University Art Gallery, New Haven. Gift of Collection Société Anonyme.

and phenomena of the "new" New York. He invited us to join him on his peripatetic tour of the city and see it through his eyes as he stood on street corners and peered out windows. But in the Cubist paintings of New York, the artist gives up his stationary position and puts himself—and us—in the middle of the maelstrom by synthesizing many vantage points and many aspects of city experience within a single canvas. Instead of observing the city from the point of view of a pedestrian, we lose our footing and are hurled into its structures, crowds, and energies, our eyes and senses bombarded with sensations

Figure 11.16 Georgia O'Keeffe, *Radiator Building—Night, New York*, 1927. Oil on canvas, 48″×30.″ Alfred Stieglitz Collection, Carl van Vechten Gallery of Fine Arts, Fisk University, Nashville.

Figure 11.17 Charles Sheeler, *New York, Park Row Building*, 1920. Photograph, 8″ × 19.″ The Lane Collection. Photo courtesy Museum of Fine Arts, Boston.

that make us dizzy and disoriented. New York City is no longer a series of discrete "views" but a certain state of being, one in which we are jostled, overstimulated, and overwhelmed. The artist presents the city as modernity itself, wondrous and exhilarating, but also strange and bewildering.

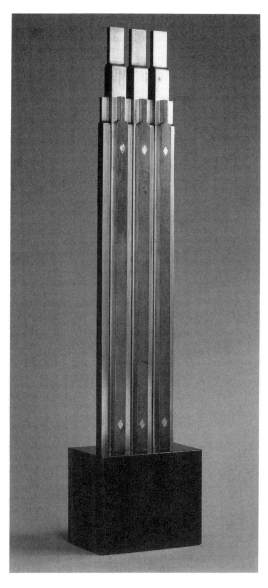

Figure 11.18 John Storrs, *New York*, ca. 1925. Brass and steel on black marble base, 25⅞″ × 5½″ × 3½.″ © 1992 Indianapolis Museum of Art, Discretionary Fund.

Modern painters of the 1920s continued to picture the modernity of New York as an awesome experience. But they did so through another kind of schematic representation of New York, one of the austere and overpowering skyscraper city. In the Precisionist works of Georgia O'Keeffe, Alfred Stieglitz, Charles Sheeler, and John Storrs, the city is rendered as if it were exclusively a man-made metropolis of superscaled buildings (Figures 11.16–11.18). Crowds, nature, and movement have vanished. Unlike earlier painters and photographers

297

who depicted the skyscraper as part of a larger city environment and tempered its contours with light and atmosphere, these artists ruthlessly boiled their compositions down to tall buildings and the razorsharp canyons between them. And when they borrowed some of the language evolved by the first generation of city painters for skyscrapers—bird's- and worm's-eye views and extreme contrasts between the bigness of skyscrapers and the littleness of people or older buildings—they used these terms with violent exaggeration, so that we now experience the city as something quite awesome and sublime, majestic and terrifying at the same time. The vocabulary used in these works is so hard-edged, geometric, and classical that the skyscraper appears as overwhelming as the pyramids of Egypt—scaleless monuments of elemental purity that dwarf everything in their presence.

By 1925, then, modernists had come up with two basic hieroglyphs to convey the essence of New York—one of crowded street life representing the city's frenzied activity and sensory overload and the other of sublime skyscrapers to symbolize the intensely man-made iron and steel city. Occasionally, artists varied what they painted of New York but not their reading of the city's essential character. When they painted the electric lights and billboards of Broadway, for example, or the lights, crowds, and amusement rides at Coney Island, they imbued the city with the sensations of a rush hour, as a chaotic, jostling, supercharged environment. Similarly, artists painted the towers and cables of Brooklyn Bridge with the same vocabulary they had devised for the skyscraper—geometric, superscaled, and sublime.

Not only American artists, but European modernists as well constructed and helped give artistic authority to these same two New York "essences." Like their fellow American artists, they were highly selective and painted only the sensory cacophony of the streets and the sweeping lines of Brooklyn Bridge and the skyscraper. In New York paintings by Picabia and Gleizes, two Parisian avant-garde painters who came to New York in the 1910s, the city is rendered as orgiastic and unrestrained, a nexus of competing sensations (Figures 11.19 and 11.20). Picabia explained to the American press that his new abstract paintings were about "the spirit of New York," its "stupendous skyscrapers" and "mammoth buildings," its "driving hurry" and "breathless haste."[6] In the 1920s when other Europeans, such as the Frenchman Bernard Boutet de Monvel and the German artist Arnold Ronnebeck, visited New York City, they had eyes only for skyscrapers and suspension bridges (Figure 11.21).

Why, one wonders, did modern artists come to "see" New York with such selective vision? Obviously, not all of New York in 1925 was skyscrapers and bridges nor was every street an experience in fast-moving crowds. New York schematized as energy and engineer-

Figure 11.19 Francis Picabia, *New York*, 1913. Gouache and watercolor, with graphite, on cream wove paper, 55.6 cm × 75.6 cm. Photograph © 1992 The Art Institute of Chicago, Alfred Stieglitz Collection, 1949.577. All rights reserved.

ing was an artistic construct, not an everyday reality for all city dwellers.

In a general sense, the question takes us back to Charles Baudelaire, who first called upon artists to see spectacle and modernity in

Figure 11.20 Albert Gleizes, *Kelly Springfield*, 1915. Gouache on board, 40⅛″ × 30⅛″ (102 cm × 76.5 cm). Gift Solomon R. Guggenheim, 1937. Photo by Robert E. Mates. © The Solomon R. Guggenheim Foundation, New York.

the forms of city life, and to Walt Whitman, who wrote so passionately about contemporary life in New York City. For decades thereafter, avant-garde poets and artists looked to cities for signs of their contemporaneity. They painted and wrote about the city's railroad stations, factories, and busy commercial streets; urban displays of new technologies, such as the car and electric light; and the city's engineering marvels, such as the Eiffel Tower in Paris and skyscrapers in

Figure 11.21 Arnold Ronnebeck, *Wall Street*, ca. 1925. Lithograph on paper, 12½″ × 16¹¹/₁₆.″ National Museum of American Art, Washington, DC. Gift of the estate of Olin Dows. Photo courtesy of Art Resource, New York.

New York. In the early twentieth century, artists and poets in Cubist and Futurist circles became almost cultist about the modernity of their age, celebrating what they perceived its great inventions—car, plane, and electric light—along with the speed and dynamism they found in modern cities. Such "modernolatry," as one historian has called it, led quite naturally to artists identifying the bustling crowds and soaring skyscrapers of New York as symbols for the new age they lived in.[7]

But it is important to understand that New York's modernity seemed

301

extravagant, even ruthless, to painters and intellectuals. It went far beyond the kinds of modernity one experienced abroad, say, in the Eiffel Tower. American modernity was "extreme modernity," as Picabia once put it, the kind that could come only from a rich country with no past to hold it back, a country where engineers not artists were its creative citizens, and where businessmen not princes and kings were in power.[8] To paint New York in the early twentieth century was not just a futurist-type exercise in modernolatry, but an effort to come to grips with a new and peculiarly American style and pace of life. Indeed, one might argue, the art that we have been looking at represents one of the first cultural recognitions of what we now commonly refer to as the "American way of life," one based on corporate business and a consumer- and market-oriented economy.

That people sensed in New York an extraordinary modernity, one unlike anything that could be experienced abroad, epitomized by skyscrapers and rush hours, is confirmed by literary descriptions of New York in the early twentieth century. This literature is vast, written by visitors as well as natives of the city. It ranges from picturesque tourist accounts and glib journalism to high-minded literary reflections by such renowned literary figures as Henry James, H. G. Wells, Rudyard Kipling, and Maxim Gorky. Some of it praises the "new" New York, some of it condemns the city. But no matter who the commentator or what the critical stance, there are two perceptions that crop up repeatedly in this literature. First, that, for better or worse, New York had become a unique and unprecedented city unlike Paris or London or, indeed, any other place in the universe; and second, that the uniqueness of the city was vested not in its past or in its cultural achievements but in its seemingly relentless modernity. New York's *métier*, explained a visitor, using common rhetoric of the day, "is to be modern, as modern as possible, not to be merely New, but ever-new, York."[9]

Like the artists, writers developed a kind of litany of sensations and sights that they found exclusive to New York. From all that New York offered, they abstracted those experiences that could not be had elsewhere. They paid no attention to the opera, museums, parks, or department stores, and looked rather at skyscrapers, Brooklyn Bridge, Broadway, Coney Island, elevators, rush hours, and modern conveniences—electric lights, central heating, plumbing, and the telephone. Often, like Henry James or Maxim Gorky, they hated these modernities, declaring them alien, extravagant, inhumane, and vulgar. But even in their ire, they spent a good amount of their creative energies trying to grapple with what they divined to be the newness and singularity of New York City.

In their efforts to explain New York, they inevitably linked the city's outlandish modernity to national characteristics. The most popular explanation was to draw upon the idea that Americans were young, both in calendar years and in spirit. America, it was repeatedly claimed, unlike Europe, was so young that it had no past to honor and hold it back. Youthfulness was used to explain the energy and the entrepreneurial spirit of the streets, the "virile young lustiness" of the skyscrapers, and the daring of the American engineer.[10] Or, if one disliked New York, one blamed the ugliness and rawness of the skyscraper on America's immaturity and lack of taste and erudition. For others, the skyscraper was explained by America's extreme wealth, practicality, and business-mindedness. These seemed like structures appropriate to a country where business and moneymaking seemed more important than spiritual goals. In Europe, it was assumed, citizens honored the past and culture over their pocketbooks.

Whether characterized as "monsters of the mere market," or as "original American architecture," skyscrapers were immediately perceived in the early 1900s as a native form of architecture.[11] The functionalism and efficiency of the tall building were said to be as reflective of American democracy and commerce as the Parthenon was of the aspirations of the Greeks. Or, it was claimed, the skyscraper was to America what the palaces and cathedrals were to Europe, an index of where power and privilege rested in a culture.[12] For some advocates, the skyscraper was indigenous because it was free from European influence. It was a national building form, said one commentator in 1907, that suits "our needs, our comfort, our landscape, without regard to any nation or civilization."[13]

It was this intimate alignment of modernity, New York, and Americanness that ultimately lay behind the growth and development of a New York iconography. Artists took on modern New York as a subject, not just because they wanted to document milieu and place or because they were driven to portray the modernity of their age, but because they sensed in the city's architecture and speeded-up life the raw, somewhat inchoate, lines of a modern American identity. An earlier national identity had been found in the frontier and wilderness, with its vanquished Indians, primeval Niagara Falls, and expansive spaces. But by the late nineteenth century, that identity was obsolete and had lost its power to inspire artists and writers. New York, one could say, became the new wilderness, the new metaphor for "Americanness." As a subject, it became a way to explore the modern as well as the hardheaded, pragmatic, and fast-paced American way of life.

The early twentieth century artist uncovered this identity, as we have seen, only slowly, through a process of invention and discovery. It began at the turn of the century when artists rather timidly ap-

303

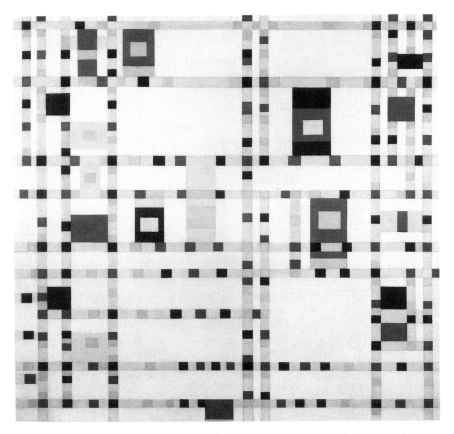

Figure 11.22 Piet Mondrian, *Broadway Boogie Woogie,* 1942–43. Oil on canvas, 50″ × 50.″ Collection, The Museum of Modern Art, New York. Given anonymously.

proached the new city and began to sort out its salient features. Appropriately, it was in the 1920s, during an era of postwar boom and economic prosperity, that Americans were proud and boastful of their international achievements, that New York found its most precise and sustaining formulation as the city of soaring "cathedrals of commerce" and rampant energies.

Space does not permit a full consideration of the degree to which these modalities, once invented for New York, were sustained in avant-garde circles. The synoptic view that reduced New York to crowds and skyscrapers became something like a tradition in modern painting and continued to be the inspiration for works of art. When Mondrian, for instance, came to America for the first time during World War II, he created a set of works about New York that restate the schema we have been tracing: they are about congestion, street energy, skyscrapers, and crowds. While he worked in his usual abstract vocabulary of straight lines, right angles, and primary colors, Mon-

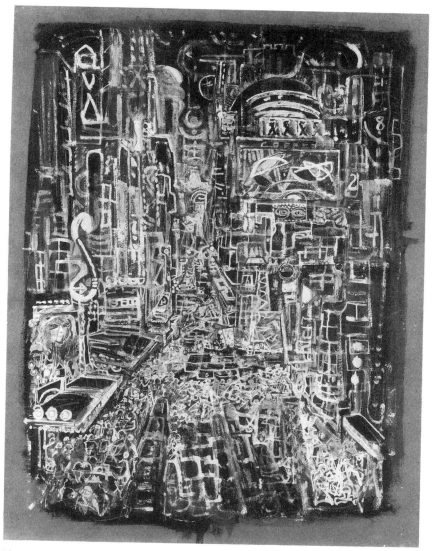

Figure 11.23 Mark Tobey, *Broadway*, 1935. Tempera on masonite board, 26″ × 19³⁄₁₆.″ The Metropolitan Museum of Art Arthur H. Hearn Fund, 1942 (42.170).

drian charged the visual fields of his New York series in new ways, making them much more dynamic and colorful. Instead of composing with thick black lines encasing large squares of primary colors, he now overlapped lines made from color—bright yellow and red—and intersected them at more frequent intervals. In *Broadway Boogie Woogie*, the most famous of these canvases, he introduced small squares of color that force the eye to dance and pulse its way across the surface (Figure 11.22). While it is generally understood that these works

Figure 11.24   Franz Kline, *The Bridge*, ca. 1955. Oil on canvas, 80″ × 52¾.″ Munson-Williams-Proctor Institute, Museum of Art, Utica, New York.

depended upon Mondrian's direct personal experience of Manhattan and his love for American jazz, it is also clear that by the 1940s, Mondrian's perceptions of this country as that of bustling energy and dense urban spaces were shaped and guided by a half-century of artistic exploration.

For the twentieth century European, Manhattan has been an occasional subject. But for Americans, New York City has been a pivotal artistic theme. And while there have been alternative visions of the city than the ones we have looked at here, particularly during the Depression years, the sustaining power of the early modernist view of Manhattan is stunning. A quick glance at city paintings by Mark

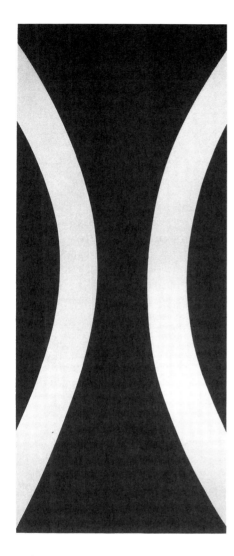

Figure 11.25 Ellsworth Kelly, *Brooklyn Bridge, VII,* 1962. Oil on canvas, 92⅛" × 37⅝." Collection, The Museum of Modern Art, New York. Gift of Solomon Byron Smith.

Tobey (1935), Franz Kline (1955), and Ellsworth Kelly (1962) shows the degree to which New York continued to be translated in avantgarde circles as thunderous energies and soaring lines (Figures 11.23–11.25). But what is most suggestive about these three paintings, all of which have New York titles, is that they come from three artists whom we generally think of in terms of very large-scale abstract paintings without ostensible "subjects." These three artists were all associated after World War II with the New York School, which achieved international acclaim for the invention of a new kind of abstract, nonreferential, "universal" painting. But one wonders, given the notions of "New Yorkness" and "Americanness" that we have uncovered here, the degree to which these ideas seeped into and shaped the vocabularies of postwar American abstract painters. A good argument can be made to show that Tobey's late canvases of abstract "white writing" began in his energetic scribbles representing the New York crowds of Broadway; and that Kline's huge abstractions of bold black strokes against white canvases are inspired by New York's much heralded modern architecture. Skyscrapers and bridges may also linger just below the surface of many of Kelly's minimalist abstractions of a later date. Though such paintings betray no specific allusions, they may indeed be there, nourished and fed by a pictorial rhetoric about American energy and engineering that had been in the making since the turn of the century. By the 1940s, American abstract artists claimed to be transnational in their concerns, but the vocabularies they used, when seen within the modernist construct of New York and New Yorkness, suggest otherwise.

Notes

1. For bibliography on the subject, see Merrill Schleier, *The Skyscraper in American Art, 1890–1931* (Ann Arbor, Mich., 1986). See also my own, "The New New York," *Art In America* 61 (July–August 1973): 58–63; and Donald Kuspit, "Individual and Mass Identity in Urban Art: The New York Case," *Art in America* 65 (Sept.–Oct. 1977): 67–77.
2. See, for instance, Rufus Rockwell, *New York: Old and New* (Philadelphia, 1909); and John C. Van Dyke, *The New New York*, (New York, 1909).
3. William Dean Howells, *A Hazard of New Fortunes* (New York, 1965), 66. Original ed. published in 1889.
4. Sir Philip Burne-Jones, *Dollars and Democracy* (London, 1904), 20.
5. Henry James, *The American Scene* (Bloomington, 1969), 83. Original ed. 1907.
6. Picabia, "How New York Looks to Me," *The New York American* (March 30, 1913), magazine section, 11.
7. Pär Bergman, *"Modernolatria" et "Simultaneità"* (Upsala, 1962).
8. Picabia, "How New York Looks to Me."
9. Richard LeGallienne, "The Philosopher Walks Up-Town," *Harper's Magazine* 123 (July 1911): 237.
10. Robert Henri, quoted in William Homer, "The Exhibition of 'The Eight': Its History and Significance," *American Art Journal* 1 (Spring 1969): 59.
11. Henry James, *The American Scene*, 80; and Giles Edgerton [Mary Fanton Roberts], "How New York Has Redeemed Herself from Ugliness—An Artist's Revelation of the Beauty of the Skyscraper," *The Craftsman* 15 (January 1907): 458.
12. See, for example, John Corbin, "Twentieth-Century City," *Scribner's Magazine* 33 (March 1903): 259–272; Sidney Allan [Sadakichi Hartmann], "The 'Flat-iron' Building—An Esthetical Dissertation," *Camera Work* 4 (October 1903): 36–49; and Giles Edgerton, "How New York Has Redeemed Herself," 458–471.
13. Edgerton, "How New York Has Redeemed Herself," 458.

Chapter 12

Avant-Garde and Conservatism in the Budapest Art World: 1910–1932

ÉVA FORGÁCS

"WHERE ARE the painters of Budapest?" asked art critic Ernő Kállai in 1947.[1] For, in sharp contrast to the many and varying representations of New York, we do not find a fascination with the cityscape of Budapest in the Hungarian art of the early 1900s. While New York, as Wanda Corn points out, "lured away American artists from the natural landscape," and even seduced artists from overseas to come and paint its freshly minted beauties, exactly the opposite occurred in Hungary.[2] Painters who were Budapest residents walked out of the city with their easels and set them up in suburbs that looked like any Hungarian village—that is how József Nemes-Lampérth painted his *Landscape* in the old Tabán district (see Figure 12.1). He wandered as far as Szentendre, a small town about fifteen miles north of Budapest on the Danube, to find the romantic idyll in nature, or just the motif he needed, far and safe from city turmoil.

While American artists were looking for dynamism and modernity in New York, identifying the city with Americanness and ignoring the huge, rural heartland of America behind it, the artists of Budapest of the 1890s–1930s wished to escape the urban milieu and ignore it as much as they could. There is, therefore, no Budapest iconography that could be comparable in some way to that of New York.

When comparing the attitude of American artists to New York and the attitude of Hungarian artists to Budapest, a series of spectacular contrasts unfolds. While modernism and innovation and speed and technology defined the dynamic rhythm of New York, there was in Budapest a desire to balance tradition and modernity, even to give

Figure 12.1 József Nemes-Lampérth, *Landscape: Horgony Street Detail,"* 1917. Oil on canvas, 98.5 cm × 106.5 cm. Hungarian National Gallery, Budapest.

priority to traditionalism. Whereas American artists hurried to possess the new spectacle offered by the skyline, the suspension bridges, and other accessories of urban development, the country, not the city, had a hold on the imagination of Hungarian artists. Instead of the future-bound optimism of New York, there was in Budapest a past-bound melancholy and nostalgia. It searched for an affirmation of the historical Hungarian identity along the cultural small streets of the old towns and in the beauties of nature. New York artists did not care what mainland America thought of them and of the sinful city they worshipped, but the artists living in Budapest were concerned with the tension between the city and country and, contrasted with the brisk and fierce self-consciousness of the New York artists, they were more concerned with Hungarianness than with Budapestness, the latter being something unidentified and suspect.

It was not only the past that had a heavy weight—unlike America, which, as Wanda Corn says, "was so young it had no past to honor and hold it back"[3]—but the very nature of this past that made the relation to modernity ambiguous in Hungary.

Modernism, in terms of social structure and industrialization, was initiated in Hungary by an act that even today brings back mixed feelings: the Compromise with the Habsburgs in 1867. Shaking hands with the Habsburgs, who defeated Hungary's thrust for freedom in 1848 and killed many Hungarians, was a historic act which, despite its obvious political realism and economic benefits, constituted a shame. Though it meant the start of modern development, it also meant betraying Hungarians for commerce; the memory of martyrs was traded for factory goods. Since 1867, there had always been something shameful about modernization, because the high price of modernization was the nation's pride and dream of sovereignty. Before urbanization and modernization could become a genuine Hungarian achievement, it had to be imported from the Austrian Empire, with all its alien habits and species—bankers, stockbrokers, and the like. The great monuments of the early nineteenth century reform era, which included building the Academy of Sciences and the Chain Bridge, did not become the emblems of a successful and autonomous national development. To the contrary, they were reminders of the aborted efforts to turn Hungary into an independent nation, and they bore the tragic connotations of defeat.

It is from this perspective that we must inspect Hungary's reluctance to accept modernization and its scene: the spectacle of Budapest as a metropolitan city that had emerged almost overnight before the turn of the century. There was Europe's first underground train line; there was the frame of the Haussmann-designed boulevards and avenues—as in Paris—with the cast-iron railway stations (one of them designed by Eiffel's office); there were museum buildings and hotels, elegant shops and lively neighborhoods where one could live cheaply; there were the stock exchange and the important marketplaces, cafés, and parks with the attendant traffic and rush hours [4]—but all this belonged to some foreign system that wanted to play its tricks with real, genuine Hungary. While Brooklyn Bridge became one of the most triumphant symbols of New York City, demonstrating the miracle of modern technology as well as modernity's beauty, the great Hungarian poet János Arany wrote a dark-toned ballad about the Margaret Bridge, depicting its inauguration as the scene of a *danse macabre*, with nightmarish figures emerging out of the dark Budapest life and plunging themselves with good reason into the river below toward death.

Nonetheless, Budapest was photographed, even if without the touch of artistic ambitions. György Klösz, a commercial photographer, took more than a hundred photos around 1896, when Hungary celebrated

311

Figure 12.2   György Klösz, *Café on Andrássy ut,* 1900, Budapest. *Budapest Anno* . . . (Budapest: Corvina, 1979).

her millenium. He went into the small curving streets, to the majestic new buildings, to the cafés, avenues, and the bridges. He seems to have been especially interested in Budapest architecture and was probably under the spell of the city's beauty and liveliness. But unlike Alfred Stieglitz, Lewis Hine, A. L. Coburn, or other New York photographers, he lacked artistic sophistication. Photography in Budapest had been looked upon as a craft; it had not been the matter of vision or inspiration. When Klösz's glass negatives were found at the end of the 1960s, they were immediately published in an album called *Bu-*

Figure 12.3 György Klösz, Market Square, Budapest, 1890. *Budapest Anno* . . . (Budapest: Corvina, 1979).

dapest Anno. . . .[5] Their publication stimulated admiration both for his qualities as a photographer and for the past dignity and beauty of old Budapest. These pictures (Figures 12.2 and 12.3) tell us that there existed a Budapest consciousness, an awareness of this city's unique situation on the Danube, of its life, even its citizens, the pipe- or cigar-smoking, coffee-drinking, daily paper-reading men, who would sit around on the open terraces of the cafés—even if all this did not appear on the painters' canvases.

The painters did not break away from nature. Tired of academicism, the first group of progressive artists followed Simon Hollósy to Nagybánya, a small village in northeast Hungary (Transylvania, today in Romania) where, undisturbed, they painted impressionistic landscapes and cosy interiors from 1897 to ca. 1905, then followed by a younger generation. This new aesthetic, which broke down the confines of academic standards, found its way to the only place where it could meet the public: Budapest. It immediately provoked hot debates there. Painting as a liberating art had been unheard of in Hungary; painters had been expected to serve the high ideals of the fatherland or religion by portraying historic scenes, allegorical events, or important personalities. As Géza Pernecsky points out, the works of the Nagybánya artists were introduced into Budapest at just the right moment to find a new, picture-buying audience ready to hang small-size landscapes on the walls of their middle-class homes.[6] Here were paintings that filled a demand in the now rapidly developing metropolis for contemporary (and still specifically Hungarian) art, which lacked the burdens of solemnity and gave pleasure to the eye. In sharp contrast to New York, where the city itself increasingly became the main spectacle in the eyes of both artists and audience around and after 1900, Budapest residents and Hungarian artists of the same years imported the countryside into the city on canvases.

The fact that Hungarians were not ready to welcome modernism in the arts was closely related to their hesitation in accepting Budapest as a modern capital city with a cosmopolitan character. All the newly erected neogothic buildings that might have become the celebrated symbols of the city—the Parliament or the Fishermen's Bastion—failed to appear in the paintings. Not even the natural beauty of Budapest, graced by her position on both banks of the Danube, was painted.

While New York grew to be the metaphor of utmost modernity through images of "soaring skyscrapers, frenzied crowds, pincushion skylines, and dazzling electric lights,"[7] there was no demand to turn Budapest into a metaphor. It could not be identified with Hungary as New York was identified with America. The ideals that New York embodied were seen as the ideals of Americanness, but Budapest was very different from the ideal of Hungarianness. In the eyes of most Hungarians, Budapest was a strange mixture of Jews and nouveaux riches, bankers and prostitutes, evil Austrians, Germans, and a hopelessly poor mob. Artists in New York were proud to identify themselves with the city and its mixtures of peoples; it would not have been popular in Hungary to identify oneself with Budapest. Nationalism was certainly more important than any metropolitan value, and being Hungarian was far more acceptable than being Budapestian— the latter not really being a popular identity before World War I. Paradoxically enough, it was the good luck of the Nagybánya artists that their artistic modernism was something apart from modern subject matters like urbanism. Had they painted cityscapes, generally seen as too harsh and poor subject matter for a painter, the press would not have brought the work of the Nagybánya artists to the public. Their art could become fashionable because it was "fresh from the country," and in addition to all the painterly values it embraced, it brought genuine Hungarianness to this strange conglomerate of a city.

The New York iconography that had evolved by 1925 was essentially a "pictorial language of New Yorkness."[8] Artistic modernism was inseparable from New York and the city's rhythm as a subject matter. Due to the ambivalent attitude to the city of Budapest and all that it had meant, modernism in Hungarian art shunned those subject matters that could be considered ipso facto modern, like metropolitan scenes and cityscapes. This caused a strange vacuum in Hungarian painting even in comparison with Berlin or Paris. Paris was loved and celebrated, Berlin rather hated and feared by the artists, but both cities challenged the painters, while Budapest failed to appear even in the most iconoclastic images painted by the new generation of artists, who appeared around 1908 and had their first important exhibition in 1910. The scandal that initially shocked the already self-confident art connoisseurs, and even those who thought they were keeping up with the new taste, was the appearance of a small group of painters in 1910, who called themselves The Eight. "We want sense in painting: disciplined human brainwork!" their leading figure, Károly Kernstok, wrote.[9] Their radicalism was extended to social thinking as well and it was shared with a group of young Budapest literati, mainly Jewish intellectuals, who formed the Galilei Circle. The Eight brought structure rather than surface into focus; they were looking for hidden essential qualities—following Cézanne in that—rather than impressionistic effects of light. Their claim was that art should reveal what was solid (though not visible) instead of clinging to superficialities and bringing cheap pleasures to the eye. They also claimed that state functionaries should not get involved in matters of art. "Our aesthetic trend is not liable to serve the ideology of the state functionaries directing our society," Kernstok wrote.[10] The cubistic-expressionistic pictorial vocabulary of The Eight, along with their leftist radicalism, was far too much for the public who went to see their pictures only to ridicule them. They, in turn, divided the public just as they divided the parameters of art, as György Lukács, their ardent advocate, put forth in his article under the title "The Ways Have Parted."[11]

The ways (i.e., the aspirations, methods, expectations of "conservative" and "modern" artists) parted, and modern art divorced all those

315

Figure 12.4 János Kmetty, *Kecskkemét Detail with Church Tower*, 1912.
Oil on canvas, 92 cm × 72 cm. Hungarian National Gallery, Budapest.

art tendencies that compromised with public taste or were not radically innovative. But radical innovation did not imply a renewed relation to the capital city in which they lived. For the most part, the content of their aesthetic innovations and radical ideas was tied to allegoric representations of heroic scenes.[12] The only cubistic cityscape that we have is from their contemporary, János Kmetty, entitled *Kecskemét Detail with Church Tower* (1912), representing a small town's typical architecture (Figure 12.4). Not even cubistic rendering

316

was married to a Budapest cityscape: Budapest simply did not inspire painters directly.

Though many art historians point out that the music of Béla Bartók was in many ways akin to, even inseparable from, the art of The Eight, his metropolitan rhythms and sounds that evoke fast-paced twentieth century city life reach back to the most ancient Hungarian traditions at the same time; they evoke more explicitly the essence of "modernity" than the speculative paintings of The Eight. Bartók distilled the kernel of urban experience into his music, whereas the art of The Eight was content with a few references to such an experience: the lyrical, descriptive, anecdotic elements were not surmounted by the quintessence of a harsh metropolitan experience. Though Budapest did appear in the literature of this period, even the epic descriptions of the city—mainly by Gyula Krúdy—focus on the small-town-like idyllic corners of the city where timeless small restaurants are populated with people who hardly ever leave their neighborhoods. The city of the big tenements and brownstone schools, of the eclectic and ambitious public buildings, of millenary monuments and broad avenues, does not surface in the pictures painted or stories told of Budapest.

Certain aspects of Hungarian history may offer some explanation for this tension between Budapest and the image of Hungarianness that dominated Hungary until after World War I. As historians point out, there was a Hungarian elite during the first three quarters of the nineteenth century whose conception of modernizing Hungary included the involvement of the Jews and the Germans.[13] In this renewed social structure, both ethnic groups would have been overrepresented, but both would have been in the service of Hungarian society. By the end of the nineteenth century, however, after the Compromise, the country's industrialization brought about a real social restructuring. In this traditionally agricultural country the industrialists and traders suddenly got rich, whereas the minor landowners, an important group among the Hungarian nobles, were on the way to rapid impoverishment. The minor landowners, accordingly, favored modernization without the Jewish and the German middle classes. It was during this period of the late nineteenth century that the Jewish-German bourgeois elite was held up in an unfavorable contrast with the more conservative Hungarian elite.

Liberal ideas guiding the country's modernization did not survive the financial polarization. The new value was financial power, and as this was mostly in the hands of Jews and Germans, traditional Hungarians pictured themselves as defenders of the "genuine" values—land and nobility—mistrusting anything and anyone else. It is true that, compared with other Eastern European countries, it was in Hungary, and mainly Budapest, where the assimilation of Jews was the most advanced (a law of 1895–1896 permitted mixed marriages[14]). But, as Laszló Varga reminds us, the Jews were allied to those *few* outstanding Hungarian intellectuals behind whom there stood nobody, especially not the Christian middle classes, a social stratum utterly hostile towards these intellectuals.[15]

Since Budapest was the unquestioned cultural center of the country, all these conflicts sharpened there: the notorious populist versus urban conflict that was set into motion translates as a conflict between the urban Jews and the "genuine," gentile Hungarians. Budapest, in the eyes of gentile Hungarians, was to a great extent identified with the urban Jews or other aliens; it was just as much "the sinful city" as was New York in the eyes of mainland America. The people who carried on commercial and financial activity were regarded with mistrust and even hatred; the Hungarian gentry that gambled their (or, rather, their bourgeois wives') money away were looked upon as truly Hungarian, sharing the nation's fate, whereas Jews (or Germans or Austrians) who invested money into business, appeared alien and undesirable.

It was the historic deed of The Eight to link the idea of social progress with aesthetic modernism, and it is symptomatic of the cultural climate that Budapest, the city in which they mostly worked, played no role in their art. It did not occur to them to embrace the city within their artistic or social innovations. After about four to five years, their radical ardor cooled. They painted more and more private, personal subjects. When World War I erupted, there appeared an even more radical group of artists (occasionally with one or another of The Eight among them) who circled around the charismatic figure of Lajos Kassák. They called themselves The Activists, a term originating with Franz Pfemfert's Berlin Communist paper, *Die Aktion.*[16]

Energetic and stubborn, Kassák, coming from a poor family and trained to be a locksmith, had become a proletarian writer and editor. He had lived in the poor factory workers' district in Northern Pest, Angyalföld (Angels' Land), and some of his poems depict this part of Budapest powerfully. But, interestingly enough, no Budapest iconography emerged from the work of these artists: both Kassák and his disciples looked much farther for the symbols that they identified with modernism.

> We'll soon set up great skyscrapers, an Eiffel tower will be our toy.
> Basalt-based bridges. New myths from singing steel in the squares
> and shrieking blazing trains thrust onto the dead tracks
> to shine and run their course like meteors dizzying the sky,[17]

wrote Kassák in his famous poem, *Craftsmen,* in 1914. In the album that he edited and published with László Moholy-Nagy in Vienna,

The Book of New Artists (1922), he included photographs of the greatest American hangar, of American grain silos, of an aerial view of New York—but none of Budapest.[18]

Ironically, Budapest, a city that proved to be too modern for the traditional Hungarian perception, was not modern enough for the Hungarian avant-garde. All they saw in the city was a fake dignity of the ornately designed apartments, the pseudo-Renaissance facades of the civic buildings, and the bulky, lazy, coffeeshop character of the city compared with the bracing modernity that they interpreted in the pictures arriving from America. They found Budapest cosmopolitanism petit bourgeois and aspired to a utopian internationalism instead of what they took for Budapest provincialism: they were thinking in terms of a cultural internationalism. They expected that the spiritual and artistic products of international movements would soon abolish all national and individual boundaries.

Kassák was a Socialist, even Communist, who repeatedly refused to join the Hungarian Communist Party in spite of the frequent urgings of György Lukács and József Révay. In 1919, Kassák wrote an open letter to Béla Kun, president of the Hungarian Soviet Republic, declaring that artists must not participate in politics, because their job was to stay independent.[19] Combining the guilelessness of the proletarian with a unique sense of organization, Kassák, who was blessed with a rare personal appeal as well as artistic talent, loomed on the scene as a completely unprecedented phenomenon in the bourgeois milieu of even radical Budapest. Most of his fellow leftist intellectuals—the members of the Galilei Circle, the Sunday Circle, and other societies—were of middle-class background, many among them Jewish intellectuals.[20] A really urban generation of the intelligentsia, they were apparently too much under the spell of radical ideas and their application to the arts to pay much attention to the city that served only as the background and site of their activity. And when it came to the arts, their leading figures—Lukács, Leo Popper, and Frigyes Antal—reached back to the Italian Renaissance; Kassák's artists had not yet been appreciated by them. With the exception of the brief period of 1905–1910/11, these intellectuals were not very much inclined to enjoy and interpret the visual arts and may have been intimidated by Kassák himself, who, as István Vas writes in his memoirs, was a person with the authority of a "tribal chief." He was not easy to approach, and he accepted alliances only if he could keep on dominating his "tribe."[21]

Kassák started to publish his first periodical, *A Tett* (The Deed) in 1915, but it was soon banned because of its militant antiwar attitude.[22] When he started *Ma* (Today), he was able to publish it continuously, even while he was an émigré in Vienna, from 1919 onward.[23]

Figure 12.5 Sándor Bortnyik, *The Red Locomotive*, 1918. Oil on Canvas, 44 cm × 33.5 cm. Legújabbkori Történeti Múzeum, Budapest.

He published radical poetry, prose, and graphics along with essays on the new art, the new society, the new world. Kassák also rented an exhibition area in Budapest's central street, Váci utca, where he showed radical modern art: the works of József Nemes-Lampérth, János Mattis-Teutsch, Sándor Bortnyik, Béla Uitz, and others. They were Expressionists and, like Uitz and Bortnyik, represented an early version of Constructivism; but when there were fresh and modern ideas there, the artists condensed them in symbols like *The Red Locomo-*

320

Figure 12.6 Béla Uitz, *Ikon Analysis*, 1922. Oil on canvas, 156 cm × 12 cm. Hungarian National Gallery, Budapest.

tive (Bortnyik, 1918, Figure 12.5) or *Ikon Analysis*, a project of Béla Uitz, 1922, Figure 12.6), showing no interest in elements of the Budapest cityscape. Their modernism was too abstract for that, and it also skipped the immediate site of their activity. Modernism, as they interpreted it, was far beyond the city limits of Budapest.

In the eyes of The Activists, Budapest was the home of an immense proletarian crowd topped with the decoration belonging to the wealthy; a city to be reformed, where social injustice should be replaced by a new and just rule, where the poverty of the factory workers should be overcome and the outrageous wealth of the few shared with the poor; it was anything but visually inspiring. For these artists, Budapest was the site of action and not an object of contemplation. In contrast, again, to New York, where the pulsing rhythm of the city was translated into the imagery of the skyline, the canyons, and the crowd, the agitation and ferment that were going on in Budapest in the first two decades of this century failed to appear in visual imagery. True, the architecture of Budapest expressed an everlasting stability like the New York bank buildings that were not chosen by the artists for representation; still, there was nothing here that appeared as extremely modern, bold, and daring, which might have grasped The Activists' imagination and become a symbol of both their radicalism and their own city.

After they had introduced antiwar expressionism to Budapest, The Activists bravely insisted on their artistic and social manifesto during the 133 days of the Hungarian Soviet Republic in 1919. They designed posters for the Hungarian Red Army and, in spite of not having joined the Communist party, they obviously supported the Republic. They undertook teaching positions in the newly opened, democratic, and tuition-free proletarian academies, and they welcomed the new, egalitarian ideals. After the defeat of the "proletarian dictatorship" in August 1919, they were forced, along with a great number of Hungarian intellectuals, to flee the country. This wave of the 1919–1920 emigration completely broke the continuity of Hungarian culture which, as we have seen, had scarcely shown much continuity in the arts anyway. The Nagybánya group had emerged out of the dark, The Eight came up with paintings unprecedented in Hungarian art, and The Activists drew their ideas and impulses from Berlin and Moscow rather than from their immediate surroundings or from local traditions. Still, had time and peace been forthcoming, all of this might have amalgamated into a tradition. But the artists were dispersed all over the world, and even if Kassák returned to Hungary in 1926 and some others also came back, the chasm could not be bridged: the main currents of Hungarian art were continued abroad, where Budapest had no role as muse.

Of those artists who stayed in Hungary, there were a few who now manifested an increased interest in the cityscape of Budapest. A small number of the paintings and drawings of Hugo Scheiber have certain parts of Budapest for their subject matter. His *Night River*, painted in 1920 (Figure 12.7), is a lyrical rendering of the majestic river, the Danube, with the Gellért Hill on the one side and with the Pest-side trees on the other. The lights of the Elizabeth Bridge are reflected on the water, and they add to the picture's intimate, inward character. Scheiber's *Downtown*, an ink drawing, that may have served as a study to his gouache painting, also from around 1920 (Figures 12.8 and 12.9), are among the rare representations of Budapest buildings and shoppers, the lights and turmoil of the city. This painting, developed out

Figure 12.7 Hugo Scheiber, *Night River*, 1920. Gouache, 19″ × 13½.″ Paul Kövesdy Gallery, New York.

Figure 12.8 Hugo Scheiber, *Downtown*, ca. 1920. Ink drawing, 20″ × 13¾.″ Paul Kövesdy Gallery, New York.

Figure 12.9   Hugo Scheiber, *Downtown* [Kövesdy label: factory], ca. 1920. Charcoal drawing, 12½" × 18." Paul Kövesdy Gallery, New York.

of the drawing, also shows a possible model for the inauguration of Budapest iconography. While the drawing is rich in details, the painting focuses on the lights and the rhythm, and even if the high building in the background is a church tower, it still adds an elevation to the main Budapest street that appears on this painting. Scheiber selected certain motifs in the city and emphasized the urban character

Figure 12.10 Hugo Scheiber, *Factory*, late 1920s. Gouache, 19″ × 18.″ Paul Kövesdy Gallery, New York.

of Budapest, unlike artists who kept wandering into the suburbs for their slow-paced idyllic scenes. He also painted factory buildings in the late 1920s, with high chimneys letting out smoke as a symbol of production (Figures 12.10 and 12.11). Scheiber seems to have been more interested in the factory as part of the urban architectural vistas, as a new and strangely colored item within the city, than in the

Figure 12.11 Hugo Scheiber, *Factory*, 1925. Gouache 16"× 19." Paul Kövesdy Gallery, New York.

social aspect of it: his two factory pictures do not seem to be close to The Activists' critical approach towards the society.

The other artist who occasionally painted Budapest was also smooth-tempered, another master of descriptive and lyrical paintings. Armand Schönberger's picture, the *The Taban* (1920, Figure 12.12), represents the hilly Buda side of the city, paying tribute to the traditional,

326

Figure 12.12 Armand Schönberger, *The Taban*, 1920. Oil on canvas,
15″ × 15½.″ Paul Kövesdy Gallery, New York.

small, yellow-painted houses, which look like village details, and
betraying nostalgic feelings for old Budapest and for her intimate, small-
scaled quarters. Schönberger's main contributions to the slowly
developing Budapest iconography were his vibrating interiors of
nightclubs, cafés, espresso houses, and cabarets, which evoke the atmosphere of the Budapest of the 1920s and 1930s (Figure 12.13). Of
these, we have hardly any visual information other than these paintings.

The image of urban life in Budapest, gathered mainly from literary
sources, has the café interior as one of the most important of all places.
Writers and poets worked in the cafés from morning until late night;
the editors had their "own" tables in their regularly attended cafés,
and that was where they were available; the authors handed in their
articles in the cafés, and they got answers there; actors and actresses
had their own corners where they gathered after shows; briefly, all

327

Figure 12.13 Armand Schönberger, *Café*, 1924. Oil on canvas, 76 cm ×
91 cm. Hungarian National Gallery, Budapest.

the species of the Budapest intellectuals had their own cafés and their
own tables in them, and a typical feature of city life was that it was
well known where everybody could be spotted. Lipót Herman, a graphic
artist who also worked in a favorite café, left behind a series of drawings that he made there about celebrities: artists, writers, poets, theater people, and others. Although his drawings have more documentary than artistic value, they still rank among the few visual renderings
of the Budapest life between the two wars.

But Schönberger's interiors are more than mere recordings. They
tell about weird people, dense cigarette smoke, and of an atmosphere
of frightful presentiments. His stylized, slightly elongated figures re-
peat the art deco fashion of the age; and the apparently easy-handed
artist's light contours suggest a volatile, unstable reality.

Both Hugo Scheiber and Armand Schönberger belonged to the Jewish middle class. They were not attached to the radical movements,

nor were they partisans or pioneers of any modernist aspiration. Their portraits of Budapest reveal a selective vision. Unlike the New York artists, who were bursting to tell all they could about their city's breathtaking sights and latest modern miracles, they painted Budapest as a landscape, as their most intimate and personal environment. They limited themselves to those few corners that they knew well, suggesting that there was something about the Budapest atmosphere that was worth describing, and to which they were so much attached. Thus, again in sharp contrast to New York's iconography featuring the more sensational sights of the city, we have private corners of urban Budapest on the few canvases that are left to us with city motifs.

It is also a significant difference that painting Budapest was never the driving force of a group here as it was for the Ashcan School in New York City.[24] Budapest representations were the private choices of just a few artists who were personally attracted to certain parts of the city. Their paintings and drawings expressed the affirmations of Jewish artists, city dwellers, whose home was Budapest and who felt cozy in it, and whose message does not go much beyond expressing this. They were not praising Budapest for any of her qualities, nor were they celebrating the city. They simply depicted it, unmilitantly, as their most immediate experience.

Had Budapest iconography had the opportunity to develop, it would certainly have become something like Paris had been for Utrillo: it would have been more likely to provoke emotional responses rather than militant appreciation or a symbolic interpretation. Judging from Hungarian literature, it would have been the hidden old houses, small squares, and the elderly people sitting on chairs put out onto the pavement in front of their tenements that would have been likely to challenge the artists, rather than the spectacular highlights of the city. Dezső Kosztolányi wrote a poem about the Üllői Road Trees (Üllői úti ják) and, in the novels of Tibor Déry, Ervin Sinkó, and Ferenc Molnár, among others, the characters walk endlessly in the streets of Budapest, deeply absorbed in their atmosphere. All this is a matter of intimate attachment, very different from the fascination, the sense of greatness, and awareness of a great future that even now New York City continues to provoke in her artists and admirers.

This is not without relation to the difference in proportions between the two countries and the two cities. It is rather the historic traditions and circumstances that seem to be responsible for the eclipse of a Budapest iconography in Hungarian art. Wanda Corn draws a straight line from Alfred Stieglitz and Childe Hassam to Franz Kline and Ellsworth Kelly. Compared to this continuity, Hungarian art, even if we disregard Budapest's lack of role as a subject matter, seems to be seriously discontinuous.[25] Not only did the art critic Ernő Kállai

329

miss the presence of a Hungarian Utrillo who would have had an eye for the Joseph-town, Ferenc-town, Christina-town, and other parts of Budapest, he could not explain why the postwar city with her new, wounded image did not appeal to artists. We can, perhaps, answer this question: Since no organic tradition could develop in Hungarian art, mainly because traditions and the events of history did not ensure the requisite peace and the time, it was not possible for the capital city to grow into a national symbol for Hungarians, artists and audience alike.

Paradoxically, it is this missing image of Budapest from Hungarian art in the first half of the twentieth century that symbolizes the lack of consensus, the lack of mutual understanding, and the lack of a nationwide solidarity in Hungary. Still, the few pictures that have been left to us with Budapest cityscapes refer to all those possible paths in Hungarian painting and culture that might have been followed, and might have led somewhere—had there been a chance for developing an unbroken, continuous culture in this part of Europe.

Notes

1. Ernő Kállai, "Hol Vannak Budapest Festői?" ("Where are the painters of Budapest?") in *Kortárs* (1947), reprinted in Éva Forgács, ed., *Művészet Veszélyes Csillagzat Alatt, Selected Writings of Ernő Kállai* (Budapest, 1981).
2. Wanda Corn, "The Artist's New York," See above, 275.
3. Wanda Corn, "The Artist's New York," 303.
4. Interestingly enough, this old Budapest appears in the richest and most colorful representation in a recent Hungarian novel, written by Péter Lengyel: *Macskakő* (Cobblestone), Szépirodalmi Kiadó (Budapest, 1988).
5. *Budapest anno . . .* A nostalgic photo album including reproductions of old postcards and many vintage photos, among them most of what had been taken by György Klösz (Budapest, 1976).
6. Géza Perneczky, *Kortársak Szemével* (With the eyes of contemporaries) (Budapest, 1967), 5–50.
7. Wanda Corn, "The Artist's New York," 277.
8. Wanda Corn, "The Artist's New York," *passim*.
9. Károly Kernstok, "A Kutató Művészet" ("Researching art") in *Nyugat* I: 95–99. This was originally a lecture that Kernstok gave in the Galilei Circle on January 9, 1910.
10. Károly Kernstok, "A Művész Társadalmi Szerepe" (The social role of the artist) in *Huszadik Század* (1912): 377–380.
11. György Lukács, "Az Utak Elváltak" (The ways have parted) in *Nyugat* I (1910): 190–193.
12. Steven A. Mansbach, "Revolutionary Events, Revolutionary Artists: The Hungarian Avantgarde until 1920," in Stephen C. Foster, ed., *"Event" Arts and Art Events* (Ann Arbor, 1988).

13. On this subject, see a discussion with the participation of Péter Hanák, Gyula Juhász, Viktor Karády, Miklós Szabó, and Laszló Varga published in *Világosság* (Budapest, June 1989), 432–443, under the title "Zsidó Kérdés Itt és Most—Gyökerek és Indák" (The Jewish question here and now—roots and branches).
14. See Viktor Karády's contribution in *Világosság.*
15. See the contribution of Laszló Varga in *Világosság.*
16. *Die Aktion* was published in Berlin from 1910 to 1932, Franz Pfempfert, ed.
17. Lajos Kassák, *Mesteremberek* (Craftsmen), 1914. English translation by Edwin Morgan.
18. Kassák and Moholy-Nagy, *Új Művészek Könyve* (Book of new artists) (Vienna, 1922). An edition of the *MA* books.
19. Lajos Kassák, "Levél Kun Bélához a Művészet Nevében" (Letter to Béla Kun in the name of art), *MA* 7 (1919): unpaginated.
20. One of the best English-language publications on the Sunday Circle and the Galilei Circle is Mary Gluck's *George Lukács and his Generation, 1910–1918* (Cambridge, Mass., 1985). On the Sunday Circle, see also *Photo Album*, by Éva Karádi and Éva Fekete (Budapest, 1986).
21. István Vas, *Nehéz Szerelem* (Hard love) (Budapest, 1973), an autobiography.
22. *A Tett* was published for one year, in 1915/16.
23. *Ma* was published in Budapest from 1916 to 1919, and in Vienna from 1920 to 1925.
24. About the Ashcan School see Wanda Corn, "The Artist's New York," 287–290.
25. See Wanda Corn, "The Artist's New York," 306–308.

Chapter **13**

The Novel as Newspaper and Gallery of Voices: The American Novel in New York City: 1890–1930

PHILIP FISHER

*T*HE HISTORY to be traced here is a paradoxical one. It is the change within the city novel from the type of victim narratives that are typical of literary naturalism to narratives of bohemian freedom; from accounts of suffering to catalogues of pleasure; from a picture of the city as a single-minded machine of indifference and destruction to a picture of a small-scale field of daily opportunities for adventure, experience, excitement—a world rich in novelties of personality and fate. If we consider the use of the so-called narrative accident we can quickly grasp this change. In the naturalist novel the classic accident is a catastrophe, a house on fire, an automobile wreck, a man killed by a stray bullet in the street. By the time of Dreiser's *A Gallery of Women* (1929), a typical accident is likely to be the unexpected meeting in a Greenwich village studio with someone who will become part of an adventure, a love affair, a whirl of activity for a brief time.

In what follows I will consider the transition from an ideology of representation that was that of naturalism or even of realism (insofar as it was subservient to political reform) to an ideology of representation that was no longer political but modernist in its central emphasis on the artist, the accumulation of experiences, the sexual, and the disconnection of moments of experience from one another.

What is paradoxical about this history is that in many cases the same materials of urban experience continue to be used but with new meanings assigned. The outsider continues to be the central figure, no longer beaten down and destroyed, but free-spirited, improvisatory, even joyfully marginal in the style of bohemian life. The novel retains an implicit norm of a middle-class way of life that is offstage and unavailable, but no longer desired; it is even held in contempt. The milieu of poverty defines both the naturalist and the bohemian novel of the city, but the meaning of material want is changed from that of desperation to that of freedom from material interest. The central characters of both naturalist and bohemian urban novels are defined by the stance of dreaming, but now the point of view of the author towards the dream or towards idealism and hope is no longer one of irony, but one of participation in the dream of art and experience.

The location of the novel in a social world where the family is no longer a working center for continuity in experience, the representation of temporary rather than enduring experiences, the turbulence of social life—its unreliability and insecurity along with its variety—are all the given conditions of such works as Stephen Crane's *Maggie* (1893) or Theodore Dreiser's *Sister Carrie* (1900) as much as of such later bohemian works as Henry Miller's *Tropic of Capricorn* (1933) or Dreiser's *A Gallery of Women* (1929). How can the identical materials suddenly appear with entirely new meanings? How does the sexual disorder of the 1890s become the sexual bohemianism of Dos Passos's *Manhattan Transfer* or Dreiser's *A Gallery of Women?* How, for example, does the simple motif of drinking change its meaning between the late nineteenth century, when it stands for despair and hopeless violence, the dead-end of experience (as it does in Crane's *Maggie*), to the glamorous world of experimentation with consciousness, the freedom from bourgeois values that alcohol and drugs represent as part of the urban milieu of Dreiser's *Gallery of Women*, in addition to the urban café, speakeasy, nightclub world of Dos Passos, Fitzgerald, Hemingway, and Henry Miller? How does the city itself pass from killing machine to playground?

It is important to note two details in advance. First, there is no political change in this period that accounts for an objectively improved, more secure, or less corrupt social scene. The "problems" of the city that had been the major topic of the novel from Dickens to Crane had not been "solved." The results of the major reforms of the New Deal and the victory of the labor unions are felt only later. It is not the success of reform politics or of revolution (and it was in the direction of the public activities of reform or revolution that the realistic and naturalistic novels tended) that could explain this change within the ideology of representation.

Second, a change in this direction is not unique to New York or even to American literature. The case of James Joyce between 1900 and 1925 is, in this, parallel to that of Dreiser. Joyce's collection of stories, *Dubliners*, written in the first decade of the century, defines the city as a uniform mechanism of destruction, of emotional and sexual frustration. The stories of *Dubliners* set up a counterpoint between the dreamer and a gray, inexorable reality. The world of Joyce's stories is a world designed around a steady march through life history—from the childhood stories with which the book begins toward a final story that is appropriately named "The Dead." Each of the stories might well have been named "The Dead," since the subject of the story is an inner blankness, a failure, a disappointment or sterility that keeps each character imprisoned in a kind of half-life of fatigue, defeat, and small-scale cowardice.

Yet, by the 1920s in *Ulysses*, Joyce has reseen the same materials through an optics of pleasure. The city is the same; the lives are as drab, cruel, and static as in *Dubliners*, but now the city is a stage for perception, for an artistic, moment-by-moment consciousness and inner vitality. "There's a touch of the artist about Old Bloom," as one of the other characters observes, and it is as an artist, as marginal observer and bohemian dreamer, that Bloom, 43-year-old hero that he is (even in banal disguise of a lower-middle-class newspaper employee and advertisement canvasser), dominates a patterned world within which he lives no less than any of the victims of *Dubliners*.

In roughly the same years (between 1900 and 1930) Dreiser went from *Sister Carrie* to *A Gallery of Women* (1929), a book that could be called a gallery of Sister Carrie's sisters. Free spirits, dreaming of art, of political revolution, or of Hollywood, moving from lover to lover, defined by energy and hope, these women live in the New York of Greenwich Village and the other edges just beyond "respectability" or the type of family life and permanence for which they and Dreiser have a horror.

When we think of the representation of New York City, the historical passage that I have traced in the case of Joyce and Dreiser begins roughly in 1890 when Howells's *Hazard of New Fortunes* or Crane's *Maggie*, along with Dreiser's climactic *Sister Carrie* (1900), defined a socially conscious sketch of the city. This social consciousness can be seen in Henry James's travel book *The American Scene* (1904) as well as in the photographs of Jacob Riis (1890 and following), and naturally, within the crusading journalism of the period. The city is seen as an array of problems that require action. Even an aesthete like James thinks of the city as the "problem" of the alien (i.e., the rising number of immigrants), the "problem" of the language, the "problem" of the new relations between men and women. Each of Jacob Riis's photographs pinpoints a "problem" for the middle-class viewers' attention: overcrowding in the slums, child labor, the street lives of children, the dirt or darkness of city slum life, the harsh working conditions of urban labor. Each "problem" can be solved; conditions can be "improved" if only the viewer will "do something to help."

The naturalist novel dealt with a level of experience beyond these photographs. Lives crushed by circumstance, by the system, by poverty; a world of inequality; the corruption of political life—these are typical of the material placed at the center of this work. But the real center is the problem of the conscience of the liberal middle class (particularly in a writer like Howells). The question of indifference to or action in the face of suffering, corruption, inequality, that is posed inside the Howells novel is the central rhetorical question between every book and its typical middle-class comfortable reader. The same question governs the rhetoric of social documentary photography from the time of Riis to the Dust Bowl photographs of the 1930s. It is the "heart" of the middle-class viewer or reader that is at stake in the ideology of socially conscious realistic or naturalistic fiction. The appeal by means of alternate doses of shock and sentiment elicits the reader's sympathies and sense of outrage or guilt in a way that is little changed from the time of the novels of Charles Dickens in the 1840s, 1850s, and 1860s.

One strange fact about the mechanisms of naturalism was that they worked almost as effectively at every level of social life. In Edith Wharton's greatest novel and the single best New York novel of the first decade of the twentieth century, *The House of Mirth* (1905), we watch an outsider lose her footing and descend until the novel ends with her solitude, drugs, and suicide. Although Wharton's is a novel of upper-class New York society, the mechanism of the plot is the story of an inexorable fall much like that of Dreiser's middle-class businessman Hurstwood in *Sister Carrie*, who flees to New York where he remains a nameless outsider in steady decline. Finally, he kills himself in a Bowery hotel, an ending with much the same tone as the suicide that ends *The House of Mirth*. At the other extreme of the social scale from Wharton, Stephen Crane's *Maggie* traces the grinding down, the "fall," and finally the death of its central figure. The report of Maggie's death that ends Crane's novella works out the same rhetorical formula as the deaths of Wharton's heroine and Dreiser's hero.

Wharton, Dreiser, and Crane are writing about three disparate so-

335

cial levels, which range from the heights of Wharton's New York society of the *Belle Epoque* to Dreiser's declining middle-class businessman to Crane's squalid tenement-dwelling, working-class, hard-drinking family. Yet, each novel's pattern is the snuffing out of a life; each author posing the Darwinian question of survival or extinction. The answer is always given in the final scene of extinction.

The pattern for this type of urban novel was invented by Zola in *L'Assommoir* (1876), in which the history of Gervaise is the history of her decline, her brave moments of illusion, her dreams, and the underlying process of wearing out (like that of a shirt which in its lifetime of washings becomes ever thinner each time it is, for a time, made to look like new). The wearing out of vitality, the decline into lethargy and indifference, was one of the great subjects of the novel of naturalism. It made the novel into a study of energy rather than that of a moral life with choices, consequences, and responsibilities. With naturalism the topic of energy replaces the topic of good and evil. "Giving up" or "giving in," surrender; agreeing to fall into bed or into a world of drinking; a lethargy that no longer resists what is inevitable—these are what remains as a kind of sensuality of defeat within naturalism.

Within the naturalist novel we find ourselves again and again with characters who can be said to have never had a chance, or, most important of all, to have never really lived. By contrast, the city novel after 1920 places at its center figures determined to live, hungry for experience, amoral in their individualism and in their egoistic relation to the possibilities around them. Dos Passos's *Manhattan Transfer*, Dreiser's *A Gallery of Women*, and Miller's *Tropic of Capricorn* define a center for this representation of New York as a chaos of values and possibilities, a chaos of perception and sexual atmosphere in which, as in Joyce's *Ulysses*, the central consciousness within experience tolerates and lives off the very urban disorder that within naturalism with its assumed background of middle-class normality (steady work, family life, home and children, economic improvement) had been lethal.

By 1925 the city novel had freed itself from loyalty or pretended loyalty to a norm of stable family life—marriage, children, home, and work. That family norm had haunted the urban novel from the time of Dickens and had permitted the realistic or naturalistic novel to display moral outrage at the many details of urban life that made that family norm more and more difficult to realize or preserve. The realistic and naturalistic novel in America was distorted in its account of urban life because it charged the city with a hostility to the norms of small town or rural life. By 1925 this family norm had vanished and a new norm of the temporary, of free-wheeling individualism, of the search for experience and excitement, of the dreamer and the artist, had taken over. By 1925 New York City was, if anything, even more hostile to the possibility of a small-town norm of family life, but it was no longer being viewed by novelists through this single-minded frame of reference.

In the analysis that follows I will discuss three models for New York urban fiction. First, the domestic model of Howells's *A Hazard of New Fortunes.* This might be called the model of the dinner table, since Howells in essence tries to extend the novel of manners so as to include the many classes, social groups, ways of life, and manners that make up the variety of city life. The round dinner table where all are equal is something of a central symbol for the novel of manners, and that is why I think of this first model as an ever-larger table where many cultures can somehow find a common language in which to communicate and act together. This model of the novel of manners, but without its snobbery, social exclusion, and feminine emphasis, is nonetheless a hopelessly middle-class form of fiction, one based on the utopian project of imagining the entire urban world as eventually subject to middle-class norms and interests.

The second model will be the modernist form of the social novel as we see it in Dos Passos's *Manhattan Transfer.* This fragmented novel, made up of nearly 150 short scenes, most of which are two or three pages long, has as its central model of experience the newspaper rather than the dinner table. In the newspaper a daily sample from every corner of the social world of the city is brought together in side-by-side juxtaposition. The aesthetics of juxtaposition, rather than that of communication, could be called Dos Passos's goal. The novel presents itself as a chaos of "stories," glimpses, and conversations over many years and more than a dozen equally important characters. The novel is a crowd of value-free equal facts—like the front page of a newspaper where we glance in ten seconds among football scores, the death of an actress, a new discovery in physics, an earthquake killing thousands in China, a three-alarm fire with no casualties, an investigation into government corruption, a story about a snowstorm that stalled traffic for three hours, the birth of quadruplets in Australia, and the launching of the first rocket to Mars. The newspaper reporter who, along with the detective, becomes the classic stand-in for the artist himself in the urban novel, and the format of the newspaper itself as a form of moral and intellectual disorder become important as a background image for the novel precisely because it is taken to mirror, in a deep way, the excitement and variety of urban life, a world of catastrophe and magic.

The third model is the new form of biography and storytelling that we can hear in Henry Miller, or earlier in the narrated lives that make up Dreiser's *A Gallery of Women.* This new talking life history, close in many ways to the endless egotistic self-description of psychoanalysis, places us face-to-face with a single life history, temperament, and language. This form of narration takes over within the novel at the moment when the technology of the radio is being introduced and at the moment of the first talking movies. The radio accustomed people to the intimacy of distant voices, whether that of the president of the United States talking in his office in Washington directly into every living room, or to the voices heard late at night from cities far away, Billie Holiday singing in Chicago, or a baseball announcer from Pittsburgh. Both psychoanalysis, which took hold in New York in the 1920s, and the new technology of the radio were forms of narrative dominated by the voice. The urban novel in this same period turned to the disembodied voice as a fundamental narrative tool.

In Dos Passos after 1925 this colloquial urban style often seems captured by a tape recorder or skilled stenographer, since the voice or voices wander on without description or analysis in page after page of brief, spoken scenes. In later writers, the tirade and the spiel produce an overall style of self-performance of the kind that Henry Miller, J. D. Salinger, and Saul Bellow make into a new style of urban intimacy not so different from hearing the life history of a stranger on a long Greyhound bus ride or a story read at night over a radio.

This feeling of an intimacy of strangers is one of the great achievements of the urban novel, since it accepts the urban solitude, the improvisatory relations among people, the unexpected and often unwanted intimacy of urban life, and converts it into a narrative form.

In the American novel the urban wise-guy, the unstoppable Ancient Mariner of his own troubles and experiences, became the key permanent narrative form from the mid-1920s to the present. The masterpieces of this urban form of talk-narrative include J. D. Salinger's *The Catcher in the Rye,* Bellow's *Herzog,* Philip Roth's many self-indulgent garrulous voices from *Portnoy's Complaint* to *My Life as a Man,* Ralph Ellison's *Invisible Man,* Joseph Heller's *Something Happened,* and the narcissistic voice of Norman Mailer in the 1960s and 1970s.

By means of these three models—the dinner table or the novel of manners, the newspaper of Dos Passos, the unseen intimate voice of Dreiser or Miller—I will sketch a history of the representation of New York City in the novel between roughly 1890 and 1930.

The Dining Room Table of Manners

The form of the social novel that Howells uses is continuous from at least the time of Jane Austen through George Eliot and Henry James and was adapted by Howells and others to a complex urban experience that is intrinsically hostile. After Howells the great novels of Edith Wharton, from *The House of Mirth* (1905) to *The Age of Innocence* (1920), take up the novel of manners form for New York society. In 1925, with *The Great Gatsby,* Fitzgerald wrote the last major work in this form as well as the first novel that reflected the new relation of suburb to city, the first Long Island–Manhattan novel, where the urban world of bootleggers, love-nest apartments, downtown jobs, and drinks in the city are seen from the perspective of a carefully manicured private world of wealth and privileged isolation, a world that is nonetheless invaded by a distraught gas station-owning husband who leaves behind a once-glamorous body floating in the swimming pool.

The novel of manners has traditionally been a literary form in which conversation and a social life defined by exchanges of visits and dining, the world of talk, dancing, courtship, and, ultimately, proposals of marriage make up the central business of the scenes. The novel of manners was traditionally a comic form, which also served to police a uniform code of behavior and public life. The novel of manners is at heart anthropological; its subject is the entrance or expulsion from society. Marriage is the ultimate act of social inclusion, banishment is at the other extreme—the ultimate form of social death.

The conversation of the novel of manners has traditionally aimed at social judgments and evaluation, which lead ultimately to inclusion or exclusion from the social set for those who are perceived as outsiders or strangers. The novel of manners is about membership, the convergence of judgments, the preservation of society from dangerous outsiders, and the enlarging of a frozen, unanimous world by including new members.

The attempt in American literature to represent the more diverse, unmanageable differences of the city within the novel of manners can be seen in *A Hazard of New Fortunes.* The central married couple of Howells's novel, the Marches, "immigrate" to New York from Boston, but in this act they stand for the wider urban fact of New York, a city of immigrants, a collection point for a variety of people born elsewhere, shaped under a variety of systems of manners, and brought together here to work out their lives in common. The novel of manners collapses in the face of this social mobility that brings together German immigrants, Midwestern money, refugees from an impoverished post–Civil War American South, and New Englanders like the Marches.

The cliché of the city as a melting pot runs up against the city as a fixed society of manners and types. The novel of manners depends, in its theory of society and in its functioning as a literary form, on small-scale voluntary associations of four to eight people like the magazine staff that Howells describes, or the people at a dinner table, or those who live together at a boardinghouse or visit together for an evening. These small groups are based on the family as a model. The novel of manners failed in the face of urban experience where this small-family-style group was no longer central. In the city novel we find the solitary individual, the sexual couple, the crowd; seldom the middle-sized four to eight person group.

Howells's is an intangible, intimate abstract world based on esteem and affection. Its center is the parlor or the dining room. Men and women are known first of all as hosts and guests, friends and suitors, potential husbands and wives, patrons and associates. Then their business and financial arrangements are added onto this world. People seem to be hired for the journal because, like Colonel Woodburn, they are found at the table of the boardinghouse where the promoter happens to eat, and where he will also find his fiancée. Relations are general, stable, and socially coded; they draw little from momentary events. They are also concentrated and overlapping to an artificial degree. Lindau, the old friend of March, is the artists' model for both Beanton and Webmore ladies. He becomes the translator for the journal, and he eats at the boardinghouse that brings together all the other characters so conveniently. The same few threads are woven and rewoven into a number of small-scale patterns. The most unnatural and contrived of these is the moment in the street near the end of the novel that brings Conrad, Lindau, and March together during the strike. This moment leads to the death of Conrad and the conclusion of the novel. Such a closed world is the mark of the Jane Austen-type novel of manners where a handful of characters from the "respectable classes" and the country gentry crisscross their way through a set of visits, dinners, dances, and outings towards a set of marriages.

Howells's world, like the world of the novel of manners in general, is free of objects and things, free of detailed settings (what the naturalist novel would call "environments"); and the novel looks closely at the outer world only in occasional, set-piece insertions like the house-hunting episode or a walk that is irrelevant to the pattern of events. The novel is free as well of decisive, large-scale matters like war, economic crisis, or other public events, and it works out the fates of its characters by means of quarrels, proposals of marriage, renewed friendships, and partings. It does so until the strike at the end of the novel shatters this world rather than creating one more causal element within it.

A type of narrative discretion or politeness sets up the model of communication, understanding, tolerance of differences, common effort, and human conscience that Howells imagines might make a tolerable, but diverse urban world. The outer world enters as a series of carefully prepared pictures as it does in this brief scene on the elevated train in Chapter 10:

> At third avenue they took the elevated, for which she confessed an infatuation. She declared it the most ideal way of getting about in the world, and was not ashamed when he reminded her of how she used to say that nothing under the sun could induce her to travel in it. She now said that the night transit was even more interesting than the day, and that the fleeting intimacy you formed with people in second and third floor interiors had a *domestic intensity mixed with a perfect repose that was the last effect of good society with all its security and exclusiveness.* He said it was better than the theater, of which it reminded him, to see those people through their windows: a family party of work-folk at a late tea, some of them in their shirt sleeves; a woman sewing by a lamp; a mother laying her child in its cradle; a man with his head fallen on his hands upon a table; a girl and her lover leaning over the window sill together. What suggestion! What drama! What infinite interest!

The outer world is seen through the window as the elevated train passes as a set of inner worlds; a set of photographs, a gallery of picturesque, Dutch genre scenes, domestic Victorian family wall pictures. What Howells supplies is a quick formula, a sketch, a distant twilight of images, and indirect narration. Even the conversation between the Marches is only reported and not literally represented. Those strangers seen at a distance for a few seconds are comforting in that their lives represent the same family values as the Marches' own genteel world: work, relaxation, young love, a child in its cradle, the laborer taking his well-earned rest. A pious and smug world, safely framed, and quickly passed, a glimpse into the "real" city without even a single disturbing detail. Certainly one of the houses that the Marches passed was not the drunken brawling home of Stephen Crane's *Maggie,* a novel published in the same year as Howells's *A Hazard of New Fortunes.*

Newspaper and Juxtaposition

Howells's novel implies that a realm of liberal, middle-class values can expand itself to take in more and more of the urban world. It can do so because that world is fundamentally the same in values and moral life. Already in 1900, in Dreiser's *Sister Carrie,* an entirely different politics of representation had taken over. The second half of Dreiser's novel is set in a New York of polar extremes, a dynamic world of rising and falling lives. The middle has fallen out, as has the model of family life, conversation, marriage, and stable enterprise. Dreiser's is a world of Broadway and Bowery, of stars and has-beens. He created the fundamental narrative for American representations of the city—a narrative in which the two extremes of glamour and despair, dreamlike wealth and homeless, drifting self-destruction replace the middle range. A narrative of juxtaposed extremes replaced a narrative of a hopeful and expanding middle class.

In keeping with the location of his material at the two extremes of the social scale, Dreiser made a key narrative invention. In the second half of *Sister Carrie* he learned to tell the simultaneous stories of two people in different worlds. He did this by alternating chapters that carried each life forward as an individual narrative, the one rising to stardom, the other falling to the Bowery and suicide. By juxtaposing each stage of Carrie's life to the corresponding stage of Hurstwood's, Dreiser created a narrative form for the tunnel existence of separate city lives. Symbolically linked at every level, parallel in surprising and subtle ways, the two life histories are free from any cheap ironic or moral relation.

It is this style of juxtaposition, of mere side-by-sideness, that Dos Passos would expand in *Manhattan Transfer* into an all-embracing way of writing. In the 1920s James Joyce in the "Wandering Rocks" section of *Ulysses* had represented the city at one hour of the day by means of twenty brief scenes, each character caught up in the local drama of the moment. This is Dos Passos's style for his novel. In the opening of *Manhattan Transfer* we can see that this alogical style operates at every level.

The opening page is made up of three separated and discontinuous paragraphs. The first is a poetic description of the arrival of a ferry boat with gulls circling above a world of debris and garbage. The second paragraph describes a nurse in a hospital bringing out a newborn child in a basket. The final line of the hospital paragraph reads, "The newborn baby squirmed in the cottonwool feebly like a knot of earthworms." The third paragraph which is set now on the ferry itself begins with the sentence, "On the ferry there was an old man playing the violin. He had a monkey's face puckered up in one corner and kept time with the toe of a cracked patent-leather shoe." Not only are the scenes harshly juxtaposed without logical connection or continuity, but within each scene we are forced into juxtapositions that are willful acts of the author. The baby is juxtaposed to earthworms. The old musician is by metaphor a monkey and by metonymy juxtaposed to the close-up detail of the "toe of a cracked patent-leather shoe." The narration works by shock and by the arbitrary acts of the writer. In one page he brings together gulls, garbage, a baby, worms, an old man playing a violin, and a cracked patent-leather shoe.

The novel as a whole simply expands this strategy of juxtaposition into an urban aesthetic. Every move is a jolt as the author passes (1) from image to object in simile, (2) from detail to whole—as in the toe of the shoe to the violinist, (3) from one scene to the next, and (4) from one moment of time in a character's life to the next, often remote, moment which is sometimes days, sometimes years later. As Dos Passos collects a dozen characters to follow through 140 brief scenes we come to know his people newspaper style—as tiny articles at widely separated, unexpected moments of time. The novel is like opening a daily newspaper and seeing that a certain rock star or well-known criminal or nearly forgotten politician has, as we say, "turned up again." He is once again "back in the news."

What is an act of genius on Dos Passos's part is to have combined the conditions of remote knowledge with the technique of intimate close-up scenes. There is a flattening of intimacy and remoteness to his technique that has much in common with a police report. An urban toughness and cynicism mark the blunt intrusive intimacy with these people who always remain strangers. The newspaper, which is the classic form of this narrative style of short, juxtaposed stories, always works through summary, description, analysis, and response. What never occurs in a newspaper is dialogue or the narrative scene. Dos Passos uses these close-up, intimate scenes within a newspaper's structure of side-by-side matter-of-factness. He implies that in the Manhattan world of 1900 to 1925 intimacy has taken on the brevity, the juxtapositions, the bluntness, and the rapid changes of the public world of baseball scores, fires, heat waves, political scandals, and juicy murder trials.

Like Dreiser, Dos Passos is still committed to telling us the life history over time of a set of characters who rise and fall, commit suicide, or become influential. He strings out for each person a set of two-page glimpses at widely separated periods of time. He operates, just as a newspaper does, with a set of types: the rising actress, the lawyer on the make, the criminal on the run, the politician, the once

343

rich but now heavy drinking drifter, the *jeunesses dorées*, the newspaper reporter, the cunning immigrant, the speakeasy bartender.

The urban aesthetic that Dos Passos invented for the novel was that of the Anatomy, the exposé. The glamorous, the amoral, the powerful, the criminal, are all seen "behind the scenes." There is an element of *National Enquirer* voyeurism to this method. It depends on that modern hunger to know the "inside story," "the real dirt." When we trace Dos Passos's individual characters back from their end point we can see that they often end up as "stories" in the newspaper meaning of the word. Bud Korpenning jumps off the Brooklyn Bridge, a story that would appear as a tiny front page story of the daily paper; Gus McNeil becomes a powerful political figure; Ellen Thatcher passes from lover to lover in her career as an actress; Stan Emery kills himself spectacularly; Anna Cohen dies in a fire in a dress factory; George Baldwin runs for mayor as a reform candidate; the ruined Wall Street financier Joe Harland drinks his way around the city, begging quarters from strangers. Each at his or her end point becomes newsworthy. What Dos Passos does is to satisfy that newspaper curiosity expressed in the sentence: "I would love to know the real story behind that!"

The novel then exposes the "real story" behind Bud Korpenning's jump from the Brooklyn Bridge, behind George Baldwin's rise as a lawyer, behind Ellen Thatcher's glamour as a starlet, behind Anna Cohen's death in a dress factory. The lurid and the glamorous, the corrupt and the "tragic" are the aesthetic categories of a newspaper age. Dos Passos, and those like Nathanael West who followed him in the thirties, took over literally the newspaper "layout" of juxtaposition; the newspaper narrative style of "following" a story; the newspaper melodrama of glamorous rise and violent fall; the newspaper equation of criminal, actress, politician, and financial wizard as all equally "famous."

When West in *Miss Lonelyhearts* tries to deepen the meaning of this urban form with symbolism, intellectual reflection, and grandiose mythmaking and irony, he only manages to make it pretentious and mannered. His one great invention is to make use of a part of the newspaper that Dos Passos had never considered, the advice column, where ordinary readers have a once-in-a-lifetime opportunity to have their own misery, suffering, problems, and hard times appear as a "story" in the day's newspaper and be read and talked about by millions of people. Ostensibly, the reason for these letters is that the writers are seeking advice. But as West's novel shows, these stories are beyond any intervention or small-scale first aid. Each letter does let one sufferer be "famous for a day" even while remaining anonymous under the pen name "Broad Shoulders" or "Sick-of-it-all" or "Desperate."

The advice column was a mechanism for democratizing the short burst of fame that the newspaper has at its command. Dos Passos's characters, like Dreiser's before him, were the classic "interests" of the newspaper reader: the businessman who robs his own safe to run away with his mistress and is found dead in a Bowery hotel; the small-town girl who becomes a Broadway star; the milkman who becomes a political power in New York; the country boy who kills his father, wanders around Manhattan, and then jumps to his death from the Brooklyn Bridge. What West had done was to see that once the aes-thetic of the newspaper had saturated the urban mind, every mind could be conceived in terms of a two-page story, crude, melodramatic, "heart-wrenching."

In *Sister Carrie* (1900) Dreiser had set a pattern for urban represen-tation that would follow in Dos Passos, West, and Henry Miller. One of its premises is the celebration of a temporary world, a world of experience rather than fixed position, a world of restlessness and change. The Chicago sociologist of the city, Lewis Wirth, described the psychology of urban experience in a way that would be essential for Dreiser and the novelists who followed him. Wirth wrote,

> The contacts are brief, impersonal, superficial, and segmental. The reserve, the indifference and the blasé attitude which urbanists manifest in their relationships may thus be regarded as devices for immunizing themselves against the personal claims and expecta-tions of others.

What Dreiser did was to reverse the moral judgments that seem im-plicit in Wirth's description.

Dreiser created the national self-portrait for an America that was urban, capitalist, scaled to opportunity and not to fixed place. It re-volved around the self-made man or woman. These people were no longer in search of family life, but linked to others only in the push of competition and the pull of sexual romance. Temporary in all things, provisional as everything must be in a society of invention, Dreiser's is a world of hotels rather than homes, affairs rather than marriages, roles and not identity. He celebrates this society of the promising and the unsettled with an enthusiasm that is one of the most strongly marked features of his best work. His is a world of the hopeful and the hopeless, of those who are promising and those who are "has beens." Rising and falling, they are women and men for whom having a place, a social position, a marriage, or a home adds up to "being stuck" somewhere in a world where it counts only to be in motion, "on the move." As Dreiser saw it, American mobility and opportunity produce a self that lacks a "sentiment of being." It is labile, externalized, and comes to view the many details of its life as more-or-less changeable outfits. Houses, relationships, jobs, and social positions count as no more than changes of clothing. At its center are characters like Carrie Meeber or Clyde Griffiths, who not only lack but are indifferent to what we call personal identity. Neither style nor personal history, neither unique plans nor strongly felt reactions, individualize them. This is a feature of a quick-change society, a society in which being "available" includes being ready to flee or grab the trappings of identities in a casual way, even where what is fled might include home, family, lovers, work—those many traditional components that gave stability to identity. Seldom does a present stage of life in Dreiser depend upon the past. Each new opportunity is literally a "break."

In the absence of any strong continuity of character or identity, Dreiser locates his women and men, changeable as they are, by means of what does remain fixed within social life: the array of types. Most often a Dreiserian description tells us that the woman or man was "one of . . . this or that: one of the new speculators in Chicago, one of those chorus girls looking for a quick break before her youth has passed, one of those formerly rich men who could not adjust to poverty." This is the language of the new sociology in which society is composed of types rather than citizens. A story by Dreiser is the account of the struggle to become an instance of a social type and to be known and seen by others as that type. Identity for Dreiser involves the act that should be called "looking around to see who I am." It is an externally referenced identity, both in its location as membership in a type and in its confirmation in the looks of others. In Dreiser there is no self-certainty at all, and it is not felt to be lacking. Uniforms and settings confirm the reality of the self: one of those people that you meet in Hollywood; the type of woman who takes afternoon tea at the Waldorf; the type of businessman who always stays at the second-best hotel. The group to which one belongs is the revealing set. The place in which one is seen or remembered by others gives the revealing setting that expresses the self better than its history or rare acts of morally decisive choice.

In a mobile society of types, the central Dreiserian woman or man is on the run or on the make, living between worlds, exposed and fragile. They are in the richest sense "worldless." That Dreiser's characters are not rebels against a society that marginalizes them, but accomplices of one that gives them a chance or perhaps no more than a hope, provides the energy of his work. His are the as-yet-outside insiders of a society. Perhaps part of the genius of American society has always been to avoid social collision by convincing almost all of its members that they are either insiders or temporarily outside insiders because the door is still slightly open. Rising or falling, the women and men of Dreiser's world have in view that slightly open door.

Dreiser, the American, had one advantage over his European contemporaries. The setting for his work was one of the most energetic and expansive stages of an as yet incomplete society. The frenzy of building, speculation, and extension of both economic and political power in every imaginable direction during the coming of age of American capitalism between 1880 and 1930 gave to his work a dreamlike setting of hope and collapse, of energy and exhaustion that had no equivalent in a Europe where empires were in decline and decay.

In tune with an incomplete society, Dreiser captures the condition of "promising lives" where the future, the possible, is not yet the focus of the mind rather than the memories or the consequences of the past. His civilization, like his best characters, was essentially hopeful, and it was therefore unsettled. Its future, like the value of land, was bound to be multiples of its present, so it might live in expectation, fantasy, and some slight dread of collapse. One of Dreiser's best images for Chicago is of streetlights turning off and on—in a prairie where no houses or neighborhoods yet exist. The lights burning all night are part of the city's imagination of itself, its confidence that in a few years there will be houses, neighborhoods, streets, and traffic where now there is only the sketch of a future in the form of these forlorn lights.

Dreiser knew best the America that, between 1880 and the stock market crash of 1929, was little more than a sketch of its own future, a future towards which it was speeding in the hope of turning out to be what it had willed itself to become. His best characters, like Carrie and the fifteen women of *A Gallery of Women*, are also hopeful and promising figures indifferent to the past and drawn almost sexually towards their own future selves for which their present is merely a rehearsal. They are characters rich with the kind of anticipation that gives them an attractive glow of incompletely fastened energy. For Dreiser the energy of promise, erotic energy, the energy of the will or of masculine power, and the energy of money which he described in *Sister Carrie* as "honestly stored energy" were convertible. At some point they converged and were indistinguishable. The play of these energies, especially the complex ways in which, once twined together, they blocked or cancelled one another, gave Dreiser the mechanism for his plots.

Dreiser discarded the traditional plot of the social novel, which aimed at conclusions of socially stable place and marriage, in favor of a pure trajectory of rise and fall. He writes for a civilization whose social space is dangerously vertical. Climbing and plunging, slipping and rising, his characters meet in love affairs where each makes the other's place insecure. Only in time can it be seen which was slipping downward, which up. Each of his plots is the tracing of the libidinal and social economy of one or of a series of love affairs.

The vertigo of the affair has as one of its features a confusion of directions, but only during the first stages of passion. As the lovers pass out of each other's sight the accelerating fall of one, the dizzying rise of the other, fixes each position unambiguously. For the early moments of love the social uniforms of rich and poor, businessman and shop girl, senator and cleaning woman, nightclub manager and actress are vaporized until at a later stage they return like a prison or, being no longer recoverable, are forfeited along with the world to which they conferred membership and identity. Mobility and self-making are the premises of his plots, but his is a world in which we find, just as often as a self-made man, his counterpart, the self-unmade man, the defector or the fugitive. Dreiser's is a reckless social world. Those on whom he fixes his attention have the addicted appetites of gamblers and, just as in gambling, most who play, lose. What is most interesting to Dreiser is not the outcome, but motion itself. Both those who rise and those who fall become in the process worldless, anomalous figures, no longer at home anywhere.

The dizzy, vertical, still unbuilt society that Dreiser takes as his setting gives special place to youth because it is the incomplete stage of the self where possibilities, opportunities, and the hold of its own future over one's self-image make up the very stuff of life. In Dreiser's stories dreaming, yearning, restlessness, and the imagination are almost civic responsibilities. His characters live in a society that invites them to experiment and to grasp themselves, as Emerson would have said, in terms of experimental lives. The actress, the drifter, the small-town Napoleon, and the outsider are each in their different ways aspects of the turbulence of the social surface. They make up for those who shake up and displace the order that has kept them out or kept them down.

Dreiser is the only American writer to have grasped, as Emerson did in philosophy, the consequences of this economic system for the self and its improvised relations. The tilt of a permanently redesignable society towards the dreamer, the improviser, the experimental life, and toward those least damaged by change or flight, those who have become immune to having the ground cut out from under their feet and have therefore come to savor the open and unpredictable, but possibly manageable speed of change: this is a central premise of Dreiser's work. He made a contribution as essential to the American mythography of the self as Walt Whitman's exemplary democratic man captured in the celebratory poet's voice, which proclaimed himself to be all men and all women. Dreiser's is the exemplary actor, or rather actress, in a world that is economic rather than political. Restless and experimental, his figures dream within a world inviting reconception and expecting each person to imagine a future that builds in a place for his or her self. To situate the self within the world requires altering the structure of the world itself since the past has no such person. This is the psychologically profound subjectivism of capitalism as a project of the self that we find in Emerson and Dreiser.

City Voices

T. S. Eliot's great poem of 1923, "The Waste Land," was at first called "He Do the Police in Different Voices." The urban world appears by means of brief scenes, many of them scenes of free-floating voices.

> My feet are at Moorgate, and my heart
> Under my feet. After the event
> He wept. He promised a "new start."
> I made no comment. What should I resent?

The disembodied voice became a means to assert a radical, freestanding experience. The voice decontextualized experience, freeing it from causality, that is, from antecedents and consequences. The free voice preserved individuality while sampling experience in a sharply truncated manner. In the years after Eliot's poem, Dos Passos in *Manhattan Transfer* wrote one of the major novels of the twenties about New York experience, a novel of almost 150 brief, glimpselike scenes, most no more than two pages long. These scenes capture the city by means of two techniques: first, overheard voices, colloquial, slangy, tough, urban voices, second, by means of a crude phenomenological descriptive practice that eliminated analysis or background so as to make the whole scene occur on the same plane. Dos Passos's novel is a heard, radiolike drama.

Ten years later Nathanael West in *Miss Lonelyhearts* produced the same effect by means of a formulaic use of letters that let each of a sample of urban sufferers speak out in a clear, simple, unliterary voice, in a single voicelike speech in which the sum total of suffering for one life could be spoken into a void from which nothing could return, no genuine help, no comforting advice.

Eliot, Dos Passos, and West had each carried forward an individualizing method of urban oral history, a life story in words. It was Dreiser who produced the first freestanding collection of what we today think of as an urban oral history. In his last great book, *A Gallery of Women*, Dreiser converted this project of the self into a series of Bohemian life histories. New York became the Greenwich Village of rope-sandaled poets, painters off to Paris, and young revolutionaries drawn to an American colony in the Siberia that the Russian Revolution would surely turn into yet another side of paradise. That future was at first a promise, as Paris was for the young who wanted to paint in the new style of Picasso and Matisse, or as New York City was for every high-energy dreamer too big for small-town life and on the run from the tedium of life once you "settled down." But the promise of all other promises was the erotic itself for which the sex appeal of money, or politics, or fame, of Greenwich Village or Paris or Hollywood was just an atmospheric setting. In this collection Dreiser wrote a dozen of the greatest stories of lives under the spell of love, sexual passion, and the variability of desire ever written in America. Like his contemporary, D. H. Lawrence, Dreiser designed a new, vitalist narrative in the aftermath of the first Freudian wave. These narratives are timed by the history of the energy of passion which glows incandescent, connects or fails to connect, but inevitably fades. Like the best of Lawrence's stories, these are accounts of lives in which the reality of passion and the reality of the aftermath of passion are the very texture of life history.

The stories of *A Gallery of Women* are stories for a promiscuous world. Each story has itself the structure of a meeting with a new and, in the story's perception, intriguing woman. The reader who "meets" or is "introduced to" Albertine, Lucia, Ellen, or Esther by the story itself has an experience that Dreiser has designed as a parallel to the stage of getting to know someone through the fascinated gaze of a new affair. The women of these stories remain conspicuously undomesticated. They appear and disappear. Their lives have gaps, other lovers, silences, blank pages. This is the narrative point of view of an affair in an easygoing world of affairs. The sexual fascination is lived through only until it dissipates or turns in another direction. The stories tell of free women or, as they used to be called, "loose" women—a term that should make us see that the alternative would be to be tied down or attached. The French would say that these are the lives of people who are *disponible,* available, ready for this or that new excitement.

At the same time, the women of Dreiser's stories are not opportunists or sensualists so much as young urban dreamers. Dream and the collapse of dreams; love and ruined love; promise and spilled promise: these are the fevers of a speculative time in love with options and risk. Dreiser makes of New York what Dostoevsky did of St. Petersburg: a city of dreamers and the debris of collapsed dreams.

In his fifteen stories Dreiser made his contribution to that poetry of Manhattan which had had its first harvest in Walt Whitman, and which had in Dreiser's own day begun to make of Greenwich Village a magical location on that American map where Walden Pond, Twain's Mississippi River, the woods of Cooper, the Mississippi towns of Faulkner, and the Arctic of Jack London have displaced mythographically whatever actual locations might be found at these spots. The city itself is a constant character in Dreiser's work, in some ways framing events and persons as a society had done in the past. It is the grid on which reality appears. With these stories he replaced the symbolic locations with which he had begun, and by means of which so much of New York narrative had operated. The lights of Broadway and the dark corners of the Bowery had in combination spelled out the politics of representation for Dreiser in 1900. By 1929 it was the dizzy freedom of Greenwich Village in its opposition to the small-town boredom of American life that located the symbolic pole around which representation takes place.

In the style of spoken history, Dreiser, along with Dos Passos, prepared the way for what we might call the city of talk, tirade, and self-performance that would follow in the work of Henry Miller, Philip Roth, Saul Bellow, J. D. Salinger, and Joseph Heller.

Chapter 14

The Role of Budapest
in Hungarian Literature:
1890–1935

MIKLÓS LACKÓ

*H*UNGARIAN literature was rooted in the provinces until the 1880s, and it has retained its provincial character to this day, though its capital city, Budapest, has long been the center of literary activity. Provincialism was a natural consequence of socio-economic developments in Hungary and of its late and limited modernization. In step with the conservative liberalism of the ruling nobility, an ideology that dominated Central Eastern Europe in the nineteenth century, Hungarian literature developed in close symbiosis with nationalism. The liberalism of the nobility differed from the more cosmopolitan Western European liberalism in its intellectual roots: in Hungary it sprang largely from the longstanding class and community consciousness of the upper classes rather than, as in the West, from enlightened absolutism.[1] Thus, in Central Eastern Europe—in Poland, Czechoslovakia, and even in Italy as well as in Hungary—literature was not so much shaped by private and individual experience as it was charged with a political mission and social meaning. Literature—or in more general terms, culture—reflected the problems of public life linked to national existence, such as the concept of nationhood and the importance of cherishing a national identity and consciousness. (Here again, the concept of nation was that imposed by the ruling nobility and by influential members of society desiring to be associated with the nobility.)

Political and social issues dominated the literary scene from the 1830s until the beginning of the twentieth century. Literature spoke of rural and provincial people and of the problems of country rather than of town. It assumed that the provincial gentry (middle-class nobility) and patriarchally depicted peasantry constituted the real prototypes of the Hungarian nation; no one else was as Hungarian as they.

When the bourgeois modernization of the country gained momentum in the last third of the nineteenth century, urbanization began in earnest, though it was long largely limited to Budapest. The popular national school was by then becoming depleted and its level sinking to vacuous epigonism; it was not able to depict the problems of modernism and the lifestyle of the rising bourgeoisie. A new urban bourgeois literature began to develop but, until the turn of the century, its emergence did not signify a radical break with the increasingly conservative liberalism of the nobility and with its literary equivalent, the popular national school. For some time, and particularly in poetry (which has always been the leading genre of Hungarian literature), the school tried to express the problems of town people undergoing modernization in a characteristic provincial idiom (e.g., the poetry of József Kiss).[2] The real breakthrough came in the novel, in the modern novella, and in the short story—that preeminently bourgeois genre which the popular national school never really managed to master. This break took place amidst internal conflicts and contradictions typical of Hungary.

In the West, the long and sweeping process of a bourgeois development, rising out of sharply heterogeneous and partly foreign elements of the population, went on for several centuries. The new class was steadily integrated with the fabric of the nation. In Hungary, however, the delayed modern bourgeois development taking place was limited but relatively quick. As a result, the new middle class was unable to become homogenized. Disparities remained between the Magyar and ethnically different (chiefly Jewish and German) layers of the bourgeoisie because of their different derivations and different mentalities. Since bourgeois development did not pervade society as a whole, layers of the nobility and of the peasantry continued to assume the role of a truly national class as against the "alien" modern bourgeoisie. In fact, it was in the interest of the nobility and the gentry that the dual origins of the bourgeoisie should not become obscured, especially not in connection with those of Jewish origin, and that the national image should apply only to the gentry and pseudo-gentry strata.[3] The Jewish bourgeoisie itself, which came partially from among the ranks of new immigrants, felt that any pretensions to a role as a leading class of the nation, that is, of the bourgeois nation, were out of place.

This process also affected cultural and literary development, especially after the 1880s and 1890s. Originally, the liberal nobility and the popular national school were not opposed to the rise of Budapest in any anti-urban sense. In fact, they were proud of their rapidly growing capital city. At the turn of the century, however, this situation started to alter; the anti-town mood critical of urban culture grew stronger and remained operative even between the two world wars when the contrast between "provincial" and city literature was actually beginning to fade. (It is noteworthy that anti-Semitism in literature became pronounced just at the time that the cultural interests and literary tastes of the different sections of Hungarian bourgeoisie were actually converging.)

Neither "provincial" nor Budapest culture were in an unequivocal position. Budapest—as opposed, for instance, to New York—was not just a very special big city: it was the capital of a multiethnic nation. A European capital, particularly one in Central Eastern Europe, had a different role and position in the surrounding system of society and culture than did a big American city.

In the nation and the period in which fast-urbanizing Budapest then found itself, its social and cultural appeal attracted an outsize intelligentsia to the capital city. This was a typical Eastern European phenomenon. In the case of Budapest, the big city as a capital city was, or had to become, the center of an entire national literature in a country where society bore the imprint of the provinces even as late as the first half of the twentieth century.

There could not have been a genuine antimetropolitanism on the part of the provinces; that would have been tantamount to the denial of their capital. It was not accidental that even Dezső Szabó, whose position was so often and so widely contested in Hungarian literature, spoke in his *The Village That Had Been Swept Away* about Budapest, "the sinful city," not as a place that should be left or leveled but as a place that should be Hungarianized. By this process, all the evil characteristics of big cities—obtrusive individualism, the excesses of capitalism and alienation—would in Szabo's opinion automatically cancel each other out. By the same token, the new bourgeoisie of the capital, and the literature that reflected this new middle class, could not have become uncritical glorifiers of Budapest. The country as a whole was still much too provincial to crown Budapest with a halo.

Attraction to the big city was never an uncritical identification as saliently expressed by literature itself. When big-city literature made its debut in the 1890s, modernity in Hungarian literature was already able to look back on some traditions. This modernity, however, and concomitant European cosmopolitanism, appeared only in the literature of a very narrow circle (Zsigmond Justh[4] and to a certain extent Zoltán Ambrus,[5] who wrote at the turn of the century); and it was largely based on foreign (often Parisian) experience. This trend infiltrated urban modernness through the sieve of the literary and art salons rather than because it was genuinely expressive of Budapest and of Hungary. The new Budapest literature that was knocking on the doors of editorial offices in the 1890s was already showing direct experience of the new problems of life in the big city, by the dissolution of realism and by the emergence of naturalism, impressionism, and incipient symbolism. At that time we were able to witness a peculiar advancement—and at the same time regression—from the point of view of modernism: this was the period when the modern life experience gained ground in the salons of the aristocracy; in the studios of artists, it became converted into direct Hungarian and Budapest experiences. This ready-to-wear modernity was gradually turned into something tailor-made for the social experience at home.

The development of a literary idiom to express the new experience in clear and comprehensive terms, and the search by freshly assimilated writers for a language that was both *Hungarian* and *modern*, marked a definite contribution to the process taking place.

Sándor Bródy, the first Budapest writer who wrote as a real big-city author yet felt himself thoroughly at home in rural Hungary, was a brilliant linguist.[6] "I was scared stiff of being immediately exposed for my deficiencies in standard usage and thought that this would be revealed to the whole world," he wrote—and no wonder, for the turn of the century resounded with fierce discussions on linguistic usage. The main argument of conservative literary critics against the new literature was that its practitioners on the whole "don't know proper Hungarian."

The "aliens" for whom the idiom of the popular national school and of Hungarian classicism was not generic did in fact play a prominent role in the development of modern metropolitan Hungarian. This was pointed out on one occasion by Endre Ady, the great and uncontestably Magyar poet who opened up a new epoch in Hungarian literature. Dezső Szomory, for instance, created the brilliant Art Nouveau Hungarian of his writings directly out of French, German, and Jewish phrases.

Characteristic of the experience of these times were the deep social divisions, the frightening social variety and new problems of the modern big city, the liberal individualism prevailing on one hand, and the sense of alienation on the other. Such experiences began to leave their imprint on literature in the 1830s and 1840s in London, Paris, and, a little later, in Berlin. They showed their first reflected literary images only in the 1880s and 1890s in Budapest (Sándor Bródy and, on a slightly lower literary level, Tamás Kóbor [7]). A little later it would be true of the work of the then young Ferenc Molnár.[8] They were above all impressed by the new social problems and spellbound by the birth of the new.

In a sketch entitled *Budapest in the Morning*, Sándor Bródy wrote:

> From the bastions of Castle Hill in Buda I am watching the dawn and [see] Buda, that old gentlemen and his wife, that saucily flirtatious young bride Pest. . . . The Left Bank itself, the big, young city of Pest, is slumbering. . . . The elegant part of town gets up late; the narrow streets are still deserted and immobile. Not so the working-class districts; they are wide awake and bustling about. *Lipótváros*, the area of business and finance, is unlocking its windowless shops. The streets have been given a wash, and lo! it is not yet seven o'clock and you see the whole mass seething and scurrying. But what a strange mass is this! It is certainly not an even mass of almost uniform usage and multistoried houses whose monotonous blocks are intermittently broken by monumental buildings for a more balanced view. The city is already big, but you can still see how it grew. There are still gardens to the private houses, and there are still tiny barrel-roofed dwellings with vast courtyards. Patriarchal-looking old trees lean against the vast bulkhead of partition walls patched with ads; holiday makers keep invading the city; and provincial little streets branch out from the elegant boulevards and from impressive elegant Andrássy Avenue. Wherever you turn your eyes, every patch is different in character, there is an orgy of various styles. . . . Villas look as if they were churches, and churches rise with fresh residential charm, easy grace and gaiety. . . . Building activity is rampant everywhere, I see people gilding domes and crosses. This is a city that is building its churches today![9]

The bliss of witnessing birth, however, did not mean ignoring the curses of the new big city. In another work Bródy writes about the sins of Budapest: "What are the typical sins of this city? Budapest is already large enough to explore them." Point by point Bródy enumerates the evils, the poverty, greedy exploitation, and other detractions, weeding out from among the sinful only the "bad girls" (characteristically, they are not called "bad women" in Hungarian). "Instead of them," he writes, "I am going to include the marriage profiteers from gentry families."[10]

Ferenc Molnár's famous novel for young people, entitled *The Boys of Pál Street*, depicts the urban character of Budapest as something that was by then already warmly familiar.[11] He writes about the development of team spirit among groups of big city schoolboys in their early teens who are fighting each other to retain the still empty building site that is their playground, or as they call it, the *Grund*. Although the characters of the novel already feel at home there, the author still reflects the unconscious awareness that Budapest is the big city of a basically provincial country:

> The Grund. . . . Oh, you hale and healthy schoolboys of the Great Plains who take just a step or two and find yourselves outside in the fresh open air of the endless flatlands, the meadows under the wonderful big blue bell of the sky, you whose eyes have grown accustomed to great distances, to a vast expanse of land over which freely roams the farsighted eye, you who do not live wedged in between tall houses, you have no idea what an empty site means to the children of Budapest. For them this is the Great Plain, an Eden of fields and meadows, of boundless flatlands. For them this is freedom and infinity. It is a piece of land hedged in from one side by a paling of tottering pickets and enclosed on the other three by the barren rear walls of tall buildings.

And elsewhere in the same novel Molnár writes:

> The boys looked over the fine big lot and the piles of wood scattered over it. The scene was gilded with the glory of a sweet spring afternoon, and their eyes shone brightly with the love of this little piece of land with the willingness to fight for it if need be. This was a kind of patriotism. They yelled "Long live the Grund!" Just as if they had shouted "Long live the fatherland."

Nor was the astonishment and bewilderment of the provincial visitor to Buda or Pest unprecedented in Hungarian literature. The first appearance of this motif was at the end of the eighteenth century. As we get closer to the turn of the century, we see, however, the colorful strangeness turning into the sensation of being at home in the city. At the same time, we are struck by a poignant new contradiction between village and town, soon realizing that in this conflict the big city is the winner despite all the traditional and patriarchal values sacrificed in the process. This experience of life was grasped by the conservative writers representing the provinces with greater insight than by the authors already acclimated to the capital city.

Géza Gárdonyi's novel, *The Old Gentlemen from the Village*, is the tragic story of a gentlemen of the landed gentry who moves to his daughter's home in Budapest and is unable to adjust to the conditions of urban life.[12] He is ill-used by his relatives who are ashamed of his countrified manners, and he finally commits suicide. At first he is impressed by the colorful variety of "this Budapest," but the astonishment of the man who has come from far away gradually wears off and turns into despair. His tragedy is actually brought about by his own newly citified family. Especially poignant are such details in the novel as the old gentleman's often losing his way in the streets and being upset because he has no one to talk to who will respond to his comments. He finds conversation only with the lower strata of the city people, among servants, the poor, and the handicapped. The narrow courtyards of the multistoried city houses give him claustrophobia. "A big house should have a big courtyard," he says. "It's a pity because otherwise this is a fine city." It is in the provincial-looking, single-story houses and inelegant streets and among the tradesmen and poor folks of the Józsefváros (District VIII of Budapest) that he feels almost at home. In his loneliness he often walks out to the fringes of Budapest to see the life-giving soil of fields; finally he starts to grow maize in cigar boxes in his attic room. (Elsewhere in his fiction, Gárdonyi complains about the fact that one sees only foreign-sounding names on the signs of Budapest shops.)

It was in this end-of-the-century period that the figures, institutions, and situations deriving from the new social conditions of urban life appeared in Hungarian letters. The elegantly worldly and demimonde life of the big city, its poverty and misery, its assemblage of queer types and of prostitutes (literary characters who preceded their Budapest incarnations fifty years earlier in Western Europe) assume particularly Budapest forms; they are practically never depicted censoriously but as pitiable developments of modern social circumstances. One can enter the city streets and the world of cafés in Hungarian letters of this time, but only rarely the metropolitan underworld. The latter is never treated in such sordid detail as in the novels of Dickens or of Balzac; here the "underworld" of gentlemen and of "gracious ladies" is much more likely to receive the limelight. On the threshold of the twentieth century, Budapest writers found more settled social conditions, circumscribed by law and order, than existed in Western Europe. There, urbanization had started half a century earlier, parallel with the Industrial Revolution.

Often portrayed in the literature of the times was the world of the theater with the actress as its focus—a *fin-de-siècle* effect. She is depicted as one of the first embodiments of independent woman (the schoolmistress is her provincial equivalent) who does not marry and does not have children, who is an equal, if not the dominant partner in love. Love is now depicted in its modern physical circumstances and even in the vitalistic-demonic form so characteristic of Art Nouveau. On the other hand, marriage is shown as a new kind of interest-linked relationship in which money and snobbery rule: young men from rural and provincial areas marry nouveau riche, middle-class wives, while the sons of the new bourgeoisie aspire to marry into old "patrician" families.

The Hungarian variants of the later types of the bohemian world made their appearance as representatives of the sections of society who found it impossible to conform. The readers of the time met Ferenc Herczeg's heros who excelled in duels, decadent gentry young men, and sleazy lawyers, and also their cultural analogues, the bohemian journalists and the moneyless self-appointed artists hanging out in Budapest cafés.[13] Later, real-life representatives of these layers were to come out with the new literature that transcended naturalism; this literature was able to apply even the decadent trends of the Western *fin-de-siècle* to the creation of a new cultural reform era and a new art standing in sharp opposition to the popular national school, an art for its own sake and abiding only by its own laws.

The central figure of the literary scene at that chronologically important point was the poet Endre Ady, who broke with the popular national school.[14] He preserved the political and public character of the Hungarian literature, but transformed it according to the criteria of modern art. In this way, Ady managed to bridge the conflict between urban and provincial literature and became the first really modern poet of the nation. (Something similar was done by Bartók when he integrated ancient folk music with modern concert art.)

The famous Hungarian periodical *Nyugat* (West), launched in 1908, soon became the forum of literary modernism. It, too, bypassed the conflict between town and country. Its distinguished poets and writers, such as Ady, Mihály Babits, Dezső Kosztolányi, and Árpád Tóth[15] (at once urban and provincial artists), worked in close intellectual alliance with the full-fledged big-city writers, like Frigyes Karinthy, Milán Füst, and Dezső Szomory,[16] no matter what their origins.

It can perhaps be regarded as a peculiarly Hungarian and Central European phenomenon that art-for-art's-sake literature, regarded as the alternative and antagonist to nationalist literature, did not lose its public and social orientation and appeal at its inception at the end of the nineteenth and the beginning of the twentieth century. As the historian Péter Hanák has pointed out, this more recent literature shifted the tradition of national and nationalistic community image to the problems connected with the new social welfare issues. The result was, of course, both good and bad. Art for art's sake became part of a radical, politically committed counterculture, but the literary trend of individualistic modernism lost its force in Hungary.

359

Walter Benjamin, that inspired student of big-city modernism, once wrote:

> If we divided every description of a town into two groups according to whether they were written by natives or not, it would probably turn out that there are much fewer of them written by local people. The exotic and the picturesque, which often serve as superficial motivation for writing, affect only strangers. To see a city as a local person does take a different and deeper drive. Those who are prompted to write by this urge will travel into the past rather than any distance. A travel book written by a local person is always related to the memoir, for the writer spent his childhood there.[17]

With some modifications, this statement holds for the Hungarian capital, too: the works with the most lasting impact were not created by those carried away by the fever of new metropolitanism, but by those who saw in Budapest the landscape of their childhood (e.g., Frigyes Karinthy), or their youth. Gyula Krúdy, for instance, "urbanized" provincial life in his writings although he cherished in the big city the nostalgic moments of his provincial experience.[18] On a more modern level, something similar worked in Dezső Kosztolányi, the son of a provincial schoolmaster, a staunch adherent of individualism and of literature free of political or social ideology. Kosztolányi tried to dethrone Endre Ady, that prophetic seer of political and public life. Ady created the unforgettable figure of Kornél Esti, an enchantingly playful bohemian, who loved to "ramble," particularly in Budapest streets.

What Walter Benjamin wrote about the "ramblers" of Berlin applies also to Kosztolányi and Kosztolányi's Budapest, for the people of the Hungarian capital, just as those of the Berlin of the 1920s, had become different.

> Their problematic pride in the capital as its founders gradually gave place to attraction to Berlin [read Budapest for Berlin] as their home. . . . It is in this situation that enters the writer who is still young enough to experience the change and is old enough to have a personal relationship with the last classics of rambling, with Apollinaire and Leautaud.

This change means the homelike appeal of the streets and public places of the city; and it often means that their past precursors haunt the writer. This is an attitude of considering the

> notable reminiscences and historical shock effects as so much litter better handled by the traveller. Such a writer will happily hand over

everything that he knows about the dens and birthplaces of artists and the palaces of princes just to be able to sniff at a doorstep, or smooth his hand over a stone slab that is just as familiar to the dogs of the neighborhood as to him.[19]

That was how Paris also became—as Hofmannsthal once described it—a "landscape built of life," a city that habit had turned into home.

The same process took place with respect to Budapest, but it was difficult and lengthy. The European metropolis, like the American big city, is a homogenizing factor, but the cities are not uniform; each has been shaped by its own individual historical past. The delayed arrival of urbanization to Central Eastern European towns, and the artistic consequences, including the peculiar piling up on each other of the various literary and art styles such as naturalism, impressionism, symbolism, Art Nouveau, and avant-gardism, introduced flashing colors into the literature of Budapest.

A special map of literary topography extends the list. I am thinking, for instance, of such alienating and at the same time intimate places as the railway stations of Budapest, where provincial Hungary meets the big city, where the sons of the provincial middle class arrive, who will become good-for-nothings (later reactionary political adventurers), civil servants, or writers and artists. It is also the first stopping point for the deprived, landless, seasonal workers and the servant girls who come from the villages. I have also in mind the City Park with its fun fairs, zoo, amusement park, and elegant promenades, where plebeian Budapest meets genteel, aristocratic, and middle-class Budapest (this is where Krúdy's heroes and heroines come for their rendezvous and where Ferenc Molnár's sentimental plebeian figures make love). The duality of the pubs and cafés is also part of this topography, with the pubs and small taverns accommodating the social strata who consider themselves authentic Hungarians while the others are frequented by the moderns. The cafés used to be the forums and agoras of alienated big-city people, where strong black coffee is still served instead of wine. Card players, salesmen, and professionals met; writers and poets also worked here—and some of them still do. Even now the cafés present an entirely different picture in the daytime than at night.

Grand Café Budapest by Lajos Nagy, published in 1935, is a relevant novel—though rather late from the point of view of our topic. It can be best compared to Alfred Döblin's *Berlin Alexanderplatz* (1929). It belongs to a late manifestation of documentary modernism in literature, as well as to a literary trend of neorealism with interest centered in sociographic detail.[20] It is a trend related to *Neue Sach-*

lichkeit. Nagy's novel, however, has no interest in any kind of enchanting "realism" since it is alien to an approach to life marked by a belief in "bearable poverty." It is filled with the savage anger of the Left and reflects on the scandal sheets, on the sensation-mongering features of the yellow press, and even the newspaper advertisements of the personal column and the weather reports—all from the angle of the proletariat.

The conflict between provincialism and urbanism is characteristic not only of a definite and relatively early period but is an ever-recurring problem of literature in the first half of the twentieth century. This problem never became completely obsolete but revived time and again according to the artistic trends and political orientation of the given period. The early twentieth century was the era of the great periodical *West,* of the literary hegemony of citified Hungary when, despite the growing dominance of urbanism, provincialism and urbanism seemed to blend harmoniously in the spirit of literary modernism and art for art's sake. This art welcomed symbolism and Art Nouveau and was patient with the appearance of avant-gardist activism, which made its debut during World War I. In Hungarian literature, however, it remained a trend confined to a rather small group.

In the first decades of the twentieth century, Mihály Babits, who was never really able to break away from his conservative provincial roots, wrote poems about the city, and the movies, versifying even the *Lichthof* (the gloomy wells of the airshafts providing the light to the bathrooms of some houses) and the windowless, barren rear walls of some high-rise, semi-detached houses. Dezső Kosztolányi, whose roots were similar, wrote an ode to the "woeful people of Pest" and offered stirring portrayals of the urban phenomenon of alienation.

A short story by Kosztolányi is about a man who, while rambling in a great town, notices a pharmacy in whose window an anti-freckles cream and a preparation to treat perspiring feet are advertised while, inside, the solitary pharmacist is twiddling his fingers, in silent despair. (In the nineteenth century world of Western bourgeoisie—and not only for Flaubert but also for Fontane—the pharmacist was the archetype of the enlightened, scientific-minded intellectual, and his shop, the pharmacy, a retreat for local people interested in small-town gossip and in national politics.) The hero enters the shop and confidentially whispers to the pharmacist that he has badly perspiring feet and needs help. The apothecary hands over his preparation triumphantly. Leaving the shop, the hero thinks that he still has not been charitable enough; he turns back from the doorstep and blushingly confesses that he also needs "something against freckles."

For an interval after the revolutions of 1918–1919 and the ensuing counterrevolutionary terror, it seemed as if rural Hungary had prevailed over the urban Hungary of Budapest. However, the provincial reaction against the revolutionary city was short-lived. With the annexation to Romania of Transylvania, such major provincial towns as Nagyvárad and Kolozsvár functioned as Transylvanian centers in Hungarian literature. After the failure of the revolutionary attempts of 1918–1919, during the autocratic Horthy era with its nostalgia for "the good old times," the liberal spirit of dualism strengthened. This attitude is reflected in the late writings of Gyula Krúdy. A *leitmotiv* of his novels and essays written in the 1920s was a nostalgia for the young Budapest: he cherishes the past—1867 "Gründerzeit," the early phase of rapid bourgeois and metropolitan development. In these nearly surrealistic pieces of literature, early capitalism and urbanization are not presented as destructive forces as in the earlier West European novels of "great realism," but as a marriage of strange elements, often unrooted in Hungary, free of any moralization. Krúdy's "Lucien Rubempre" (we have his novel *Hét Bagoly* [Seven owls] in mind) remains a free bohemian; his disappointment makes him move from a rich downtown neighborhood of Budapest to the world of the "men of the street."

Even the new populist/rural-sociologist literature developed, for all its anti-city, intellectual elements, in Budapest. Its aim was to Hungarianize the capital city in a spirit only a little more modern than the earlier intentions of Dezső Szabó.

In a work entitled *The Conquest of Budapest*, László Németh declared that the inflow of provincial Magyars to Budapest, parallel with the decrease in the birthrate of Jews, should Hungarianize Budapest even without the anti-Jewish laws of Fascism.[21]

Zsigmond Móricz, originally a provincial, middle-class writer who focused on the gentry and the peasantry, sized up the situation more accurately.[22] In his novels written during the worldwide economic crisis of the 1930s, he depicted the symbiosis of Budapest and the provinces, with Budapest definitely being the "host organism." In *The Caged Lion*, his heroes retain the memory of provincial life though they now represent the social layer of civil servants. They live largely in the streets around the National Museum on the Pest side where the aristocracy once resided and where later, high-ranking government officials had their homes. The principal character of the novel, a provincial type in his sixties, is the husband of the now aging daughter of a gentry family; he falls in love with a young girl from Pest and consequently finds himself passionately fond of Budapest, too. The lovesick man is depicted in a Baudelairean mood in an episode in which he notices a young woman he does not know in the street:

> He stopped on Calvin Square. While he was waiting for the policeman directing the traffic to wave him on, he gazed on his favorite landmark, the fountain on the square. . . . This was probably the first instance when one of the sights of Budapest struck him as beautiful. It is beautiful that it is so big and asymmetrical. . . . This square was like the meadow where they held picnics in May during his student years. The massive blocks of houses all around constituted the woods. The thought appealed to him; it was a thread following which he might get his bearings in this city. Indeed, it was like a forest. And full of big game. . And how many beautiful women. . . . So many little female wild fowl.

It is at this point that he notices the beautifully built, slim and tall blond woman.

> He felt a glow and a seething sensation in his innermost being. He would like to meet this woman. But what was she doing down town? And why did she look so sad? . . . What ails such a young and wonderfully attractive woman? To be sure. Pest is a strange and unpleasantly oversized city. . . . Now if this woman lived in a small town, he would surely know her. He felt a constriction in his heart; it was painful that this woman whom he had consumed until his soul was brimming with her would simply disappear in the crowd and he would never but never see her again. . . . What would have to happen for the two of them to meet?

In *She Has Her Say*, another novel written almost simultaneously with *The Caged Lion*, Móricz describes how people become accustomed to the big city. Here he writes about ordinary people from the provinces who live on the fringes of District IX of Budapest in a small two-room apartment in the rear courtyard of a big house close to Üllői Avenue. "Opposite the window there is no wall and no house to stop the eyes. One sees the garden of the neighboring house off the other side of the street, where the trees are still black and bald like an engraving. The branches are black from the soot deposited on them." (Only two decades earlier Dezső Kosztolányi was inspired to write a nostalgic poem about the same trees.)

> "You know what is interesting," he called out to his wife who was standing behind him, doing something in the room. "Haven't you noticed that the leading people—and not only in public life—have

come up from the villages. . . . It is strange that in Pest everybody is from the country."
"What is so interesting about that?"
"Well, it is interesting that in Budapest that is only natural."
"If something is natural, it is surely no longer interesting."

In addition to reflections on the relationship and conflicts between the metropolis and the countryside, the image of Budapest as a home becomes more and more current. From the late 1920s on, these literary trends, turning away from avant-garde modernism, moved, following the main stream of European literature, towards neorealism. One of the last works of avant-garde modernism was Tibor Déry's strongly surrealistic novel, *The Play of Clouds in Pest.*[23] Lajos Kassák, the greatest exponent of Hungarian avant-garde constructivism, also took this path in his novels.[24] His novel, *Angyalföld* (The field of angels [a working-class district in Budapest]), and his autobiography *Egy Ember Élete* (Life of a man), deal with the life of Budapest workers to whom he also originally belonged. He wrote about *Angyalföld*:

This is one of my most favorite novels, I love it because I think I managed, in a concise style, to describe in it what the largest industrial district in Budapest suggested at its very core. I was not born there, still I was an original dweller in this world of crumbling walls, smoky air, echoing steam-hammers but sometimes also merry laughter and drunken yells.[25]

This realism (Kassák uses the term *plastic* instead of realistic), which characterized not only the work of Kassák, had nothing to do, however, with the mandated Socialist realism of the Soviet Union in the 1930s.

Notes

1. Miklós Szabó, *A Dualizmuskori Szellemi Élet Néhány Kérdéséről* (On some problems of intellectual life during the age of dualism), manuscript.
2. József Kiss (1843–1921), poet, editor.
3. Miklós Szabó, On some problems of intellectual life during the age of dualism.
4. Zsigmond Justh (1863–1894), writer.
5. Zoltán Ambrus (1861–1932), writer.
6. Sándor Bródy (1863–1924), writer and journalist.
7. Tamás Kóbor (1867–1942), writer and journalist.
8. Ferenc Molnár (1878–1952), writer and playwright.

9. Sándor Bródy, "Budapest Reggel" (Budapest in the morning), *Fehér Könyv* (White book) (Budapest, June 1900): 77–79.
10. Sándor Bródy, "Budapest Bűnei" (The sins of Budapest), *Fehér Könyv:* 155–156.
11. Ferenc Molnár, *A Pál Utcai Fiúk* (The boys from Pal Street) (Budapest, 1907).
12. Géza Gárdonyi (1863–1922), *Az Öreg Tekintetes* (The old gentleman from the village).
13. Ferenc Herczeg (1863–1954), writer and editor.
14. Endre Ady (1877–1919).
15. Mihály Babits (1883–1941), poet and a leading personality of the review *Nyugat* (West); he was its co-editor from 1919; from 1933, writer; Árpád Tóth (1886–1928), poet.
16. Frigyes Karinthy (1887–1938); Milán Füst (1888–1967); Dezső Szomory (1869–1944).
17. Walter Benjamin, *Die Wiederkehr des Flaneur*, Gesammelte Schriften III (Frankfurt, 1972), 194.
18. Gyula Krúdy (1878–1933), writer.
19. Walter Benjamin, *Die Wiederkehr des Flaneur*, 195.
20. Lajos Nagy (1883–1954).
21. László Németh (1901–1971), writer and essayist.
22. Zsigmond Móricz (1879–1942), writer. The *Rab Oroszlán* (Lion imprisoned) was published in 1936; *As Asszony Közbeszól* (The woman interferes) in 1934.
23. Tibor Déry (1894–1977). *Pesti Felhőjáték* (The play of clouds) was published in 1927.
24. Lajos Kassák (1887–1967), writer, poet, and painter.
25. Lajos Kassák, *Az Angyalföld Születése* (The birth of Angyalföld); *Könyvbarát* (Bookfriend), 1957.

Historical Perspectives
and National Cultures

CARL E. SCHORSKE and THOMAS BENDER

THE COMPARISONS of New York and Budapest yielded by this study are far from comprehensive. Nor are they derived from two general histories of the two cities built on a single meta-narrative. Neither group of historians attempted to construct a consolidated account of their city's development; indeed, the very choice of the city as focus was prompted by the search for an object of study which, though bounded in space and time, was a social entity sufficiently multifaceted to be responsive to the many forms of illumination that our pluralized contemporary discipline of history could play upon it.

Among both Hungarian and American historians today divisions of professional concern and method are present: political historians concentrating on the relations among institutions, social structures, and political behaviors; social historians tracing power relations and cultural values through the uses of city space for residence and leisure; historians of elite culture concerned with the decipherment of artistic products as contemporary interpretations of modern urban life and society. Yet these several approaches to the analysis of metropolis are not present in the same proportions in the two national groups of historians. With due allowance made for the accident of individual selection in the distribution of historical methods within our national teams, the differences in the cultural and political formation of historians and their functional identity in Hungary and in the United States since World War II have produced differences in the weighting of methodological approaches to urban history. They have also affected the way in which even commonly shared methods are employed.

The reader of the Hungarian and American papers will have discovered some of these differences directly. Yet we should like to delineate a few features of historiographical difference of which the participants themselves became aware only through the process of collaboration. Two major differences in historical disposition affect at its very source the search for meaning in the two metropolitan histories. The first of these is, in the widest sense, political; the second, categorical, i.e., the weighting of time and space as coordinates of historical understanding.

For the Hungarian historians, "political" involved an analytic concern for the impact of the nation and the state on the city. Concomitently, periodization played a stronger role for the Hungarians than for the Americans. Whether in the sphere of ethnic relations, the social use of space, popular culture, or literature and painting, the Hungarian historians tended to derive the periodization of the city's history from the turns in the national and international destiny of Hungary as a whole. Attentiveness to the temporal dimension of history and, with it, the recourse to a narrative construction of historical experience accompanied logically the primacy of the political. Synchronic relations within urban society were of less concern to the Hungarian than to the American historians. For the synchronic web of associations among the various constituents of Budapest social life was rent and reshaped under the hammer-blows of political events: revolution, invasion, dictatorship, intervention, occupation.

The Hungarian historians perceive and study Budapest as a city struggling for a modern and liberal identity against feudal and provincial forces, social and cultural, that penetrate the fiber of its being, its very consciousness of self. The national and international context in which they view their historical object is, naturally enough, the one in which their own outlook was defined and where their own values—generally those of an updated Budapest progressivism dating from the turn of the century—were challenged, compromised, and all too often defeated by the nationalist right or the dictatorial left and the overwhelming pressure of foreign powers.

Within the general framework of this common subliminal democratic-progressive outlook, however, one can distinguish generational differences. The professional formation of the older historians took place in the immediate postwar era, when history was placed firmly under the sign of politics, with Marxism-Leninism, with whatever degree of acceptance or critical resistance, constituting the framework within which historical questions were defined and pursued.

368

These historians infused into the prevenient dominant political tradition of Hungarian historiography a new concern with social and economic substance as well as interpretation, even as they tended to employ the political norms of the left liberal intellectual movements of the early twentieth century.

For the next generation of historians, whose intellectual formation took place after the shattering experiences of 1956 and 1968, neither Marxism nor the optimistic dimension of bourgeois progressivism held much charm. Turning away from Marxism in all its forms, they explored the neo-positivist "New Histories" generated in the West, especially in France, where a social history without an evident national politics struck a resonant chord. Yet in our own conference, even the second-generation historians continued to define many of their urban problems in national terms. (See Chapter 6 by Teplán on the housing development of St. Imre, which was designed to accommodate bureaucratic and Magyar middle-class émigrés from Transylvania after the Romanian annexation.)

Compared to the essays on Budapest, those on New York are signal for their lack of direct concern for the national context. Where the Hungarian historians study Budapest's transformation under the pressure of forces from without, the Americans examine a New York remaking itself as it generates largely from within the social, political, and cultural forms to integrate its own pluralized content. The city is seen to construct an autochthonous modern identity from within as well as to offer its own democratic, world-metropolitan social myth as a model for a cosmopolitanized America. Where the Hungarian historians examine in Budapest the workings of a logic of domination strongly articulated through politics, the American historians of New York pursue the identification of a dynamics of inclusion, with a heavier stress on culture even in the study of politics. Thus, David Hammack charts New York's passage from a politics of the Anglo-Saxon elites to one of multiethnic and multiclass participation, even when the economic elites continued to shape much of municipal policy. The American analysts of popular culture for their part show the creation, through commercial intervention, of an acceptable New York metropolitan identity out of a multicultural, multiethnic society. The press, vaudeville, film, and popular dance all seem to trace the same trajectory: a passage from the expression of a European subcultural group consciousness to the construction of a culturally differentiated but integrated metropolitan identity. In this reading of metropolitan history, not politics but culture, fueled and organized by economic enterprise, builds an integrated New York from within the city itself. Power conflicts are there, to be sure, but they are muted by being transacted on the stages of the common public life, from the street and the housing development to the park and the newspaper, not only through the formal political system.

The Hungarian and American historians acquired from each other a new awareness that behind their professional visions of their respective cities in history lay different formative experiences of their generations. If most of the Hungarians construct an urban historiography of liberal defense, many of the Americans create one that displays the power of alternative culture. The American historians, children of an America that had become a major imperial power but was riven by new forms of open social conflict, were formed in a world where it was assumed that an autonomous cultural realm *could* be constructed. Although some American historians were affected by the civil rights movement of the 1950s and 1960s, others by the deep inner conflicts of the Vietnam War and the student movement, most of the younger group participated in a growing disillusionment with America's traditional institutional politics and nationalist ideology as the primary vehicles of American self-realization. Against the attempt of their professional elders to define a "consensus history" that would safeguard American unity against the disruptive claims of class and foreign threats, the younger generation of American historians posited a pluralized history "from below"; i.e., a history created from the experience of the lower strata of society. Rejecting the dominant groups and the traditional national ideology associated with them, they often identified with the minorities—blacks and European ethnics who had learned to defend their existence by means of culture. Fortified by the work of E. P. Thompson in England, the *Annales* school in France, and their own pioneers of ethnic social history, Herbert Gutman and Eugene Genovese, the younger generation began to find in the history of America's minority communities the lineaments of "alternative cultures" to which they had often become drawn as students.

A second source for the historical study of broader cultural themes lies in the New Deal era fascination with the lives and culture of the "people." The Depression of the 1930s, like the Vietnam War and the student movement, had created an earlier skepticism about the value of official culture and stimulated research into vernacular traditions and popular modes of expression. This impulse, which was institutionalized academically in the interdisciplinary American Studies movement in the 1940s and 1950s, provided a base for historical exploration of various levels and forms of culture. Initially, this work looked more to regional than to urban cultures, sometimes with an enthusiastic sense of discovery, sometimes from an urbane, detached, or even ironic point of view. Only later, in the 1970s, did this tradition of scholarship associate itself with urban studies, exploring the cultural plurality of big-city life.

Finally, to this intellectual inversion of traditional, politics-centered history was added another new concern: the interest in pleasure-oriented American consumer culture. Since the 1970s, commerce has become recognized by historians as a powerful agent in the construction of American popular culture. Whether affirmed for its democratizing, integrating power and its sexually liberating features, or castigated for its destruction of values, business enterprise became a constituent in the enlarged armamentarium of American sociocultural history. While professional interest in politics, social movements, and the organization of the life of work diminished, new vistas were thus opened for the historical understanding of society through the exploration of the life of leisure, of affective and symbolic culture.

If our self-analysis as historians formed by two different, long separated societies has any truth, then the diptych of Budapest and New York must be considered in its light. From the start, we conceived our collaboration as a critical encounter in which Hungarians and Americans would learn from each other. But the lessons learned were as often about the nature of our respective historical visions as about the methods of analysis related to them. The Hungarians saw in much of the American work a kind of indomitable social optimism which the American historians—some of whom considered themselves to be radicals beyond illusions of progress—would hardly posit of themselves. The separate pieces in the Americans' kaleidoscope of New York in transformation produced a pattern of surprising uniformity: a multiethnic society which redefined, through politics, business, and culture, the terms of being an American beyond the traditional cultural norms set by the Anglo-Saxon Protestant hegemony. A solid tone of hopeful affirmation sounds beneath these scrupulous investigations of different aspects of a metropolitan society in which immigrants, without denigration of their foreign birthright and with the help of an inventive commercial culture, forged a New York identity that could stand as a model for a new, cosmopolitanized but multicultural America. Is this historiography part of an "alternative culture" becoming national? Does the work here brought to focus on New York herald a new "consensus history" for the nation, one built from the experience of the multiform culture of the modern metropolis?

The American historians particularly noticed in the Hungarian approach the strong light which their attention to national factors could shed on the process of metropolitan transformation, cultural as well as political. Thus, Miklós Lackó identified as a major question of the Budapest artistic intelligentsia: "Who defines the Hungarian?" His pursuit of this question in Hungarian writers shows the power of ideology in the life of letters and also demonstrates a continuous dialectic between provincial and rural culture and new cosmopolitan urban values. Such analysis stands in contrast with the more strongly textual focus of the American treatment of the arts, in which extra-urban cultural problematics receive scant attention. Philip Fisher, in his analysis of the unfolding of an attitude of personal liberation and urban affirmation in the maturing literature of modern New York, leaves unspoken the residues of heartland-American values in the new writer's consciousness. A comparison of Wanda Corn's and Éva Forgács's papers on painting in the two cities shows the difference between an American scholarship centering on symbolic representation and a Hungarian focus on the social and national formation and function of schools of art.

Our collaborative project produced with stunning force a self-consciousness among all those who participated about the continuity of history and historiography, about how professional academic discourse is culturally situated. A heightened awareness of the perspectives with which the two national historical professions approach the history of the metropolis could and should raise doubts about the very validity of the scholarly comparison: Are the findings on Budapest and New York presented here so strongly affected by the conceptual screen of the investigators that the differences and similarities lie not in the cities themselves but rather in the eyes of their beholders? The work of collaboration which opened this question in the end turned it away from radical doubt to the firmer ground of skepticism born of mutual enlightenment. The historians of New York, for example, became aware of the potential for enrichment of their subject by the application to their city of the national-contextual perspective of the Hungarians. The Hungarians similarly came to appreciate what the American-style analysis of ethnic cultural experience could contribute to recasting problems in the history of Budapest.

In the essays, and even more in reflection on the issues they raise, the poison of political isolation and methodological exclusiveness became transmuted into the elixir of enriched historical interpretation. As in the social history of both our cities, so in their modern historiography: the mutual integration of the other out of a recognition of intellectual complementarity provides a new and sounder basis for a widened historical understanding.

**Papers Presented at the Conference
on the Comparative History
of Metropolitan Transformation
of Budapest and New York: 1870–1930**
(Budapest, 1988)

Báron, G. "The Movies in the Metropolis"

Bender, T. "The Emergence of the New York Intellectuals: Modernism, Cosmopolitanism, and Nationalism"

Blackmar, E., and R. Rosenzweig. "The Park and the People: Central Park, 1870–1914"

Borsányi, G. "Class Location and Voting Behavior During the Interwar Years"

Buzinkay, G. "The Budapest Joke and Comic Weeklies as Mirrors of Cultural Assimilation"

Corn, W. "The Artist's New York, 1900–1930"

Fisher, P. "The Novel as Newspaper and Gallery of Voices"

Forgács, É. "Avant-garde and Conservatism in the Budapest Art World, 1910–1932"

Gyáni, G. "Uses and Misuses of Public Space Around the Turn of the Century"

Gyori, P. "Community Housing and Housing Policy in Budapest, 1873–1941"

Hammack, D. "Political Participation and Municipal Policy: New York City, 1870–1940"

Hanák, P. "The Reign of the Gypsy Baron, the Merry Widow and the Csardas Princess in Vienna and Budapest"

Harris, N. "Covering New York: Journalism and Civic Identity"

Jackson, K. "Transportation, Housing, and Government Policy in the Expansion of New York City, 1900–1945"

Karády, É. "The Sunday Circle and Budapest"

Kasson, J. "The Transformation of the Performing Arts and Their Audiences in New York, 1880–1930"

Lackó, M. "Modern Budapest in Hungarian Literature"

Lengyel, G., and B. Nagy. "Spatial Distribution of the Entrepreneurial Class in the Interwar Period"

Moore, D. "Class and Ethnicity in the Creation of New York City Neighborhoods, 1900–1930"

Musser, C. "Comedy, Ethnicity, and the Early Films in New York"

Nagy, Z. "Changes in the City Politics of Budapest, 1873–1941"

Peiss, K. "Vicarious Promiscuity: Gender, Class, and the Geography of Urban Leisure, 1900–1930"

Rosner, D. "Voluntary Providers of Health Care in New York City, 1920–1950"

Scobey, D. "The Streets and Social Order: The Class Politics of City Building in New York, 1870–1914"

Shefter, M. "The Incorporation of Jews and Italians into New York City's Democratic Party"

Sipos, P. "Spatial Distribution of the Working Class in the Interwar Period"

Snyder, R. "Ethnicity, Race, and Popular Culture: The New York Vaudeville Stage, 1880–1930"

Szegedy-Masák, M. "Literary Modernism and the Modernization of Hungary"

Teplán, I. "St. Imre Garden City: An Urban Anthropological Approach"

Tímár, L. "The School System and Social Mobility in Budapest, 1873–1941"

Trachtenberg, A. "Surveying the City: The Documentary Mode"

Vásárhelyi, M. "Budapest and Its Press"

Zeke, G. "Residential Segregation and the Jews of Budapest"

Thomas Bender, university professor of the humanities at New York University, is a historian of the United States whose work has focused upon cities, intellectuals, and cultural history. His books include *Toward an Urban Vision* (1975), *Community and Social Change in America* (1978), *New York Intellect* (1987), and *Intellect and Public Life* (1992). He is editor of *The University and the City* (1988).

Elizabeth Blackmar is associate professor of history at Columbia University and author of *Manhattan for Rent, 1785–1850* (1989) and, with Roy Rosenzweig, *The Park and the People: A History of Central Park* (1992).

Géza Buzinkay, director general of the Budapest Historical Museum, is a cultural historian with a particular interest in the history of the press and in jokes and caricatures. His publications include *Borsszem Jankó és Társai* (Hungarian comic journals and their caricatures in the second half of the nineteenth century) (1983).

Wanda M. Corn is an art historian on the faculty of Stanford University. She presently serves as the Anthony P. Meier Family Professor and Director of the Stanford Humanities Center. She is the author of *The Color of Mood: American Tonalism, 1880–1910* (1972) and *Grant Wood: The Regionalist Vision* (1983).

Philip Fisher is professor of English and American literature at Harvard University. His recent books include *Making and Effacing Art: Modern American Art in a Culture of Museums* (1991) and *Hard Facts: Setting and Form in the American Novel* (1987). He has also edited *The New American Studies* (1991).

Éva Forgács is an assistant professor in the Hungarian Academy of Crafts and Design. Her field of interest is Central European art in the early twentieth century. Her publications include *Collage and Montage* (1976) and *Bauhaus* (1991). She has also edited the writings of É. Kállai.

Gábor Gyáni, senior research fellow at the Institute of History of the Hungarian Academy of Sciences, is a social historian with a special concern with cities. His books include *Család, Háztartás és a Városi Cselédség* (Family, household and urban domestics) (1983), *Bérkaszárnya és Nyomortelep. A Budapesti Munkáslakás Múltja* (Rent-barrack and slum. The past of Budapest workers' housing) (1992).

David C. Hammack, professor of history at Case Western Reserve University, has published widely on urban history and the development of social institutions in the United States, including schools and nonprofit organizations. He is the author of *Power and Society: Greater New York at the Turn of the Century* (1982, 1987), and *The Russell Sage Foundation: Social Research and Social Action in America, 1907–1947* (1988).

Péter Hanák is one of the founders of the Institute of History of the Hungarian Academy of Sciences, where he is senior research advisor. His numerous publications include *Ungarn in der Donaumonarchie: Probleme der bürlichen Umgestalung eines Vielvölkerstaates* (Hungary in the Danubian monarchy: Problems of the bourgeois transformation of a multinational state) (1984).

Neil Harris, Preston and Sterling Morton Professor of History at the University of Chicago, is a historian of American culture. His books include *The Artist in American Society: The Formative Years, 1790–1860* (1966), *Humbug: The Art of P. T. Barnum* (1973), and *Cultural Excursions: Marketing Appetites and Cultural Tastes in Modern America* (1990).

Miklós Lackó is a senior research adviser of the Institute of History of the Hungarian Academy of Sciences. He has published a monograph on the historical changes in the social composition of the Hungarian working class. For the last two years his major research interest has been in twentieth century Hungarian cultural history. His works include *Válságok-választások* (Crises-choices) (1975) and *Korszellem és tudomány* ("Zeitgeist" and scholarship) (1988).

Deborah Dash Moore, professor of religion at Vassar College and director of its American Culture program, is a historian of American Jews in the twentieth century. She has published two books, *At Home in America: Second Generation New York Jews* (1981) and *B'nai B'rith and the Challenge of Ethnic Leadership* (1981). She has edited *East European Jews in Two Worlds* (1989), and with Ronald Dotterer and Steven Cohen, *Jewish Settlement and Community in the Modern Western World* (1991).

Zsuzsa Nagy is scientific advisor at the Institute of History, Hungarian Academy of Sciences and university professor of history at the Lajos Kossuth University, Debrecen. Her books include *A Budapesti Liberális Ellenzék* (The liberal opposition in Budapest, 1919–1945) (1972), *The Liberal Opposition in Hungary, 1919–1945* (1983), *Szabadkomuvesség a XX. Században* (Freemasonry in the twentieth century) (1977), and co-author, *Iparosok és Kereskedok Magyarországon a Két Világháboru Kozott* (Artisans and shopkeepers in Hungary between the two world wars) (in press).

Roy Rosenzweig is professor of history at George Mason University. He is the author of *Eight Hours for What we Will: Workers and Leisure in an Industrial City* (1983), and the co-author with Elizabeth Blackmar of *The Park and the People: A History of Central Park* (1992). He is co-editor of *Presenting the Past: Essays on History and the Public* (1986) and *History Museums in the United States: A Critical Assessment* (1989).

Carl E. Schorske has been concerned with the relationship between the development of high culture and social and political change in modern Europe. Emeritus professor of history at Princeton University, he is the author of *German Social Democracy, 1905–1917* (1955) and *Fin-de-Siècle Vienna: Politics and Culture* (1980).

Robert W. Snyder is the author of *Voice of the City: Vaudeville and Popular Culture in New York* (1989). He is currently serving as co-curator of an exhibition on the Ashcan artists and turn-of-the-century New York for the National Museum of American Art and researching the history of crime in American politics and culture.

István Teplán holds a research position at the Center for East and Central European Studies. His most recent work in the urban field is "The City of Totalitarianism—the Monumental City: Dictatorship as Visual Experience" (1992). He also holds an administrative position at the Central European University.

Boldface numbers refer to figures and tables.

[B] = Budapest

[NY] = New York

I